ENGLISH SURNAMES SERIES

THE SURNAMES OF
DEVON

ENGLISH SURNAMES SERIES

Edited by D. A. Postles

Department of English Local History
University of Leicester

DEVON

Principal places mentioned in the text

ENGLISH SURNAMES SERIES

VI
The Surnames of
Devon

by
David Postles

with a Chapter contributed
by
Richard McKinley

LEOPARD'S HEAD PRESS

1995
Published by
LEOPARD'S HEAD PRESS LIMITED
1-5 Broad Street, Oxford OX1 3AW

ISBN 0 904920 25 9

*This is the sixth volume in the
English Surnames Series
which is published for the
Marc Fitch Fund*

Typeset by Denham House, Yapton, West Sussex
and printed in Great Britain by
Progressive Printing (UK) Limited, Leigh-on-Sea, Essex

Contents

List of Figures

vii

List of Figures

List of Tables

List of Tables

xi

List of Tables

Abbreviations

Ashburton CW Accounts	A Hanham, ed., *Churchwardens' Accounts of Ashburton 1479–1580*, (D&C RS, ns 15, 1970).
BL	British Library.
Book of Fees	*Liber Feodorum. The Book of Fees, commonly called Testa de Nevill*, (2 vols., 1920–31).
Canonsleigh Cartulary	V M London, ed., *The Cartulary of Canonsleigh Abbey*, (D&C RS, ns 8, 1965).
Caption of Seisin	P L Hull, ed., *The Caption of Seisin of the Duchy of Cornwall*, (D&C RS, ns 17, 1971).
Crown Pleas Devon 1238	H Summerson, ed., *Crown Pleas of the Devon Eyre of 1238*, (D&C RS, ns 28, 1985).
D&C Exeter Archives	Dean and Chapter Exeter Archives.
D&C Notes and Gleanings	*Devon and Cornwall Notes and Gleanings.*
D&C Notes and Queries	*Devon and Cornwall Notes and Queries.*
D&C RS	Devon and Cornwall Record Society.
Dartmouth Records Computer Database	A computer database incorporating the information in H R Watkin, *Dartmouth*.
Devon Taxes	T L Stoate, ed., *Devon Taxes 1581–1660*, (1988).
Dorset Lay Subsidy 1327	A R Rumble, ed., *The Dorset Lay Subsidy Roll of 1327*, (Dorset Record Society, 6, 1980).

Dorset Lay Subsidy 1332	A D Mills, ed., *The Dorset Lay Subsidy Roll of 1332*, (Dorset Record Society, 4, 1971).
DRO	Devon Record Office.
ESS	English Surnames Series.
Exeter Freemen	M M Rowe and A M Jackson, eds., *Exeter Freemen 1266–1967*, (D&C RS, Extra Series 1, 1973).
Feet of Fines Devon	O J Reichel, ed., *Devon Feet of Fines*, (2 vols., 1912 and 1939).
Feudal Aids	*Inquisitions and Assessments relating to Feudal Aids . . . 1284–1431*, (6 vols., 1899–1920), I.
Finberg, *Tavistock Abbey*	H P R Finberg, *Tavistock Abbey. A Study in the Social and Economic History of Devon*, (reprint 1969).
Hearth Tax 1674	T L Stoate, ed., *Devon Hearth Tax Return Lady Day 1674*, (1982).
Hoskins, *Devon*	W G Hoskins, *Devon*, (1954).
Kowaleski Database	Computer database compiled by Dr Maryanne Kowaleski of Fordham University, relating to the inhabitants of Exeter in the later middle ages (from, *inter alia*, the Mayor's Court Rolls).
Launceston Cartulary	P L Hull, ed., *The Cartulary of Launceston Priory*, (D&C RS, ns 30, 1987).
Lay Subsidy 1332	A M Erskine, ed., *The Devonshire Lay Subsidy of 1332*, (D&C RS, ns 14, 1969).
Lay Subsidy 1524–5	T L Stoate, ed., *The Devon Lay Subsidy Rolls 1524–7*, (1979) (using here only the data of 1524–5).
Lay Subsidies 1544–5	T L Stoate, ed., *The Devon Lay Subsidy Rolls 1543–5*, (1986) (using here only the data for 1544–5).

Longleat MSS Uplyme court rolls computer database	Computer database incorporating data from the court rolls of Uplyme in the Longleat MSS. Used only where the information derives from many rolls; otherwise precise references are given.
McKinley, *Lancashire*	R McKinley, *The Surnames of Lancashire*, (ESS, 4, 1981).
McKinley, *Norfolk & Suffolk*	R McKinley, *Norfolk and Suffolk Surnames in the Middle Ages*, (ESS, 2, 1975).
McKinley, *Oxfordshire*	R McKinley, *The Surnames of Oxfordshire*, (ESS, 3, 1977).
McKinley, *Sussex*	R McKinley, *The Surnames of Sussex*, (ESS, 5, 1988).
Oliver, *Monasticon*	G Oliver, *Monasticon Dioecesis Exoniensis*, (1846).
PND	J E B Gover, A Mawer and F M Stenton, *The Place-Names of Devon*, (English Place-Name Society, 2 vols., 8–9, 1931–2).
PRO	Public Record Office.
Reaney, *DBS*	P H Reaney, *A Dictionary of British Surnames*, (reprint 1987).
Reaney, *Origin*	P H Reaney, *The Origin of English Surnames*, (reprint 1987).
'Somerset lay subsidy 1327'	F H Dickinson, ed., *Kirkby's Quest for Somerset . . .* (Somerset Record Society, (3), 1889).
TDA	*Transactions of the Devonshire Association.*
Tudor Exeter	M M Rowe, ed., *Tudor Exeter. Tax Assessments 1489–1595 including the Military Survey 1522*, (D&C RS, ns 22, 1977).
Watkin, *Dartmouth Records*	H R Watkin, ed., *Dartmouth*, 1 (1935).

Abbreviations

West Country Shipping	D M Gardiner, ed., *A Calendar of Early Chancery Proceedings relating to West Country Shipping 1388–1493*, (D&C RS, ns 21, 1976).
Wreyland Documents	C Torr, ed., *Wreyland Documents*, (1910).

Acknowledgements

This volume, the sixth in the English Surnames Series, is the product of continued collaboration between the Marc Fitch Fund and the Department of English Local History in the University of Leicester. Without the support, both financial and moral, of both these bodies, the research and publication would have been the lesser. Many individuals in both organisations have provided much needed and appreciated advice, knowledge and interest. In particular, Roy Stephens, of the Fund and Leopard's Head Press, has been constantly understanding and helpful. Charles Phythian-Adams, Professor and Head of the Department of English Local History, has been continuously involved in the maintenance of the Survey. Dr Maryanne Kowaleski very generously placed at my disposal much of the data relating to her own research into Exeter in the later middle ages, which is shortly to appear as a book. This kindness included printout of her databases relating to inhabitants of Exeter. My further debt to her is reflected in the numerous references to her published work. The greatest academic and personal debt, however, should probably be attached, despite his reluctance, to Dr Harold Fox, for information, interpretation, and amusement. My hours in front of a monitor would have been unremitting toil without the friendship and levity of Paul Ell and Linda McKenna, who were also chained to the terminals to the mainframe in the Computer Room at Marc Fitch House. To them, I owe what little sanity remains. Consequently, I wish them both inordinately well with their own intriguing and interesting research. The pivot of the Department is Pauline Whitmore, and, like so many other things here, this book could not have been written without her efficiency in the affairs of the Department. She additionally input the chapter on heritability into the mainframe.

Richard McKinley has brought the Survey to such a stage of fruition in four previous volumes in this series, that I have felt foolhardy and impetuous enough to attempt some different approaches. These changes are more of emphasis than radical departure, and would not have been possible without the tremendous interpretation which he had already achieved. He has, indeed, contributed a substantial part of the chapter relating to the genesis of hereditary surnames. The entire framework of this book,

Acknowledgements

and the series, is his initiative. Although she is not related to this University or the Series, I have drawn inspiration and insight from the pioneering and perceptive publications by Cecily Clark, who stands as the doyenne of anthroponymy.

Many archivists and reprographics personnel have facilitated my research by their efficiency, kindness and tolerance, particularly at the British Library and Public Record Office. I hope that I have not abused their helpfulness. Equally helpful, kind, and incredibly efficient, were Angela and Kumlash in Audio-Visual Services in this University, who transformed my inchoate and ineffective doodlings into real maps and diagrams, despite their unrelenting workload. I am greatly in their debt.

Finally, I owe numerous personal debts, both to many of those mentioned above, and to others. I invidiously and selfishly single out the most important to me. To my wife, Suella, I owe more than I can express. My mother and late father provided the foundation for everything which I have managed to produce, despite their hardship. I am truly grateful.

1995   D.A.P.

Introduction

Bynames and surnames are simply descriptors of human beings. Consequently, questions relating to the generation, adoption, and diffusion of these names are matters of human activity and culture, and can be approached from the perspectives of the historical sociologist and the social anthropologist, although the techniques of genealogy are important for establishing the correct etymology and the mechanics of distribution. The significance of personal names, however, resides in the wider issues of the relationship between culture, agency and society; between individuals and the rest of society; to social organisation and kinship; and, indeed, to other variables. Thus the adoption and diffusion of *cognomina* concern cultural diffusion in a broad sense. Differences of time, social group and region within this process reflect the complexity of cultural diffusion vertically (through society) and horizontally (through region). This calculus embraced also dialect and regional variations. It is tempting to conceive a single cultural system in the middle ages, to be excessively deterministic, to allow only of cultural integration, cultural coherence, a hegemonic culture, central values, or dominant ideology. At the centre, the perception might involve causal consensus, and, concomitantly, logical consistency. Cultural integration would involve some sort of elision of values, based upon either downwards or upwards conflation or central conflation. The alternative explanation would present a picture of pluralism, of variation and inconsistency within cultural phenomena.[1] The actual nature of culture in the middle ages is not clear. The best-fit suggestion would be, perhaps, that there was some degree of conflation, largely, but not exclusively downwards. Vertical diffusion of naming patterns in the Middle English (ME) period thus included a large element of donwards conflation, although the mechanism of this influence is not always visible. It may have involved imitation and fashion, but also some functionalist aspects of socio-legal norms. On the other hand, there may well have been some aspects of upwards conflation or diffusion, such as through popular attitudes to personal naming during the later middle ages (as well as also, perhaps, aspects of popular religion). It as as well to be mindful also of that immense upwards diffusionism which was forged and forced from below between the tenth and twelfth centuries.[2] The adoption of firstly bynames and subsequently hereditary surnames by and large, however, permeated downwards through social group. The relative

1

timing of that process was influenced by a number of variables, including social group and region. At the beginning of the ME period, therefore, the tendency towards heritability of surnames was more protracted amongst some social groups and in some regions than in others. For example, unstable patronymic forms of bynames were still widespread in county Durham in the fifteenth century, with the resultant difficulty of establishing the identity and relationship of individuals in court rolls. Equally, at the commencement of the ME period, the gradual supplanting of Old English (OE) personal names by recently introduced Continental-Germanic (CG) personal names, which had a profound effect on the development of bynames, varied by time and region and social group.[3] Such differences, *inter alia*, contributed to regional variations in naming patterns.

The diffusion of bynames and surnames spatially depended thus on such variables as mobility, patterns of migration, mean household and family size, changes in demographic patterns, inheritance customs, settlement patterns and topography, the localization of society, and, in some cases before the end of the middle ages, lordship and seignorial control (either as positive or negative influences) — in fine, the socio-legal or functional aspects of society which inter-related with culture. Recent research has illustrated that medieval and early modern society, despite some restrictions on personal mobility, had some degree of movement and turnover.[4] The framework of migration may have involved several patterns: 'chain'; 'betterment'; 'localized'; 'circular' or 'career'; which varied according to social group — as well as the natural disposition of 'movers' and 'stayers'.[5] Stimuli to migrate may have encompassed such push factors as household and family size, expectations of inheritance, and economic opportunities (the latter also a pull factor). Changes in these variables over time affected the degree of aggregate migration and distances moved. Kinship ties may have induced movement as well as immobility. Indeed, some of the very longest distance migration may have been assisted by extended kinship ties.[6] Migration may have been shaped by the pattern of 'open' and 'closed' parishes and communities, and by the different requirements for labour within varied regional economies. Commercial linkages may have formed a duct for 'chain' migration at the level of the merchant elite. The needs of formal education for clerical (and other) careers, especially by the later middle ages, may have contributed to 'circular' migration.

During the middle ages, lordship may have acted more frequently as a negative force, restricting personal mobility, but occasionally also as a positive factor. Where seignorial estates were dispersed, bynames were associated (to some degree) with the freer and wealthier sections of the population. A high level of locative bynames in medieval lay subsidies may thus result only from the fact that the wealthier formed a disproportionate number of the taxed. The poorer inhabitants, precisely those excluded from the taxation, may have borne other types of byname. Lay subsidies before the stability of surnames may thus tend inherently to exaggerate the level of locative bynames at the expense of other forms. The extent to which this sociological influence on the formation of locative bynames operated within Devon is discussed further below, where it is suggested that locative bynames were not as deterministically related to social group in Devon as in some other counties. Regional variation, arising from the distinctive pattern of settlement of some *pays* of Devon, meant that there were other influences on the formation and use of locative bynames.

The question of under-enumeration in the lay subsidies is still critical. Where contemporary rentals exist, the extent of the problem can be elucidated, but few are extant. The best examples may relate to Axminster and Uplyme. For the former, there is a series of rentals culminating in that of 1334; for Uplyme, an extent of the early fourteenth century survives.[18]

Table 1.1

Comparison of the Lay Subsidy of 1332 and some Survey-type Documents
Axminster and Uplyme in the early fourteenth century

Manor	Lay subsidy 1332		'Survey'	
	taxpayers	bynames	tenants	bynames
Uplyme	31	26	67	41
Axminster	30	27	101	63

* Taxpayers denotes the number of different taxpayers; tenants the number of different tenants; bynames the number of different bynames.

The rental of Axminster thus contained some 47 bynames not enumerated in the lay subsidy for Axminster, although four of these do occur in appurtenant Membury. Similarly, the lay subsidy omitted 28 bynames which were included in the contemporaneous extent of Uplyme. Moreover, the rentals reveal the extensive network of some bynames, not indicated by the lay subsidy. Thus, the bynames Pyw and Wrang were held by several tenants in Axminster, but this is concealed by the lay subsidy. The byname Pyw equally occurred in the court rolls of Uplyme, but was excluded in the lay subsidy. The rentals thus reveal the serious extent of under-representation of both tenants and bynames, and yet rentals themselves are recognised to have serious limitations, since they almost consistently omit under-tenants and undersettles.[19] Court rolls assist in assembling more comprehensive listings, especially of the high numbers of transients in communities in Devon, since suit of court, trespass, debt, covenant and the assize of ale (effectively a licensing system) required many to appear in court.[20] Even court rolls, however, have their deficiencies.[21]

The problem of a simple comparison of the lay subsidies of 1332 and 1524-5 is more complicated still. Both taxable constituencies were only a small proportion of the global population of the county. The basis of taxation was different for the two subsidies (see further below). The taxable constituency in 1332 was some 10600, that of 1524-5 some 28000. The total population of Devon, however, was probably lower in 1524–5 than in 1332, so that the proportions of the population taxed in each diverge widely. In short, although the taxable population increased by a factor of 2.6:1 (comparing 1524 with 1332), the global population of the county probably diminished between those dates (possibly by a factor of 1:1.5 (comparing 1524 with 1332). This calculation assumes that the population of the county followed broadly those estimates which have recently been made of national demographic change between 1348 and 1540 (see further below). The sample sizes and hence the nature of the samples are thus entirely incompatible. These static comparisons, moreover, do not allow for changes in the social and economic circumstances of the life-cycle of individuals and kinship groups during the vicissitudes of the later middle ages. This complication affects any attempt to correlate bynames and surnames within communities and between the populations of the county at the two dates, since the taxable populations in effect consist of different samples.

References

[1] G Tengvik, *Old English Bynames*, (Nomina Germanica, 4, Uppsala,1938).

[2] G Fellows-Jensen, 'Some problems of a maverick anthroponymist', in H Voitl, ed., *The Study of Personal Names in the British Isles*, (1976), 52.

[3] O von Feilitzen, *The Pre-Conquest Personal Names of Domesday Book*, (Nomina Germanica, 3, Uppsala, 1937).

4 T Forssner, *Continental-Germanic Personal Names in England in Old and Middle English Times*, (Uppsala, 1916).

5 For example, the journal *Nomina* prefers toponymic; J C Holt, 'Feudal society and the family in early medieval England: II, notions of patrimony', *Transactions of the Royal Historical Society*, 5th ser, 33 (1983), 193-220; *idem*, 'Politics and property in early medieval England', reprt. in T H Aston, ed., *Landlords, Peasants and Politics in Medieval England*, (1987), 69-70; *idem*, *What's in a Name: Family Nomenclature and the Norman Conquest*, (1982). Others prefer the term habitative byname or surname.

6 J Jönsjö, *Studies on Middle English Nicknames. I. Compounds*, (Lund Studies in English, 55, 1979).

7 *Lay Subsidy 1332*, 2-3, 16, 99, 112, 122.

8 In some cases, Kingman may have represented real office, as at Dartmouth, where the byname Kingesmey existed in the early fourteenth century: *Lay Subsidy 1332*, 111, and Dartmouth Records computer database. Other Kingmans, however, are less likely to have had this derivation: *Lay Subsidy 1332*, 86, 125 (Bampton and Venn Ottery); and at Sidbury where the surname proliferated amongst the unfree tenantry *c*. 1350-94 (Richard, Nicholas, Robert, all customary tenants holding messuages and small holdings, and John and Thomas holding half-ferlings) — D&C Exeter Archives 2944-2945.

9 BL Add MS 28838, fos 77v-84v.

10 BL Add MS 28838, fos 80v and 83v.

11 *PND*, I-II, *passim*.

12 *PND*, II, 677.

13 *PND*, II, 374, 377, 435.

14 *Lay Subsidy 1332, passim.*

15 J F Willard, *Parliamentary Taxes on Personal Property*, (Cambridge, Mass, 1934), 87-92; for a more cautious view about how far the lower peasantry escaped, J R Maddicott, 'The English peasantry and the demands of the Crown 1294-1341', in T H Aston, ed., *Landlords, Peasants and Politics in Medieval England*, (1987), 294.

16 A Jones, 'Caddington, Kensworth and Dunstable in 1297', *Economic History Review*, 2nd ser, 32 (1979), 316, 319-22, 324; A T Gaydon, *The Taxation of 1297*, (Bedfordshire Historical Records Society, 39, 1959 for 1958), xxxiii.

17 B M S Campbell, 'The population of early Tudor England: a re-evaluation of the 1522 Muster Returns and 1524 and 1525 Lay Subsidies', *Journal of Historical Geography* 7 (1981), 145-54.

18 *Lay Subsidy 1332*, 47, 126; BL Arundel MS 17, fos 48v-49r; BL Add MS 37053, fos 273-279.

19 Jones, 'Caddington . . .'; Gaydon, *The Taxation of 1297*.

[20] J B Post, 'Manorial amercements and peasant poverty', *Economic History Review*, 2nd ser, 28 (1975), 308-9; N Denholm-Young, *Seignorial Administration in England*, (1937), 89-91.

[21] L R Poos and R M Smith, ' "Legal windows onto historical populations?" Recent research in medieval history', *Law and History Review*, 2 (1984), 128-52, and ' "Shades still on those windows": a reply to Zvi Razi', *ibid*, 3 (1985), 409-29; Z Razi, 'The use of manorial court rolls in demographic analysis: a reconsideration', *ibid*, 3 (1985), 191-200.

CHAPTER 2

DIALECT AND LOCAL USAGE

The inflection -a, -ia, -ya; fricative f/v; s/z interchange; high
front lengthened vowel (week); suffix -ing (especially
topographical forms); suffix -er (topographical forms);
suffix -man; occupational forms with -ster; similar forms
with -maker; some dialect words; from syndetic to asyndetic
topographical forms as an indicator, including elliptical
by-; instability of surnames in the later middle ages;
patronymics and the genitival -s.

As in other regions, the formation of bynames and surnames was
influenced to some degree by dialect and local usage during the
Middle English period (c.1100–1500). In general terms, Devon
comprised the westernmost extension of Southern ME dialect,
which ran eastwards to Sussex, Cornwall (mainly) and Kent having
their own particular dialects. Nevertheless, some of the dialectal
influence in Devon also obtained in parts of Cornwall; some influences seem also to have been specific to these two counties. The
isoglosses between Southern ME and Cornish followed a rather
elliptical route along the valleys in the confluence of the Ottery,
Tamar and Linher, resulting from the fluctuating success of the
westward expansion of Wessex during the late OE period. OE thus
extended into Cornwall in the north-east and south-east, in the
hundreds of Stratton and East, but east central Cornwall, in the
valley of the Linher, adjacent to west central Devon, remained
solidly Cornish, a division reflected in the formation of placenames
in these areas.[1]
The dialectal influences in Devon were manifested in some inflections, the interchange and pronunciation of some vowels and
consonants, and the use of some and paucity of other suffixes. Some
dialect terms were also used more prevalently in Devon than in other
counties, although their stem was to be found in OE. These dialect
terms were mainly topographical, but some occupational, and a few
related to relationship; all thus affected the formation of some
bynames.

One of the distinctive particularities of some bynames in Devon and Cornwall, through much of the ME period, was the inflection -a, -ia, or -ya, and related forms (sometimes, possibly, simply -y(e) as Ralph Wodye, a customary tenant of Stokenham in 1278). For example, Cole occurred as Cola, White as Whita, Cade as Cadia. Some 270 taxpayers in 1332 bore bynames inflected in this way.[2] The form appeared in both urban and rural parishes, for example Frya, Kena, Piria, and Tyla in Totnes.[3] In many places, the inflection was used inconsistently, so that Cole and Cola, White and Whita, Cade and Cadia, occurred simultaneously in the same or adjacent parishes. In Colyton hundred, Cada (bis) and Gylla were concurrent with Cole (several), Vele, Scute and Cobbe.[4] Perhaps, however, the inflection occurred slightly less frequently in the lay subsidy of 1332 in the South Hams and east Devon. Its incidence may have been correspondingly higher in mid- and west Devon: in Roborough hundred (30 taxpayers); Witheridge hundred (24); Black Torrington hundred (23).[5] In Plymouth, in 1332, a nascent borough in the south-west, the taxpayers then included Stipa, Bagga, Broda, Folia, Bonda and Pepa.[6] In these areas, the inflection was formed mainly on simple, uncompounded bynames, often from personal names, such as Goda, Frya, Lagga, Grygga, Tippa, Greta. Of the 167 occurrences in west Devon, only a few comprised dithematic or disyllabic forms, such as Louera, Whetena, Godhyna, Slyuera, Swatela, Shurreua, Luuesta.[7] An inflection was also used, however, in many locative bynames in several sources, complicating the issue.

The inflection was employed from the inception of ME and persisted in rural areas through to the fifteenth century in some places. In c 1193-1217, William, earl of Devon subinfeudated Robert de Wortha, son of Hawyse de Wortha, in land in Fairby in Tiverton.[8] In feet of fines of 1198-9, conusors and conusees included Hay de Wika, Nicholas de Forda, Richard de Cumba, and, in 1219, Richard de Yerda.[9] Numerous jurors in the Crown Pleas of 1238 had bynames incorporating the inflection: for example, Nicholas de Cumba, Hugh and Alan de Morba, Roger de Spina, Henry Cobba, Richard Stranga, Richard Beta, Benedict Bunta, Robert Peccha, John Watta, Walter Surreva, *et al*.[10] The clerk who compiled the charters of the Thorne family, of Somerset, in favour of Canonsleigh Priory, from *c*.1215, used the form Thorna, although by the fourteenth century the form had become normalized in the charters as Thorne. In the same charters, the bynames of other beneficiaries from Somerset were inflected: Nicholas Bagga, Richard and William Capa; as also were those of some donors from Devon: William Homa and Richard Stranga, as well as all locative bynames.[11] The extent of Berry Pomeroy in 1292 listed Stephen Bolda, Adam Frya, Thomas le Boya, John Coula and Richard de Forda.[12] In 1310, Matthew Veala was admitted to the freedom of Exeter.[13] In the same year, Walter Gydie and Robert Gydia were placed in mercy for trespass in the wood and pasture at Buckland.[14] In the late thirteenth century, William de Spina issued letters obligatory at Modbury.[15] Amongst the list of tinners taxed in 1339 were enumerated those bearing the bynames Lappa, Hokka (bis), Cola (but also Cole), Rugga (but also Rugge), Huta, Coula, Prouta (three), Patya, Stowka, Taccha, Calwa (from calwe, bold), Louera (bis), Kena (but also Kene), Brenta and Wighta.[16] In the late fourteenth century, Thomas Coppa was murdered at Bradninch and Richard Bela outlawed.[17] Thomas Attewilla brought an action to outlaw Robert Willa and John Forde in the mid fifteenth century.[18] In 1432, John atte Clyva junior was involved in a case of trespass at Yarcombe.[19] The rental of Modbury of *c.* 1398 included Walter Prata, William Frya, William Golda, William Spyna, and Simon Loda.[20] At Stoke Fleming, the surname Trende occurred alternately as Trenda in the later middle ages. Walter Trenda occurred in the court rolls from 1393 almost consistently as Trenda, but in the early fifteenth the form alternated between Trende and Trenda. From then, through the 1440s, Roger Trenda appeared in the same rolls with the inflection. In the court rolls of the same manor, the byname Slota was always inflected.[21] At Werrington, in west central Devon, the surname Love constantly occurred in the court rolls throughout the fourteenth and fifteenth centuries in the inflected forms Louia, Louya, or Louie, until its disappearance from the manor in the 1490s. In the same court rolls, actions were brought or presentments made against John Spera (1385), Alana Grove (1385), Alana wife of Walter Cadya (1386), Walter Cadia himself (1392–6), Walter Whyta (1395); Nicholas Bata died there in 1396, his administrator being John Bata; William Bribba appeared in 1384–95 (but subsequently as Bribbe); Richard Vela appeared in 1395 and William Bata in 1385–95.[22] John Nude *alias* Nuda attended Exeter College in Oxford from 1382 to 1388.[23] The inflection was thus constructed throughout rural Devon on the bynames of all social groups, by local clerks as well as by clerks of county officials acting on behalf of the royal administration.

This inflection persisted in some of the boroughs towards the end of the middle ages. The churchwardens' accounts of Ashburton mentioned John Wylla in 1504–5, whilst William Mace was entered variously as Masy, Macy and Masi in the 1490s, a surname which became stabilized there as Macye (thus inflected) by the 1580s.[24] At Dartmouth, a thriving community on the eastern, more cosmopolitan, seaboard, bynames were consistently inflected during the

thirteenth and fourteenth centuries. Charters mentioned Richard de
Cumba (c.1210), Roger Cumba, Walter de Comba, Ilary de Cumba
(c.1235), Roger Tubba alias Tubbe (c.1210–20), Adam Cada and
Walter Wita (c.1243), William Gora (1278–1318), Walter Wyta
(c.1300), John Wyta (1333), Gilbert Willa (1325), Adam Cada
(c.1300), John Calna alias Calnya (1311) and others. The byname
Rurde appeared there alternately as Rurda, but increasingly without
the inflection after c.1290. By c.1340, the inflection generally had
declined in Dartmouth, although it still surfaced occasionally, as
with John Colta (1348), John Bigga (1354), John Forda (1399), and
William and Piers Reda in the poll tax of 1377. The predominant
forms in Dartmouth by the late fourteenth century, however, were
uninflected: Burde, Cote, Gode, Wybbe, Colte, Cade, Swete, Rurde,
Stibbe, Cole, Hobbe, Forde, Rede.[25] In metropolitan Exeter, some
inflected surnames occasionally surfaced in the later middle ages:
John Berya (1390–1), Baldwin Bolla (1349–50), John Brenta (1349),
John Fulscha (1394–5), John Reva (1349), Robert Tubba (1494), and
William Vela, the common clerk (1505–6).[26] In Tavistock, Reginald
Strepa was churchwarden in 1385–6, and the families of Brenta,
Hunta and Libba resident there in the mid fifteenth century, whilst
John Wysa attested a charter relating to property there in 1402.[27]
Generally, therefore, the use of the inflection had declined in
boroughs by the end of the fourteenth century, except perhaps in
the medium sized boroughs such as Ashburton, which were also
located in the uplands. The residual incidences of the inflection may
represent stabilization of some surnames with the inflected form, or,
in some cases, perhaps immigration from some rural areas.

The inflection did persist in some rural parts of Devon through
into the fifteenth century. By 1524, its survival was circumscribed in
specific areas, represented by a few residual entries in the lay subsidy
of 1524–5: John Bela at Lifton, William Bybbye at Haccombe,
Nicholas Bolla at Holsworthy, Henry and John Cadda in Welcombe,
John and Richard Cragga in Milton Abbot, John Dybba, Simon
Tybba and John Tybby all in Hartland, Nicholas and Stephen Tody
in Marytavy, Stephen Tody in Milton Abbot, Thomas Dogga (but
John and Roger Doygge) in Milton Abbot, Thomas Cady in Hartland, Richard Wella, John and Richard Whyta and Sampson Frya in
Werrington, and William Laka in Dunsford. Additionally, the
surname Facye had become established in several places and Vele
had become stabilized in its inflected form (Vela, Vely) in some
others (Broadwoodwidger, Hartland, Sampford Courtenay,
Tetcott). By 1524, it seems, inflected surnames survived only in
north and west Devon, particularly in Hartland Hundred, somewhat remote.[28] Here, for example, in Hartland itself, Vele was still

occasionally inflected, existing there as a core surname represented strongly in the survey of the manor in 1566.[29]

The inflection existed in adjacent Cornwall in the later middle ages. For example, Henry Gartha was a tenant on the manor of Liskeard in 1427.[30] Almost a century earlier, the caption of seisin of the Earldom estates included numerous tenants whose bynames were inflected: Langa, Densha, Broda, Whita (several), Chubba, Witha (several), Prouta (several), Bonda, Plegha, Penta, and many others. In 1357, Anger Hunta was one of the conventionary tenants at Trematon, and, in 1382, an inquisition at Liskeard mentioned Walter Wada and Richard Nuda.[31] By contrast, the inflection hardly existed in the lay subsidies of Dorset in 1327 and 1332, with only isolated examples (Vaga, Toly-bis, Tilie-ten, Cady-*bis*), but many consistently uninflected bynames (Golde-33, Dodde-10, Rugge, Tibbe, Bonde, Dabbe, Cole, Bole, Bagge, Bibbe, Tudde *et al*). The lay subsidy for Somerset about the same time (1327) also exhibited few examples of inflection.[32] The inflection seems, therefore, to have been a distinctive feature of bynames in Devon and Cornwall.

Explanation of its incidence is complicated. Locative, and some topographical, bynames may simply have been declined as feminine Latin nouns (de Cumba, de Forda). Thus a writ-charter of Matilda was directed to her *ministri* at Lyftona (*c*.1100–1107); a charter of slightly later date was attested by Ralph de Lega (but also by Hamelin de Leigh); charters were issued by Robert de Wyka in 1176 and 1199–1207; another charter of 1174–1184 referred to land in Brenta, land held by Augustine de Brenta; and William, bishop of Exeter, issued an *actum* confirming the church of Hatherleya in 1225.[33] Such an explanation may also account for those few inflected bynames derived from office or status, such as Shurreua or Bonda. A suggestion which must be discounted is that the inflection of locative bynames represented the OE dative singular.[34] These 'Latinized' bynames, however, comprised only part of the corpus of inflected names. Another proportion may have derived from OE personal names, such as Dobbe or Bagge, in which case there may be a persistence of OE inflection of weak nouns, and, in a few cases, such as Cade, of OE hypocoristics of Celtic personal names.[35] Equally probable, however, given the timing of the inflection, is the influence of the levelling of ME inflections. During the ME period, the OE analytical inflections gradually declined, to be replaced in many syntactical cases by a levelled inflection, -e. In southern ME, the pronunciation of this levelled inflection may have been voiced -a or -ya, and this explanation seems most likely for many of the inflected bynames in Devon.[36]

The interchange of fricative initial f and v was widespread in southern ME.[37] Its existence in Devon is evident from the twelfth century, for example in the person of Martin de Visacre (Fishacre) in Dartmouth, where also resided William atte Vosse in 1327. In the later middle ages, other inhabitants of that borough included William Venton, who attested three charters in 1414, and John Voule, who attested as Voule, Foughell and Fouhell in 1417 and 1423.[38] Amongst the freemen of Exeter were John le Velter (1288), two burgesses with the same occupational byname le Vissere (1302) and le Vyssher (1308), whilst the military survey there in 1522 mentioned Richard Fyncent.[39] The churchwardens' accounts of the smaller borough of Ashburton referred to the obit for Joan Varwell in 1509–10, to her husband John Varewell in 1508–9, and to Richard Veyremouthe in 1522–3, the latter also being entered as Fayremouthe. One of the jurors for Ashburton at the great stannary court on Crockerntor in September 1494 was Richard Voxforde (*alias* Foxford).[40] This interchange persisted throughout the later middle ages in urban Devon.

It was equally prevalent in rural Devon. In the east, the change occurred at Uplyme, where the court rolls mentioned Robert le Voghelere in 1307–8 and John le Vrenshe de Axmouthe in the 1370s.[41] In the South Hams the mutation is well attested at Stoke Fleming, particularly in John Vincent, fl *c.*1450–1470. He occurred in the court rolls there initially as John Fyncent, but later consistently as John Vynsent *alias* Vincent *alias* Vyncente, but, by contrast, Henry Fynsent appeared contemporaneously.[42] In the west, at Werrington, the court rolls enumerated John Foleslo *alias* Voleslo, both forms being used almost equally in 1395. From 1479 to 1496, John Vogler made appearances in court, on five occasions as Vogler, but on seven as Fogler. Another tenant there with a locative surname derived from Fentrigan in Cornwall appeared as Ventrigan.[43]

In the lay subsidy of 1524–5, the interchange was extensive, listing taxpayers named Verlegh (3), Velacot (3), Ven(n) (7), Venicombe (8), Venman, Venner (16), Venning (7), Venton (4), Verchild (3), Visher, Vischleigh, Vorseman (i.e. Furseman), Vosse (5), Vowler (3), and Voxhill.[44] Not surprisingly, many of these surnames related to locative or topographical derivations from Fenn. The form of the placename stabilized in Devon as Venn, but the derivative surname fluctuated between Fenn and Venn, more usually Fenn in the lay subsidy of 1332. The interchange was not exclusive to Devon, but pertained more widely to southern ME; thus in Dorset, in 1327, taxpayers included Visshere, le Vader (but also Fader), le Visere, Vromond and le Vaire.[45]

Nor was the interchange restricted to the voicing of initial characters. Medial v and f were also interchanged. Thus, at Ashburton in the 1480s, John Cleve provided ironwork for the tabernacle of St Mary in the aisle of the parish church, but his name was entered in the accounts variously as Cleve, Cleffe, and Clyffe, but predominantly as Clyffe *alias* Cliffe.[46] At Yarcombe, the same transliteration occurred in the fourteenth and fifteenth century in the court rolls: Richard atte Clyve (1321-31), Robert de Wytecliue, Agnes atte Cliue, Thomas Curreclyue, John atte Clyue (variously as Clyue, Cleue, Cleve and Clyfe) (1327-1436).[47] Similarly, in 1238, Richard de la Clive was presented at the eyre.[48] Taxpayers in 1332 included amongst many others Thomas and Letice atte Clyue in Tavistock, Robert and Walter atte Clyue in King's Nympton, Walter Uppeclyue at Withycombe Raleigh, Adam atte Clyue at Yarcombe, Richard Bynytheclyue at North Molton, Thomas atte Clyue and Thomas Wyteclyue at Burrington, and William atte Clyue at Kingsbridge.[49] In 1524-5, taxpayers included *inter alia* two Chafes and one Chave at Uplowman, and seven Lyffes and one Lyve at Stokenham.[50]

Double mutation happened only infrequently, particularly with the locative or topographical byname Thorn. At Stoke Climsland in Cornwall, a dispute in 1361 concerned a free tenant who held unfree land, John Vorn son of John Vorn.[51] Taxpayers in Devon in 1332 included two called Vorn.[52] The mutation here developed through (θ) to (ð) to (γ). Double mutation between v and w, which occurred minimally, may have been a corruption of the interchange between u and v. Thus at Yarcombe, the rector of Punchardon, John atte Vatere,[53] was presented for default of suit; at Ottery St Mary, Richard Wenman was presented for brewing in 1379 and admitted as tenant of a house in 1380, in this case suggesting a mutation from f to v to w. In recapitulation, the interchange between fricative f and v was extensive throughout the whole area in which southern ME obtained. It affected the form in which some surnames became stabilized in Devon.[54]

The mutation between initial s and z occurred much less frequently. Bynames and surnames had an initial s rather than z. In fact, the substitution of z for s seems to have been more prevalent in the sixteenth century than earlier. In the lay subsidies for 1542-5, the taxpayers included William Zewarde at Uplyme, William, Agnes and Bridget Zeward at Combe Pyne, Richard, Andrew and Thomas Zewarde at Axminster, and John Zewarde at Woodbury. In the earlier subsidy of 1524-5, the taxpayers at Stokeinteignhead had included two Zewardes and two Sewardes, and nine Zeves. Few earlier examples of this interchange can be found.[55] Initial interchange between y and g was more significant, especially, for example, in yate or yeat (gate), a widespread topographical byname in Devon. The interchange also occurred medially, as in degher for dyer, heghes or heghen for hays. This interchange may have involved the frequency of yogh (ȝ) in the south-west.[56]

The high front lengthened vowel was important in Devon for one particular topographical or locative byname. In Devon, OE *wicu* developed as ME weke, wyke or week, both as placename (such as Week St Mary, Highweek, Germansweek) and as byname. This evolution contrasts with those regions, particularly northern and north-west England, where the prevalent form was wich.[57] Thus, in the Crown Pleas of 1238, the byname occurred eleven times as de Wike and once as de Wiche.[58] In 1332, the byname occurred constantly as (de) Wyke (38 taxpayers).[59] In 1524–5, 31 taxpayers bore the surname Weke(s), four Wyke(s), one Wike, one Wecke, three Wekys, and one Whyke.[60] The common form in the later middle ages is represented by Walter Weke, who was presented by the homage of the small manor of Colebrooke in mid Devon, for allowing his bakehouse to fall into disrepair and for not inhabiting his tenement (1499–1500).[61] The surname subsequently evolved as Week(s) in Devon.

The transition of OE reflex -y- into ME followed the general pattern of southern ME. The convoluted forms did not depend on whether the document was compiled centrally or locally, the form varying widely in both.[62] In *c.*1205, Reginald de la Putte, a leper, issued a charter in favour of Tavistock Abbey 'pro terra de Putte'.[63] In a rental of Ottery St Mary in *c.*1381, the customary tenants of the hamlet of Putt ('Pitte custumarii') included Roger de Pitte, who held two ferlings. The customary tenants of the hamlet of Hill included Michael at Hille, who held three ferlings.[64] In the late sixteenth century, Joan Hull, widow, of Exeter, was party to a deed with the Magdalen Hospital.[65] The admissions to the freedom of Exeter from the fifteenth to the eighteenth centuries included burgesses called Hylman and Hilman.[66] At Yarcombe in 1393, John Pytman appeared in the manorial court.[67] The transformation of reflex -y- in ME occurred indiscriminately as -i-, -u- and still -y-, even within locally produced documents.

A form of byname and surname which seems to be quite distinctive of Devon is a topographical one with the suffix -ing. A number of bynames in Devon were seemingly OE personal names with the associative element -ing, reflecting an earlier formation. The most frequent of these were Brouning and Batyn, which were borne by 24 and 25 taxpayers respectively in 1332, and continued throughout the late middle ages.[68] Other, less frequent, examples of this type included Whityng, Snellyng, Godyng, Pippyng, Baddyng, Dobyn, Collyng, Loueryng, Poddyng, Croppyng, Dollyng, all occurring between one and four times in 1332.[69] More unusual, however, were later, topographical bynames which incorporated this element: Bryggyng; Torryng (4 taxpayers in 1332); Forssyng; Dounyng (7); Stonyng; Knellyng and Knollyng (4); Hillyng (2) and Hullyng; Pittyng (3); Bromyng; Comyn(g) (5); Worthyn (2); Moryn(g) (5); Willyng (2); Fennyng; Thornyng (3); Beryng (from O E *bearu*) —which all occurred in 1332.[70]

During the later middle ages, these topographical forms abounded. In the court rolls of Stoke Fleming, in the fifteenth century, occurred Fennyng, Dounyng, Pittyng, Stonyng and Hillyng.[71] Isabella Wallyng appeared in court at Stoke Canon in 1455.[72] At Feniton, in the late fourteenth century, John Dounyng was attached to perform fealty and suit of court.[73] Numerous inhabitants of Ashburton had similar surnames between 1480 and 1521: Roger Torryng, Joan Knollyng, Richard Knollyng, John Torryng, William Knollyng, Thomas Torryng, Alice Torryng, John Comyng, William Brokyn, John Brokyn, William Cullyng, Alice Brokyng.[74] Similarly at nearby Wreyland, the tenants included John Comyng (fl 1437-8), John and Roger Torryng (fl 1479-87), and John, William, Thomas and Michael Wallyng.[75] At Modbury, *c.* 1398, one of the tenants was John Torryng.[76] In the late fifteenth century, Martin Ferrers levied a fine with John Fennyng concerning two messuages, two gardens, 30 acres arable, 20 acres pasture, one acre of wood, and 20 acres of furze in North Alvington.[77] John Hillyng of Staverton compounded for his tithes with the Dean and Chapter of Exeter in 1441.[78] Freemen of Exeter between 1319 and 1497 bore the surnames Downyng, Stonyng (4), Thornyng, Hillyng (2), Burghyng, and Comyng.[79] Much earlier, in 1238, cases before the Devon eyre involved Robert Wiking, Henry and Sampson Culling. The Cullyng family had become established at Tavistock by 1306 and later provided Abbot Thomas Culling (1381-1402).[80] In 1366, the murder of Thomas Cotyng atte Yoo was presented.[81] In 1461, Henry Combyng committed an assault at Dawlish and was outside the tithing. John Hillyng of Houghton was involved in a dispute over a tinworking in the early fifteenth century; Robert Thorning was one of the largest tinners at Chagford in 1550. In 1394, John Stonyng was a small unfree tenant at Sidbury.[82] Many other tinners taxed in 1339 had borne bynames of this type.[83]

By 1524-5, a high proportion of topographical surnames had the suffix -ing: Downing (*alias* Dunning) (3); Comyng (17); Moryn (4); Hyllyng (11); Stonyng (16); Thornyng (6); Pittyng (6); Knollyng (11); Hellyng (heel, a quarry); Townyng; Torryng (12); Wyllyng (12); Brokyng (12); Crossyng (3); Fossyn; Vennyng and variants (11); and Burryng. In a few places, there was a concentration of such surnames; at Yealmpton, of 109 taxpayers, four had the surname

Thornyng, two Brounyng, eight Deryng, two Brokyng, and two Dabyn. On the nearby manor of Plympton Grange, c.1524 and through the late sixteenth century, the Brokyn(g), Torryng and Wyllyng families persisted.[84]

An explanation of this form of surname is not absolutely clear-cut. The earlier forms, particularly those involving ostensibly OE personal names, must have represented the OE associative element - ing. Another explanation may reside in the OE weak plural form - en, but this suggestion probably only applied to a few surnames derived specifically from minor placenames: Pitten in Yealmpton and Willing in Rattery, for example.[85] The surnames Worthen and Heghen probably also resulted from this influence, but the latter never occurred with a final -ing.[86] Rea and Ewen advanced the notion that the element represented 'a meadow', but this hypothesis seems unusual.[87] The OFr diminutive -en would more normally have been appended to personal names.[88] For Devon, there is a corpus of about a dozen topographical bynames and surnames which assumed the element -ing. Of these, Reaney commented on three, defining Hilling as 'hill-dweller', Coming as deriving from the personal name Cumin, and Dunning as a patronymic of Dun (although for Walding, not encountered in medieval Devon, he gave the etymology as 'forest-dweller').[89] There seems little doubt, however, that all these forms are topographical, and that their implication is possibly inhabitant in that feature, so that topographical bynames with -ing may be an equivalent of such bynames with the suffixes -er or -man. These different suffixes, -man and -er, occurred also in Devon, -man almost as frequently as -ing in topographical forms, -er more rarely.

The suffix -er in topographical bynames was extremely rare in Devon, by contrast with some other counties, such as Sussex.[90] In the lay subsidy of 1332, only three potential examples occurred: Thomas le Comere at Sampford Peverell; Thomas Comer at Tavistock; Richard Comere at Crediton.[91] This particular byname, however, is ambivalent, since it could also be occupational, associated with woollen cloth. By the lay subsidy of 1524–5, a wider, but still limited, range of topographical bynames with -er becomes evident: Comer (11 taxpayers); Ryxer (living by the rushes) (9); Whyker or Weker (7) and possibly also Whycher and Veker; Slader (8); Shuter (ambivalently); Rogger repeatedly, but also ambivalent; Gater (3); Venner (13); Brygger; Lyer (from lye, a variant of ley) (7); Leker (*alias* Laker).[92] Confirmation that Comber could be topographical is found at Dartmouth. There, John Combe attested innumerable charters in the mid fifteenth century, described six times as Comber between 1435 and 1446. The surname of John

Holcomber, who also occurred in Dartmouth in 1410, may also be indicative.[93] Shuter is complicated by the corruption of the occupational byname Suter, as at Stoke Fleming during the fifteenth century.[94] The occurrence of Rogerman suggests that at least some instances of Rogger could be topographical as well as surnames derived from personal names.[95] Gater and Brygger could be equally occupational surnames.[96]

Other incidences of these forms occurred during the later middle ages. At Exeter, the burgesses included Comere (1352 and 1364) and Rogger (1429–54, four times).[97] John Whyker was admitted to the freedom in 1368 and died in 1375, but his son succeeded him and lived until the 1390s.[98] Matilda, the widow of Robert Wycher occurred in the Mayor's Court Rolls in 1314.[99] In the lay subsidy of 1498 and military survey of 1522 were listed, within the City, John Slader, a Holmer, Ligher and Ryxer.[100] At Yarcombe, Walter Comer appeared in court in 1331–3.[101] The list of those in tithing or paying recognition at Stoke Fleming in the early sixteenth century included Peter Weller.[102] One of the manorial jurors at Uplyme in the mid thirteenth century was Geoffrey le Comere *alias* Komere, who held a virgate as a customary tenant.[103] Although instances can be elicited, therefore, yet this form of byname was particularly unusual in Devon.

The element -man may have had different applications in different regions. The suggestion that, when combined with a personal name, the element signified a servant, does certainly not apply to Devon.[104] In this county, the element almost exclusively denoted a topographical or occupational sense.[105] The element was also, in accordance with southern ME, always reproduced as man, by contrast with, for example, the dialectal mon in the west Midlands.[106]

In the lay subsidy of 1332, some 60 taxpayers had this form of byname. A number were obviously occupational: Chisman (*bis*); Botman; Clouterman; Deyman (*bis*); Shepesman. Coteman probably reflected economic status.[107] Deyman became a fairly widespread occupational byname and surname within Devon, related to the dairy production which expanded during the later middle ages; the surname was particularly important in the west, especially in Hartland.[108] Hyredman in 1332 was one of the few indicators of the extent of wage labour in Devon in the later middle ages.[109]

The majority of the usages of -man, however, were topographical: Hayman; Fenman; Holeman; Hegheman; Heleman; Lakeman; Leyman; Pitman; Shuteman; Tounman; Waterman; Wodeman; Yetman; Crosman; Fordeman; Polman; Courtman; Rodeman (although a few of these might also be occupational).[110] In most cases, the implication was that the original bearer had lived by one of these features rather than held an occupation related to that feature. Only Nyweman had locative implications.[111] A smaller number of bynames may have represented status, but were more likely to have originated as nicknames: Kyngman; Richeman.[112] More definite nicknames included Fairman, Godman, Truman, Whiteman, Stilleman, Yoldeman and Yolleman.[113] Selyman was a frequent example of this type of nickname.[114] Compounded names of this sort only involved female gender once: Stelewomman.[115] The most frequently occurring bynames of this type in 1332 were Chepman (17), Godman (10), Holeman (8), Selyman (7), and Nyweman (6). The frequency of Chapman reflected the pattern of rural trading in Devon, where, because of the topography, there was considerable petty exchange through broggers, despite and because of the high number of small towns and market vills.[116]

Many other sources establish the level of occurrance of surnames with -man in Devon during the later middle ages. One of the jurors at the Crown Pleas for the borough of Bradninch was William Porteman.[117] At Stoke Fleming, during the fifteenth century, appearances in court were made by Lakeman, Crosseman, Fursman, Holman, and Bryggeman, as well as Schepeman *alias* Shipman, Horsman, Hogman, Deyman, Chapman and Wenman. John Shipman was listed in the extent of 1374, and he and John junior recurred in the court rolls in the 1390s. Two siblings of the family, Thomas and Richard, were *fugitivi* from the manor. Horsman was introduced to Stoke during the fifteenth century.[118] The surname also occurred in the terrier of Uplyme in 1516 (Horsman *alias* Stere), where John Horsman held a fardel and other lands and was a tithingman in 1530-6.[119] This surname seems to have occurred more frequently during the later middle ages, although Palfreyman had occurred in 1332.[120] The wider usage of the surname Horsman may reflect the increased use of horse-drawn transport, especially packhorses, in the later midle ages, especially as its incidence seems to have been highest in those areas adjacent to the ports of east Devon and the South Hams.[121]

Topographical forms with -man occurred in most communities in Devon during the later middle ages. At Wreyland, Thomas Leyman claimed a stray foal in 1489.[122] Cecily Beryman had the farm of her own tithes in Staverton.[123] In the largest towns, the element often reflected rural topography, as at Dartmouth, where charters referred to Heyman (1466), Leyman (1379-88), as well as the occupational Chepman (1430), and possibly occupational Wodman (1409-37) and Scherman.[124] In late medieval Exeter, the admissions to the freedom included a Biriman (1315), Hethman (1378, 1417), Hilman (1455), Poleman (1458) and Puryman (1429).[125]

Countless incidences occurred on rural manors during the later middle ages. John Cheseman inhabited Kingston in the mid fifteenth century. John Bereman was a seafarer and merchant from Topsham (fl 1475–80). John Deyman held two ferlings at Ottery St Mary in *c.* 1381. Richard Belaman and John Blakeman were tenants of Berry Pomeroy and Stockleigh Pomeroy in 1293; John Holman of Tavistock at the end of the fourteenth century; John Hayman at Feniton at the end of the fifteenth. Subscribers to the Guild of St Katherine of Tinners included Henry Peryman and Joan and Richard Hilman. At Sidbury *c.* 1350, the customary tenants included Peter Rodman, and John, Nicholas and Richard Kingman.[126] The frequency is best illustrated at Werrington. Forsman was borne here by Ellis in 1368, John, who was a pledge in 1384, Walter, who was constantly involved in litigation about debt from 1384 to 1396, and Robert, who was amerced for brewing. Thomas Holman was presented for hue and cry in 1384–5, whilst John Holman brewed in the 1460s and 1470s. Margery Horsman appeared fleetingly in the manorial court in 1385 for trespass. John and Thomas Burman appeared in 1385, Thomas later being presented for an offence against the tithing in 1395, when Robert also appeared as Burgheman. William Berman was presented for withdrawing suit of mill in 1395. Nicholas Parkeman, who died in 1395, had held a free tenement in Werrington.[127]

By 1524–5, the relative proportion of topographical forms had increased. More than 60% of the surnames with -man were topographical, only 23% occupational, 9% nicknames and 4% generic locative (such as Frenshman). At this time, some 2% of the taxpayers bore surnames which were compounds of -man.[128] The highest concentration in 1524–5 seemed to be in the west and north, in the hundreds of Shebbear, Fremington, Hartland, Lifton and South Molton. In these hundreds, between 2–3% of taxpayers bore this type of surname. The most frequent surnames comprised Hayman (27 taxpayers), Beryman (22), Leman (28), Fursman (15), Holman (26) and Crosseman (13). Peryman was apparently concentrated in East Budleigh Hundred (7 of 15 instances), whilst Bowrman similarly in Hemyock Hundred (8 of 15, but 7 in Hemyock parish), reflecting the localized fortunes of some kinship groups.[129] These topographical forms were much in evidence during the later sixteenth century. William Lakeman, Peter Bawman, Stephen Hayman and John Peryman were all customary tenants on the manor of Plympton Grange. William Beryman of Iddesleigh was a joint-stock partner in a ship trading to Portugal in 1585. The Bowreman surname continued to be associated with Hemyock. In 1566, Isabella, Richard and James were all tenants there, as were Christopher and Isabella Knolman. Amongst those submitting tin for coinage at

Chagford in 1523 were John Leyman of Ashburton, whilst William Knapman was a substantial tinner at mid century. In 1547, he sold tin valued at more than 83 pounds to a merchant of Exeter, and received a mortgage of two manors as collateral for the sale of other tin. He was described as a gentleman of Throwleigh. William Dayman was a copyholder at Colwell and Sutton Lacy in the 1560s.[130] This surname persisted at Ashburton through the sixteenth century. At Hartland, Daymans continued there from the sixteenth to the twentieth centuries, and distant kin returned from Canada for a Dayman funeral there at the turn of this century.[131] The element -man thus contributed highly to the formation of surnames in Devon, increasingly within topographical surnames, but also occupational and nickname.[132]

Alternative forms, equivalent to -man, were insignificant in Devon. The element -grom was frequent in Dorset, as also in Southampton and Surrey and other areas of southern ME.[133] It occurred much less frequently in Devon: only Whitegrom and Redegrom amongst the taxpayers of 1332.[134] Equally, -wyne was uncharacteristic of Devon, featuring only in some of the boroughs, such as at Exeter, Ottery St Mary, Great Torrington and South Molton (Godewyne, Ryddewyne, Redwyne and Bylewyne).[135]

A further unusual form in Devon was occupational bynames with the suffix -ster. When this form did occur, the context was usually very specific, relating to (independent) women pursuing petty trades, often, but not exclusively, in urban centres. In the later middle ages, this form reflected a continuing instability of surnames in this limited section of the community, since these women assumed their *cognomina* from their actual occupation. Whereas, by the late fourteenth century, the surnames of the majority of the population had become hereditary and stable, these female hucksters continued to have bynames relating to their actual occupation. This instability perhaps related to the rather wider opportunities for women in the urban economy of later medieval England, although still restricted to petty trading.

In 1332, Isabel Shipstere paid tax at Bovey Tracy, but she is the only occurrence of this type in that lay subsidy. Most probably, however, most female petty traders would not have accumulated enough taxable wealth to be assessed for the subsidy.[136] At Uplyme, Joan la Crokesterre was reported in 1340 as having been a former tenant of a messuage and two and a half acres of land. Also in a rural context, Avice and Margery Kemistere were involved in cases of trepass in Yarcombe in 1347.[137] Although in a rural context, their trades were petty ones.[138] More importantly, in late fourteenth century Exeter, the petty hucksters included Joan Shippestere,

Isolda Spynnestere, Joan and Cecily Kemestere, Kathleen Broude-stere, and Agnes and Juliana Shippestere.[139] Those assessed in the poll tax for Dartmouth, in 1377, included Gonne Tappesterre, Margery Scheppestere, and Alice Sheppestere.[140] An alien taxed in the mid fifteenth century was Christine Spinster, who had migrated from Scotland to Northam, a petty borough.[141] Her byname reflects the instability not only of female petty traders, but also of aliens.[142] Her social position was reflected by her assessment for 6d. levied on aliens *non tenens hospicium*, and therefore probably in lodgings or living-in. In other towns of southern England, such as Oxford and Westminster, the suffix -ster had the same specific interpret-ation.[143]

Occupational surnames with the suffix -maker were introduced into Devon during the later middle ages. Their introduction seems also to have occurred initially in an urban context. Although they intruded during the later middle ages, yet they still seemed to represent the actual occupation of their bearers, another example of instability amongst specific sections of the community during the later middle ages. These bynames also seem to relate to new designations for trades. In 1377, John Cardemaker was assessed to the poll tax in Dartmouth.[144] Thomas Cardemaker was admitted to the freedom of Exeter in the same year.[145] Admissions of burgesses with this type of name, however, did not become frequent until the late fifteenth century, such as: Anthony Hatmaker (1480-1); John Cardemaker (apprenticed 1501-2). Taxpayers at Exeter included Nicholas Hattemaker (1489) and John Cardmaker (1524-5).[146] To some extent, these new forms may have been associated with aliens, who may have introduced the trades. Thus, amongst those enumerated in the military survey of Exeter in 1522 were John Hatmaker, born in Brabant, James Hatmaker, born in Lucca, James Shoemaker, born in Holland, and Claret Shoemaker, a Dutch-man.[147] This association may have obtained by the mid fifteenth century. Amongst the aliens taxed then were Henry Clokmaker, a Dutchman, at Dartmouth; William Orgemaker, another Dutchman, in Exeter; Peter Stolemaker, a Norman in Sidmouth; and Peter Cardemaker, a Frenchman in the small borough of Bradninch.[148] At the same time, new occupational surnames were developing in the urban context. Glasier became a new surname in Exeter in the late fourteenth century.[149] Cordwainer was associated with aliens, especially Dutchmen, in the mid fifteenth century, alongside the indigenous forms of clouter and *sutor*.[150] The formation of surnames with the element -maker provided only a very minor part of the stock in Devon, but their significance resided in their association with alien craftsmen during the later middle ages.[151]

Some dialect words persisted in use throughout the middle ages. Principal amongst these was the topographical byname and surname yeo and its variants, common throughout the south-western counties. In the Crown Pleas of 1238, seven of those who were impleaded or were suitors had the byname (de) (la) Ya, whilst only one was known as Atewater.[152] The proportion of taxpayers with these respective forms in 1332 was rather different; 14 were called atte Watere, whilst 23 were known by the byname Yo and its variants.[153] At Uplyme, the byname in the early fourteenth century was exclusively atte Watere. During the later middle ages, Yeo seems to have become more prevalent than atte Watere. An inquisition into the lands in Yeo of Joan, daughter of Thomas atte Yeo, was held in *c.* 1388, because of her disability.[154] By the early sixteenth century, Yeo had become a very common surname in Devon.

Some other topographical terms, derived from OE, contributed to the pattern of naming in Devon. Bear, from *bearu*, was a common alternative to wood (OE *wudu*). Burgh or Burrow (*beorg*, a mound) occurred frequently as a byname and surname. Other dialect terms which were integrated into naming, were occupational, although they were broadly dialectal in relating to the south-west as well as Devon: crocker, tucker, helier. The dialect term of relationship, yem or eym (uncle) occurred a few times in the lay subsidy of 1332, in a rental of the fourteenth century, and was represented by Richard Yeme, Abbot of Tavistock (1490–2), although, like all bynames and surnames of relationship in Devon, it was not significant quantitatively.[155]

One of the major changes in the form of bynames and surnames during the later middle ages was the transition from syndetic to asyndetic forms. The chronology of this change, from forms with a preposition to those without, is represented by the mutation in topographical surnames, since these persisted with some syndetic forms into the sixteenth century and later (whilst other forms of surname will be discussed below). The process is illustrated by changes at Werrington. Here, locative surnames had become asyndetic by 1368; the court rolls, for example, referred to John Coulecote, Adam Bradeburgh, Walter Yundecote, William Ayrigg, Robert and Richard Godecote, Robert Douneworthie, Henry and Emmota Churcheton, William Eggebere, Robert Bolepitt, John Pattecote, Richard Wynguecote, Jocelin Wyledon, Walter Ventregan, Ralph Clobury, Thomas Panston, and Henry Pyntesslo, in 1368. Only a few locative surnames were still syndetic: John de Raddon, Richard de Sutton, Richard de Wynguecote, John de Sotton, and Henry de Churcheton. By contrast, topographical surnames continued predominantly in syndetic form, such as Richard atte Pole,

Figure 1
The Distribution of the Topographical Bynames Water and Yeo in 1332.

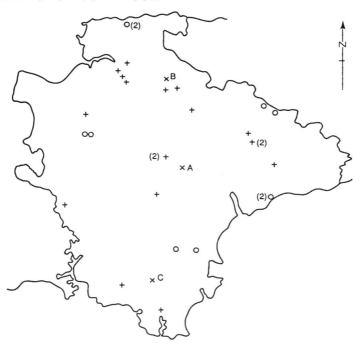

Key:

+	yeo, yea, yo, ya
o	atte Watere, de aqua
x	both elements in one location

A Crediton	atte Watere (1)
	atte Ya (1)
	atte Yo (1)
B S Molton	atte Watere (1)
	atte Yoo (1)
C Ugborough	atte Watere (2)
	de la Yeo(2)

The map excludes more specific bynames such as atte Broke, Biestewatere etc.
Figures in brackets denote the number of occurrences.

John atte Legh, Matilda Byesteway, Hamelin atte Brigge, John atte Weye, John Bythemour, Nicholas atte Hele, in 1368; in 1369, litigants and suitors to the manorial court included John atte Hamme, Robert att' Ford, Richard attemore, John atteford. Syndetic forms of topographical surnames continued to appear in the court rolls throughout the later middle ages: Miles atte Hele (default and relaxation of suit in 1384); Richard atte Hamme (1384–95); Felicia atte Bear (1385); John atte Court (1392–6); Richard atte More (1392); Joan atte Hele (1392); William atte Hamme (1462). About 1462, asyndetic forms became more prevalent. In that year, John Court occurred in the court rolls eight times in asyndetic form, by contrast with John atte Court, who had been presented for brewing and involved in a case of covenant in 1392–6. In this form, the court rolls recorded his surrender of his lease of a messuage and half acre in 1463. After two initial entries as William atte Hamme, William appeared consistently thereafter as William Hamme, as did Thomas Hamme in 1463–9 and John Hamme, in 1469.[156]

The persistence of syndetic forms of topographical surnames was as strong at Stoke Fleming. Stoke Fleming was located on the east coast of Devon, in the South Hams, in contrast with Werrington, which was land-locked on the western extremity of Devon. The court rolls of Stoke Fleming continued to contain syndetic forms of topographical surnames well into the fifteenth century.[157] From 1475, John at Court(e) was frequently presented as a brewer, or for default of court, twice as John A Court in the 1480s. William at Combe was another persistent brewer in the 1480s, but was also entered as William A Comb and William Comb. Philip A Comb *alias* Philip Comb was also presented for brewing in the 1490s. In the early sixteenth century, John A Comb served as one of the *xij pro Rege*, and was presented as a brewer as John Acomb.

At Ottery St Mary, *c.* 1381, all the topographical surnames listed in the rental, which was compiled locally, were syndetic: at Burgh (several); at Hille (several); at Wer (several); at Pitte; at Wode; at Brigge; at Stone; at More; at Lane (several); Bynethewaye; at Will (*bis*); at Slade; at Thorn; at Heys.[158] Only two tenants occurred, each once, in asyndetic form: John Burgh and Richard Hille.[159] Documents produced for central government also contain predominantly syndetic forms, such as Thomas Attewilla in the mid fifteenth century and Joan daughter of Thomas atte Yeo in the late fourteenth.[160]

At Dawlish, syndetic forms persisted into the sixteenth century. In 1385, the court rolls enumerated trespasses involving Agnes atte Stone, Richard atte Pytte, Adam atte Pyne, Isabella atte Beare, Alice atte Yete, Richard atte Berne, Bartholomew atte Aller (*alias* de Alre), and Henry atte Yurde. Similar forms were repeated in 1461: Thomas att' Bern, Roger att' Aysh. Even in 1514-15, the court rolls preferred some syndetic forms, such as John at Barn (*alias* To Barne *alias* John Barne), Thomas atte Barne, Maurice atte Yeate. Some asyndetic forms had appeared, however, as John To Waye was described more frequently as John Waye, whilst William To Will was the defendant in a case of debt impleaded by Thomas Will.[161] At Sidbury, *c.*1350, all the topographical bynames in a rental occurred in the syndetic form; they persisted in this form into the rental of 1394. A further rental of the fifteenth century contained the same forms: Nicholas atte Pyn', William at' Pyn, William atte Rode, John Knoll but also John Atteknoll, John Att Woode, Walter Atteknoll, and Ralph atte Pate.[162]

Syndetic forms of topographical surnames continued to be used in the borough of Ashburton into the sixteenth century. The churchwardens' accounts, written locally, referred to William At Combe (1488-9), William at Wille (1490-1), Thomas and Joan At Weye (1499-1500), William At Waye (1502-3), Alexander At Wode (1510-11), Henry At Fenne (1512-13), William Atway (1514-15), Richard Atcomb (1515-16), William To Way (1516-17), Margery At Way (1516-17) and William At Way again in 1536-7.[163] Ashburton, although a borough, was located on the periphery of the moors, so that change may have been less precocious there.

Nevertheless, even at Exeter, some freemen were occasionally admitted in the very late middle ages with syndetic topographical surnames, such as Nicholas a Burne in 1482-3 and John a More in 1504-5.[164] It might be assumed that these may have been immigrants to the borough, but some other syndetic forms existed in Exeter at that time, and, indeed, came to be stabilized in that form. In the early decades of the seventeenth century, William Towill *alias* Atwill, of Stokeinteignhead, husbandman, was a tenant of the Magdalen Hospital.[165] Gilbert Tohill, tailor of Exeter, acquitted a debt to the Court of Orphans in 1643-4, whilst, about the same time (1643-5), Katherine Brooke *alias* Tohill was the executrix of her late husband, William Brooke.[166] These were, however, residual elements in the pattern at Exeter.

The extent of the persistence of syndetic forms of topographical surnames is confirmed by the lay subsidy of 1524-5. In particular, a number had the preposition To as an alternative to Atte.[167] Later in the century, these forms still existed in rural areas. Thomas Acourte was a customary tenant of Lord Dinham at Hemyock in 1566. John Abancke held 32 acres called Chapel Land in Colyton in the middle of the century. Richard Attwell produced all the 302 lbs. of tin for coinage at Plympton in September 1647.[168]

Amongst some of the lesser gentry, syndetic forms still existed in the late middle ages. The list of those holding knights fees in 1428, contained innumerable surnames of this type: Attewode, atte Wyll, at Wode, Attrewyn, att Torre, at Forde, Attecombe, Atbear, atte Mede, Atehole, Atlegh, atte Thorne, and many more.[169]

Topographical surnames thus survived in syndetic form much later than other forms of bynames in Devon. In some cases, consequently, they became stabilized as surnames in that form, such as Acourt and Acomb. In the later middle ages, and particularly the early sixteenth century, the preposition To became an alternative form to atte, and this form too occasionally became stabilized as in Tohill.

By the sixteenth century, the two principal residual prepositions in topographical surnames were atte and to, the latter more recently introduced. At an earlier time, a wider range of prepositions had been employed, such as by-, inthe-, up-, under- and binithe-. These forms were more transient than atte, and tended to disappear by the end of the fourteenth century. In the Crown Pleas of 1238, cases were presented which involved John Binorthdone in South Tawton Hundred and William Byalla in Crediton Hundred.[170] At Stockleigh Pomeroy in 1293, four customary tenants bore the byname Binytheton, as well as Richard Underdown. At a later date, other tenants of Newenham Priory and Plympton Priory included Stephen Bysouthway, Cecily Bisoutheton, and Walter Bysouthewode, being both conventionary and customary tenants.[171] Admitted to the freedom of Exeter in 1331–8 were burgesses named Biteyng, Byestecote, and Inthehaye.[172] Alleged tinners taxed in 1339 included William Bithebrok and Thomas Bithelak (Cornwood), William Bynytheclyue (Sourton), Philip Uppehill and William Inthetrawen (in the trees) (Whitchurch), and William Inthecomb and William Uppehull (Sampford).[173] These syndetic forms tended to disappear during the late fourteenth century, although a few instances still persisted later, such as Cecily Inthecomb, who compounded for her tithes with the Dean and Chapter of Exeter in 1441 at Staverton, and John Nytheway, who was one of the larger customary tenants at Sidbury in the late fourteenth century. Consequently, these surnames existed in 1524–5 as Estbroke, Estecherche, Estlake, Estway, Westbroke, Westlake, Westlane, Westway, Northway, Northwood, but a few as Indebroke, Bickhill, Bicklake, Bidlake and Bidwill.[174]

The most common of these less frequent prepositions was the elliptical by-, which occurred in 59 bynames in the lay subsidy of 1332, representing thus 4% of taxpayers with topographical bynames and 0.6% of all taxpayers. In the same taxation, only about seven of those assessed had bynames compounded with 'beneath' and a smaller number with 'beyond' (Byundebroke, Byundelake).[175] A recent interpretation of bynames compounded with the elliptical by- in the lay subsidies of 1327 and 1332 for Lincolnshire has suggested that: 'Each is clearly a descriptive term used as a byname or surname. None is in any sense a place-name, and we have not found any of these names, subsequently, used independently as minor place-names.'[176] This conclusion related more particularly to bynames in which were compounded by-, a point of the compass and a topographical feature. A number of these forms existed in the lay subsidy of 1332 for Devon: Biestewatere; Byestechurch; Bye-stecolmp; Byestelake; Byestewaye; Bynorthechurch; Bynorthdoune; Bynorthemille; Bynorthmor; Bynortheweie; Bynorthewode; Bysouthebear; Bysouthebroke; Bysouthecolmp; Bysouthedon; Bysoutheweie; Bysouthewode; Bywestedon; Bywestlak; Bywes-teweie; *et al*. The tenants of Cowick Priory in the early fourteenth century included Robert Byestecolm.[177] In some of these cases, the evidence concurs with that from Lincolnshire; the byname simply reflected one who lived to the west of the church, east of the lake, east of the way. In others, however, a different interpretation is necessary, taking into account the nature of dispersed settlement in some regions of Devon. In some caes, therefore, the byname did represent a minor placename, so that they may have been locative rather than topographical. In Broadhempston, in 1332, some tax-payers were known as Bythelake and Bywestedon, which can be correlated with the minor placenames Lake and Down. At Brixham, two other taxpayers had the byname Bysouthedoun(e), consistent with the minor placename Southdown. The name Bysoutheweye in Tamerton Foliot evidently derived from the minor placename Southway, as did the byname Bynortheweie in Monkleigh with the placename Northway. The taxpayer called Bysoutheya in Culmstock may have resided in the minor settlement there called Southey, and similarly the taxpayer called Bysouthewode in relation to Southwood Farm in Rockbeare.[178] The pattern of dispersed settle-ment in Devon thus elicited a different explanation of some of these topographical bynames which incorporated elliptical prep-ositions.

Although bynames in Devon had developed into fully heritable surnames through almost all sectors of society by the middle of the fourteenth century, some instability still persisted amongst some few specialised groups. Instability was associated with gender and occupation in the form of the -ster element, noted above, par-ticularly in urban communities. The same instability may have been attached to the -maker bynames introduced during the later middle ages, also remarked upon above. These -maker names may have been associated with alien immigrants in the fourteenth and fifteenth centuries.

Perhaps the largest group containing a high element of unstable surnames were exactly these aliens in the later middle ages.[179] In the middle of the fifteenth century, these aliens were taxed, 342 assessed at 16d since they held *hospicia*, and 333 at 6d since they did not hold an *hospicium*. Analysis of their bynames is tabulated below. A proportion came to be referred to by generic locative bynames, such as Norman or Frenshman. Of those holding an *hospicium*, 7% had this form of byname. Of those who did not own a residence, a very much higher proportion, 30%, had generic locative bynames. The remainder of those with bynames, assessed both at 16d. and 6d., had very largely been attributed the common surnames borne by Devonians. Fewer held locative and topographical bynames, however, by comparison with the indigenous population. Most of the locative and topographical surnames of aliens were distinctly Devonian: Gonsales de Plymmouth' (a Portuguese); John Okebeare; Thomas Stanlynche at Brixton; John Dounyng (from the Isle of Man); William Crosse (a Norman at Sidmouth); John Fenneman (a Norman at Brixton); John Hegheman (a Norman at East Budleigh). A higher proportion held occupational bynames, which were predominantly those usual in Devon, such as Hoper and Webber. Even nicknames and bynames from personal names comprised a high percentage of common Devonian forms.

Nevertheless, the aliens did bear some different forms of byname. Some nine locative bynames held by aliens taxed at 16d derived from Devon, but another 17 were introduced from outside the county, such as Cardeff (2), Penwardyn, Cork, Cardigan, Appledore, Winton'. Of those assessed at 6d, nine bore locative bynames of Devon extraction (for example, Brixham, Hoiwyssh), but three external locative bynames. Some of the occupational bynames differed from the normal Devon stock at that time, such as Cordener and Weuer. Several aliens held the -maker form of bynames, especially Dutchmen, whilst four bore the byname Glasier, which had been introduced into Exeter apparently *c.*1377. Whilst many nicknames conformed to existing Devonian types, a large number of Anglo-Norman forms were also introduced, which do not seem to have occurred earlier, such as Malet, Peaufrere, Teste, Gorget, Purquay. Similarly, some of the bynames from personal names were ostensibly foreign: Gillam, Pattrykke, Poterell, Mughell, *et al.*, but some at least of the Continental-Germanic personal names had been introduced into Devon at an earlier time. A small number of aliens, in particular Dutchmen, also bore patronymic forms with the element -son, which had not previously been contained within the pattern of naming in Devon.

The significant aspect of the naming of the aliens, however, was the flexibility and instability, by which they were seemingly accorded new names for the purposes of the taxation. A large proportion were attributed Devonian bynames which they presumably had not previously held, others were simply referred to by generic locative bynames, again which were applied because of their specific circumstances.

Table 2.1

Analysis of the Bynames of Aliens in Devon
Source: PRO E179/95/100

Taxonomy	A(%)	B(%)
Generic locative	7	30
Locative	13	10
Topographical	11	6
Occupational	15	14
Nickname	15	18
Metonymic	2	
Personal name	29	15
Patronymic		3
Relationship		1
No surname	3	
Uncertain	5	4
Total	100	100

A — relates to those holding a residence (taxed at 16d).
B — relates to those not holding a residence (taxed at 6d), but excludes those specifically described as servants since they by and large were not assigned bynames (see further below).

Table 2.2

Analysis of those taxed at 6d.

Servants with no surname	168	(50%)
Servants with a surname	19	(6%)
Not servants, having a surname	142	(43%)
Not servants, having no surname	1	
Servants with no names	3*	
Total	333	(100%)

* *duo homines et j mulier* who were servants at Mowlish and of French origin.

Amongst those aliens assessed at 6d, 56% were servants, of whom the vast majority were not accorded a byname. These servants were presumably known by the byname of their employer, who was usually specified in the assessment. Female servants in Exeter between 1373 and 1393, comprising 37% of known female inhabitants of the City, had the same pattern.

Table 2.3

Names of Female Servants in Exeter 1373–93

Forename and employer's surname	74%
Forename and surname of husband or father	6%
Forename and own surname	20%
N = 160.	

Source: M Kowaleski, 'Women's work in a market town: Exeter in the late fourteenth century', in B A Hanawalt, ed., *Women and Work in Pre-industrial Europe*, (1986), 153.

In the lay subsidy of 1524–5, 109 of those assessed were also described as servants, although this figure must be a considerable underenumeration, since the taxation probably omitted many whose wages fell below the taxable threshold of wages of 20s. *per annum*. The concentration of these servants in the trading communities, with 20 at Plymouth, nine at Dartmouth and six at Totnes, implies that these were household servants rather than servants in husbandry.[180] Servants in husbandry, residing in the household of their employer, and regarded as part of the household, may have assumed the surnames of their employers.[181] Of the 109 (household) servants denoted in the lay subsidy of 1524–5, 31 (28%) were designated by their own surnames, whilst 78 (72%) were not known for the purposes of the subsidy by a surname, and so were presumably known by that of their employer. Only one, David Durnex, servant of William Durnex of Ottery St Mary, was explicitly assigned the surname of his employer. The suffix -man was not employed at all to denote servants in Devon.[182] Where servants were assigned surnames, they were predominantly topographical or occupational. Labourers, who usually lived in their own accommodation outside their employer's household, may be recognised perhaps by the high numbers of taxpayers who were assessed at 20s. on wages in 1524–5. Labourers were known in the taxation by their own surnames. Concomitantly, apprentices in Exeter usually retained their own surname, although a small proportion did apparently receive that of their employer.[183]

Amongst these groups, that is servants and apprentices, some instability in naming persisted into the early modern period, although not in a substantial way. Instability in the surnames of some other Devonians resulted less from belonging to a particular group than from individual circumstances. Thus the proportion of formal aliases seems to have increased during the later middle ages, although encompassing only a small part of the population. The percentage of aliases did not attain the same level as, for example, on the estates of Ramsey Abbey in the east Midlands about the same time.[184] Before *c.*1350, the informal instability of bynames meant that one person might be known, in different circumstances, by a number of bynames. In the later middle ages, this flexibility of bynames had been replaced by the stability of surnames. Aliases, however, came to be used as a formal qualifier, usually as a result of specific circumstances. The cause of aliases is perhaps more easily explained in the urban context. Many aliases in Exeter, for example, related to occupation, although the reliance on the register of freemen for this purpose may be a self-fulfilling prophesy. The register consequently included: John Dene *alias* Barbour (1403); John Carwythan *alias* Coteler son and heir of Stephen Carwythan *alias* Coteler (1417); Robert Langbrig' *alias* Webbere (1420); Robert Forde *alias* Hosyer (1421); John Gayr' *alias* Hostyler (1422); Thomas Puryman *alias* Helyer (1429); John Glasyer *alias* Bernewyke (1469). Implicitly, these freemen practised the trade which formed their alias. Some apprentices, as noted above, assumed the surnames of their masters, but it is sometimes difficult to establish whether they might, indeed, have been sons as well as apprentices: thus John Wilford apprentice of Robert Wilford; and Roger Shapleigh apprentice of John Shapleigh. There is the more explicit case of Roger Doly, son and apprentice of Roger Doly senior. In yet other instances, it seems fairly evident that the apprentice had assumed the master's surname, as Baldwin Barbour *alias* Warde apprenticed to Janin Barbour in 1429, Henry Hilman *alias* Salter apprenticed to John Salter, saddler, in 1455, and, with a complicated mutation, John Bawyer *alias* Holmore apprenticed to John Yoode *alias* Bawyer in 1498-9.[185]

Aliases occurred also on rural manors during the later middle ages. At Werrington, few formal aliases were registered in the court rolls, Richard Paynter *alias* Lucas appearing fleetingly in 1474-5. At Stoke Canon, Thomas and John Bonour had the formal *alias* Bolour in 1456, but this may have represented only a variant spelling. At Uplyme, the court rolls mentioned transiently John Webbe *dictus* Keeting in 1369, but also Thomas son of John Holcombe *dictus* Skyttysh in 1373, who continued to be known thereafter as Thomas Skyttysh. He was listed as a *garcio* in 1368 who had left his holding

(*reliquid tenementum suum*). John son of William Hollyng *dictus* Voode
was enumerated as a *garcio* in 1408. By contrast, aliases proliferated
in Uplyme in the early sixteenth century. In the terrier of the manor
in 1516, 37 tenants bore 36 surnames (including aliases); of these 37
tenants, eight bore aliases: Denys *alias* Rychard; Gamyge *alias*
Smyth; Haukyns *alias* Sampson; Richeman *alias* Symons *alias*
Symms; *et al*. In the 1530s, the tithingman was John Horseman *alias*
Stere. Few of these surnames had existed at Uplyme before *c*.1408,
but there is a large hiatus in the documents between then and 1516.
A small proportion of the taxpayers in the lay subsidy of 1524–5,
about 30, bore aliases, but the subsidy does not illuminate the
reason. In some of these cases, the presumed reason for the alias
may have been inheritance of or accession to land, but this is far
from clear, unlike many instances on the estates of Ramsey Abbey.
Only a few specific instances of this causation have been discovered
in Devon. In *c*.1408, William Tolchet *alias* Fokeray held a fardel *per
seruicium militare*, which was late (*nuper*) that held by William Fokeray.
In this, and the few other, cases, Tolchet had acceded to the tenure
from outside the nuclear family, although his exact relationship
(whether extended kin or 'adopted heir') is unclear. In any case, he
adopted as an alias the surname associated with the tenement. This
association of surname and tenement may have been more
important amongst free tenures than customary tenures during the
later middle ages, as in this specific case.[186]

Finally, the incidence of patronymic bynames and surnames was
rare in Devon, as is discussed further below. In particular, the formation in the vernacular with -son was unusual at all times, and was
probably introduced as an external influence in the mid fifteenth
century, possibly through commercial linkages. Patronymics in the
vernacular form -son, the Latin form (*filius x*), or Anglo-Norman
form (*fitz*) were not significant at any time in the pattern of naming in
Devon, although they may have been slightly more prevalent in the
twelfth and early thirteenth century than at a later time. It has been
suggested that forms with a genitival inflection -s may have existed in
southern England as an alternative to patronymic forms in -son.[187]
Initially, however, this genitival form was not strictly a patronymic
form in the south west, but reflected wider relationships and
kinship. More especially, it was associated with gender, and was
commonly borne by women. An exception was William Peters, a
tenant of Berry Pomeroy in 1292.[188] By contrast, on the manor of
Uplyme in the early fourteenth century, all the bynames with a
genitival -s were borne by women: Felicia Riueles, Alice Riueles,
Matilda Riueles; in contrast with the form of the byname when
borne by the male kin, simply Riuel.[189] In the court rolls of this same

manor, in the early fourteenth century, the genitival -s is almost exclusively associated with women: Joan Cosynes; Agnes and Matilda la Meyes (by contrast with Henry, John and Adam le Mey); Isabella Parkeres; Edith Propechauntes (but Hugh Propechaunt); Alice (le) Pywes (but John Pyw); Is' la Smythes; and, as late as 1367–8, Joan Hobbes, daughter of William Hobbe, and Agnes Rauwes. It was only in the later fourteenth century on this manor that the genitival -s became used in conjunction with males and thus stabilized in surnames: for example, Robynes and Ricardes. This transition first occurred in the 1340s and 1350s and stabilized in the later part of the century.[190]

Despite its usage on the manor of Uplyme, few instances of the genitival -s occurred in the lay subsidy of 1332. The few instances were all associated with women: Christine Leches (Brixton); Agnes Canynges (Parkham); Alice Steuyns (Colyton Hundred); Alice Smithes (Lupridge); and Mariota Mayouns (Colyton Hundred).[191] This same association with gender occurred in the lay subsidy of Dorset in both 1327 and 1332, but there the genitival -s was encountered much more frequently, constantly associated with women. There were thus some 29 instances in 1327, such as Matilda Shurreues, Joan Richmans, Letice le Tanneres, Agnes Crokkeres, and Helen Comeres.[192] This correlation was less precise, however, in the lay subsidy of Somerset in 1327, since there the bynames with the genitival -s were also held by male taxpayers, and not exclusively by women. Thus, whilst the subsidy enumerated Matilda Cuperes, Agnes Thomases, Edith le Smithes and Matilda Richemans, it equally included John Hobbes, Richard and Henry Stephenes, William and Laurence Ricardes, William and Benedict Phelippes, Osbert le Smythes, Edward Germannes and many more similar male taxpayers.[193] In Wiltshire, some women certainly bore bynames with the genitival -s, but its full extent is not known: thus, at Longbridge Deverill and Monkton Deverill, Alice Semannes paid 2s for merchet to marry outside the manor (*pro se maritanda extra*) and Agnes la Brokkes 3s. 4d. for the same licence; in 1307, on the same manors, Alice la Bakeres was fined, and so also Agnes le Brasors (and Hamond le Brasour), Matilda Packeres (and William and John le Packere), Agnes *Relicta la Packeres* and Alice Soteres.[194] There is thus a strong indication that bynames with the genitival -s were often associated with women (probably as widows or daughters) in some parts of the south west, so that this inflection was not simply an alternative to a patronymic form of byname. Only in the later fourteenth century did the genitival -s develope into a strictly patronymic form, but by then the -s may have been incipiently inorganic and stabilized in some surnames.

By the early sixteenth century, the proportion of bynames with a final -s was still insignificant in Devon, such surnames being borne by just over 140 taxpayers out of a total of more than 26,000 in 1524 — that is, by less than 1% of all taxpayers.[195] By this time, the inflection was usually on a surname derived from a personal name, often a hypocoristic form such as Harris (21 taxpayers) or Wattes (11). In the early fourteenth century, the inflection had been appended on other types of bynames when held by women, particularly occupational bynames, but also bynames derived from nicknames. At no time, however, was this form of byname and surname of any quantitative significance in medieval or early modern Devon.

To a certain extent, therefore, the formation and development of bynames and surnames in Devon was influenced by localized usages and dialect. Some of these influences pertained generally to southern ME dialect; others, although only a few, were more specific to Devon (and parts of Cornwall). Some of the influences diminished during the course of the middle ages, some to be almost extinguished by c.1400, although a residual influence persisted in some areas, often the west and north, through the later middle ages. Other influences persisted more vitally into the early modern period, and thus became formalized in the naming pattern of Devon. Yet other aspects had not been characteristic of Devon before the later middle ages, and were introduced at that late time. These late accretions did not make an enormous impact on naming in the county.

References

1 O Svensson, *Saxon Place-Names in East Cornwall*, (Lund Studies in English, 77, 1987), 8-10.
2 *Lay Subsidy 1332, passim*; PRO C134/16, m 9.
3 *Lay Subsidy 1332*, 111.
4 *Ibid*, 43.
5 *Ibid*, 15-18, 28-32, 65-71.
6 *Ibid*, 15.
7 *Ibid, passim.*
8 R Bearman, 'The charters of the Redvers family and the earldom of Devon in the twelfth century', unpub. PhD London, 1981, 410.
9 *Feet of Fines Devon*, I, 10-11, 21, 53 (nos 10, 11, 29, 95).
10 *Crown Pleas Devon 1238*, 1-3, 5-8, 20-1, 25, 35, 37-40, 44-5, 56, 65-6, 74, 81, 89-90, 94, 102, 104, 113, 116, 125-7 (in all about 44 instances throughout Devon).

[11] *Canonsleigh Cartulary*, 27 ff, 33, 39, 43-4, 47-51, 53, 56, 59, 61, 63-7.

[12] O J Reichel in *TDA*, 28 (1896), 372, 375, 377.

[13] *Exeter Freemen*, 11.

[14] DRO M1277.

[15] E(ton) C(ollege) R(ecords) 1/32, fo3v.

[16] PRO E179/95/15.

[17] PRO Chancery Miscellanea Bundle 55, file 5, no 6, and file 6, no 230; see also B H Putnam, *Proceedings before the Justices of the Peace* (1938), 64, 75, and 79 (John Bonda, theft, 1351; John Chopa, clerk, 1353; Robert Cadie, 1353).

[18] PRO Chancery Miscellanea Bundle 55, file 6, no 229.

[19] DRO M1429.

[20] ECR 1/139.

[21] DRO 902M/M4-19.

[22] DRO Bedford MSS Werrington court rolls computer database (Richard Slota, *c.*1398; Walter Hyna, *c.*1384; Walter Wytha, 1395).

[23] Boase, *Registrum Collegii Exoniensis*, (Oxford Historical Society, 27, 1894), 20.

[24] *Ashburton CW Accounts*, 6, 33 and 186-7.

[25] Dartmouth Records computer database; M Kowaleski, 'The 1377 poll tax for Dartmouth', *Devon & Cornwall Notes & Queries*, 35 (1985), 290-1.

[26] *Exeter Freemen*, 64.

[27] J J Alexander, 'Tavistock in the fifteenth century', *TDA*, 69 (1937), 250, 271 and 273.

[28] *Lay Subsidy 1524-5, passim*.

[29] DRO 217/3/19 ('Survey of Lord Dinham's Lands'), fos 51r-70v.

[30] H S A Fox, 'Devon and Cornwall: peasant farming', in E Miller, ed., *The Agrarian History of England and Wales*, forthcoming.

[31] *Caption of Seisin*, 16-17, 36-8, 50-2, 100-4, 114-15, 129-30; *Register of Edward the Black Prince Part IV (1351-1365)*, (HMSO, 1933), 125, 216.

[32] *Dorset Lay Subsidy 1327*, 124 and *passim*.

[33] H P R Finberg, 'Some early Tavistock charters', *English Historical Review*, 62 (1947), 354, 364-5, 367, 374-6. For the medial inflection in some Devon placenames (e.g. Billacott, Brazacott, Trillacott, Winnacott), mostly in west Devon, see *PND*, I-II, *passim*. The medial phonetic change is also encountered in some bynames, as Robert de Uppaheie in Axminster in the late thirteenth century: Bodl Libr MS Top Devon d 5, fos 31v-32v, 35r-36r.

[34] *PND*, I, xxxvi.

[35] Forssner, *Continental-Germanic Personal Names*, 261 n1; M Redin, *Studies on Uncompounded Personal Names in England in Old and Middle English Times*, (Uppsala, 1919), xxxv-xxxvi; O von Feilitzen, 'Some Old English uncompounded personal names and bynames', *Studia Neophilologia*, 40 (1968), 1 (Cade).

[36] I owe much to discussion with Beverly Boyd and Claude Luttrell amongst others. See also, A C Baugh and T Cable, *A History of the English Language*, (3rd edn., repr. 1987), 159-61.

[37] Baugh and Cable, *op. cit.*, 191; M F Wakelin, *English Dialects. An Introduction*, (repr. 1981), 91.

[38] Dartmouth Records computer database.

[39] *Exeter Freemen*, 3, 10; *Tudor Exeter*, 23.

[40] *Ashburton CW Accounts*, 37, 48; T A R Greaves, 'The Devon tin industry, 1450-1750', unpub. PhD Exeter, 1981, 380.

[41] Longleat MSS Uplyme court rolls computer database.

[42] DRO 902M/M19-21 and 27.

[43] DRO Bedford MSS Werrington court rolls computer database.

[44] *Lay Subsidy 1524-5, passim*.

[45] *Dorset Lay Subsidy 1327*, 38, 50, 73, 96, 125, 127.

[46] *Ashburton CW Accounts*, 6, 11, 13, 20, 25.

[47] DRO M1429.

[48] *Crown Pleas Devon 1238*, 114, 229, 443, 451.

[49] *Lay Subsidy 1332, passim*.

[50] *Lay Subsidy 1524-5*, index, sn Chafe, Lyffe.

[51] *Register of Edward the Black Prince, Part IV*, 175.

[52] *Lay Subsidy 1332*, 78.

[53] DRO M1288 and 1429; also Walter atte Clywe in Sourton, *Lay Subsidy 1332*, 62.

[54] Compare Wakelin, *English Dialects*, 27; the letters written by John Shillingford, mayor of Exeter (1447-50) had already lost traces of such aspects of local dialect as the voicing of f and v and s and z.

[55] *Lay Subsidy 1524-5*, index, sn Seward/Zewarde; the interchange occurred medially only occasionally, for example Dorzed for Dorset: *Ashburton CW Accounts*, 34.

[56] *Ashburton CW Accounts*, xxi; see also Walter at Yeate at Ottery St Mary *c.*1380 (DRO M1288); the byname Yete occurred 21 times in the lay subsidy of 1332: *Lay Subsidy 1332, passim*. The medial gutteral interchange as in degher and heghen is too frequent to document, but, for example, Geoffrey de Heghen at Ottery St Mary *c.*1381 (BL Add MS 28838, fo 80v), Hugh de Heighe of Uffculme (*Crown Pleas Devon 1238*, 2). In 1332, the byname Heghen occurred 17 times, Heghes three, and Hayne five; in 1524-5, Hayne *alias* Heyne 26. These numbers exclude com-

pounds from placenames, which were prolific. Compare the
bynames Felyceheis, Uppeheie, Wrangeheie and Childheie in
Axminster in the late thirteenth centrury (Bodl Libr MS Top
Devon d 5, fos 28v, 31r-v, 32r, 35r-36r, 45r-47r, 112v-113r). For
degher/dyer, see , for example, William Degher and John Dyer
alias Degher both at Ottery St Mary in 1379–80 (DRO
M1288).

57 G Kristensson, *A Survey of Middle English Dialects 1290-1350. The Six
Northern Counties and Lincolnshire*, (Lund Studies in English, 35,
1967); *idem, A Survey of Middle English Dialects. The West Midland
Counties*, (Publications of the New Society at Lund, 78, 1987).
58 *Crown Pleas Devon 1238*, 5, 7, 35, 49, 69, 78, 87, 93.
59 *Lay Subsidy 1332, passim.*
60 *Lay Subsidy 1524-5, passim.*
61 Nottingham University Library Dept of MSS MiM 6/173/272:
'Homagium ibidem presentat quod Walterus Weke permisit
pistrinum suum esse ruinosum et debile . . . Et quod Walterus
Weke non trahit moram suam super tenementum suum quod
tenet secundum consuetudinem manerii sicut concessio in se
exigit . . . Walterus Weke habet diem ad commorandum super
tenementum suum citra festum Natalis domini proximum
futurum sub pena forisfacture tenementi sui.'
62 P McClure, 'Lay subsidy rolls and dialect phonology', in F
Sandgren, ed., *Otium et Negotium. Studies in Onomatology and Library
Science Presented to Olof von Feilitzen*, (1973), 188-94.
63 H P R Finberg, 'Some early Tavistock charters', 375.
64 BL Add MS 28838, fos 77v, 79v.
65 DRO Magdalen Hospital Deed 121(b).
66 *Exeter Freemen*, 52, 70, 349; *Tudor Exeter*, 1-5. In the tenth of 1489 in
Exeter, the taxpayers included Robert Hylle *alias* Hull *alias* Hill,
John Colshull, Henry Hull, William Hyll, John Hull and Ralph
Hill *alias* Hyll.
67 DRO M1438. Note also medial -e- instead of reflex -y- in Cleve
alias Cleffe in *Ashburton CW Accounts*, 6.
68 *Lay Subsidy 1332, passim.*
69 *Ibid.*
70 *Ibid.* Alexander, 'Tavistock in the fifteenth century', 247-85;
Finberg, *Tavistock Abbey*, 277, n3 (Culling could, however, derive
from the personal name Culling or *cull*, a deep valley).
71 DRO 902M, *passim.*
72 D&C Exeter Archives 5007.
73 BL Add MS 28838, fo 176r.
74 *Ashburton CW Accounts*, 1, 3, 10, 14, 19-21, 26-7, 32, 35, 60-1, 67.
75 *Wreyland Documents*, 1, 4, 21-2, 27, 37, 41, 66, 71.
76 ECR 1/139.

77 BL Add MS 28838, fo 44v.
78 D&C Exeter Archives 5249.
79 *Exeter Freemen*, 9, 16, 18, 22, 28, 33, 39, 40, 44, 49, 62; David and Clement Comyn were presented for engrossing and forestalling grain in 1352: Putnam, *Proceedings before the Justices*, 68.
80 *Crown Pleas Devon 1238*, 64, 90 (nos 374 and 542).
81 PRO Chancery Miscellanea Bundle 55, file 5, no 163.
82 D&C Exeter Archives 2945 and 4785; Greaves, 'Devon tin industry', 31, 291.
83 PRO E179/95/15 (Richard, William and John Dounyng at South Tawton); DRO 14294/PW2 (John Dounyng and John Comyng, *c.*1496–1525); H P R Finberg, 'The Stannary of Tavistock', *TDA*, 81 (1949), 173-5, 177-80 (William Comyng, Thomas Wallyng, John Dounyng, Nicholas Thornyng, William Brokyng, John and William Torryng, all in 1523); C W Bracken, 'The manor of Plympton Grange: a court roll and rental', *TDA*, 70 (1938), 235-9, 243-5; and so, later, Benedict Hillinge in 1566, the most substantial tenant at Venn Ottery: DRO 217/3/19, fos 39v-40v; Thomas Crossing, alderman of Exeter in 1639: DRO Borough Charity Deed 327; and the late William Crossing who produced extensive publications on Dartmoor and Devon between 1888 and 1912.
84 *Lay Subsidy 1524-5, passim.*
85 *PND*, I, 263, 311; H P R Finberg, 'Some early Tavistock charters', 357-8, 367 (1155-84) referring to Edwin Coaching and *terra Coaching.*
86 *Lay Subsidy 1332*, 20, 27, 32, 38, 50, 55, 60, 61, 63, 65, 75.
87 Rea *TDA*, Ewen.
88 For example, *Dorset Lay Subsidy 1327*, 73; *West Country Shipping*, 23 (no 22); Forssner, *Continental-Germanic Personal Names*, 113, 278-9.
89 Reaney, *DBS*, 81, 90, 106, 177, 368.
90 G Fransson, *Surnames of Occupation 1100-1350*, 192-202; McKinley, *Sussex*, 152-9, where such forms were much more widespread.
91 *Lay Subsidy 1332*, 40, 85, 115, 119.
92 *Lay Subsidy 1524-5*, e.g. 9, 19, 20, 23, 25, 34-5, 52-3, 57, 60, 64, 68, 72, 80, 89, 91-2, 94-6, 101-3, 106, 110, 113, 116, 119, 120, 123, 125-7, 177-8, 181, 189, 197, 201-2, 204, 207-8, 214, 231, 237.
93 Dartmouth Records computer database.
94 DRO 902M/M8, 19: Richard Shuter; John Shuter who died in this year; his wife and executrix, Joan Shuter. An occasional variant was Sweter.
95 *Lay Subsidy 1524-5*, index, sn Rogerman.
96 *Ibid*, index, sn Gater, Brigger.
97 *Exeter Freemen*, 30, 32, 47.

98 Kowaleski computer database.
99 DRO MCR will 1314 (ex inf M Kowaleski).
100 *Tudor Exeter*, 4, 8, 15, 27.
101 DRO M1432-1433.
102 DRO 902M/M33.
103 BL Add MS 17450, fo 218r-v.
104 Reaney, *Origin*, 193-7.
105 Fransson, *Surnames of Occupation 1100-1350*, 204-7.
106 I Hjertstedt, *Middle English Nicknames in the Lay Subsidy Rolls for Warwickshire*, (Acta Universitatis Upsaliensis, 63, 1987), 26-7.
107 *Lay Subsidy 1332*, 3, 25, 72, 87, 100, 108-9, 112.
108 DRO 217/3/19, fos 51r-70v; H Fox, 'Peasant farmers, patterns of settlement and *pays*: transformations in the landscapes of Devon and Cornwall during the later middle ages', in R Higham, ed., *Landscape and Townscape in the South West*, (Exeter Studies in History, 22, 1989), 62-4; Finberg, *Tavistock Abbey*, 135-44; M R Bouquet, 'The sexual division of labour: the farm household in a Devon parish', PhD thesis, Cambridge, 1981, 57, 75-6.
109 *Lay Subsidy 1332*, 24.
110 *Lay Subsidy 1332, passim.*
111 *Ibid*, 32-3, 119.
112 *Ibid*, 86, 96, 125.
113 *Ibid*, 11, 13, 15, 21, 27, 35, 53, 68, 76, 77, 81, 84, 85, 95, 111, 127.
114 *Ibid*, 15, 33, 65, 79, 86, 98, 121.
115 *Ibid*, 51.
116 *Ibid*, 7-8, 19, 29, 38, 47, 68, 76-8, 81, 103, 108, 120, 124.
117 *Crown Pleas Devon 1238*, 6, 112.
118 DRO 902M/M4, for example.
119 Longleat MSS 10757, 10833; BL Eg MS 3134, fos 216-227.
120 *Lay Subsidy 1332*, sn Palfreyman.
121 *Lay Subsidy 1524-5*, index, sn Horsman; J Langdon, 'Horse hauling: a revolution in vehicle transport in twelfth- and thirteenth- century England', in T H Aston, ed., *Landlords, Peasants and Politics in Medieval England*, (1987), 33-64.
122 *Wreyland Documents*, 47.
123 D&C Exeter Archives 5249.
124 Dartmouth Records computer database.
125 *Exeter Freemen*, 13, 34, 52, 53.
126 PRO Chancery Miscellanea Bundle 55, file 7, no 224; *West Country Shipping*, 103 (no 87); BL Add MS 28838, fos 49r and 77v; *Book of Fees*, ii, 1309, 1315; *Calendar of Inquisitions Post Mortem 7-15 Ric II*, 438; DRO 14294/PW2; D&C Exeter Archives 2944.
127 DRO Bedford MSS Werrington court rolls, *passim*.
128 *Lay Subsidy 1524-5, passim.*

129 *Ibid*, index, sn Bowrman; DRO 217/3/19, fos 12r, 15v, 17r.
130 C W Brackley, 'The manor of Plympton Grange', 243-4; *Chancery Proceedings: Supplement Elizabeth I* (List & Index Society, 202, 1983), 126; *Chancery Decree Rolls*, (L&I Society, 198, 1983), 46; DRO 217/3/19, fos 12r, 15r-18r, 117r; H P R Finberg, 'Stannary of Tavistock', 173-6; Greaves, 'Devon tin industry', 55.
131 See below, 'Isonymy and community'; for the Dayman funeral at Hartland, Bouquet, 'The sexual division of labour', 127.
132 Fransson, *Surnames of Occupation 1100-1350*, 204-7.
133 *Dorset Lay Subsidy 1327, passim; Surrey Taxation Returns*, 21, 65, 84.
134 *Lay Subsidy 1332*, 10, 66.
135 *Lay Subsidy 1332*, 10, 66, 110, 116, 118, 124.
136 *Ibid*, viii.
137 Longleat MS 10773, m4; DRO 346M/M1; see also another rural woman with a -ster byname who was a tenant of a small holding, Margaret la Scheppestere *tenens unum Cotagium et Curtillagium* . . . in Longbridge Deverill in 1307: Longleat MS 9657.
138 See further below.
139 M Kowaleski, 'Women's work in a market town: Exeter in the late fourteenth century', in B A Hanawalt, ed., *Women and Work in Pre-Industrial Europe*, (1986), 153.
140 M Kowaleski, 'The 1377 Dartmouth poll tax', *D&C Notes and Queries*, 35 (1985), 286-95.
141 PRO E179/95/100 (18 Henry VI).
142 For the instability of bynames of aliens, see below.
143 See also J E Thorold Rogers, ed., *Oxford City Documents*, (Oxford Historical Society, 18, 1891), 13, 15, 17, 22-3, 26-31, 33, 36, 39 (poll tax 1380); H E Salter, ed., *The Cartulary of Oseney Abbey*, III (OHS, 91, 1931), 119, 124, 135, 145 (rentals, 1280-1317); G Rosser, *Medieval Westminster 1200-1540*, (1989), 197, 198 nn121 and 124, and 196-201; D Keene, *Survey of Medieval Winchester*, ii (Winchester Studies, 2, 1985), 1345-6, 1356; C Spiegelhalter, 'The surnames of Devon III. Occupative names', *TDA*, 70 (1938), 277-96 (Emma la Scyppestere at Totnes; Juliana Shapster in Dartmouth; Joan Harpestre in Totnes; Cecily Bakestere in Barnstaple; but also Richard Webbestere in Exeter in 1375 and Edward Bagester in 1549, who may, however, have been immigrants, since this sort of byname was not usually associated with males in Devon).
144 M Kowaleski, 'Dartmouth poll tax', 290.
145 *Exeter Freemen*, 33, 40.
146 *Ibid*, 58, 63; *Tudor Exeter*, 1, 39; D Keene, *op. cit.*, 1256 (Hatmaker in the 1490s, the first evidence of intrusion of this form of byname).

147 *Tudor Exeter*, 9, 11, 15, 16.

148 PRO E179/95/100.

149 *Exeter Freemen*, 34.

150 PRO E179/95/100.

151 Spiegelhalter, 'The surnames of Devon III', 277-96 (Clokmaker at Barnstaple, 1424; Netmaker there, 1507; Pochemaker in Exeter, 1374; Hatmaker in Barnstaple, 1541; Sopemaker in Totnes, 1448; Waxmaker there, 1481; Naylmaker, 1377; Carpetmaker in Barnstaple, 1507; Sackmakere there, 1303, *sic*). The constant connection seems to be with urban communities which may have attracted alien immigrants during the later middle ages.

152 *Crown Pleas Devon 1238*, 1, 26, 96, 98-9, 104, 112.

153 *Lay Subsidy 1332, passim.*

154 PRO Chancery Miscellanea Bundle 55, file 9, no 350.

155 *Lay Subsidy 1332*, 74, 88, 99, 120; Alexander, 'Tavistock in the fifteenth century', 281; Finberg, *Tavistock Abbey*, 277; BL Add MS 3660, fo 149v (Richard le Yem, *nativus*, at Hockford).

156 DRO Bedford MSS Werrington court rolls, *passim.*

157 DRO 902M/M25-34.

158 BL Add MS 28838, fos 77v et seqq.

159 *Ibid*, fos 80v and 81r.

160 Chancery Miscellanea Bundle 55, file 6, no 229, and file 9, no 350.

161 D&C Exeter Archives 4784-4786.

162 D&C Exeter Archives 2944-2945, 2961.

163 *Ashburton CW Accounts*, 12, 15, 27-8, 42-3, 46, 52-3, 55, 61, 100.

164 *Exeter Freemen*, 59, 64; see also a Legh, a Wode, a Bancke, a Mownt and a Courte in the lay subsidy of 1524-5: *Lay Subsidy 1524-5, passim.*

165 DRO Magdalen Hospital Deed 124(h).

166 DRO Court of Orphans Papers Inventories items IV and 11.

167 *Lay Subsidy 1524-5, passim* (To Yeate, To Wode, To Fosse, To Pen, To Wyll, To Myll, To Ward, To Bow, all mainly in east Devon, it seems).

168 DRO 217/3/19, fo 18r; *Chancery Decree Rolls: Elizabeth I*, 49; Greaves, 'The Devon tin industry', 38-9.

169 *Feudal Aids*, I, 443, 445, 448-52, 454-5, 457, 459, 463-4, 468-70, 472, 480, 489.

170 *Crown Pleas Devon 1238*, 68 and 72 (nos 401 and 428).

171 *Book of Fees*, ii, 1315; BL Harley MS 4766, fo 9r; BL Arundel MS 17, fo 33v; BL Harley MS 3660, fo 143r.

172 *Exeter Freemen*, 3, 20, 23.

173 PRO E179/95/15.

174 D&C Exeter Archives 2961 and 5249.

[175] *Lay Subsidy 1332, passim*, but also 30, 50, 52, 105 (beyond), 18, 21, 43, 44, 64, 96, 124 (beneath); *Lay Subsidy 1524–5*, 13, 46-7, 49, 50, 55, 58, 59-61, 63, 65, 67, 71, 74, 76-8, 82, 84, 102, 105, 119-20, 134-7, 139-45, 147-9, 151, 163, 172-8, 183-4, 192, 197, 203, 207, 209, 212, 214, 219, 224-7, 230, 237, 243, 249, 251.

[176] K Cameron, 'Bynames of location in Lincolnshire Subsidy Rolls', *Nottingham Medieval Studies*, 32 (1988), 156-64.

[177] *Lay Subsidy 1332*, 3, 6-7, 9, 13, 16, 20-2, 27, 28, 33-4, 38, 40-2, 44, 49-50, 52, 54-5, 60, 69, 86, 97, 104, 113, 118, 122; Oliver, *Monasticon*, 157.

[178] *Lay Subsidy 1332*, 3-4, 16, 22, 38, 104; *PND*, I, 100, 243, and II, 509-10, 594, 613.

[179] PRO E179/95/100.

[180] *Lay Subsidy 1524–5, passim*.

[181] A Kussmaul, *Servants in Husbandry in Early Modern England*, (1981).

[182] Reaney, *Origin*, 193-7.

[183] *Exeter Freemen, passim*.

[184] E B DeWindt, *The Liber Gersumarum of Ramsey Abbey, passim*.

[185] *Exeter Freemen*, 36-7, 39, 42-4, 47, 52, 56, 61.

[186] DRO Bedford MSS Werrington court rolls computer database; Longleat MSS Uplyme court rolls computer database; D&C Exeter Archives 5008; *Lay Subsidy 1524–5, passim*. E B DeWindt, *op. cit., passim*, for example, 114, 133, 140, 240, 255, 262, 269, 303, 359, 372 (nos 1220, 1491, 1576, 2937, 3123, 3197, 3278, 3649, 4331, 4365); for Devon, BL Harley MS 4766, fo 8v (William Tolchet *alias* Fokeray).

[187] C Clark, *Nomina*, 3 (1979), 113-14, reviewing McKinley, *Oxfordshire*.

[188] O Reichel, note in *TDA*, 28 (1896), 374.

[189] BL Add MS 37053, fo 278.

[190] Longleat MSS Uplyme court rolls computer database.

[191] *Lay Subsidy 1332*, 12, 20, 43-5, 100.

[192] *Dorset Lay Subsidy 1327*, 24-6, 28, 32, 38, 49, 70, 77-8, 93, 95, 98-9, 102, 108, 114-15, 117, 121, 123, 125, 133; *Dorset Lay Subsidy 1332*, e.g. 2, 7, 9, 11, 16.

[193] 'Somerset Lay Subsidy 1327', 80-1, 105, 114, 119, 122, 126, 134, 161, 194, 232. See also Christine Grigories at Mells in 1334-5: Longleat MS 10755.

[194] Longleat MSS 9647, 9657, 10618.

[195] *Lay Subsidy 1524–5, passim*.

CHAPTER 3

MIGRATION AND MOBILITY

The diffusion and distribution of surnames within and outside Devon from the later middle ages, after the establishment of the heritability of surnames and their stability, depended partly on the fortunes of particular families and partly on patterns of migration by individuals. The fortune of individual families was a passive agent, deciding whether a surname would survive in particular communities, the intensity of that survival vis-a-vis other surnames within the same community, and the so-called 'ramification' of surnames within a circumscribed locality. Patterns of migration determined the distribution of surnames over wider areas, whether in localized networks or social locations (groups of kinship networks in groups of parishes), or along more linear routes.

Models of patterns of migration have been constructed for the early modern period, which can, cautiously, be applied to the later middle ages.[1] 'Circular' migration is perhaps epitomized by the clergy in the later middle ages and early modern period in Devon. In the early modern period, this pattern also obtained for farm servants.[2] Its application to servants in husbandry, and also agricultural labourers in the later middle ages is more difficult to address. 'Chain migration' occurred along established routeways.[3] Linkages along commercial routes were extremely important in late medieval and early modern Devon. The impact of these commercial linkages varied by region within Devon, and between urban and rural contexts, and between large and small towns. In the early modern period, it has been suggested that kinship ties were an important element in migration and the assimilation of newcomers, especially into towns. An example from Devon is John Pinney, born in Dorset, who worked in Exeter, then joined his kinswoman, Sabina Pinney, at Chudleigh, and subsequently established his own household as a cordwainer.[4] Immigration from Ireland to Devon, and the existence of bands of itinerant Irish in the early modern period, may also have represented the influence of extended kinship. Migration from Devon to the New World may have conformed to the pull of extended kinship.[5] It is important, therefore, to attempt to establish patterns and routes of migration of people in late medieval and early modern Devon, as an agency for the diffusion and introduction of surnames. Of equal importance is the establishment of 'information fields' which may have ultimately induced migration. It should be emphasized, however, that, although the migration of surnames depended on the movement of people, the distribution of surnames is not direct, precise or reliable evidence of personal mobility and movement of individuals, especially after the heritability and stability of surnames.

One of the principal considerations of the study of surnames is the rate at which they migrated through different regions. This dissemination may reflect the continuance of very localized social organization and networks, and then the subsequent change to more inter-regional social organization, assisting the transmission and confusion of different cultures, and, ultimately, resulting in a common rather than regional popular culture and national identity. The very tightly localized nature of many surnames throughout the middle ages and early modern period, and indeed in some regions until quite recent times, has been perceived as a reflection of the intense localization of society or societies. The rate of migration of surnames over time is, therefore, an indicator of wider social organization and affinities.

The migration of surnames should not be considered in isolation; the actual migration of people can act as a 'control' by which to measure the migration of surnames. Unfortunately, the migration of people in the middle ages is elusive, especially in Devon, where the sources are both defective and reticent. The patterns of migration perceived below are therefore inevitably patchy, but an attempt is made to assess how localized was society at that time, particularly at the lower social margins. The concentration on the lower social groups is deliberate. An exception is the analysis of the pattern of migration of the clergy, which constituted a special career group (but possibly of pluralistic social origin), but which, in fact, confirms the concept of intensely localized social contacts and networks. In the case of the clergy, patterns of migration were stimulated by patterns of patronage and careerism, but these forces too may have been localized. The clergy may have been theoretically a career open to all, although recruitment from the lowest social group, the unfree, depended on seignorial permission and specific licence (since ordination was tantamount to manumission). The process of migration is thus offered below as an empirical yardstick against which to measure the migration of surnames.

Evidence of migration and mobility amongst lower social groups in Devon is fragmentary. Customary carrying services suggest a theoretical 'information field', but it is not certain whether the services were still performed. Thus the tenants of Stokenham had a theoretical obligation to carry fish to Stoke in Wiltshire and to use their own boats to transport wine between Totnes, Kingsbury, Dartmouth and the manor.[6] The principal indicator for the later middle ages is the presentment of *fugitivi* in manorial courts, that is, of those unfree peasants who had left the manor without the lord's licence or payment of chevage. This evidence suggests the persistent movement of small numbers of villeins within circumscribed areas. For example, *nativi* fled from Waddeton to Kerswell, Churchston Ferrers and Galmpton between *c.*1370 and *c.*1430; from Ide to Dawlish; from Ashwater to Sheepwash, but also into Somerset and Dorset. The sons of William Bosce, of Shilhall in east Cornwall, migrated just over the county boundary, one to Plympton in service with a merchant, another to Plymouth in service with a mariner, another to Lamerton as a farm servant.[7] The extent of this sort of migration seems to have been more a trickle than a flood in Devon, by comparison with some regions of eastern England at the same time.

Table 3.1

Villein Fugitivi *from some Manors in Devon*

Manor	Dates	No of *fugitivi*
Uplyme	1307–1536	12
Stoke Fleming	1384–1521	11
Werrington	1365–1498	17
Stoke Canon	1454–1455	3
Yarcombe	1338–1433	6

N.B.: Most of the series of court rolls are broken and some are fragmentary.

The problem of such entries in court rolls for manors in Devon is that they do not often specify the new place of residence of the fugitive. A small number of entries do provide this information, and may be used cautiously as evidence of distances of migration. Six entries from Uplyme identify the new place of sojourn in the later middle ages as Musbury (less than four miles from Uplyme), 'Colewey' and Bruckland (three to four miles), 'Netherlym' (two miles), and the local 'le Haselbear'. The court roll for the same manor in 1536 contains more evidence, the new places of refuge being Musbury, Colyford (five miles away), Axminster (four miles), and Colyton (five miles). By implication, therefore, migration of villeins from Uplyme was exclusively to other places in east Devon, within a radius of five miles. Only two entries in the court rolls of Werrington are as specific; in both cases, migration was localized, as that to Bradstone, less than five miles distant. A fugitive from Stoke Canon was reported to be living at Thorverton, less than three miles away. The rolls of Stoke Fleming only indicate the place of residence in two cases, in both of which the flight was to the adjacent borough of Dartmouth. Two *nativi* from Clayhidon were living at Yarcombe in *c.*1486. What evidence there is thus suggests that there was probably only a small amount of movement, which took place within a very circumscribed area of migration. Distance of migration may have become even more circumscribed in the later middle ages, as economic and landholding opportunities became more locally available as a result of the demographic contraction of the later middle ages.

The exact status of the fugitives is sometimes revealed; they were predominantly sons, and a few daughters. Their position correlates with the *garciones* in the court rolls of Uplyme, who were predominantly sons, either allowed to leave the manor on payment of chevage to seek work elsewhere, or staying on the manor as farm servants on payment of recognition. The lists of *garciones* decline after *c.*1350 as internal opportunities became available at Uplyme. Throughout the period, however, the lists included sons of core families, such as Gache. By contrast, the fugitives from Uplyme before *c.*1500 mainly consisted of the offspring of the less substantial families — Peynte, Lombes (*bis*), de Shotecomb, Rychardes, Meyes, de Graveston, Pert (four), Hobbs and Nog. Similarly at Stoke Fleming, fugitives were drawn from the less influential families, such as Wade, Hillary, att' Worthi, Wodeby, Whisleigh, Pareys, Shipman (*bis*), Slegh', atte Wille (*bis*) and Lakeman. Thus at Uplyme, John, son of John Rychardes was repeatedly presented as a fugitive from 1366 to 1375, from age 20 to 27. Joan, daughter of William Hobbs was presented there in all courts between 1366 and 1369. Both were the offspring of the lesser tenantry. Similarly, four children of the minor tenant, William Pert, absconded simultaneously, Robert, John, William and Alice. Some of the daughters absconded without licence to marry, such as the sisters, Alice and Christine Lombes, Agnes, daughter of Reginald de Shotecomb, and Matilda Meyes, although the payment of merchet to marry outside the lordship was common at Uplyme. Joan Hobbes from Uplyme and Agnes Maiour from Werrington, probably fled because they were pregnant, as they were also fined leyrwite specifically for being pregnant. Over half the fugitives from Uplyme were female, about a third from Werrington (five of 17), but only two from 11 from Stoke Fleming. When, in 1536, five *nativi* were presented as fugitives from Uplyme, however, the pattern seems to have changed, since all were sons of core families, three sons of William Gache and two sons of John Lyllyng.

The earlier pattern at Werrington had been quite different, since a number of fugitives had derived there from core families, even from the Tommas and Louya families (four fugitives).[8]

Because of their status as siblings, the fugitives did not cause the surname to be subtracted from the manor, although they would have been responsible for its migration in a localized framework. The surname was left behind on the manor in the form of parents or other siblings, but occasionally with a *consanguineus*. Thus, the court rolls specify that a father or *proprinquior consanguineus*, usually bearing the same surname, will be responsible for securing the return of the fugitive. The profile of the fugitives is fairly consistent; they were young or adolescent. At Werrington, as in the case of Richard Medere *alias* Modere and Joan Maiour, they were adolescents seeking employment, in these two cases with parish clergy. Four non-resident villeins at Uplyme in 1536 were aged 21, 13, 18 and 27.

The evidence of fugitives depicts a pattern of adolescent migrants moving in a localized society. Other, more miscellaneous, evidence in the court rolls, elucidates further the nature of movement, comprising cases of breaches of the peace, trespass and theft. In particular, the pleas from Werrington illustrate short-distance impermanent movement over the county boundary from Cornwall, although there were only a few instances. In 1474, the jurors at Werrington presented that Thomas Veele *de Boyton in Comitatu Cornubie clerke* had poached rabbits in the lord's warren at Webworthy. In two other presentments, tenants of Werrington were placed in mercy for prosecuting suits, involving other tenants of Werrington, outside the manorial court in courts in Launceston. In 1365, it was presented there that Thomas Coulecote had abducted thirteen lambs from the land of John Coulecote and driven them into Cornwall.[10] In 1479, the jury presented that on Christmas eve in 1478, John Wolffe of Ashwater, husbandman, Thomas Courteys of the same place, labourer, and William Esseworthy of Werrington, husbandman, *cum aliis ignotis*, stopped William Robyn, late of Carey, labourer, on suspicion of felony, and discovered that he had 60 lbs. of stolen wool.[11] Carey Barton is a hamlet in the parish of St Giles on the Heath, the parish adjacent to Werrington. In a case in the manorial court of Uplyme, in 1369, William Vyne counted that Henry Gache had taken his horse further than Musbury, into the country (*patria*), losing two shoes from the horse, Musbury being about four miles from Uplyme. The court rolls of Yarcombe, close to Uplyme, reveal that thefts and burglary there were committed by *homines suspesiosi* from Buckland in Somerset and from Monkton and Honiton.[12] Some migration was forced by external circumstances, by push factors. In 1334, the assessment on Ottery St Mary under the new quota system, was raised from £15 10s. 7d. (1332) to £20, because, it was maintained by the taxpayers of Ottery, the chief assessors had a grudge against the Dean and Chapter of Rouen, who held the manor; consequently, 26 of the 134 tenants abandoned their lands and the manor. A petition of the men of Budleigh in 1347 complained that French raiders had carried off many of the richest merchants and seamen of the township, with the result that those remaining were obliged to pay the full weight of taxation; some had had to resort to begging and others were on the point of leaving their holdings.[13] This movement of peasants was all very localized.

The migration of females was probably also within very short distances. On many manors in Devon there was no restriction on females marrying outside the lordship, provided that merchet was paid. Female-led migration may have been a constant factor in the later middle ages, but circumscribed in terms of distance because of the fewer economic and social opportunities.[14] Neither did it involve the loss of surname from the manor or even the permanent migration of the surname into other communities. Pledges for the payment of merchet indicate that the surname always remained on the manor. Thus, at Uplyme, Joan and Agnes, the eldest and youngest daughters of William Lyllyng, gave merchet to marry outside the manor, their pledge being their father, William. Peter atte Watere provided merchet for his daughter, Isabella, to marry outside Uplyme, the pledges being Robert atte Watere and Richard atte Watere. Isabella Kene paid her own merchet to marry outside, her pledge being John Kene.[15]

Impermanent migration by agricultural labourers may have become an increasing feature of the rural economy of the county during the later middle ages. Some peasants of Ashwater migrated in autumn 1346 *usque les Southammys* for harvest work, some from Sidbury to 'eastern parts', and others from Bratton Clovelly 'away from the county'.[16] At Uplyme, at an earlier date, the lord, Glastonbury Abbey, was allowed the services of 'strangers' or 'foreigners' at both boon ploughings and boonworks for reaping, suggesting that these may have been migrant labourers.[17] The nature of some services, established at an earlier time and possibly when the pattern of settlement was different, also contributed to movement; thus the tenants of Stokenham owed suit to the mill of Blackawton, some five miles and two parishes away.[18] The development of regional economies of the county during the later middle ages may have induced further impermanent movement, such as the droving of cattle over longer distances. Concomitantly, the effects of the demographic contraction, resultant new economic opportunities, and moderation of seignorial control in the later middle ages, may have allowed wider movement within the county.[19]

Figure 2
Some Movements of Criminals and the Commission of Offences in 1238 and *c.*1280–1500.

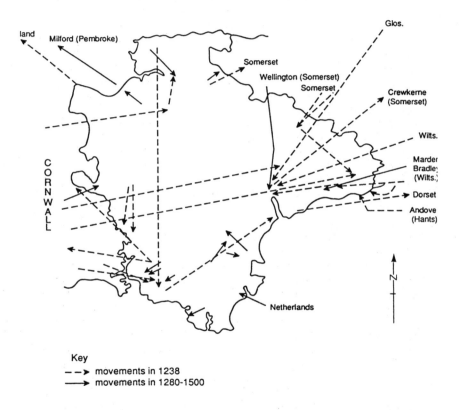

Key
- – → movements in 1238
——→ movements in 1280-1500

The arrows relate to: (a) routes where victims were murdered; or
(b) relationship of place of offence to usual place of residence of the offender;
(c) migration of criminals after the commission of offence.

Source: Chancery Miscellaneous volume VIII (List and Index Society, 26, 1967)
(Bundle 55 passim), c1280-1500.
Crown Pleas Devon 1238, passim.

The migration of criminals and the location of crime is an ambivalent indicator of movement, since the mobility of the perpetrators after the offence, usually involving sanctuary, abjuration and outlawry, was involuntary. In one respect, however, criminal activity seems to have had a direct impact on bynames. Some criminals were accorded nicknames reflecting their delinquency, thus Ralph Ronneaway, Robert Godbithamungus, William Routaboute, William Swengebagge, John Luggespurs and William le Wykkede, appear among those prosecuted in the late thirteenth century. The committal of crime often involved movement. Thus in 1258, the vagrants who committed murder included contingents from Cornwall, Somerset, Dorset, Ireland, and particularly Wales. Welsh cattle thieves featured heavily in the crown pleas in that year.[20]

The pattern of movement involved in crime in 1238 and in some miscellaneous prosecutions during the later middle ages is represented on the map above. For example, Ralph de Cruke, an offender in 1238, was a stranger who had lived in Exeter, had abjured the realm, but was, in fact living in Crewkerne in Somerset. William de Criditreu, of Exeter, had received goods stolen in Dorset. Vagrant thieves in Exeter included Thomas Capun from Wiltshire and William Ernis from Gloucestershire. The body of Thomas Anderbode was found by his nephew, from Dorset, Thomas. John le Brokere, Gilbert Hamun, Adam Kerl, Geoffrey Coppe, William Giuwold and William Gutt, all from Lyme Regis in Dorset, were presented for taking wreck at Uplyme. Emelota a thief from Cornwall sought sanctuary in the church at Honiton. The jurors of Honiton also presented Walter de Boteilerheie who had killed Nicholas de la Furse, and had lived in Waringstone in Hemyock Hundred. The jurors of Colyton Hundred presented that Walter Spere had been murdered on his way to Exeter with cloth, and that Nicholas Pain had been killed as he returned from a scot ale in Dorset. Those of Hemyock Hundred reported that Gerald de Tottewrthe had fallen from his horse on Widecombe Moor on his way from Somerset. William Herm, who sought sanctuary in the church at Kentisbeare, had lived in Stockland, a detached tithing in Dorset. Miles de Calklewdele denied an appeal on the defence that he had been living in Ireland for a year. At Cliston, the death was reported of Sarah, daughter of William Grameire of Cornwall. In Budleigh Hundred, it was presented that William de la Pitte had been outlawed in Dorset, and that William *pistor* of Exeter had been killed by Hugh de Cockewille at Bishop's Clyst, but that Hugh was now living in Exeter. Godfrey de la Leghe was found dead in Lifton Hundred, but his murderers lived in Sampford in adjacent Black

Torrington Hundred. Similarly, Roger Cidie had been killed at Okehampton by other inhabitants of Black Torrington Hundred. Walter son of Richard Burri, presented by South Molton Hundred, fled across the nearby county boudary into Somerset. Braunton Hundred reported that Walter de Dureville had hanged himself in Plympton. The jurors of Barnstaple maintained that, whilst Ralph *faber* had killed a young boy there, he belonged to the tithing of Horwood in Fremington Hundred. John de Bido, a thief from Cornwall, was arrested in Great Torrington. Roborough Hundred reported that Edward Calwe, a murderer, had been arrested in Launceston, just over the county boundary, and that Amadas de Wike and Walter de Wyke had abducted Robert Sparke across that boundary to Killigorrick. Two thieves from Cornwall, Ralph le Potter and Alice, were presented at Plympton. A youth presented at Axmouth maintained that he came from the region around Andover. The pattern revealed in 1238 both short- and longer-distance migration, involving both perpetrators and victims. The pattern includes the movement of offenders in perpetrating the crime, their movements after the offence, and the movement of victims at the time of the offence. The movement of victims and of criminals before the offence was voluntary, that of criminals after the offence forced by circumstance.[21]

The pattern can be reinforced by the evidence of miscellaneous offences committed between *c.*1280 and *c.*1500. One victim, Robert le Peschur, was en route between Wellington in Somerset, Bradninch and Exeter, when he was murdereed. Philip de Stakepole and others were outlawed on appeal for offences committed as far away as Milford in Pembrokeshire. John van Selesburgh, a Dutchman, was murdered in Dartmouth. A number of cases involved Londoners. An inhabitant of Plymouth was outlawed on the action of William Totewill of London, but the latter's surname seems to be a Devon one. In another case, men from Winchelsea and Sandwich had plundered ships in the harbour at Dartmouth.[22] These later incidents reveal the patterns of communications developing in later medieval Devon through the expansion and consolidation of commercial linkages.

A special linkage had been developed between Devon and the advowson and rectory manor of Bampton in Oxfordshire, which provided a specific route for migration.[23] This chain migration involved two processes, presentation to the living (clerical careerism) and appointment of estate officials (lordship). Thus, in 1326, Walter de Blackeworthy, whose byname was a locative one from Devon, acted as bailiff at Bampton, and another Walter de Blackeworthy, a Fellow of Exeter College in Oxford in *c.*1333–7, may have been a relative.[24] Earlier, in 1296, William le Deveneys had collected the rents from Bampton.[25]

Unfortunately, it is not possible to obtain more than the slightest imputation of the significance of lordship. In the early fourteenth century, Richard Schyrewold was amerced several times in the manorial court of Uplyme for stray beasts and also leased additional pasture for his sheep between 1300 and 1314.[26] His occurrence and his byname were transient in the court rolls and accounts for the manor. The element -wold in this locative byname suggests that it originated outside Devon. The same byname occurred in Glastonbury and adjacent Baltonsborough and Harptree in the lay subsidy of 1327 for Somerset.[27] Moreover, the accounts for some manors of Glastonbury Abbey reveal the localization of the byname around Glastonbury. At Baltonborough, Agnes daughter of Robert Shirewold paid merchet in 1314-15; William son of Margery Schirewold paid an entry fine of nine pounds for a messuage and half virgate, at the same time as Margery Schirewold paid merchet of 20s. *pro se extra maritanda*, and Walter and Adam Schirewold paid smaller entry fines (all 1314-16). Reginald son of Walter Schirewold paid an entry fine of ten pounds for a messuage and virgate and other parcels there, and Henry Schirewold almost simultaneously paid an entry fine of ten pounds for a similar amount of land (*c.*1348-50).[28] It seems probable, therefore, that Richard Schyrewold originated from around Glastonbury, and migrated as an official of the Abbey to its manor in Devon at Uplyme.[29] Conversely, a few of the tenants of the Abbey in Somerset bore the byname Devenish.[30]

During the later middle ages a connection was established between Oxford and Devon, creating an avenue for linear or chain migration of people and bynames. Before the foundation of Exeter (Stapleton) College in Oxford, the relationship remains obscure. The secular chapter at Exeter had its own schools which enjoyed a high reputation in the twelfth century. Thomas de Marlbergh, who became a monk at Evesham *c.*1194-1200, had taught both laws at both Exeter and Oxford; his byname was almost certainly a locative one relating to Marlborough in the South Hams. By 1159-60, the Exeter schools may have gained an international flavour, with the presence of Nicholas of Flanders and Gilbert of Ireland. The school may have enjoyed this reputation until the 1230s.[31]

Some Devonians migrated in the thirteenth century to be educated at Oxford. William de Exeter was one, a Franciscan Friar (fl 1289-1306); Walter de Bronescombe, who became bishop of Exeter in 1258, had studied in Oxford. John Gervais de Exonia had become a *magister* by 1234, and may also have studied at Paris, but his clerical career commenced with the rectory of Bridford in Devon (and was completed when he was elevated to the see of Winchester in 1262). Master Richard le Deveneis seems to have been at Oxford *c.*1222–1228. Augustine Devoniensis was presented for trespass in Shotover Forest in 1231. Richard Devoniensis was a Franciscan who, early in his career, assisted in establishing new convents in Oxford and Northampton. The illustrious William de Excestre *alias* Newetone received licences to study *c.*1319–23 , becoming DM by 1327 and DTh by 1336. He returned to Devon as rector of Stokeinteignhead and was appointed a canon and prebendary of Exeter from 1331 to 1351, but also held similar offices in York and Lincoln.[32] In these cases, the migration through Oxford did not involve more than the transient migration of bynames. The more permanent migration of the byname Devenish into Oxford is elucidated below.

Ecclesiastical preferment thus provided one route for the temporary migration of people. Before the Reformation, such migration of people would not have induced the permanent migration of surnames because of clerical celibacy. After the Reformation, the path was clear for migration of people and surnames to proceed hand in hand. The pathway for ordination for Devonians was quite predominantly through Exeter College, founded as Stapleton Hall in *c.*1312–15. Up to 1530, some 392 fellows and members of the College can be identified. Of these, 203 originated from Devon and 96 from Cornwall — about 75% from the south-western diocese. The vast majority of these returned to livings in the south west because of the pattern of patronage and localized ties.[33] Even after the Reformation, the College continued to admit mainly from the south-west, a pattern which persisted into the seventeenth century. Most graduands continued to enter the church, despite the new opportunities in secular professions such as the law. Although the potential for the migration of surnames existed now, because of clerical marriage, most graduates of the College still returned to livings in the south west. For example, Henry Dotyn, whose family had a tradition of ecclesiastical office, was admitted to the College in 1553/4, was vicar of Bampton in Oxfordshire by 1558/9 on the resignation of his uncle, John Dotyn, but ended his career as rector of Stokeinteignhead from 1569. Thomas Upham became rector of East Worlinton from 1591–1603 and vicar of St Andrew's, Plymouth, where he died in 1603. George Hakewill, after an illustrious career, which, however, ended ignominiously, returned to be rector of Heanton Punchardon, where he died in 1649. William Hele became vicar of Bishop's Teignton and Rattery from 1620–7, dying at the latter in 1627. John Hakewill, who was baptised at

Barnstaple in 1616, became rector of Heanton, where he died in 1654/5. All these clerics from Devon had attended Exeter College. They all bore distinctive surnames from Devon, but all returned to their county of origin.[34]

An exception to this pattern was established through the linkage between Devon, Exeter College and the living at Bampton in Oxfordshire, held by the Dean and Chapter of Exeter. During the middle ages, many of those presented to this living originated in Devon, some through Exeter College, a few through Oriel: Philip de Exeter (instituted 1272); Mr Nicholas de Totnes (*c.*1236–58); Mr Richard de Exeter (*c.*1296–1316); Mr Robert Bythewall *alias* de Exon (1316–1342/5); Mr Thomas Dyer *alias* Dyra, son of John Dyra of 'Critton' in Devon (1393–1405); Mr Robert Alyngton (1522–   ); Mr Edmund Willesford (1498–1506); and, later, Mr Edmund Crispin (1547-9); Mr Richard Crispin (1523–   ), Mr Thomas Plymiswood, Mr Robert Holcot (1481—   ), John Dotyn (1543–59), and Henry Dotyn (1559–   ). In 1401, Thomas Plymiswood exchanged his living at Bampton with John Wydelond, vicar of Heavitree. Thus the locative surname, from Widlond in Modbury, migrated from the South Hams to east Devon and into Oxfordshire. Conversely, Robert Holcot resigned Bampton to be inducted as rector of Goodleigh in Devon (1492–1500). After the Reformation, the migration of people may have involved the movement of surnames permanently to Bampton. John Dotyn, from Harberton in Devon, became a Fellow of Exeter College (1528–39), and subsequently rector of Bampton (by 1543). From 1558 until his death in 1561, he was rector of Kingsdon in Somerset, where he was buried. In 1568, however, he sold property in Bampton to his kinsman, Andrew Dotyn, of Bampton in Oxfordshire, yeoman. His successor in the living at Bampton, Henry Dotyn, also passed through Exeter College. By his will, Henry left legacies to the poor of this Bampton, but also to the poor of Alphrington and Stokeinteignhead, the Lazars of Totnes, and the Magdalen House at Teignmouth. Amongst his bequests in his will (1590, proved 1591) were household goods in both Bampton and Stokeinteignhead. The surname Dotyn thus became established over generations in Bampton through the linkage with the living.[35]

Internal migration within Devon to the regional capital, Exeter, during the later middle ages is represented in the origins of some apprentices in the City, constituting perhaps 'betterment migration'. This migration was not only rural-urban, but also from some of the other boroughs to the City, from Plymouth, Barnstaple, Dartmouth, Tavistock, Totnes and Crediton. The origins are stated from 1413. Some apprentices derived from Cornwall; some from

Figure 3
The Origins of Apprentices in Exeter from 1413.

From outside Devon

Cornwall:

Cornwall (2);	Guernsey (2)
Bodmin (1);	Snaith (Yorks) (1)
Tregeny (1);	Rousham (Suffolk) (1)
Liskeard (1);	Christchurch (Hants) (1)
S. Petherwin (1);	Croydon (Surrey) (1)
	Birmingham (Warws) (1)

Guernsey followed established commercial linkages. A very few originated from further afield: Snaith (Yorks); Christ Church (Hants); Croydon (Surrey); Birmingham (Warws); and Rougham (Suffolk). Most of the apprentices, however, were induced from a wide geographical area within Devon, reflecting the increasing regional importance of Exeter in the south west. More explicit evidence of this expanding status of the City is provided by details of the origins of some incomers listed in the military survey in 1522, with a more significant pull on Somerset as well as the large numbers of aliens.[36] In the mid sixteenth century, a small leakage of apprentices escaped Devon. Between 1542 and 1565, some 27 apprentices in Bristol originated from Devon, comprising, however, only 0.9% of all the apprentices in Bristol, but more than from Dorset (18) or Cornwall (9).[37]

Contacts outside the county extended along the south coast and with alien merchants, through chain migration in both directions, inwards and outwards.[38] The port books of Southampton reveal the details of ships and merchants from the ports of Devon trading to that entrepot. In 1439, the 'Antonius' from Dartmouth, owned by the merchant John Blakesclat of Dartmouth, and a ship from Exeter owned by William Dewke, traded there; in 1440 a ship from Plymouth and ships from Kingsbridge imported 10,000 slates from Devon; a ship from Ottermouth brought fish under the mastership of William Helyer; a ship from Kingsbridge carried wine. The brokage books of Southampton also reveal the overland trade from east Devon: Thomas Shote of Axminster bringing 26 dozen straits on his three horses; Walter Smyth of Cheriton with 600 *ferri* in his own cart; Henry Vrye and Robert Wylly returning to Honiton with woad and alum for the cloth industry.[39] In 1435-6, the port books listed John Combe of Stokenham transporting 24,000 slates, John Gillis of Dartmouth with wine, several ships from Ottermouth with ling, herring and other fish, merchants from Honiton with wine, woad, soap and paper.[40]

These same commercial contacts explain the inwards migration of aliens into Devon. When taxed in the mid fifteenth century, some 45% of the aliens in Devon originated from Normandy, with an additional 15% described as Frenchmen and 4% as Bretons. The Irish comprised 14% of aliens resident in the county, whilst small numbers of Dutch, Guernseymen and Flemings exercised an important commercial function. The assessment listed some 342 aliens taxed at 16d. as they held *hospicia* and 333 at 6d. as they did not hold an *hospicium*. About 56% of those assessed at 6d. were servants. The concentrations of aliens was by and large in the trading communities of the east and South Hams, although they were

Figure 4
The Origins of Some Inhabitants of Exeter (1522 Military Survey).

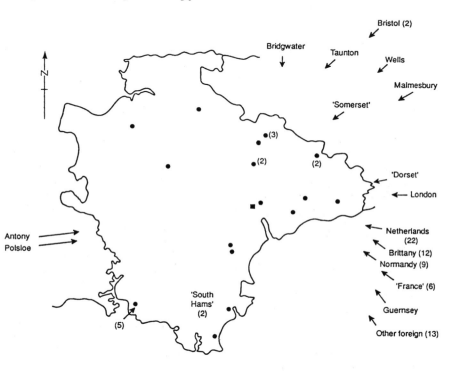

Source: <u>Tudor Exeter.</u>

The data relate to specific statements of origins. A dot represents one person unless a figure is given in parenthesis.

Other foreign: Picardy, Brabant (2), Cleves (2), Lombardy, Lucca, Friesland, 'Fleming', Flanders (2), Utrecht, Cologne.

dispersed in small numbers in communities throughout Devon. The Dutch were located primarily in Dartmouth and Exeter. Exeter had the greatest variety of aliens resident with *hospicia*. The Irish tended to be concentrated more in north Devon, but they also formed a contingent in Plymouth.[41]

Table 3.2

Analysis of the Provenance of Aliens in Devon in the mid fifteenth century

Provenance	Taxed at 16d		Taxed at 6d					
	No.	%	Servants		Non-servants		Totals	
			No.	%	No.	%	No.	%
Normandy	141	41	81	47	75	53	297	45
Frenshmen	45	14	36	21	19	13	100	15
'Hibernicus'	31 } 19		4 } 8		7 } 11		42 } 14	
Irishman	32 }		10 }		9 }		51 }	
Flemings	11	3	16	9	2	1	29	4
Guernseyman	4	1	10	6	4	3	18	3
Dutchmen	22	7	7	4	10	7	39	6
Breton	18	5	4	2	6	4	28	4
Misc*	13				20			
Unknown provenance	23		—————13—————				36	
Totals	342	51			333 (49%)		675	100

* De Vascon' (2), Gascony (4), Flanders (2), de Franc' (10), Scotland (1), Gallicus (2), de Beme (2), Isle of Man (4), Spaniard (1), Hollander (1), de Britannia (1), Selander (1), de Seland (1), de Spruys (1), Portugal (1), de Burdegalia (2), de Saxonia (1).

During the later sixteenth century, commercial linkages within the county developed further, particularly with the increased need for the countryside to sustain the expanding towns. Connections with London also increased.[42] Some of these patterns are reflected in Figure 5.[43] Overseas, the trade to Portugal became more significant, including the export of cloth.[44] Numerous Londoners became involved in disputes, not only for debt, but also relating to land in the county.[45] Numerous cases of litigation involved profits from maritime enterprises and joint-stock organization.[46] Victualling assumed even more importance. John Andrewe, a merchant of Great Torrington, was embroiled in a dispute with a baker of Penryn in Cornwall about the sale of defective 'biscuit bread'.[47] A yeoman of

Table 3.3

Concentrations of Aliens in Devon in the mid fifteenth century
(more than five aliens in one community)

Settlement	N	H	I	D	Fl	Br	Fr	Others
Ilfracombe	1	5						
Churston Ferrers	4				1			
Brixton	1		1			1		5
Newton Ferrers		2				1	2	
Dartmouth	6		2	5			1	
Stonehouse	3	1	1	1		6	3	1
Plymouth	6	1	2			2	1	3
Plympton	4		2	1	1	1	7	
Exeter	8		3	10				13
Sidmouth	8							
Woodbury	5							
E Budleigh	14							
Littleham	16							

Buckerell proceeded against George Serell, baker of Exeter, for non-payment for wheat in 1600.[48] To some extent, this evidence is misleading, since the source, suits in Chancery, would tend to exaggerate the level of wider commercial connections. Below this level, there must have existed a base of localized transactions. The cases in Chancery reflect, however, the widening contacts and horizons which may have affected some social groups in some of the more accessible and open communities in Devon by the later sixteenth century. Such influences may have been exerted unevenly, so that the more isolated and remote regions may have remained unaffected.

The commercial connections with Southampton did not seem to have induced much permanent emigration from Devon even by the seventeenth century.[49] Only four out of 650 apprentices in Southampton between 1609 and 1740 had origins in Devon, from Aylesbury, Bickley, Dartmouth and Plymouth.[50] Indeed, most recruitment of apprentices in Southampton was localized, from Hampshire, and only 84 (2%) came from the western counties, mainly from Wiltshire, Dorset and Somerset, but none from Cornwall.

Some evidence of internal migration in the county in the early sixteenth century is provided for limited areas in the lay subsidy of 1524–5. In a few hundreds, the collectors indicated the new place

Figure 5
Some Commercial Linkages *c.*1570–1603.

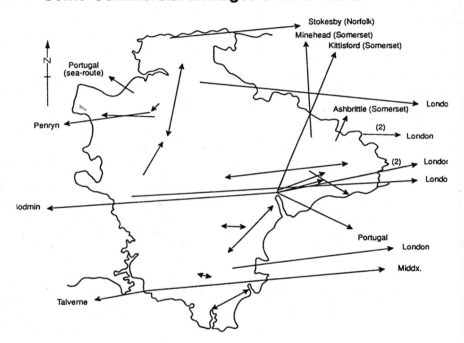

Stokesby (Norfolk)
Minehead (Somerset)
Kittisford (Somerset)

Portugal
(sea-route)

Londo

Ashbrittle (Somerset)

(2)

Penryn

London

(2)   Londor

Londo

lodmin

Portugal

London

Talverne

Middx.

Commercial linkages: mainly debt and detinue, a few land.

Sources: Chancery Proceedings, Supplement Elizabeth I (List and Index
Society, 202, 1983)
Chancery Decree Rolls: Elizabeth I (List and Index Society, 198, 1983)

of residence of taxpayers who had migrated between 1524 and 1525. The total of individuals involved was 72, but no destination is specified for 23. In one other instance, a taxpayer known as Iryshman had returned to Ireland from Sidmouth. Of the 58 whose destination is recorded, 19 (27%) moved to an adjacent parish. A large number also migrated to parishes at a short remove or within the same hundred. A few female migrants moved over longer distances for marriage, from Sidmouth to Honiton, Sidmouth to Farway, Buckland Brewer to Morwenstow in Cornwall, and Ashprington to Dorset. Most migration in east Devon was, however, extremely short-distance, but in north Devon some longer movement was involved.[51]

In rural communities in the seventeenth century, migration was still localized. The marriage horizons of inhabitants of Ipplepen between 1612 and 1813 exhibited this pattern. The small number of partners who came from outside the parish originated predominantly from within a radius of 3.5 miles. There was a particularly strong connection with Totnes, to which Ipplepen seems to have looked rather than to Ashburton, which was slightly closer.[52]

The movement of vagrants in the late sixteenth and seventeenth centuries is not truly representative of the entire lower social groups, and may perhaps be an extreme pattern of migration. Between 1598 and 1638, 59 vagrants apprehended in Salisbury claimed to have come from east Devon, along the important Exeter-London route, and thus comprising about 9% of the total of vagrants apprehended in Salisbury.[53] The origins of vagrants arrested in Devon and Cornwall between 1634 and 1638 are presented in tabular form.

Table 3.4

Origins of Vagrants apprehended in Devon and Cornwall 1634–8

1 — Profile of status

Single men	166
Single women	56
Couples	26
Children	48
Total	296

2 — Distances (miles) between places of origin and punishment of vagrants (%)

Miles	0–20	21–40	41–60	61–80	81–100	101–50	151–200	200+
%	21.6	10.6	8.3	5.7	5.7	9.5	34.8*	3.8

* Mainly accounted for by bands of Irish wanderers, as, for example, 15 adults and 14 children apprehended together in Colyton.

Figure 6
Exogamous Marriages at Ipplepen 1612–1813.

EXETER (5)

Sourton (1)

Kenn (1)

10 miles

Bovey Tracey (2)

Widecombe in the Moor (3)

Ilsington (3)

5 miles

Tavistock (1)
(2 miles)

Kingsteignton (4)   Teignmouth (1)

Bickington (2)   Highweek (2)

Newton Abbot (3)   Combeinteignhead (5)

Holne (1)   Ashburton (6)

E. Ogwell (2)   Woolborough (10)   Stokeinteignhead (3)

Woodland (4)   W. Ogwell (2)

Abbotskerswell (6)

Denbury (5)   Kingskerswell (5)

Buckfastleigh (2)

Torbryan (9)   St Marychurch (1)

IPPLEPEN

Broadhempston (13)   Staverton (15)   Cockington (4)

Littlehempston (18)

Rattery (2)   Marldon (8)

S. Brent (1)   Berry Pomeroy (18)   Paignton (13)

Totnes (19)

Churchston Ferrers (4)   Brixham (3)

Plymouth (2)   Dittisham (1)

Plymstock (1)   Modbury (2)   Dartmouth (3)

Wembury (1)   E. Allington (1)   Kingswear (1)

Aveton Giffard (1)   Stoke Fleming (1)

Stokenham (1)

0   5   10
MILES

Outside Devon
Wareham (Dorset)
Portsea (Hants)
Liverpool (Lancs)
Poplar (Middx)
Bodmin (Cornwall)
London (Middx)
Jamaica

3 — Origins of vagrants

Devon	Cornwall	Ireland	Counties to the east of Devon	Total
34	26	77	75	212

Source: P Slack, 'Vagrants and vagrancy in England, 1598–1664', in P Clark and D Souden, eds., *Migration and Society in Early Modern England*, (1987), 55–6 (Table 2), 59, 61–2.

About a third derived from within the two south-western counties, a third from counties east of Devon, but another third in bands of roaming Irish kinship groups. About a third of the poor apprehended in Somerset between 1607 and 1636 originated from Devon and Cornwall. The punishment of the poor in the south-western counties confirmed the predominant movement from west to east.[54]

Slightly later (1654–62), some 87 individuals from Devon and Cornwall migrated to the New World as indentured servants and nine others as apprentices, through Bristol, comprising 3.5% and 0.9% respectively of emigrants of those types from that port. Of the 87, about six came from Barnstaple and ten from Exeter, the remainder from throughout the county. Of some 2885 emigrants to New England between 1620 and 1650, whose origins have been discovered, 6% derived from Devon, although no Devonians travelled in Winthrop's fleet of 1630. In terms of the numbers of emigrants from counties, Devon ranked ninth, but considerably lower than the counties in East Anglia and south east England and the triangle of Dorset, Somerset and Wiltshire.[55]

Table 3.5

Migrants from Devon to New England 1620–50

Destination	Mass.	Conn.	NH	RI	Maine	LI	Unknown	Total
Numbers	82	0	17	5	50	2	5	161

Notes: the sample is that of Banks (2885 individuals) as analysed by D H Fischer, *Albion's Seed. Four British Folkways in America*, (1989), 34–5.

Society in some parts of Devon continued to be very localized and constrained. Even in those parts open to influence from other parts of England and the continent, much of the movement was over very short-distances. Although the volume of movement increased in the early modern period, only a tiny amount involved distances of any length. The west, interior and parts of the inland north of the county long remained isolated from external influences and contributed little to out-migration. The more open regions, in the middle ages as later, were the trading communities and other accessible communities in the South Hams and east Devon.

The migration of bynames and surnames out of Devon self-evidently depended on the emigration of Devonians outside the county. Even for the later middle ages, however, only limited appreciation can be gained of this process of the out-migration of people and bynames and surnames, but some of the nuances can be perceived. First, the migration of surnames outside the county seems to have been limited, even during the early modern period. Secondly, the surnames tended to be concentrated both in adjacent counties and in the trading communities of southern England with which there existed established commercial linkages. Third, the primary (almost exclusive) byname or surname outside Devon during the late middle ages was Devenish and its variants. Bynames from specific placenames in Devon (rather than Devenish or variants) were more likely to occur in urban communities, such as in London, Winchester, Southampton, Bristol and Taunton.

In Dorset in 1327, Henry and William Deuenysche were assessed to the lay subsidy at Wool and Bexington in Punchknowle and William Deuenysche at Gillingham. In 1332, the taxpayers in that county included additionally John Deuenyssch at Godmanstone and Alexander Deuenyssh at Burton Bradstock. More ambivalently, Gervase and William de Wydecombe were assessed in 1327 at Burleston, but their locative bynames may have derived from, for example, Widdecombe in Somerset or one of the other Widdecombes. At Clifton Maybank, in 1327, Robert and Nicholas Hewysh were assessed, this byname also occurring at Hillfield and Dorchester; and at Corfe Mullen, John Wyndelsore. In 1332, Robert de Tauton was taxed at Winterbourne Houghton. Some of these locative surnames may have derived from the eponymous places in Devon.[56] The lay subsidy for Cornwall in 1327 may contain some seven locative surnames from Devon, including four from Tavistock, all concentrated in east Cornwall.[57]

The concentration of these bynames may, nevertheless, have been higher in Somerset. Those assessed in 1327 included Joan le Devenishe at Newton, Geoffrey le Devenysse at North Cadbury, Ralph Barstaple at Yeovil, Richard le Devenisch at Wells, Henry de Tyverton, John de Hembury and Ivo de Yartecombe, all in Taunton, John de Modbure at Dunster, John Hembure at Mulverton, Walter de Merkesbury, John de Axebridge and Simon de Plymtone all in Bristol, John de Membury at Shipton Montagu, William de Hywysh and Richard Hiwysh at Thurlbury. Hiwysh and variants may, however, have related to any of the numerous settlements with this name in the south-west.[58] In 1305–6, William le Deueneys paid an entry fine of 20s. at Rimpton to marry the widow of Robert Kybbel with her land. In 1307, John le Deuenyssch was a *garcio* at Nettleton and William le Deueneis of similar status at Brent.[59] The level of concentration of such bynames in Wiltshire is less clear. By 1375-6, chevage was paid by John Bratton and John Wynkelegh at Longbridge Deverill, but these may not have originated from placenames in Devon.[60] In 1279, Robert le Deveneys was a party to a final concord relating to 12 acres in 'Overtoneacr'' in Wiltshire. Another Robert le Devenisse was received into the manor of Highworth, a small borough in Wiltshire, in 1282. [61] The byname Deueshyre and variants appeared also in the west Midlands during the early fourteenth century. Two taxpayers called John de Deuesschyre *alias* Deuesshire were assessed at Wolricheston and Bretford in Warwickshire in 1332. Richard Devnych' was assessed at Dailsford in Worcestershire in 1327 and William Devening at Sodinton in the same county *c.*1280.[62]

Perhaps the most important linkages were those along the south coast, to other trading communities. In the early fourteenth century (1312-13), the burgesses of Bristol included four with locative bynames from Devon, from Pinhoe, Barnstaple, Great Torrington and Plymouth. Bristol had assumed the status of a regional capital, with a concentrated influence within a 'primary radius' of 20-25 miles.[63] These locative bynames from Devon had migrated from 56 to 100 miles. By 1332, three locative bynames from Devon occurred amongst the taxpayers of Sussex, that is, Devenyssh, Exccetr' and Mogridge.[64] In a contemporary lay subsidy for London, three burgesses bore locative bynames from Devon, from Combe Martin, Exeter and Woodbear. Other locative bynames from Devon are also known to have been in the capital, however. In 1275, the will of Richard de Exemue was proved in the Hustings court, in which his principal real estate was a capital messuage. More affluent was William Bukerell, whose will, proved in 1278, mentioned a drapery in West Cheap and houses in Aldermanbury, Grub Street and many rents. This byname seems to have become hereditary in London, for other, later wills of Bokerels were also proved in the Hustings court. Isabella, wife of Stephen (father of William above), died in 1280. Her will, presumably relating to her holdings in dower, enumerated many houses and rents. The will of Denis Bokerel in 1295, however, gave his father's name as Peter Gysors.[65] As early as 1244, Richard de Totenesse had a house in the capital, to which he added a solar, causing a nuisance, and, in the same year, the sheriff broke into this house, committing an assault, on the suspicion that Richard's wife, Beatrice, was harbouring thieves.[66] Walter de Deuenschire attested a charter in Canterbury *c.*1177. By 1524-5, the taxpayers in Sussex

included Antony Deuenyssh at Hailsham, Richard Deuenyss, one of
the commissioners, and John Exetter (but described as an alien) in
the borough of Lewes. By 1551, Ralph Devonisshe had been elected
to the Common Council of Romney.[67]

During the middle ages, bynames from Devon had thus migrated
as far as the south eastern coast of England, but the most important
connection may have been that in Winchester. By 1148, Richard de
Exon' and William Exon' had become established there. Robert,
William and another William de Excestre all inhabited that City in
the high middle ages (fl 1222–48, 1319–33, and 1340–43 respectively). Henry Barstaple was a merchant-brewer there c.1377–1415,
having entered the guild merchant in 1377–8, and become a citizen
by 1407. Hugh Hemyock inhabited the city in 1414–17, Richard
Hemyock, a clerk, c.1396. Simon de Membury, another clerk in holy
orders, who was instituted to many livings in the south west, arrived
in Winchester c.1396, and became Treasurer of Wolvesey in 1410–
19, and was deceased by 1423. William Wydecombe lived in
Winchester c.1426–9, but his byname was possibly derived from a
Widecombe outside Devon.[68]

The most influential commercial connection in Winchester was
undoubtedly the generations of the Devenis(c)h merchant house.
Nicholas Devenish *alias* (de) Excestre (fl 1309–60) was an important
merchant in cloth, wool and wine in the city. John le Devenish
(fl 1303–66) was another wool merchant there, who held lands in
rural Hampshire, was a citizen by 1303, bailiff of the borough in
1309–10, mayor successively in 1317–18, 1326–7 and 1330–1, and
MP for the borough in 1326–7 and 1329–30. Nicholas Devenish II
(fl 1334–50) traded in wool and spices. Succeeding generations
continued the byname and surname in Winchester until at least
John Devenysshe (fl 1471–2), an urban innkeeper.[69]

In nearby Southampton, the byname de Toteneys appeared
amongst holders of burgage tenements by c.1200. Roger attested
several charters before 1217. Later, Bernard de Toteneys held
tenements there, was bailiff in c.1280–90, and attested charters
between 1270 and 1290. In the later middle ages John Devoniensis
(*alias* Devynnys *alias* Devonschyre) also held burgage property there.
In 1443–4, those importing and exporting by sea included John
Devenex and John Hewyshe.[70] The locative byname had thus
migrated along the south coast in connection with the commercial
linkages.

The special relationship between Oxford and Exeter may have
also induced migration of the bynames. By c.1228, Mr Richard
Deveneis witnessed charters in the borough relating to burgage
tenements. Stephen le Deveneys attested charters relating to

tenements in the parish of St Peter in the East and in 'Kibaldestrete' in *c.*1242-73, in which he was described as a mason. William le Deveneys was established as a tenant of burgage property in 1279-80, and attested a charter relating to property in the parish of St Thomas in 1296. William le Deveneys was involved in litigation in the portmoot in 1294-5, in a case of trespass. At the same time, William le Deveneys junior, a tailor, acted as a pledge for William de Horspath. A year or so earlier, Richard de Deuonschyr' had compromised his action against Thomas de Bristoll', and Philip le Deueneys was a pledge for John le Poleter. The byname had thus become established in Oxford during the thirteenth century, perhaps through chain migration.[71]

The pattern of outward migration of bynames from Devon during the later middle ages thus correlated closely with the pattern of actual migration, in particular through chain migration along the south coast in close correlation with commmercial linkages and through the specific relationship with Oxford. The sparsity of the incidence of these bynames outside Devon, except in adjacent counties such as Somerset, suggests, however, that the diffusion of bynames outwards was an extremely slow process.

References

1   P Clark & D Souden, 'Introduction' in Clark and Souden, eds., *Migration and Society in Early Modern England*, (1987), 11-48; L R Poos, 'Population turnover in medieval Essex: the evidence of some early fourteenth-century tithing lists', in L Bonfield, R Smith and K Wrightson, eds., *The World We Have Gained*, (1986), 3-5.

2   Clark and Souden, *op. cit.*, 16-17; A Kussmaul, *Servants in Husbandry in Early Modern England*, (1981).

3   Clark and Souden, *op. cit.*, 17.

4   *Ibid.*, 24-5 and 272.

5   A Guillemette and J Legaré, 'The influence of kinship in seventeenth century immigration to Canada', *Continuity and Change*, 4 (1989), 79-102.; Cressy, *Coming Over* (1987).

6   PRO C134/16, m 9.

7   H Fox, 'Peasant farmers, patterns of settlement and *pays*: transformations in the landscapes of Devon and Cornwall during the later middle ages', in R Higham, ed., *Landscape and Townscape in the South West*, (Exeter Studies in History, 22, 1989), 47, 68 (n 41); BL Add Ch 64453; PRO SC2/168/61; I owe these references to the kindness of Dr H S A Fox.

⁸ L R Poos, 'Population turnover in medieval Essex: the evidence of some fourteenth-century tithing lists', in L Bonfield, R Smith and K Wrightson, eds., *The World We Have Gained*, (1986), 3-5.

⁹ *Ibid*; for the movement of the peasantry in Cornwall, J Hatcher, *Rural Economy and Society in the Duchy of Cornwall 1300–1500*, (1970); *Register of Edward the Black Prince Part IV (1351–1365)*, 44 and 175 (bondmen withdrawing from manors in Cornwall to the Isles of Scilly in 1353; petitions by John Vorn and John Gyneis, tenants of villein lands, as to their free status, their having migrated to Cornwall from Middleton in Devon and Gascony, 1361).

¹⁰ DRO Bedford MSS Werrington court rolls.

¹¹ *Ibid.*

¹² Longleat MSS 11182, m 25d; DRO CR 1445.

¹³ J R Maddicott, 'The English peasantry and the demands of the Crown 1294–1341', in T H Aston, ed., *Landlords, Politics and Peasants in Medieval England*, (1987), 298-9, 336, 353.

¹⁴ P J P Goldberg, 'Marriage, migration, servanthood and life-cycle in Yorkshire towns in the late middle ages: some York cause paper evidence', *Continuity and Change*, 1 (1986), 141-69.

¹⁵ Longleat MSS 10771, m 52d, 11252, m 1d.

¹⁶ H S A Fox, 'Peasant farmers, patterns of settlement and pays: transformations in the landscapes of Devon and Cornwall during the later middle ages', in R Higham, ed., *Landscape and Townscape in the South West*, (Exeter Studies in History, 22, 1989), 47 and 68 (n41).

¹⁷ BL Add MS 17450, fo 221r ('Notandum quod dominus potest habere precariam vij carucarum bis per annum de hominibus extraneis . . . Et ad precariam messionis sue v homines extraneos . . .').

¹⁸ *Feet of Fines Devon*, I, 313 (no 615).

¹⁹ H S A Fox, 'Peasant farmers, patterns of settlement and *pays*', 61.

²⁰ H Summerson, 'Crime and society in thirteenth century Devon', *TDA*, 119 (1987), 80-1.

²¹ *Crown Pleas Devon 1238*, *passim*; compare B Hanawalt, *Crime and Conflict in English Communities 1300–1348*, (1979), 168-71.

²² PRO Chancery Miscellanea Bundle 55, file 5, nos 139, 169, file 6, nos 197, 223, 224, file 8, no 288, file 9, no 320.

²³ See below.

²⁴ Rev C W Boase, *Registrum Collegii Exoniensis*, (Oxford Historical Society, 27, 1894),3.

²⁵ I owe this information to the kindness of Dr John Blair.

²⁶ Longleat MSS Uplyme court rolls computer database; Longleat MSS 10655 mm 68-70, 10656 mm 85-88, 11215 mm 74-75,

11216 mm 66-68, 11271 mm 47-48, 11272 mm 84-85 (account rolls in which the entries mainly occur in the *Exitus manerii*).

[27] 'Somerset lay subsidy 1327', 204-6, 231, 266.

[28] Longleat MSS 10656, 10766, 10785, 11185.

[29] Miss L Marston confirmed that the Schirewolds were officials of the Abbey. It is possible that they were related to Reginald de Schyr, Edmund de Schyr and John de Schyr, resident on another manor of the Abbey, Longbridge Deverill in 1307: Longleat MS 10725, m2.

[30] See p.73.

[31] K Edwards, *The English Secular Cathedrals in the Middle Ages*, (1949), 189-90.

[32] A B Emden, *A Biographical Register of the University of Oxford*, (3 vols, 1957-9), I, 279, 575, 659-61, II, 757.

[33] Boase, *Registrum Collegii Exoniensis*, 1-59; J R L Highfield, 'The early Colleges', in J I Catto, ed., *The History of the University of Oxford, I, The Early Oxford Schools*, (1984), 228.

[34] *Ibid*, 68, 81, 93, 103. In the early sixteenth century, the diocese of London depended on attracting ordinands from other dioceses; thus between 1490 and 1529 some 1522 priests were derived from outside London, but only 45 (less than 3%) originated from the diocese of Exeter: R L Storey, 'Ordinations of secular priests in early Tudor London', *Nottingham Medieval Studies*, 33 (1989), 122-33, esp. the Table at 132-3.

[35] I again owe this information to the kindness of Dr John Blair.

[36] *Exeter Freemen, passim*; *Tudor Exeter*, 7-33.

[37] A Yarborough, 'Geographical and social origins of Bristol apprentices, 1542-1565', *Transactions of the Bristol and Gloucestershire Archaeological Society*, 98 (1980), 113-29.

[38] *Ex inf* Dr M Kowaleski.

[39] H S Cobb, ed., *The Local Port Book of Southampton 1439-40*, (Southampton Record Society, 5, 1961), 11, 14, 35, 39, 46, 51; O Coleman, ed., *Southampton Brokage Book 1443-44*, (2 vols, SRS, 4 and 6, 1960-1), 31, 37, 90, 181, 250. See also, M Kowaleski, 'Port towns and their hinterlands in fourteenth century Devon', in B Greenhill, S Fisher and J Youings, eds., *The New Maritime History of Devon* (forthcoming).

[40] D Foster, ed., *Local Port Book of Southampton 1435-36*, (SRS, 7, 1963), 10, 40, 42, 48, 76.

[41] PRO E179/95/100 (18 Henry VI). For trading by the Irish in Plymouth, *Register of Edward the Black Prince Part IV*, 115, 131 (1357).

[41] *Chancery Proceedings: Supplement Elizabeth I* (List and Index Society, 202, 1983), 1, 28, 105, 114, 119, 126.

[43] *Ibid*, 105, 131, 162; *Chancery Decree Rolls: Elizabeth I*, (List and Index Society, 198, 1983), 6. These cases related to embezzlement of kerseys in 1579–87, involving a London draper; kerseys sent for finishing from Uffculme to Minehead in 1578–9; cloth sent to Portugal in 1558; a case of debt between a dyer of Ottery St Mary and a fuller of Exeter in 1591.

[44] *Chancery Proceedings: Supplement Elizabeth I*, 126, 131; *Chancery Decree Rolls: Elizabeth I*, 6.

[45] For example, lands in Devon as collateral for a statute staple in 1574, *ibid*, 28.

[46] *Ibid*, 99, 119, 126, 177.

[47] *Ibid*, 2.

[48] *Ibid*, 94.

[49] For migration to late medieval Winchester, see below, p.74.

[50] A J Willis and A L Merson, eds., *A Calendar of Southampton Apprenticeship Registers 1609–1740*, (SRS, 12, 1968), *passim*, but esp xxix (Table D), 17, 25, 31, 38.

[51] *Lay Subsidy 1524–5, passim.*

[52] W Phillimore, ed., *Devonshire Parish Registers. Marriages I*, (1909), Ipplepen, *passim.*

[53] P Slack, 'Vagrants and vagrancy in England, 1598–1664', in Clark and Souden, eds., *Migration and Society in Early Modern England*, 63, 70.

[54] Slack, 'Vagrants and vagrancy', 55-6, 59, 61-2; A L Beier, *Masterless Men*, (1985), 34 and 72.

[55] D Souden, ' "Rogues, whores and vagåbonds?" Indentured servant emigrants to North America and the case of mid seventeenth century Bristol', in Clark and Souden, eds., *op. cit.*, 158-9; D H Fischer, *Albion's Seed. Four British Folkways in America*, (1989), 34-5.

[56] *Dorset Lay Subsidy 1327*, 11, 24, 44, 56, 132, 137; *Dorset Lay Subsidy 1332*, 7-8, 13, 25, 81.

[57] O Padel, 'Cornish surnames in 1327', *Nomina*, 9 (1985), 82.

[58] 'Somerset lay subsidy 1327', 86, 95, 99, 105, 119, 131, 141, 168, 208, 215, 251, 272, 274, 275, 277, 278.

[59] Longleat MS 11252; Hants RO Eccles 2/159321 (I owe the latter reference to the kindness of Dr C Thornton).

[60] Longleat MS 9593.

[61] R B Pugh, ed., *Abstracts of Feet of Fines relating to Wiltshire Edward I and Edward II*, (Wiltshire Archaeological Society, Record Series, I, 1939), 11 (no 46); *idem*, ed., *Court Rolls of the Wiltshire Manors of Adam de Stratton*, (Wiltshire Record Society, 24, 1970 for 1968), 139 (no 147).

[62] W F Carter, ed., *Warwickshire Lay Subsidy 1332*, (Dugdale Society, 6, 1926), 38, 43; *Lay Subsidy Rolls 1280–1603*, (Worcs Historical Society, 8-13, 1893–1901), vol 8, 60.

[63] S A Penn, 'The origins of Bristol migrants in the early fourteenth century: the surname evidence', *Transactions of the Bristol and Gloucestershire Archaeological Society*, 101 (1983), 128, 130.

[64] McKinley, *Sussex*, 103, 118.

[65] Reaney, *Origins*, 347; the will of William de Combemartyn, a very affluent burgess, was proved in the court of Hustings in 1318, that of Michael le Deueneys, tailor, in 1308, adding to Reaney's description: R R Sharpe, ed., *Calendar of Wills Proved and Enrolled in the Court of Hustings, London, AD1258–AD1688*, (2 vols, 1889), I, 199, 276. For the wills of Exemue and Bokerell, *ibid*, 26, 36, 49, 122.

[66] H M Chew and M Weinbaum, *The London Eyre of 1244* (London Record Society, 6, 1970), 75, 98, 144 (nos 186, 239, 410).

[67] J Cornwall, ed., *Lay Subsidy Rolls 1524-5*, (Sussex Record Society, 56, 1956), 97, 108, 112-13; F Hull, ed., *White and Black Books of the Cinque Ports*, (Kent Records, 19, 1966), 243; W Urry, *Canterbury under the Angevins Kings*, (1967), I, 405.

[68] M Biddle, ed., *Winchester in the Early Middle Ages*, (Winchester Studies, I, 1976), 194; D Keene, ed., *Survey of Medieval Winchester* ii (Winchester Studies, 2, 1985), 1155, 1202, 1259, 1296, 1392.

[69] D Keene, *op. cit.*, 1214–15.

[70] H S Cobb, ed., *The Local Port Book of Southampton 1443-4*, 90, 181; J M Kaye, ed., *A God's House Miscellany*, (SRS, 27, 1984), 8; *idem*, ed., *The Cartulary of God's House, Southampton*, I (SRS, 19, 1976), 13, 19, 21, 30-1, 47, 53-4, 66-7, 127, 171, 230, 254, 256, 264, 363, 405.

[71] H E Salter, ed., *The Cartulary of Oseney Abbey*, 2 (Oxford Historical Society, 90, 1929), 386; *idem*, ed., *A Cartulary of the Hospital of St John the Baptist*, (2 vols, OHS, 66 and 68, 1914–15), I, 212-15, and II, 122; Oxford City Archives D17/1(b); W Illingworth, ed., *Rotuli Hundredorum tempore Hen II & Edw I*, II (Record Commission, 1818).

Chapter 4

THE EVOLUTION OF
HEREDITARY SURNAMES IN DEVON

R. A. McKinley

Beginnings of hereditary surnames

Bynames were in use in Devon before the Conquest. In Domesday some of those listed as holding land under Edward the Confessor have bynames, and some pre-Conquest landholders not given bynames in the Exchequer Domesday are recorded with bynames in the Exon Domesday. For instance, Undercleave was held under King Edward by Edric *mancus* (possibly 'the maimed'); in 1086 the same holding was in the hands of Edward son of Edric, so that Edric's byname was evidently not hereditary.[1] Under the Confessor, Ermington was held by Asgar *contractus* ('the cramped'?),[2] and Iddesleigh by Alware *tet,*[3] according to the Exon Domesday. Several other pre-Conquest landholders were recorded in the Exon Domesday with bynames.[4] So far as can be seen, these bynames were not hereditary. Most of those mentioned in pre-Conquest sources were people of some standing, and it is impossible to say how widespread the use of bynames may have been at that period among the population of the county as a whole. The great number of personal names in use may have made the widespread employment of bynames unnecessary.

Domesday provides much more information about the names of landholders than is available for earlier periods. One of the difficulties of using Domesday for the purpose of investigating hereditary surnames, however, is that many landholders listed there, especially subtenants, were not given surnames or bynames even where it could be seen from other sources that surnames or bynames existed. It seems probable that the surnames or bynames of many subtenants were eliminated from the record in the process of the completion of the Exchequer Domesday. In the case of Devon and some other south-western counties, the Exon Domesday listed surnames or bynames for some tenants which were not given in the Exchequer Domesday, so that rather more evidence is available about the names of subtenants in Devon than for some other counties.

81

Out of the tenants in chief in 1086, several had names which subsequently survived as the hereditary surnames of landowning families in the county. The names of Walter de Claville, Robert Bastard, Ralph Paganel, Ralph de Pomerai, Robert de Albemarle, and Osbern de Salceid all became hereditary surnames in Devon. It is difficult to be certain how far these were hereditary surnames in 1086, in the sense that the Domesday tenants had inherited them from previous generations of their respective families. Ralph Paganel was the son of William Paganel, who had held land in Devon before 1086, and Ralph in turn had a son, Fulk Paganel.[4] Ralph de Pomerai had a brother, William *capra*. (*Capra* is probably a Latin translation of the Old French *chevre*).[6] Ralph de Pomerai transmitted his name to his descendants, who were for long an important landed family in Devon, but it does not appear that his name was already hereditary in 1086. One of the more important of the Devon tenants in chief, Judhael of Totnes, had a byname from the town which was the principal place in his English possessions; obviously he had acquired a byname after the Conquest from his lands in England, like a number of other French landholders. Judhael was succeeded by a son, known as Alfred son of Johel or Alfred of Totnes, so that the name may have been tending to become hereditary, despite the fact that Judhael had lost possession of Totnes.[7] Judhael was also referred to as Judhael of Barnstaple, or as Judhael *de Meduana*, from Mayenne (Dept. Mayenne), in France, so that like some other landholders at the time he had no stable byname.[8]

Some Devon tenants in chief in 1086 thus had names which were at least in the process of becoming hereditary, but this was not true of all. A number of tenants in chief were given no bynames of any kind in Domesday, and although this negative evidence is not conclusive proof that they were without bynames, it is probable that they had no settled bynames of any sort. Several others were referred to in 1086 merely as the son of some other person; Latin phrases such as *Tetbaldus filius Bernerii, Odo filius Gamelin'*, and so forth were used. It is unsafe to assume that such Latin phrases were always, or even usually, translations of vernacular bynames beginning in 'Fitz', such as FitzBerners, FitzGamelin, etc., unless there is contemporary evidence for such forms being in use. Apart from these instances, there were cases in 1086 of tenants in chief with bynames which did not become hereditary. One of the largest Devon landholders at that time was Baldwin *vicecomes* ('the sheriff'). As he was the sheriff of the county this was probably rather a description of his rank than a byname. He was also known as Baldwin de Brionis (he was a son of the Count of Brionne), and as de Moles (from Meulles, dept. Calvados), and as de Clare.[9] Another Domesday tenant in chief,

Walter de Douai, who held Bampton in 1086, was succeeded by a son, Robert of Bampton, one of the many examples of a Norman obtaining a byname from English estates.[10] Robert's heir was a daughter, and neither his byname, nor his father's, became hereditary. Walter was also mentioned as Walter Flandrensis, so his byname was evidently not fixed. Ruald Adobed ('the dubbed') another tenant in chief in 1086, had a byname which does not recur in Devon.[11]

The descendants of Domesday subtenants were in general more difficult to trace than those of tenants in chief, but several subtenants in 1086 had bynames which became hereditary in the county. Robert de Pont Cardon was the ancestor of the Punchardon family, landowners in Devon over a long period, and Rainald de Vautortes (so named in the Exon Domesday, though not in the Exchequer Domesday), was the ancestor of the Vautort, or Valtort, family, landowners in Devon and Cornwall during the twelfth and thirteenth centuries.[12] Ralph *de Brueria*, another Domesday subtenant, was succeeded by Anthony *de Brueria*, and was the ancestor of the de la Bruere family who were still tenants by knight service in Devon during the thirteenth century.[13] Another subtenant, William *Pictaviensis* ('the Poitevin'), appears also to have transmitted his name to his descendants, for the lands which he held in 1086 were later in the hands of tenants with the same surname.[14] The William listed in the Exchequer Domesday as the tenant of Talliscombe, under the Count of Mortain, is identified in the Exon Domesday as William de Lestre.[15] He was the ancestor of a family which held land in Devon and Somerset, with a surname variously given as Del Estre, de Lestre, et al., and frequently translated into Latin as *de Atrio*, a translation probably based on a mistaken etymology of the vernacular name.[16] Robert de Beaumont, another subtenant in 1086, was succeeded by Thomas de Beaumont, so that his name became hereditary.[17]

Many other subtenants of 1086, on the other hand, had no traceable descendants, and their bynames do not seem to have survived in Devon. In one or two cases, hereditary surnames evolved in the course of time from the names of those subtenants of 1086. The Rogo who was a tenant of Baldwin the sheriff in 1086 was the ancestor of a Devon landholding family known during the twelfth and thirteenth centuries by a surname rendered in Latin as *filius Rogonis* or *filius Roges*.[18] The Latin phrase was used for several generations of the family, and was evidently a translation of a surname which had become hereditary.[19] It is clear that the expressions *filius Rogonis* or *filius Roges* were used over a long period for men who were not in fact the sons of someone named Rogo, even

though the Christian name did recur in the family.[20] It is difficult to
be sure what was the vernacular form; a form such as FitzRogo may
possibly have been used in speech at times. Holcombe, one of the
estates held by Rogo in 1086, became known as Holcombe Rogus.[21]
The form Holecombe Roges occurred in 1281,[22] so that Roges is
likely to have been established as a surname for the family before
that date. The form Roges is found as a surname during the
thirteenth century, and was evidently then hereditary, but it
continued at that period to be used alongside *filius Rogonis*[23]. It is
clear that in this instance a surname evolved from the personal name
of a Domesday subtenant, even though the use of Latinized versions
obscures the precise course of development.

The surname FitzPaine, that of another landholding family in
Devon, can be traced back to Domesday subtenants. Roger *filius
Pagani* and Ralph *filius Pagani* were listed, so named, in the Exon
Domesday as subtenants in Devon; the Exchequer Domesday
omitted their bynames.[24] In all probability they were in fact the sons
of someone named Pain, a fairly common personal name in
Normandy then and later, and their bynames were not hereditary.
There is no clear evidence of any relationship between the two,
though one seems likely, and it must be uncertain just what vernacular name is translated by the Latin phrase used in 1086. It may
well have been FitzPaine, but some caution is required when dealing
with Latin translations of Old French or Old English names. Roger's
descendants appear over a long period in the twelfth and thirteenth
centuries, with the Latin *filius Pagani* as a surname.[25] The surname
occurred in the form FitzPaine at a later period, and in this case
there is little doubt that the vernacular form FitzPaine is concealed
behind the Latin phrases used, probably from at any rate the twelfth
century, if not earlier.[26] The village of Cheriton FitzPaine derived its
manorial modifier from having been held by the family over a
long period.[27]

In contrast to such cases, some Domesday subtenants had no
bynames which can be discovered. It may be rash to conclude that
all of them were without bynames at all, since the Exchequer
Domesday frequently omitted subtenants' bynames, and there can
be no certainty that the Exon Domesday gave all the bynames which
were in use. It is evident, however, that by 1086, Devon had a group
of landholders who included many families with names which were
hereditary in the sense that the bynames of the tenants of 1086 were
transmitted to their descendants as hereditary surnames. There does
not seem to have been any significant difference in this respect
between tenants in chief and subtenants, and there is nothing about
the situation in Devon to differentiate it from the position in other
counties at the same period.

Between 1086 and *c.*1200 a number of new landholding families with hereditary surnames appeared in the county. One of these was a family named de Tracy, from one of the places in France called Tracy. Henry de Tracy acquired, under circumstances which are not entirely clear, lands in Devon which had been held by Judhael of Totnes. Henry had probably inherited his name de Tracy from his father.[28] Henry was succeeded by his son, Oliver de Tracy or de Trazi, and Oliver in turn was followed by his son, another Oliver de Tracy.[29] It is not necessary to trace the descent of the family further, but it is clear that it had an hereditary surname during the twelfth century. The case of another, distinct, landholding family, also called de Tracy, illustrates the general lack of uniformity which existed during the twelfth century in the descent of surnames. The lands in Devon which had been held in 1086 by William *capra* were granted by Henry I to one of his many illegitimate children, William de Tracy. The name of William's mother is not known, and it is impossible to say why he acquired his byname. Possibly he may have been born at one of the places called Tracy. William died without male heirs, leaving a daughter who inherited his lands. She married a Gloucestershire landholder, John de Sudeley. The elder son of this marriage, Ralph de Sudeley, inherited his father's name, and lands in Gloucestershire; the second son, another William, assumed his grandfather's name of de Tracy, and succeeded to lands at Bradninch and elsewhere in Devon, and to some lands in Gloucestershire. The younger William de Tracy was one of the murderers of Thomas Becket. William's descendants continued to bear the name de Tracy.[30] A good many other cases are known from other parts of England where surnames have descended through females in this fashion during the twelfth and thirteenth centuries.[31]

Two other natural sons of Henry I acquired lands in Devon. One of these was Robert, mentioned in a variety of sources as Robert *filius Regis*, who obtained through marriage the lands once held by Baldwin the Sheriff.[32] The Latin *filius Regis* may be a translation of some vernacular byname such as Fitzroy or Fil de Rey, but that is uncertain. Robert left no male heirs, so any byname which he may have had did not become hereditary. In this instance a man who was one of the principal landholders in Devon for much of the twelfth century was without a hereditary surname. Another illegitimate son of Henry I who held land in Devon appeared as William *de marisco*.[33] It is not known how William's byname originated, and no descendants have been traced.

The Nonant family, who acquired large estates in Devon under William II, had a hereditary surname. Roger de Nonant was granted Totnes, and other lands in the county, by King William early in his reign.[34] The lands thus given to Roger had been held in 1086 by

Judhael of Totnes, who was still alive, and who was holding land in Devon at a later date. It is not known why Judhael was replaced by Roger de Nonant, and the episode illustrates the way in which the Norman kings were able to interfere with the possession, and descent, of fiefs. Roger was succeeded by Wido (or Guy) de Nonant, who was holding Totnes under Henry I.[35] Wido was in turn followed by a second Roger de Nonant.[36] It is clear, without pursuing the history of this important family further, that a hereditary surname was in use from the eleventh century onwards.

Two other families significant for the history of Devon were those of de Redvers, or de Reviers, and de Courtenay. Baldwin de Reviers, who was created the first Earl of Devon in or about 1141, was the son of Richard de Reviers. It is uncertain if the family's surname was hereditary before Richard, though it has been suggested that a Hugh de Redveris, living in the late eleventh century, may have been related to Richard.[37] Richard was granted large estates in Devon and elsewhere by Henry I.[38] He appeared with the name de Redvers in a considerable number of documents.[39] Baldwin the first earl, his son Richard, the second earl, the same Richard's son, Baldwin the third earl, and another Richard, brother of the third earl — eventually the fourth earl — all used the surname de Reviers (or de Redvers). It seems from this that the family had a well established hereditary surname during the twelfth century. How erratic the usage about surnames was at this early period can be seen, however, by the fact that the fifth earl, William, who was a younger son of the first earl, was generally known as William de Vernon. In one of the few instances where any explanation for a byname is given in medieval sources, the fifth earl's name is said to have been due to the fact that he had attended the schools at Vernon (probably Vernon, dept. Eure). It is doubtful if this is an accurate explanation, for William's grandfather, Richard (father of the first earl) was the lord of Vernon (Eure), and was possibly the son of an earlier William de Vernon.[40] The fifth earl was, however, also mentioned in contemporary sources as William de Redvers.[41] The surname is from a French place-name, Reviers (Calvados). William's descendants and successors, the sixth and seventh earls of Devon, used the surname de Reviers.[42] The seventh earl was also described as Baldwin *de Insula*, no doubt from his having been lord of the Isle of Wight.[43] The case of the de Reviers family shows how the surnames of major landholders could remain unsettled in the twelfth and thirteenth centuries, even where a family had used one surname peristently over a long period.

The Courtenay family have been great landholders in Devon since the twelfth century, and held the earldom of Devon since the fourteenth. Renaud (or Reginald) de Courtenay, at one time lord of Courtenay (Loiret) in France, was in England by 1161.[44] He acquired by marriage the honour of Okehampton, which had been held by Baldwin the sheriff, and subsequently by Robert *filius Regis*. His descendants regularly used the surname Courtenay.[45] Hugh de Courtenay, a descendant of Renaud just mentioned, and in the female line descended from the de Reviers family, was recognised as Earl of Devon in 1335,[46] and the family have retained the title to the present. It is not clear that the family had a hereditary surname before coming to England, since the designation of de Courtenay might be merely a description of their position as lords of one of the places so called, but Renaud de Courtenay lost his French fief, and from the late twelfth century onwards the family must be considered as having a hereditary surname.[47]

During the course of the twelfth century, a number of landholding families of knightly rank appeared in Devon with hereditary surnames, some of them families which were to be established in the county for centuries. Among the families listed in 1166 as holding by knight service in the county, in addition to those already mentioned, were those of de Boterell, Coffin, Cruwys, le Daneis (sometimes given in a Latinized form as *Dacus*), Hiddon, Pine, de Reigny, Tremenet (Latinized as *de Tribus Minetis*), and Vipond (Latinized as *de Veteri Ponte*),[48] all families with names which survived as hereditary ones. Among other knightly families with hereditary surnames, present in the county before about 1250, were those of Raleigh,[49] Clist,[50] Fortescue,[51] Monk (often occurring as le Moyne in medieval sources),[52] Kelly,[53] Boty (or Buty),[54] Calloway,[55] Chambernon (Latinized as *de Campo Arnulfi*),[56] Ferrers,[57] and Satchville (Latinized as *de Sicca Villa*).[58]

The circumstances under which some landed families acquired hereditary surnames were obscured by the use of Latin phrases in twelfth and thirteenth century sources. Reference has already been made to the family of FitzPaine in this connection. One such family appears over a long period with a surname represented by the Latin *filius Martini*.[59] The family, descended from a Martin living in the late eleventh century, obtained some lands in the twelfth.[60] It might be supposed that the Latin phrase just mentioned was translating the vernacular surname of FitzMartin, but although such a vernacular name has been attributed to the family in secondary works, no contemporary instance of it in use has been found, and during the late thirteenth and the fourteenth centuries the family's name occurred as Martin.[61] It seems likely that the Martin family had a hereditary surname (probably in the form Martin) from at least the mid twelfth century, but it is difficult to be sure about this. Other landed families can be found in Devon during the twelfth and thirteenth centuries with their names given in similar Latin forms, such as *filius Stephani*. During those periods a family with a name given in that form held by knight service from the honour of Totnes, though none of those so styled seems to have had a father named Stephen.[62] Early in the thirteenth century forms such as Fuiz Estephene and Fitzesteve appeared,[63] and a locality in Broadwoodwidger, where the family held land, was mentioned as More Estevene in 1303.[64] It is probable that the family had the hereditary surname of FitzStephen from the twelfth century, though this is concealed by the Latin forms generally used in the twelfth and thirteenth centuries.

Despite uncertainties about the nature of surnames in the case of some families, it seems probable that by the mid thirteenth century most landed families of any consequence in Devon already possessed hereditary surnames, many of them surnames which had arisen in the late eleventh century or the twelfth. Even among this relatively small section of the population, hereditary surnames were not universal. During the twelfth and thirteenth centuries, one family used at times the byname Wangeforde, at times that of Espus.[65] A family who held land at Blackawton and elsewhere in Devon during the thirteenth century was without a hereditary surname; some members of the family appeared with a name Latinized as *filius Mathei*, and this may have been a translation of FitzMatthew, but if so it was not a stable hereditary surname.[66] Or, to give another example, in 1241 Dodbrook was held by Ruald son of Alan, but in 1276 it was held by Alan son of Rowald, and in 1285 by Henry son of Alan.[67] Or, to cite another case, William Giffard, a tenant by knight service, had a son named Joel de Buketone, living *c.*1230 and later.[68] Very probably this was a case of a kind which can be paralleled in other counties, of a younger son from a landed family using a byname different from the family's hereditary surname. In another example, land at Rocombe was held in 1284–86, by knight service, by Ralph son of William, and in 1346 by Ralph's son, William son of Ralph. Ralph appears to have been a son of an earlier William son of Ralph, who was living in 1241.[69] In this case a minor landed family was still without a hereditary surname in the mid fourteenth century.

The more important landed families in Devon thus acquired surnames over a long period, and even as late as 1300 the process was not complete. Where families of such standing were concerned, the situation in Devon was not substantially different from that in other counties during the period between the Conquest and about 1300. This is not surprising, since the county's landholders were in no way isolated from their counterparts elsewhere. Many landed families in

Devon had holdings outside the county, and many families whose main estates were elsewhere had some lands in Devon. The hereditary surnames of some landed families have left a permanent mark on Devon place-names in manorial additions derived from surnames, such as Clyst Hydon, Lew Trenchard, Holcombe Rogus, Cheriton FitzPaine, Upton Pyne, Heanton Punchardon, Heanton Satchville, Berry Pomeroy, Ashreigny, or Cruwys Morchard, while Craze Loman preserves, in a much altered form, the surname of the de Claville family.

Surnames of smaller freeholders

Landed families are inevitably the best documented section of the medieval population, and although it is not always possible to get a complete view of how hereditary surnames evolved among that social group, the quantity of evidence in existence is considerable, and the difficulties of dealing with the names of any other part of the community are considerably greater; in particular, there is a shortage of information for the period before about 1200. Even during the thirteenth century, though there is more evidence, it is by no means easy to discover how widespread hereditary surnames were among the lesser freeholders. It is not too difficult to find instances, among that social group in Devon, where sons had the same surnames as their fathers, or to discover cases where particular individuals clearly did not have hereditary surnames. For instance, Roger Mirabel, a tenant by sergeanty at Skerraton in 1228, was the son of David of Seyredon (that is, of Skerraton).[70] Mirabel is a byname from a feminine forename, and Roger may well have had a byname from his mother's first name. Henry the chaplain, an outlaw in Devon in 1238, was the brother of Richard Redeman.[71] Whether Henry's designation was a byname, or merely a description of his profession, is uncertain, but evidently the brothers did not share a hereditary surname. Roger de la Bere (1270) was the son of William de la Hole.[72] William le Geg, a derogatory nickname, was the son of Ailward Sampson.[73] Both lived in 1238.[74] William Dogefel, also living in 1238, was the son of Thomas de Uppecote.[75] Thomas le Bere, slain in or before 1238, was the brother of Walter de Farebi.[76]

Some of these instances come from the records of the Devon Eyre, held in 1238. Eyre records often deal with people of little wealth or standing, who may be poorly represented in medieval records generally, and provide some evidence about the names of the poorer sections of the community. It is noticeable in the Devon Eyre of 1238 that there were many persons mentioned who had occupational names derived from the trades or crafts which they were actually pursuing, and these names are unlikely to have been hereditary.

Similarly, examples can be cited for the thirteenth century where among the same social group surnames were hereditary, at least for a generation or two. A family called *de Marisco* (probably a translation for Marsh) at Godcott (probably in North Petherwin) had a hereditary surname for several generations in the mid and late thirteenth century. The family's possessions included a house and a carucate of land, so that they were substantial free tenants.[77] William le Arper, a freeholder *c.*1230–50, was the son of Peter le Harper, and William Parl, also a local freeholder, was a son of William Parl the elder.[78] The court rolls of Modbury show the existence on that manor during the thirteenth century of a family with the surname atte Trawen (sometimes Latinized as *de Arboribus*), evidently a hereditary one, and derived from a local place-name, Traine in Modbury.[79]

Besides instances like these, of which more could be cited, there were cases in the thirteenth century where new surnames seem to have been developing, often from personal names. For example, Reginald Martin de la Heie, of Lamerton, mentioned in 1238, was the son of a man named Martin, as a first name, while Ivo Angot and William Angot, of Ermington Hundred, also in 1238, were the sons of a man with the first name of Angot.[80] Angot was then rare as a personal name in Devon, which leaves little doubt that Ivo and William had bynames from their father's first name. Ralph Humphrey, a tenant at Netherton early in the thirteenth century, had a father with the first name of Humphrey. Ralph Humphrey was probably the same person as a Ralph Pynnok, also mentioned at Netherton about the same time.[81] Pynnok is a byname of the nick-name type, from a word for the hedge sparrow, and very probably Ralph's name was still unsettled. William Sanguin, a free tenant at Whimple *c.*1250–80, seems to have been a son of an earlier tenant there, Sanguinus de Whimple, or Sanguinus son of Robert.[82] Similarly, a family named Walrand or Walerond, who held land at Uffculme and also at Exeter, during the thirteenth and fourteenth centuries, were descended from a man with the personal name of Walrand, living apparently early in the thirteenth century, whose first name had thus given rise to a hereditary surname.[83]

This evidence indicates that hereditary surnames were developing quite frequently among families in this social group during the thir-teenth century, and it seems likely that many families acquired hereditary names during the period. It was, however, still quite common in the thirteenth century for families of free tenants to be without hereditary names, and it is difficult to make any realistic estimate of what proportion of the small freeholders of the county had hereditary surnames by, say, about 1300. The evidence is also not sufficiently comprehensive to enable accurate comparisons to be drawn between different parts of Devon. In such a large and diverse county it might be expected that there would be significant differences between one part and another where the evolution of surnames was concerned, but the evidence for the thirteenth century is too incomplete to allow such divergencies to be properly assessed.

During the first half of the fourteenth century instances can still be found in Devon of free tenants without hereditary surnames. In 1328, for instance, Thomas Twynne was listed as the son of Henry Pynde.[84] In the subsidy roll of 1332 for Devon, there were a relatively small number of taxpayers, who must at least have been people of sufficient means to contribute to the subsidy, who were described merely as the son of some other person, without any surname or other byname.[85] There were also in the same record instances of men being described merely as the servant of another, such as Richard servant of Reginald le Baker,[86] or William servant of Walter Benet.[87] Similar descriptions of taxpayers as servants can be found in the contemporaneous subsidy rolls for other counties, and it is generally not clear whether these were really cases of men without bynames at all, or whether some people were described in such a way in the rolls merely because it was a convenient way of identifying them.

Such evidence shows that there were still Devon families in the fourteenth century without hereditary surnames, but it does not show what proportion of the free population in the countryside was still in that position, and generally the evidence suggests that by about 1330 a considerable proportion of the free tenants in the county had hereditary surnames. In the lay subsidy of 1332, only a small proportion of the taxpayers listed were without surnames or bynames at all. The taxpayers were likely to have included all but the poorest free tenants, though the status of those listed was not normally given, and some of those listed were probably villeins. There were also instances in the same subsidy roll which suggest that surnames were beginning to ramify locally. There were, for instance, six taxpayers named Haukerigge at Clannaborough, three named atte Hangre at Fardell, four named de Trendelbear and four de Sercheslond at South Tawton, and four named de Kenewode at Kenton.[88] Subsidy rolls do not of course list the whole population, but only taxpayers, most of them adult males, so that it is unlikely that all those with any one surname would be recorded. None of the surnames mentioned were at all common, and these examples look very like cases where surnames had already been hereditary for a generation or two before 1332, and had begun to ramify to a modest extent.

This evidence indicates that a considerable section of the rural population of the county were likely to have had hereditary surnames by 1332. It is not possible to estimate accurately what proportion had surnames, but in general terms it seems likely that by the middle of the fourteenth century at least half of the rural free population had hereditary names. Many surnames or bynames to be found in Devon during the first half of the fourteenth century, in sources such as subsidy rolls or manorial records, disappeared, and are not to be found in the county at later periods. This is no doubt due to some extent to families dying out in the male line, and to a certain amount of migration out of the county, while the heavy mortality from the pestilences of the mid and late fourteenth century must have led to the extinction of some established hereditary surnames. On the other hand, some manorial records, such as the court rolls of Uplyme, show that some surnames survived among the tenantry for much of the century.

It is probable that by about 1400 it was unusual for families in the class of small free tenants not to have hereditary surnames. Clear examples of families with names that were not hereditary are not generally found in Devon during the fifteenth century and later, and it is likely that the evolution of hereditary names was largely complete among that section of the population by the end of the fourteenth century.

Hereditary surnames of serfs

Evidence about the names of the unfree part of the population is scantier than that for the names of small free tenants. In particular, there is very little evidence about bondmen's names until manorial records start to become available after the middle of the thirteenth century. Evidence from some other counties shows that serfs there began to acquire hereditary names at much the same period as small free tenants, or slightly later, but it cannot safely be assumed that in Devon the position was the same as elsewhere.

Such evidence as there is indicates that families of unfree tenants were coming to possess hereditary surnames during the late thirteenth century and the first half of the fourteenth, but probably not earlier. The evidence of some pedigrees from the assize roll of Devon in 1239 detailed serfs at Buckland Brewer, apparently living in the early thirteenth century, none of whom were given surnames or bynames at all.[89] Villeins named at Berry Pomeroy under Edward

I included Roger, Richard, and William Garland, and this looks very much like an instance of a family with a hereditary surname. The bond tenants also included William Dulle Sparke (evidently a nickname), and William Dulle Sparkson, obviously a case where a son had a byname from his father's nickname.[90] At Uplyme, the manor court rolls show that pledges often had the same surnames as those for whom they gave surety during the first half of the fourteenth century; in view of what is known about pledging procedures in manorial courts generally, this has very much the appearance of persons summoned before the manor court being supported by their kin, with all members having the same, probably hereditary, surname.[91] At Stoke Canon, an unfree tenant, Joel Bysouthecolm, died in 1307, and his daughter, Joan by southecolm, claimed, though unsuccessfully, the right to succeed him in his holdings.[92] In this case a hereditary surname existed, or perhaps was at the point of emerging.

This somewhat fragmentary evidence would suggest that during *c.*1300–1350 many of the unfree peasantry were acquiring hereditary surnames. It is difficult to be sure just how far this process had gone by the mid fourteenth century. There may well have been significant differences between one manor and another where serfs' names were concerned. It seems likely, however, that by about 1350 a majority of unfree tenants had hereditary surnames.

Hereditary surnames of townspeople

Much of the evidence about the names of the urban population in Devon relates to the City of Exeter, much the largest place in the county during the Middle Ages. There is only fragmentary evidence about the names of the citizens before the admissions of men to the freedom of the city started to be recorded in the late thirteenth century. A few instances show that hereditary surnames were arising in the City from at least the early thirteenth century. William Sukespic, who occurred in Exeter documents in the late twelfth century, and who acquired land at Clyst St. George outside the city, had a son and heir, Robert Sukespic, who inherited land at Exeter and at Clyst, and who was living in 1221. Robert was in turn followed by his son and heir, Jordan Sukespich, living *c.*1240. The name Sokespitch continued to appear at Clyst later, probably as the name of Jordan's descendants. The origin of the name is not clear; it has been suggested that it meant 'suck spice', and that the family were originally spicers, but this seems conjectural.[93] To give another example, Maurice Coleprest, or Coleprust, and William Coleprust, property owners at Exeter about 1230 and later, were the sons of an earlier William Coleprust.[94] (The name is one of a number formed from compounds of 'priest', probably nicknames in origin). Another family, called de Okeston, one of whom was a mayor of Exeter, had a hereditary surname from at least about 1250 onwards.[95] Cases like this show that hereditary surnames were already coming into existence at Exeter by about 1250, but give little indication of how common such names may have been there.

Instances can also be found at Exeter of people during the thirteenth century with names which were clearly not hereditary. For instance, William Goding, Richard Kene, Matilda and Alice (apparently both without bynames), owning land at Exeter in 1263, were all the children of Juliana de la Lane.[96] It is, however, not until more systematic information about freemen's names becomes available that it is possible to form a more general view of the position. The names of men admitted to the freedom of the city have been preserved from the late thirteenth century onwards. The records of admissions to the freedom are incomplete, but it is unlikely that there was any significant difference between those whose admissions were noted on the city records, and those whose admissions were left out, where the heritability of surnames was concerned. In many cases where the names of freemen were recorded, there is no evidence whether the surnames were hereditary or not. Sometimes, however, men were admitted in succession to a male relative, often a father, less frequently an elder brother or uncle, and it is then usually possible to tell if a surname has descended from one generation to another, or if there was plainly not a hereditary surname. Freemen were also admitted otherwise than by succession to a relative, generally by paying a fine, and in a minority of cases, when men were admitted by fine, the names of their fathers were recorded. People admitted in succession to a relative who had been a freeman earlier are obviously very likely to have been natives of Exeter. People admitted by fine must have included many who had migrated into the city from outside.

Between 1286 and 1299, inclusive, there are thirteen examples of men being admitted to the freedom who had the same surnames as those of their fathers or other male relatives, and eight cases where men had bynames different from those of the relatives they succeeded. There were also three cases where men newly admitted were described in terms which suggest that their bynames were not stable or hereditary, as, for instance, in the case of 'Adam called Duk, skinner', admitted in 1297, or 'Peter called le Lung of Cobbaton', admitted in 1286,[97] probably someone who had migrated into Exeter. This limited body of evidence suggests that in the late thirteenth century a good half of the City's freemen had hereditary names. Between 1300 and 1349 there were 53 instances where men admitted to the freedom by succession had surnames which were the same as those of their fathers or other male relatives, and there were a further 11 where men admitted otherwise than by succession were noted to have had the same surnames as their fathers. As against this, among the men admitted by succession there were only 13 with bynames different from those of their predecessors, and five cases of men admitted other than by succession who were noted to have had bynames different from those of their fathers. There were a further six instances of men, none admitted by succession, whose names were given in a way suggesting that they were not hereditary, as described above. This evidence indicates that by the first half of the fourteenth century a large majority of freemen had hereditary surnames. As many of those who acquired the freedom other than by succession are likely to have been immigrants to the city, often from other parts of Devon, it appears from this evidence that hereditary surnames were becoming common in the county among the sections of the population who were likely to become traders or artisans.

Some examples show that new bynames were being formed from personal names at Exeter during 1300–1350. John Davy, for instance, became a freeman in succession to his father, David Gascoyng, in 1323, and John Roland succeeded his father, Roland FitzRauf, in 1349.[98] John Davy, son of John Davy, admitted freeman in 1341, may have been a son of the John Davy mentioned above, though as Davy is a fairly common name it is difficult to be sure.[99] From 1350 onwards there are very few cases where men admitted to the freedom at Exeter clearly did not have hereditary names. Ralph de Shyllyngford, for example, admitted in 1354, was the son and heir of Thomas FitzRauf.[100] Ralph's byname was probably from one of the places in Devon named Shillingford, and though the son of a freeman he may have lived outside the city for a time.[101] It seems likely from the evidence of freemen's names that by the late fourteenth century the great majority of Exeter freemen had hereditary surnames.

This evidence of course only concerns the City's freemen, who on the whole were the more prosperous part of Exeter's inhabitants. Other sources, such as title deeds, tend to refer mostly to much the same group. It is much more difficult, at Exeter, and in medieval towns generally, to discover very much about the names of unskilled labourers and other poor, property-less sections of the urban community. Occasional references suggest that the poorer part of the urban population adopted hereditary names later than freemen. For example, in 1332 John Pers and Nicholas (or Richard, for his first name is given differently at various points) Coch, both sons of Florence le Maughestere, were accused of breaking into a stall at Exeter.[102] Obviously neither had a hereditary surname. Isolated instances like this, however, do not provide any good general view of the position about the names of the poorer sections of the population.

References

1 A Farley, ed., *Domesday Dook, seu Liber Censualis* (1783), i, fo 100.
2 H Ellis, ed., *Libri censualis, vocati Domesday Book* (1816), iii, 78.
3 *Ibid*, 78, 101.
4 See, e.g., Aluuard *mertus* or *merta*, or Aelfric *piga*: *ibid*, 315, 362, 363, 447.
5 *VCH Devon*, i, 553.
6 *Ibid*, 560; H Ellis, *op. cit.*, iii, 65, 376.
7 C Johnson and H A Cronne, eds., *Regesta Regum Anglo-Normannorum*, ii (1956), 239, 291; J H Round, *Feudal England* (1909), 483; J Hunter, ed., *Magnum Rotulum Scaccarii, vel Magnum Rotuli Pipae, Anno Tricesimo-primo Regni Henrici Primi* (1833), 153; *TDA*, 12, 162; 29, 233.
8 Johnson and Cronne, *op. cit.*, 2, 185, 222.
9 J H Round, *Feudal England* (1909), 473.
10 *VCH Devon*, i, 563; W Illingworth, *Placitorum in Domo Capitulari Westmonasteriensi Asservatorum Abbrevatio* (1811), 92.
11 C and F Thorn, *Domesday Book: Devon* (1985), 2, section 23.
12 Farley, *op. cit.*, i, fos 100, 105; *VCH Devon*, i, 570; H Hall, *Red Book of the Exchequer* (1896), i, 261, 259; *Book of Fees*, 2, 1297-98; J H Round, *Calendar of Documents Preserved in France* (1899), i, 437; L C Loyd, *Origins of some Anglo-Norman Families* (Harleian Soc, 103, 1951), 83. The name de Pont Cardon, later Punchardon, is from Pont Chardon (dept. Orne); the name Vautort, or Valtort, is from Vautortes (dept. Mayenne); G Tengvik, *Old English Bynames* (1938), 108, 117.
13 *VCH Devon*, i, 555; H Hall, *op. cit.*, i, 252; *Book of Fees*, i, 399; ii, 756, 763; H Ellis, *op. cit.*, iii, 266, 271, 273, 290; *Feudal Aids*, i, 318.
14 H Hall, *op. cit.*, i, 260; *Book of Fees*, ii, 762, 791; C and F Thorn, *op. cit.*, ii, section 34.
15 Farley, *op. cit.*, i, fo 105.
16 H Ellis, *op. cit.*, iii, 74, 192, 250; H Hall, *op. cit.*, i, 231-32, 260; *Book of Fees*, ii, 769, 782; *Great Roll of the Pipe for the Thirtieth Year of Henry II* (Pipe Roll Soc, 33, 1912), 78; *Great Roll of the Pipe for the Fourth Year of King John* (Pipe Roll Soc, 53, 1937), 253.

[17] *VCH Devon,* ii, 556; Book of Fees, ii, 98; J Hunter, *op. cit.,* 155.

[18] Farley, *op. cit.,* i, fos 107, 108.

[19] See e.g., H Hall, *op. cit.,* i, 251; *Book of Fees,* ii, 784; *Feudal Aids,* i, 318, 363, 381; W Illingworth, ed., *Rotuli Hundredorum* (1812–18), i, 64; *Great Roll of the Pipe for the 34th Year of Henry II* (Pipe Roll Soc, 38, 1925), 166; *Great Roll of the Pipe for the 10th Year of Richard I* (Pipe Roll Soc, 47, 1932), 180; H C Maxwell-Lyte et al, *Two Cartularies of the Augustinian Priory of Bruton and the Cluniac Priory of Montacute* (Somerset Record Soc, 8, 1894), 126, 176-81.

[20] Maxwell-Lyte, *op. cit.,* 176-77, 179; *Canonsleigh Cartulary,* xxi.

[21] Farley, *op. cit.,* i, fo 107.

[22] *PND,* II, 535.

[23] *Canonsleigh Cartulary,* 5-7, 26, 49, 55-56, 65; *Book of Fees,* i, 98; ii, 759, 786; *Feudal Aids,* i, 369, 415, 432.

[24] H. Ellis, *op. cit.,* 3, 65, 290, 316.

[25] *Book of Fees,* ii, 758, 768, 775; *Feudal Aids,* i, 311, 313, 318; *Feet of Fines Devon,* i, 202-3, 287, 334; *Great Roll of the Pipe for the 9th Year of Richard I* (Pipe Roll Soc, 46, 1931), 6; *Great Roll of the Pipe for the 14th Year of Henry III* (Pipe Roll Soc, 42, 1927), 29; W Illingworth, ed., *Rotuli Hundredorum,* i, 90, 92; *Close Rolls of Henry III, 1234–37,* 504.

[26] *Feudal Aids,* i, 426; *Feet of Fines Devon,* ii, 105, 253.

[27] *PND,* II, 414. The form with the addition FitzPaine occurs in 1354.

[28] L C Loyd, *op. cit.,* 105.

[29] *VCH Devon,* i, 557; I J Sanders, *English Baronies* (1960), 104; H Hall, *op. cit.,* i, 255; *Great Roll of the Pipe for the 11th Year of Henry II* (Pipe Roll Soc, 8, 1887), 81; R Howlett, ed., *Chronicles of the Reign of Stephen, Henry II, and Richard I* (Rolls Series, 1884–9), 3, 52, 134.

[30] H Hall, *op. cit,* i, 254; W H Hart, ed., *Historia et Cartularium Monasterii Sancti Petri Gloucestriae* (Rolls Series, 1863–67), ii, 180; F Barlow, *Thomas Becket* (1986), 235-36.

[31] See, e.g., McKinley, *Oxfordshire,* 182-83, 185, 186.

[32] J Hunter, *op. cit.,* 152; H Hall, *op. cit.,* i, 251-54; J H Round, *Geoffrey de Mandeville* (1892), 124-25; J H Round, *Calendar of Documents Preserved in France* (1899), 219.

[33] H P R Finberg, 'Some early Tavistock charters', *English Historical Review,* 62 (1947), 365; *Great Roll of the Pipe for the 30th Year of Henry II* (Pipe Roll Soc, 33, 1912), 74; W Stubbs, ed., *Chronica Rogeri de Houedene* (Rolls Series, 1868–71), ii, 134-35.

[34] Johnson and Cronne, *op. cit.,* ii, 50, 400.

[35] J. Hunter, *op. cit.,* 154; Johnson and Cronne, *op. cit.,* ii, 785; H W C Davis, ed., *Regesta Regum Anglo-Normannorum* (1913), i, 299.

[36] I J Sanders, *op. cit.*, 89; H Hall, *op. cit.*, i, 31, 43; *Book of Fees*, i, 98.

[37] Johnson and Cronne, *op. cit.*, ii, 272; Vicary Gibbs et al, *Complete Peerage* (1916), iv, 309-311.

[38] *VCH Devon*, i, 551.

[39] See, e.g., Johnson and Cronne, *op. cit.*, ii, 13, 14, 23, 24.

[40] *Great Roll of the Pipe for the 6th Year of Richard I* (Pipe Roll Soc, 43, 1928), 166; *Great Roll of the Pipe for the 8th Year of King John* (Pipe Roll Soc, 58, 1942), 137; Vicary Gibbs et al, *op. cit*, iv, 309-10.

[41] *Great Roll of the Pipe for the 6th Year of Richard I* (Pipe Roll Soc, 43, 1928), 171; *Great Roll of the Pipe for the 1st Year of King John* (Pipe Roll Soc, 48, 1933), 199; *Great Roll of the Pipe for the 2nd Year of King John* (Pipe Roll Soc, 50, 1934), 232.

[42] H R Luard, ed., *Matthaei Parisiensis, Monachi Sancti Albani, Chronica Majora* (Rolls Series, 1872–83), v, 616; *Close Rolls of the Reign of Henry III, 1256–59*, 30, 33; Vicary Gibbs et al, *op. cit.*, iv, 318-20.

[43] *Close rolls of Henry III, 1256–59*, 30; *Calendar of Patent Rolls 1232–47*, 328, 338.

[44] H Hall, *op. cit.*, i, 36; *Great Roll of the Pipe for the 10th Year of Henry II* (Pipe Roll Soc, 7, 1886), 43.

[45] See sources cited in note 47 below.

[46] *Calendar of Patent Rolls, 1334–38*, 214.

[47] *Great Roll of the Pipe for the 23rd Year of Henry II* (Pipe Roll Soc, 26, 1905), 3; *Great Roll of the Pipe for the 5th Year of King John* (Pipe Roll Soc, 54, 1938), 79; *Great Roll of the Pipe for the 14th Year of Henry III* (Pipe Roll Soc, 42, 1927), 26, 28.

[48] H Hall, *op. cit.*, i, 248-61.

[49] *Great Roll of the Pipe for the 7th Year of Henry II* (Pipe Roll Soc, 4, 1884), 27; *Feet of Fines Devon*, ii, 65, 71, 236, 332-33.

[50] *Book of Fees*, i, 396; ii, 777; *Feet of Fines Devon*, i, 19-20; *Great Roll of the Pipe for the 14th Year of Henry III* (Pipe Roll Soc, 42, 1927), 19.

[51] *Book of Fees*, ii, 770; *Feet of Fines Devon*, i, 50, 245; ii, 443; *Great Roll of the Pipe for the 24th Year of Henry II* (Pipe Roll Soc., 27, 1906), 15; *Great Roll of the Pipe for the 31st Year of Henry II* (Pipe Roll Soc, 34, 1913), 162; Hoskins, *Devon*, citing the cartulary of Modbury Priory.

[52] *Great Roll of the Pipe for the 24th Year of Henry II* (Pipe Roll Soc, 26, 1906), 15; *Book of Fees*, ii, 772; *Feet of Fines Devon*, i, 189, 223, 326.

[53] *Great Roll of the Pipe for the 6th Year of Richard I* (Pipe Roll Soc, 43, 1928), 170; *Book of Fees*, ii, 756, 784.

[54] *Canonsleigh Cartulary*, xx, 3, 5, 12, 13, 14, 15, 17, 21, 22; on origins, see G Tengvik, *Old English Bynames* (1938), 214.

55 *Book of Fees*, ii, 758, 780; *Canonsleigh Cartulary*, 3, 22; F W Weaver, ed., *Cartulary of Buckland Priory* (Somerset Record Soc, 1909), 147; Reaney, *Origin*, 71; *Great Roll of the Pipe for the 6th Year of King John* (Pipe Roll Soc, 56, 1940), 85.

56 *Great Roll of the Pipe for the 8th Year of King John* (Pipe Roll Soc, 58, 1942), 144; *Book of Fees*, ii, 778; *Feet of Fines Devon*, i, 251, 333, 357; DRO, Exeter City Records, Misc. Roll 5, m 6.

57 *Great Roll of the Pipe for the 22nd Year of Henry II* (Pipe Roll Soc, 25, 1904), 146; *Great Roll of the Pipe for the 6th Year of Richard I* (Pipe Roll Soc, 44, 1928), 171; *Great Roll of the Pipe for the 7th Year of Richard I* (Pipe Roll Soc, 44, 1929), 128; *Great Roll of the Pipe for the 1st Year of King John* (Pipe Roll Soc, 48, 1933), 190, 194, 199.

58 *Book of Fees*, i, 433, 435; ii, 757-58; *Canonsleigh Cartulary*, 24, 44, 47; *Great Roll of the Pipe for the 22nd Year of Henry II* (Pipe Roll Soc., 25, 1904), 148; *Great Roll of the Pipe for the 7th Year of Richard I* (Pipe Roll Soc, 44, 1929), 129; *Great Roll of the Pipe for the 1st Year of King John* (Pipe Roll Soc, 48, 1933), 191; J H Round, ed., *Ancient Charters* (Pipe Roll Soc, 10, 1888), 100; *Feet of Fines, 1182–1196* (Pipe Roll Soc, 17, 1894), 86.

59 H Hall, *op. cit.*, ii, 558; *Book of Fees*, i, 98, 432; ii, 764, 766; *Feet of Fines Devon*, i, 275; *Rotuli Hundredorum*, i, 66, 95; *Great Roll of the Pipe for the 8th Year of Henry II* (Pipe Roll Soc, 5, 1885), 6.

60 J H Round, ed., *Calendar of Documents Preserved in France* (1899), xxxv; *VCH Devon*, i, 565.

61 *Feudal Aids*, i, 349, 415; *Calendar of Inquisitions Post Mortem*, iv, 24; vi, 446; *Feet of Fines Devon*, ii, 25, 54, 224.

62 H Hall, *op. cit.*, i, 258; *Book of Fees*, ii, 755, 757, 765, 770; *Great Roll of the Pipe for the 5th Year of Henry II* (Pipe Roll Soc, 1, 1884), 42; *Feet of Fines Devon*, i, 193, 195, 346.

63 *Ibid*, 74, 78, 94.

64 *Feudal Aids*, i, 355.

65 *Feet of Fines Devon*, i, 206; *Crown Pleas Devon 1238*, 4, 50.

66 *Feudal Aids*, i, 332, 349; *Book of Fees*, ii, 790; *Calendar of Inquisitions Post Mortem*, iii, 146.

67 *Feudal Aids*, i, 332; *Book of Fees*, ii, 786; *Rotuli Hundredorum*, i, 90.

68 *Crown Pleas Devon 1238*, 101.

69 *Feudal Aids*, i, 313, 387; *Feet of Fines Devon*, i, 368.

70 *Rotuli Hundredorum*, i, 79; *Close Rolls of the Reign of Henry III, 1227–31*, 62; *Crown Pleas Devon 1238*, 97.

71 *Crown Pleas Devon 1238*, 94.

72 *Feet of Fines Devon*, i, 373.

73 Reaney, *DBS*, 142.

[74] *Crown Pleas Devon 1238*, 89.
[75] *Ibid*, 67. The surname Doggefel is probably from an unidentified place-name.
[76] *Ibid*, 65.
[77] DRO, Exeter City Records, Misc Roll 5, m 1.
[78] *Canonsleigh Cartulary*, 59-63.
[79] *Eton College Records*, 1/32, fos 5, 7-8, 18.
[80] *Crown Pleas Devon 1238*, 12, 93-4, 105.
[81] *Canonsleigh Cartulary*, 59, 60, 61, 64.
[82] DRO, Courtenay Cartulary, 131, 135-36, 137, 139, 140-41.
[83] *Canonsleigh Cartulary*, 26, 68, 69, 73; *Crown Pleas Devon 1238*, 24, 25, 28, 123; *Feet of Fines Devon*, i, 278, 367; ii, 300, 316.
[84] A J Howard, ed., *1332 Assize Roll: County of Devon* (1970), 2, 7.
[85] See, e.g., Ralph son of Thomas (*Lay Subsidy 1332*, 55), John son of Richard (*ibid*, 119), or John son of Philip (*ibid*, 123).
[86] *Ibid*, 112.
[87] *Ibid*, 121.
[88] *Ibid*, 79, 98, 121, 122.
[89] W G Hoskins and H Finberg, *Devonshire Studies* (1952), 98.
[90] O J Reichel, 'The Devonshire "Domesday" ', *TDA*, 28, 374-75.
[91] Longleat MSS 10770, 11252.
[92] Exeter D & C Archives 1712–1714.
[93] Hoskins and Finberg, *op. cit.*, 111-117.
[94] *Canonsleigh Cartulary*, 7, 26, 66, 67-8.
[95] *Ibid*, 46, 67, 72, 75; *Crown Pleas Devon 1238*, 6, 59, 121.
[96] *Feet of Fines Devon*, i, 325.
[97] *Exeter Freemen*, 1, 5.
[98] *Ibid*, 18, 29.
[99] *Ibid*, 25.
[100] *Ibid*, 30.
[101] *PND*, ii, 503, 532.
[102] A J Howard, *op. cit.*, 3, 6, 9. Maughestere is an occupational name in a feminine form.

Some further reflections on the heritability of surnames amongst the free and unfree peasantry

David Postles

Heritability of surnames was achieved amongst some social groups below the higher and lower nobility at different times in different regions. Heritable surnames were most precocious amongst the civic elite in some boroughs, particularly Exeter. This burghal elite had established hereditary surnames by the middle and late thirteenth century in Exeter. In Dartmouth too, a burghal caucus had hereditary surnames before the majority of other burgesses. In the early fourteenth century, in both communities, many burgess families had now established hereditary surnames, although some still had more fluid bynames. During the early fourteenth century, however, most burgess families came to hold hereditary surnames in boroughs of all sizes within the urban hierarchy.[1]

The development of hereditary surnames amongst those of free status in rural communities followed a similar pattern. Some of the free tenantry certainly had incipiently heritable surnames by the mid and late thirteenth century in east Devon and the South Hams. The evolution of the surname atte Trewen around Modbury illustrates this process. In 1260, William *de arboribus* held land from Modbury Priory *que vocatur De arboribus in parochia de Modbyr'*. Before then, the Priory had granted a lease for eight years of land at Wyke to Helewysia, widow of Terricus *de arboribus*. Letters obligatory of 1298 made mention of William *de arboribus filius et heres predicti Terryci*, and a subsequent quitclaim of right in the lands at Wyke was made by the same person, styled as William atte Trawen.[2] The surname atte Trawen continued at Modbury thereafter.[3] At about the same time, the surname (de) Bacalr' was becoming hereditary around Axminster in east Devon. In 1269, Newenham Priory gave a corrody to Walter de Bacalr' in return for his gift of land in 'Bacalr' '. In charters of similar date, other gifts were made by Thomas Bacalr' son of William de Bacalr' senior, confirmed by Thomas's brother, another William de Bacalr', and by Adam de Bacalr' (two and a half acres to sustain a light in the church).[4] Rentals of 1260 and the late thirteenth century enumerated further Robert Bacalre, who held thirteen acres and one acre of meadow, and William Bacalre, who was another tenant there. In 1332, John Bacalr' was assessed there at 2s.[5] In the same place, the surname de la Lane may also have become hereditary about the same time. In 1296, Henry 'known as de la Lane' (*cognomento de la Lane*) gave two and a half acres in Axminster to Newenham, as well as other small gifts. Another charter styled Henry as Henry de la Lane son of Gilbert de la Lane (*filius Gilberti de la Lane*); this surname recurred in rentals of Newenham's lands in Axminster. In 1334, both Thomas atte Lane and Walter atte Lane held land there.[6] These surnames, however, may have been polyphyletic as they were locative and topographical, that is, several unrelated tenants may have assumed their bynames from the place or feature. On the other hand, there is some evidence of relationships of the bearers of the bynames. At the same time, charters of Newenham relating to land in Axminster referred to John de Milebrok' son and heir of Ralph de Milebrok' and Richard de Coteheie son and heir of Haydof de Coteheie, although these transmissions were, as far as is known, only between two generations.[7]

The establishment of hereditary surnames around Axminster is best illustrated by the surname Pie or Pyw, borne by an expanding family there. In 1260, Nicholas and Gilbert Pie held land there; slightly later, tenants there included Gunnilda, Laurence, Edith and William Pie, the latter a son of Laurence Pie; in 1316, William Pie son of Laurence Pie was enumerated again in a rental, as were another William, Henry, Walter and John Pie *alias* Pyw; in 1332, John and Henry were assessed in the lay subsidy; in 1334, tenants now comprised Henry, Joan, John, Alice widow of William, and *Relicta Walteri Pyw*.[8] The byname Pie *alias* Pyw also occurred in nearby Uplyme in the early fourteenth century in the guise of John (le) Pyw and Alice (le) (*sic*) Pywes, who may have been related to the Pies of Axminster.[9] In Axminster, the surname Wrang(he) was also held over several generations.[10] In east Devon and the South Hams, therefore, hereditary surnames were evolving amongst the free tenantry in the late thirteenth century, but this process may have been more protracted in mid and west Devon.[11] By 1339, bynames of some tinners had become stabilized in south west Devon, since some bore occupational names derived from activities other than tin-mining.[12]

Hereditary surnames may have existed incipiently amongst the unfree peasantry of east Devon by the early fourteenth century, amongst some kinship groups, although not necessarily all or even the majority. At Stoke Canon, a byname was inherited by a daughter in 1306–7. Joel bysouthecolm felled and sold forty oaks, which he sold to Stephen le schumere of Exeter. He was arraigned by his lord, who claimed that he was an unfree tenant. Joel defended his status and his right as a free tenant, but subsequently admitted he was of unfree status. He requested to be readmitted to his tenement, but was allowed to resume it only for the term of his life. On his death in 1307, his daughter, Joan by southecolm claimed her inheritance, but she was refused admission since she had previously left the manor without the lord's licence.[13] Although the byname had been transmitted over only two generations, it had been retained by a daughter after the death of her father.

More extensive evidence for east Devon exists for the manor of Uplyme. In an extent of the mid thirteenth century, all the customary tenants were assigned bynames; two tenants, however, were designated simply Maci and Salmay, but these *cognomina* may have been bynames rather than forenames.[14] Entries in the court rolls of the early fourteenth century implicitly reveal the development of hereditary surnames there. When Peter atte watere paid merchet for his daughter, his pledges were Robert atte watere and Richard atte watere. Such topographical bynames may have been polyphyletic but the personal pledging suggests some relationship between the parties. In 1307-8, Richard Scote senior and Richard Scote junior were both placed in mercy; John de bosco senior and junior were amerced for trespasses respectively by avers and sheep. Implicit in these affixes are two generations of the same family. There is more explicit evidence of the transmission of a byname over two generations of an unfree family in Uplyme. In *c*.1315, John atte Rode, son of Thomas atte Rode junior, surrendered his messuage and ferdel *atte Rode*, which Thomas had previously held. Thus a topographical byname associated with a tenement until 1315, had been passed over at least two generations.[15] Several simultaneous male bearers of other names may also suggest an hereditary surname: thus in 1307, Thomas, John and William Lilling; James, John and Peter Nog; John, Edward and William le Kyng. During the early fourteenth century, several surnames were held over several generations: Curteis *alias* Curteys (1307-1408); Dounheigh *alias* Dounhey (1315-1408); Gache (1307-1536); de Holcombe (1307-1375); de Canyngton (mid thirteenth century to 1340); (le) Mey(es) (1307-75); Kene (1308-1380s); Lilling (1307-1536); Slug (1307-75); atte watere (1307-50); and Morgan (1313-1408).

The process of stabilization is illustrated by the evolution of some patronymic and metronymic surnames in Uplyme. John *filius Juliane* appeared also as John *filius Joyote* and John Julianesone (1307-8). The byname Joyote was subsequently held by several other individuals before 1340: Isabella, Walter, Thomas and John, suggesting a family surname. Thomas *filius Sibille* appeared in court in 1307, the lay subsidy listed John Sibilie in 1332, and William

Sybeli occurred in court in 1350–2. Similarly, John *filius Clementis* was listed as a *garcio* in 1315, whilst a John Clement occurred in the 1340s and 1350s. In 1340, the personal pledge for William Hobbe junior was William Hobbe senior, a surname borne also by other members of this family, including a daughter.[16] The surname Lilling represented a core kinship group in Uplyme from the early fourteenth century; a Thomas Lilling also occurred in nearby Axminster fleetingly in the rental of 1316.[17] In nearby Awliscombe, the persistence of the byname atte Pille suggests that it became hereditary there in the first half of the fourteenth century. A different Henry atte Pille was mentioned in charters of *c.*1316 and *c.*1354–9, and a Henry Pille in 1418. This topographical byname thus became associated with a tenement called Pyle, even when that holding had come into the hands of the Preng family.[18]

In the South Hams, some bynames may have become hereditary about the same time. In Berry Pomeroy in the 1290s, three customary tenants, holding between them four and a half ferlings, were known as Garland (Roger, Richard and William). One of the burgesses there was William Sparke, whilst the customary tenants included William Dulle Sparke and William *filius Willelmi Sparke*. In contemporary Stockleigh Pomeroy, four customary tenants (Geoffrey, Ydelot, John and Christine) bore the byname Binythetone, which may have been assigned to them separately or may represent a relationship.[19]

In the extreme west of Devon, bynames evolved into hereditary surnames by the 1360s, represented by the transformation in the court rolls of Werrington, which are extant from that date. Stabilization may have occurred before then, but there is no extant evidence. Thus, when William Briton died in 1365, his heir was Joan, the daughter of Robert Briton, who was allocated custody of his daughter. In the same year, William Carpenter died, and his son, John Carpenter was distrained to assume the holding.[20] When also in 1365, Matilda Baron left the manor illicitly, Richard Baron was made accountable for her. Similarly, William Godefray was made responsible for the flight of William Godefray junior, as was William Mayour as *proprinquior consanguineus* for the fugitive Joan Maiour, all in 1365. Walter Salle was heir to William Salle, who died in 1369. In the same year, William Besant de Topehull died, a *nativus* who had held a ferling, to which succeeded his youngest son, Ralph Besant junior, according to the custom of the manor.[21] At the same time, John Besant was placed in mercy for trespass in a case with Ralph Besant (senior). William Bribb junior found as surety his father, William Bribb.[22] In other cases, a surname was held simultaneously by at least three tenants. Thus in 1369, John Cotel de Radeford acted as a pledge for John Cotel de Wytston, whilst William Cotel was placed in mercy for withdrawing his suit of the mill. In 1365, William Kye, *nativus*, died, and his daughter, Alice, was placed in wardship. In 1369, Alice died, whose heir was Joan Kyea, one of whose pledges was Richard Kyea. Matilda Hamelyn was amerced in 1369 for detinue of half an ox against Robert Hamelyn; at the same time, John Hamelyn, who held a tenure by the right of his wife, Matilda, died, as also in that year did Richard Hamelyn, *nativus domini*. In 1365, John Louye, as *proprinquior consanguineus*, was made responsible for the chattels of his sister, Juliana Louye, who had died. From *c.*1365–70, several other tenants bore this surname: Roger, *nativus*, who held one and a half ferlings and died in 1365; Robert who held a ferling; John, the principal member of the kinship group, who accumulated multiple tenures; John, servant of Robin atteforde; and Matilda, a vendor of tap ale.[23]

In the very east of Devon, bynames had developed into hereditary surnames earlier, apparently, than in the west. Virtually all the bynames mentioned in the court rolls of Yarcombe from 1321 became hereditary by the 1330s, if not before. These included atte Stoute (later Stote), Rodayn, Twetyng, Bras, Kybbel, Kywer, Brouning, Underdoune, Bonde, Boulogne, de Bradelegh, de Bremeler, Bek, Prodomme, Viroun, mostly held by customary tenants, although including a small number of free tenants and *censarii*. These surnames persisted on this manor and in these court rolls throughout the fourteenth century, some well into the fifteenth and early sixteenth. Even in 1321, Rodayn was borne by William, Alice and John, all amerced separately in the court; Twetyng similarly by Philip, Alexander and Peter; Kybbel by Richard, Robert and Walter; atte Stoute by Henry, Nicholas and Matilda (although such a topographical byname may have been simply polyphyletic, held by more than one individual holding a tenement there; but it did become hereditary and persist in the manor). More explicit evidence derives from inheritances of land. In 1321, John Kyckard paid an entry fine of 10s for the tenement formerly held by his mother, Christine *relicta Walteri Kyckard*. In 1327, William Rodayn and his wife, Blissota, were admitted to the half ferling held by Richard Rodayn, who had died. In 1331, William atte Wode paid for an inquisition to decide whether he had any right in the tenement *apud la Wode*, which his mother, Edith att' Wode, had held. Later, in 1338, another inquisition reported that in 1332, Ivo Prodomme, father of Walter Prodomme, had held a customary tenement in Yarcombe.[24]

The unfree peasantry of Devon had thus acquired hereditary surnames by the middle of the fourteenth century. The process had been uneven in several senses. Some kinship groups in some communities developed hereditary surnames before other families.[25] Hereditary surnames may also have been conceived amongst the unfree peasantry earlier in some parts of Devon, such as east Devon, than in others.

References

1 See below, pp.255-8.
2 E(ton) C(ollege) R(ecords) 1/32, fos 4v-5v, 7r-8v, 18v.
3 ECR 1/139.
4 Bodl Lib MS Top Devon d 5, fos 30r, 33r, 42r-45r.
5 BL Arundel MS 17, fos 35r-v; *Lay Subsidy 1332*, 126.
6 Bodl Lib MS Top Devon d 5, fos 29r, 30v-31r, 32v, 33v; BL Arundel MS 17, fo 49r.
7 Bodl Lib MS Top Devon d 5, fos 38v, 39r.
8 BL Arundel MS 17, fos 34r, 36r-v, 47r-v, 49r; *Lay Subsidy 1332*, 126.
9 Longleat MSS Uplyme court rolls computer database.
10 BL Arundel MS 17, fos 33v-48v.
11 See also the transmission of hereditary surnames in the cartulary of Canonsleigh (BL Harl MS 3660, in preference to the calendar in London, *Canonsleigh Cartulary*): de Aysforde (fos 36r-38v); William le Arper *filius et heres Petri le Harper* (fos 83r-86r); William Parl *filius et heres Willelmi Parl de Bromlegh'* (fo 87r); although the de Aysforde and Harper families may have held knights' fees in 1242-3. At Uplyme, the free families of dę Carswell (1275-c.1370) and Ryuel (1267-1360s): A Watkin, *The Great Cartulary . . .*; Longleat MSS Uplyme court rolls computer database.
12 PRO E 179/95/15.
13 D & C Exeter 1712-1714 (*Processus Curiarum de loquela que fuit inter homines de Stoke et . . . dominum ibidem*).
14 BL Add MS 17450, fos 218-221.
15 Longleat MS 10771, m 52d: 'Johannes atte Rode filius Thome atte Rode iunioris . . .'
16 Longleat MSS Uplyme court rolls computer database; *Lay Subsidy 1332*, 47.
17 BL Arundel MS 17, fo 47r.
18 *Devon and Cornwall Notes and Gleanings*, 4 (1894), 39.
19 *Book of Fees*, ii, 1311, 1315.
20 'Et venit Johanna filia Roberti Briton et cepit eandem terram . . . Et predictus Robertus custos dicte Johanne . . .' This and all subsequent references from DRO Bedford MSS

Werrington court rolls. 'xij presentant quod Willelmus Carpenter natiuus domini qui tenuit unum ferling' terre ... obiit ... Et distr' Johannem Carpenter filium et heredem dicti Willelmi Carpenter ad satisfaciendum domino ...'

21 'Et venit Radulphus Besant natiuus de stipite junior filius et heres predicti Willelmi secundum consuetudinem manerii.'

22 'Willelmus Bribb invenit Willelmum Bribb patrem suum ...'

23 DRO Bedford MSS Werrington court rolls.

24 DRO CR 1428-1438, 1441–1450. For example: 'Johannes Kyckard venit et dedit domino pro tenemento habendo .x.s. quod fuit Christine relicte Walteri Kyckard ad terminum vite sue.' (DRO CR 1429, 1321).

25 Charters in the late thirteenth century could still refer to villeins by forenames only as BL Harl MS 3660, fos 35r, 77r, and 80v: two ferlings in Clanfield *quos Falco tenuit*; one ferling in Waterslade *cum homine qui illum tenet nomine Elye et uxore et facultate sua*; a croft in 'Estwill' *quam (sic) Godefridus tenuit*. But the context may not have required bynames, although the tenants may have been assigned bynames in other contexts.

CHAPTER 5

CHANGE DURING THE LATER MIDDLE AGES

Changes in the proportions and nature of locative and occupational bynames and surnames; those from personal names; the surname Cole; patronymic forms; Anglo-Norman and Middle English forms of bynames and surnames, including surnames from nicknames.

The pattern of bynames and surnames changed radically during the later middle ages, in Devon, as in many other counties. Its causation owed much to several variables. The principal change was the decline in the proportion of locative surnames between 1332 and 1524. Reasons for this specific change are multiple. The contraction of population and settlement in the long run over the later middle ages may have contributed to this decline, especially in the loss of small settlements in the dispersed pattern of settlement.[1] Such a cause may not be the exclusive instrument of change, since many locative surnames from these settlements had already entered the stock of bynames and surnames before demographic decline. Depopulation of and vacancies in some of the small hamlets and dispersed tenements, however, may have constituted one cause of change. A wider agent of change may have been cultural transition, both vertically and horizontally. There may thus have been a change of naming attitudes away from locative bynames to other forms of bynames, coinciding with the transition from unstable bynames to hereditary surnames, from an incipient form of naming to a later form. If vertical cultural influences were a cause of the decline of locative bynames, then it must have been an inverse social relationship, since it is generally assumed that the higher and freer social echelons tended towards locative bynames and that the lower social groups tended to have non-locative forms.[2] If the movement was away from locative surnames during the later middle ages, then cultural diffusion may have been upwards rather than downwards. Such considerations, however, need to be pursued in the regional context, and are discussed further below. Other cultural influences were certainly exerted on the pattern of surnames in the later middle ages, but perhaps only to a minor degree. The introduction of patronymic surnames with the element -son during the later middle ages was intrusive from other regions of England and even other parts of Europe. The infusion of new types of occupational byname had the same general origins. By and large, however, the pattern of naming in Devon, although influenced in a minor way by these external influences, was changed more by seemingly internal than external influences, and remained a localized and self-contained stock. Another explanation of the decline of locative surnames may be the nature of the sources. The lay subsidy of 1332 may have had a tendency to identify taxpayers by their locative byname, rather than any other by which they may have been known, so that change may have been slightly compounded by the nature of the sources. Finally, of course, the transformation of the pattern owed something to the fortunes of individuals, life-cycle, family and kinship groups during the demographic vicissitudes of the later middle ages. These influences are discussed further below in an attempt to illustrate the changes which occurred in naming patterns in Devon during the later middle ages.

The most significant change during the later middle ages was the relative decline of locative surnames, and the corresponding increase in the proportions of other forms. About 34% of taxpayers on average throughout Devon in 1332 bore locative bynames; by 1524, the figure had declined to 26%. There is some evidence to suggest that this pattern of bynames in 1332 related to the pattern of dispersed settlement in Devon. This ascription can be illuminated by comparing the pattern of bynames in Devon and adjacent Dorset in the early fourteenth century.

Table 5.1
Structure of Bynames in Devon (1332) and Dorset (1327)[3]

	Devon (%)	Dorset (%)
Locative	34	16
Topographical	15	16
Occupational	10	21
Personal	15	19
Nicknames	18	16
Relationship	>1	2
Uncertain	7	10

The figures here and throughout relate to numbers or percentages of taxpayers with a byname or type of byname.

The principal difference is the level of locative bynames in each county. In Devon, there was a much higher level of dispersed settlement than in Dorset, although some parts of east Devon and the South Hams had less polyfocal settlement than other parts.[4] The same contrast holds true with much of the pattern of bynames in Somerset in 1327, although there too there were regions of dispersed settlement.[5] The pattern in Devon was very similar to that in Cornwall in the lay subsidy of 1327, recently elucidated by Padel, which also related to the level of dispersed settlement in that county.[6]

Thus the structure of bynames in Devon resembled that of some other counties which contained some regions with higher levels of dispersed settlement — not as high as the 52% of locative bynames in Lancashire, but slightly higher than Staffordshire (29%), Warwickshire (30%), and the West Riding of Yorkshire (28%). The difference between Devon and these counties was the decline of the proportion of locative surnames during the later middle ages in Devon, compared with their persistence in the early sixteenth century in Lancashire (25–60% in different parts of the county), Staffordshire (30%) and Yorkshire (40%).[7]

Given these contrasts from the same sources, the extent to which the nature of the lay subsidy of 1332 affected the ostensible pattern in Devon is complex. The taxable population in 1332 encompassed some 10,614 persons; in 1524–5, over 28,000 taxpayers were assessed. Reliance on the two subsidies provides only broadly valid notions of change. The lay subsidies were wealth-specific, excluding those below a tax threshold.[8] The subsidy of 1332 was levied on those with disposable personalty — in excess of that required for subsistence — valued at more than 10s. The subsidy of 1524–5 was collected on wages, goods, and land valued at 20s. or more. By 1524–5, as surnames had become hereditary, the distortion may not be too great. In 1332, however, when bynames were still unstable and formative, considerable distortion may been induced by the nature of the taxation. The proportion of bynames in the taxation may have been influenced by the socio-economic status of those taxed and those excluded, if, as has been shown for some other counties, locative bynames tended to be held by the freer and wealthier, and other forms of bynames by the poorer social groups. In those counties, locative bynames were associated with free status, frequently because the mobility of freemen was not constrained by seignorial restriction. There, locative bynames were related to personal mobility.[9] In Devon, however, as will be shown below, locative bynames were not only attached to the higher and freer social groups; since these forms derived from dispersed settlement, they were held by unfree and free tenants, related to tenures in dispersed settlements and tenements. The regional influence here may have complicated the sociological. On the other hand, the organisation of the subsidy may have distorted the levels of different forms of byname. The subsidy was collected by parish, so that those holding land in dispersed hamlets or tenements may have tended to have been identified for the purpose of the subsidy, by a locative byname relating to their place of residence within the parish of assessment. In other documents, before hereditary surnames, they may have been identified by other bynames. In this case, the administrative arrangement of the subsidy combined with the dispersed pattern of settlement may have conspired to corrupt the levels of different forms of byname in 1332.

About a third of taxpayers in Devon in 1332 bore locative bynames, including generic locative bynames, such as Wals(c)h(e), Waleys, Cornysh, Cornwaille, Irische, Irreys, Irlaunde, Gascoigne, Peuteuyn, and variants. The relative distribution of these taxpayers was as follows:

Table 5.2
Relative Distribution of Taxpayers with Locative Bynames in 1332

	Total taxpayers	Taxpayers with loc	Loc as % of total
Rural hundreds	8991	3084	34.3
Ancient demesne	600	186	31.0
Boroughs	1023	258	25.2
Total	10614	3528	33.9

The methodology adopted here is to assess the distribution of these taxpayers by parish and by hundred. The hundred has been taken as an intermediate level of analysis with some misgivings, since the hundred might not correlate to *pays* or region. On the other hand, some hundreds of Devon are very small, and the hundred was the intermediate level of assessment, organisation and collection. In some cases, moreover, the lay subsidy was collected for an undifferentiated hundred, that is the level of assessment and collection within that hundred was not taken down to the level of the parish. For example, the assessment for the hundred of Colyton was for the entire hundred, not by individual parishes.[10] In many cases, the hundred is fortuitously very closely related to relief, topography and *pays*. It is also possible to group the hundreds discretely into the principal distinctive regions of Devon, such as east Devon, the South Hams *et al.*

Figure 7
The Distribution of Locative Bynames in 1332 as Percentage of Total Taxpayers.
(Excluding Boroughs and Ancient Demesnes.)

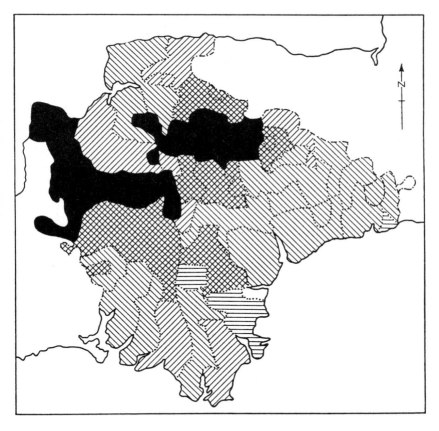

⏐⏐⏐⏐ below 15%	20–30%	40–50%
15–20%	30–40%	over 50%

Figure 8
The Distribution of Topographical Bynames in 1332
as Percentage of Total Taxpayers.
(Excluding Boroughs and Ancient Demesnes.)

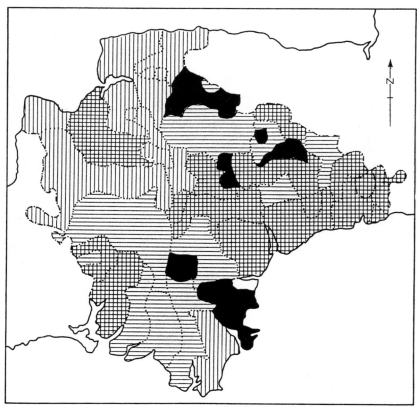

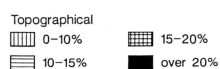

Topographical
- 0–10%
- 10–15%
- 15–20%
- over 20%

The distribution of taxpayers with locative bynames (as a percentage of all taxpayers) is illustrated in the map. The greatest concentration occurred in the centre, north and west of the county, especially in the hundreds of Black Torrington, Hartland and Witheridge, where locative bynames were borne by more than 50% of the population. In the hundreds of Teignbridge, Lifton, Crediton, North Tawton, South Molton and Tiverton, some 40–50% of taxpayers held such bynames. This high proportion of locative bynames is seemingly related to the high level of dispersed settlement in these regions, compared with the slightly more nucleated pattern in east Devon and the South Hams. The nature of this distribution is reflected further in the histograms, which indicate the proportion of locative bynames which derived from within the parish (CP), from other parishes within the hundred, and from outside the hundred. Locative bynames from minor placenames within the parish represent dispersed settlement; those from places in other parishes within the hundred reflect short-distance migration. Some short-distance migration also occurred between adjacent parishes in different hundreds; for example, in the small hundred of Molland (now in South Molton Hundred), fourteen taxpayers bore locative bynames relating to places in South Molton Hundred, of which twelve were minor settlements in the parish of Knowstone.[11]

The histograms represent the proportions of locative bynames which resulted from dispersed settlement (CP) and short-distance migration within the same hundred. These two elements account for almost all the locative bynames in rural settlements. The highest proportions occurred in the hundreds with the highest levels of locative bynames. Thus, in Teignbridge Hundred, 66.7% derived from dispersed settlement and 24.6% from short-distance migration; in Lifton Hundred, respectively 66.3% and 17.8%; in Black Torrington Hundred 56.6% and 25%; in Hartland Hundred 74.5% and 8.8%; in Witheridge Hundred 75% and 14.9%; in North Tawton Hundred 56.5% and 24.6%; in South Molton Hundred 62% and 27.3%; and in Tiverton Hundred 60.4% and 14.6%. In many hundreds, more than 50% of locative bynames derived from dispersed settlement.

The predominantly local nature of migration is illustrated by the composition of locative bynames in some parishes. Eighteen taxpayers in Bradworthy bore bynames from placenames in other parishes in the same hundred, of which nine were located in the parish of Pancrasweek. In Werrington, fourteen bore these bynames from other places in the Hundred, but six were from minor settlements in the adjacent parish of North Petherwin. Twenty-one

Figure 9

Locative Bynames as a Percentage of the Total Taxpayers by Hundred in 1332.
(Excluding Boroughs and Ancient Demesnes.)

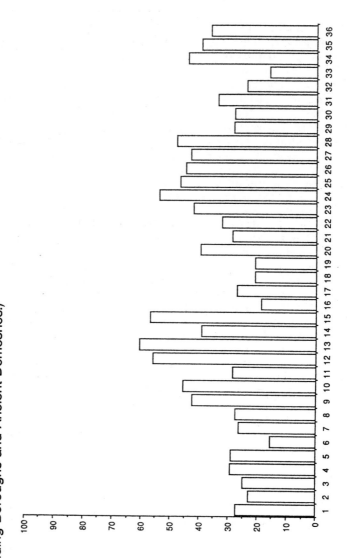

Figure 10
The Composition of Locative Bynames by Hundred in 1332.

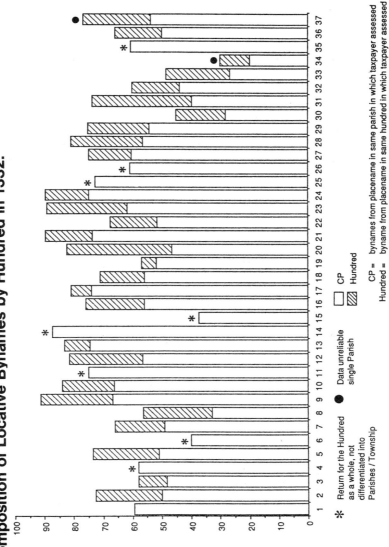

CP = bynames from placename in same parish in which taxpayer assessed
Hundred = byname from placename in same hundred in which taxpayer assessed

CP ☐

Hundred ▨

● Data unreliable
  single Parish

✳ Return for the Hundred
  as a whole, not
  differentiated into
  Parishes / Township

taxpayers in Umberleigh had similar bynames, of which eleven were from places in the parish of High Bickington. In Abbotsham, ten of the thirteen taxpayers with bynames from places elsewhere in the hundred, had ones relating to small settlements in the adjacent coastal parish of Alvington. Similarly, Littleham and Buckland Brewer were adjacent litoral parishes. In Littleham, eighteen taxpayers had bynames from other places in the same hundred, including thirteen from settlements in Buckland. Where locative bynames did represent migration, therefore, the movement was intensely localised.[12]

The nature of the settlements from which many of these locative bynames evolved, might imply that some bynames may have been monophyletic rather than polyphyletic. In 1428, some hamlets in east Devon contained fewer than ten inhabitants.[13] In 1332, it is possible that some dispersed settlements, especially dispersed tenements and farmsteads which had been attributed formal minor placenames, may have consisted of no more than one or two kinship groups bearing a byname from the placename. Thus the byname de Porrecombe (Parcombe) may have been monophyletic.[14] Although the vast majority of English bynames were polyphyletic, some few locative bynames from such small settlements as there were in some regions of Devon, may have been monophyletic. A multitude of minor settlements in Devon, however, received their placename from topographical features. The consequent locative *cum* topographical bynames were polyphyletic, since the same placenames recurred throughout Devon. For example, at least 22 places were called Stone; 23 Week; 14 Well; 22 Pitt; 14 Aller; 19 Ash; 15 Beara and 16 Beer; 14 Berry; nine Borough and 13 Burrow; 22 Bowden; 12 Brook; 22 Cleave; 82 Combe; 18 Down; 53 Ford and seven Forder; 22 Hayne and six Hay; 18 Hele and seven Heal; 39 Hill, four Rill and seven Rull; 30 Hole; 22 Knowle; 16 Leigh, 13 Lee, one Lea and 12 Ley; 27 Moor; 14 Pool; 19 Lake; 18 Slade; six Shute; 22 Thorn; 12 Tor; 30 Venn; 12 Way. Consequently, innumerable taxpayers in 1332 bore bynames from these minor placenames, such as 44 Bear or Bere, 38 Wyke or Week, 80 Hole, 33 Stone.[15] Whereas some locative bynames from very small settlements may have been monophyletic, those from these locative *cum* topographical placenames were exceptionally polyphyletic.

By 1332, locative bynames were becoming asyndetic, losing, inconsistently, the preposition *de*: thus Thomas Borbrok' in Tawstock from Bourbrook; Robert Punchardon in Colmpton; Stephen Bakelaford of Battleford; William Spichewyk of Spitchwick; John Wydymore of Withymore; John Nottecomb' of Nutcombe; Margery Merlegh from Marley. Similarly in Dartington, those enumerated included Matthew Byllyngheghe, John Driarugg', John Bealle, and Thomas Wascomb' (Billany, Croridge, Belleigh, Westcombe); others comprised, for example, Ralph Moriheued (Moors Head), Henry Lasborne (Lisburn), Robert Corndoune (Corringdon), Robert Yolleland (Yolland), William Barlecomb' (Barleycombe), Richard Hurburneford (Harbourneford) and William Kylleburi (Kilbury).[16] In all, some 384 taxpayers in 1332 bore locative bynames in the asyndetic form, comprising about 13% of all locative bynames. Asyndetic and syndetic forms co-existed: 12 of 23 in Tiverton were asyndetic.

The extent to which locative bynames reflected actual migration from eponymous places of origin, even before *c.*1350, is complicated. Even before this date, the bynames of some social groups, including some freemen and unfree tenants, had developed into hereditary surnames. Some bynames must also be treated cautiously because they are associated with the higher and lesser nobility, and must therefore be equivocal *noms d'origine*.

The Norman *noms d'origine* provide problems as well as the English ones. Perhaps the least ambivalent is Dinham, which is almost exclusively associated with the nobility. The same association may have persisted in the case of Ferrers, a cadet family from Ferrières in Manche, which did not appear in Devon until 1168.[17] Pomeray was quite different. The family which was a tenant in chief in 1086 and mesne tenant of the earl of Mortain, probably originated in La Pomeraye in Normandy.[18] The byname Pomeray, however, recurred in Devon by the early fourteenth century and through the later middle ages. The transformation of the social composition of the gentry in the later middle ages may have led to the diffusion of this byname, but it also seems clear that the byname had another etymology unconnected with the nobility and Normandy (see below).

Even more complicated are some locative bynames derived from English placenames. The most contentious is possibly Wellington (Somerset). A family of this name had become mesne tenants of the Honour of Plympton (earl of Devon) by 1242–3, Ralph de Welinton having married a ward of the earl in 1199. In 1242–3, Ralph held fees in Langleigh, Stokes and Beauford, and at Gridsham from the earl of Gloucester. By the mid fourteenth century, Sir Henry de Welyngton had become steward of the earl of Cornwall, and held three Cornish acres at Helston in Trigg in 1337, as well as other land from the earl at Penmain. In 1428, Wellingtons held fragments of fees in Combe and Morleigh, Langleigh, Gidsham, Uplowman, Beauford and Stoke Rivers.[19] The surname occurred, however, amongst other social groups. Thus at Yarcombe, in 1393, a

Welington was amerced in the manorial court for brewing; in 1238 Ranulf de Wellintone appeared before the Crown Pleas in Shirwell Hundred; the surname entered Dartmouth in the late fifteenth century.[20] In 1524–5, the surname was concentrated in the north and north-east of Devon hard by the boundary with Somerset. Its distribution in Devon thus emanated from two separate sources: the Wellington family of the higher and lesser nobility, and migration.

The distribution of the surname Arundel in Devon was confined both geographically and socially, always associated with the family of the lesser nobility. This extended kinship group held fees in Cornwall, Devon and Somerset (e.g. Sampford Arundel in Somerset). In 1242–3, John de Arundel held fees in Loventor, Hempston, Ash and Beer, and William a fragment of a fee in Orchard. In 1428, John Arundel held parts of fees in Bigbury, Buckland, Pidickwell, and Yulford.[21] The incidence of the surname in Devon does not therefore reflect direct migration from Sussex. The surnames de Cirencestre, de Sancto Albino and Kendale have the same cautionary explanations. Thomas de Cirencestre held fees in Woodhuish and St Marychurch in 1242–3; Stephen de St Alban a fee in Mattingho.[22] The existence of the surname Kendale in Devon may be related entirely to the family which became retainers of the earl of Cornwall, of whom John was receiver from 1351, at the same time as Richard occurred at Launceston. In *c*.1381, however, a Richard Kendale held one hide (16 ferlings) in socage at Holcumbe, part of the discrete manor of Ottery St Mary, as well as a half virgate there enumerated amongst the *customarii* of the hamlet of Combe.[23]

Other surnames became vaguely associated with the lesser nobility and gentry. David de Clotesworthi was the plaintiff in a final concord in 1256 concerning one fourteenth of a fee in Clotworthy in South Molton. In 1428, Thomas Clotworthy, with various co-parceners, held fragments of fees in Anstey, Aure, and East Bray, in South Molton Hundred, whilst Robert de Clotworthy had previously held part of a fee in Rowleigh in Shirewell. In the lay subsidy of 1332, only Oliver de Cloteworth' had been assessed, in South Molton. By 1524–5, the surname remained extremely localized: Christopher and Robert were assessed on wages in the borough of South Molton; four different Johns on goods and wages in the rural manor of South Molton; Oliver on wages at nearby Chittlehampton; Thomas on goods at Wembworthy; Baldwin on the same in Tavistock and William similarly in Bideford. John Clatworth was involved in a dispute over land in North Molton in 1563. Another John Clotworthy, however, had migated south-west to Werrington in the late fifteenth century, had accumulated multiple tenures, but only, it seems, during his own life-cycle. By 1566, another John Clotworthy had migrated westward to Hartland. In 1572, John and Anthony Cloteworthe became embroiled in litigation concerning an annuity from lands in Sheviok (Cornwall) and Shobrooke and customary lands in Sheviok. The surname was thus disseminated painfully slowly through north and west Devon, for a very long time concentrated around the hamlet of its origin, Clatworthy in the parish of South Molton, where it had been associated to a small degree with the lesser nobility.[24]

In the later middle ages, the surname Chichester became attributed to the lesser nobility, so that in 1428 John Chichester was a co-parcener in fees in Aveton, Stodbury, Trendeslo, Filleigh, and Whitworthy, scattered throughout Devon. In this case, however, it seems that the byname had entered Devon much earlier through the South Hams and east Devon, and only later became associated with the lesser nobility.[25]

These cautionary examples show that a proportion of locative surnames in Devon, whether from placenames inside or outside the county, do not always reflect actual patterns of migration of people, even at a time when other locative bynames can be assumed to reflect general patterns of personal migration.

Even so, some locative bynames became persistently associated with their place of origin, and so reflect the continuous localization of surnames in the county. This connection of surname and eponymous placename is most frequently associated with the smaller dispersed settlements, even after the development of hereditary surnames. In the late fourteenth century, Richard at yea was re-granted the tenement at le yea.[26] In c.1498, John More was listed as the tenant of two tenements in Colesworthy and Feniton which had been held previously by William Collesworthy.[27] In the rental of Ottery St Mary in c.1381, some customary tenants continued to be associated with eponymous hamlets. At Putt's Farm ('Pitte'), one of four tenants was Roger de Pitte, who held two ferlings. At Rill ('Hill'), Micheal at Hill, amongst four tenants, held three ferlings. At Borough and Wood's Farm ('Burgh et Wode'), the two tenants were Walter at Wode (seven ferlings) and Henry at Burgh (two ferlings). At Woodford Barton, Thomas Woodford held two ferlings, a parcel of meadow and five acres. At Morcombe, Stephen Morcomb held one and a half ferlings of demesne (barton) land. At Burcombe, Thomas Burcomb held a messuage, a curtilage and two ferlings, and at Wonscombe, Thomas Wynscomb held a ferling of demesne land. All these customary tenants held standard holdings and were core families.[28]

In 1388, an inquisition was held into the land of Joan daughter of Thomas atte Yeo at Yeo.[29] At Werrington, in 1368, Hamelin atte brigge, a conventionary tenant, held half a Cornish acre in Bridge, but the continuity of association was lost as the tenement lapsed into the lord's hands after the heavy mortality of that year. There also, Richard Grove died about 1490, having held half a Cornish acre in Grove in free socage. In c.1366, the tithingman and tithing there were placed in mercy for concealing that Roger Knight was an unfree tenant, not of free condition. At the same time, Knight paid for an inquisition into his right to a holding at Knightscote.[30] In the fifteenth century, in a rental of Sidbury, John Pleeford senior and junior each held a ferling in the hamlet of Playford, and William atte Rode a ferling in the hamlet of Rode.[31] In the early fifteenth century (c.1407–8), a number of free tenants of Plympton Priory, many of them holding in return for residual and fragmentary knight service (*per seruicium militare*), also still held surnames associated with the hamlet or tenement, such as Nicholas atte More who held lands and tenement *apud le More iuxta Columpton'*, Roger Forde holding similarly *apud le Forde*, John de Wybbeton holding lands and tenement *in Wybbeton' nuper Rogeri de Wybbeton'*, John Blakmanscomb' who held a ferling *in Blakmanscomb'*, John Ayschrygg who held a tenement and two ferlings in Ashridge late (*nuper*) of Thomas Ayschryg. At Thrushelton, another manor of Plympton, John Rysdon held at Rysdon, John Blakgroue at Blackgrove, Richard Thorne at Thorne, and Ralph att' Hylle *apud le Hille*. On the central manor of Plympton Grange, Udo att' Fenne held *apud le Fenne*, William Wodmanston at the hamlet of his surname, Joan widow of Roger Chancey in 'Chanceycomb' ', William Hetfyle *in Hetfyle*, the heirs of John Scobhull in Scoble ('Scobhill'), William Halswill at Halswill, William Swyneston in that hamlet, William atte Pytte in 'Pytte', the heirs of Walter atte Pytte *apud le Westerpytte*, those of Geoffrey Nyttherclyf inherited land *apud Nytherclyf*, and John Lurcomb held *in lurcomb' iuxta Bukyngton.*[32]

Some qualifications do need to be advanced. In some of the cases in the late fourteenth century, the continuity of association was still very young, and hereditary surnames only recently developed, especially in west Devon. In many cases, however, the continuity of association persisted after the mortality which caused the general disassociation of land and family in some regions.[33] The second caveat relates to free tenures. The greater sense of patrimony and the bond between land and family amongst free tenants may have induced greater continuity of association of surname and eponymous holding amongst this social group.[34] Nevertheless, the examples of continuity of association are striking and testimony to the very intense localization of society in Devon. In some few cases, this association persisted into the sixteenth century; thus Andrew Pytte paid rent *pro pytten* in a rental of Plympton Grange in the late sixteenth century.[35]

With these problems in mind, some attempt can be made to describe and explain the decline of locative surnames as a proportion of the taxonomy of surnames in Devon during the later middle ages. Overall this diminution was from an average of 34% of taxpayers in 1332 to 26% in 1524-5.

Table 5.3

Analysis of Locative Surnames in 1524

Total number of legible taxpayers — 26159
Total taxpayers with locative surnames — 6663
Locative as a % of total taxpayers — 26%

CP	Total 867 (13% of total locative)
Hundred	Total 1660 (25% of total locative)
Devon	Total 3626 (54% of total locative)
Outside	Total 510 (8% of total locative)

Where CP represents surnames from places within the same parish where the surname occurred; Hundred those from parishes in the hundred; Devon those from other hundreds in Devon; Outside those from places outside Devon.

These global figures, however, obscure the localized changes. In 1332, there had been a wide diversity between the levels in different hundreds. In a number of hundreds, especially in the South Hams and east Devon, the level of locative bynames fell below 30%, as in Haytor, Stanborough, Plympton, Roborough, Colyton, Axminster, Wonford, Exminster, and East Budleigh. The highest concentration of locative bynames was in the west and north, as in Witheridge (54%), Black Torrington (56%), Hartland (60%) and Molland (57%). These hundreds with high incidences were generally areas where dispersed settlement was most predominant. By 1524-5, the differences between hundreds had narrowed; the range then was both lower and less differentiated, from 15% (Hartland) to 37% (North Tawton). In only eight hundreds did more than 30% of taxpayers bear locative surnames. The structure of locative surnames within and between hundreds had thus altered radically.

124   *The Surnames of Devon*

Table 5.4

Ranges of Locative Surnames by Hundred: 1332 and 1524–5

	1332	1524–5
Low	27% (East Budleigh)	3% (Fremington)
High	75% (Hartland, Witheridge)	32% (Hartland)
Median	34%	12%
Mean	34%	14%

In all hundreds the proportion of locative surnames related to dispersed settlement had diminished. In thirteen hundreds, this contraction was by more than ten percentage points: South Molton; Witheridge; Crediton; West Budleigh; Tiverton; Lifton; Tavistock; Black Torrington; Hartland; Winkleigh; Coleridge. In some hundreds, the decline was even more severe: in South Molton from 62% to 12%; Witheridge 75% to 23%; Lifton 66% to 16%; Black Torrington 56% to 18%; Hartland 75% to 32%; and North Tawton 57% to 4%.

Conversely, the percentage of locative surnames derived from other places within the hundred increased, as in Haytor Hundred (20% to 33%); Stanborough (7% to 20%); Roborough (5% to 33%); Witheridge (15% to 42%); Wonford (17% to 28%); Lifton (18% to 29%); Black Torrington (25% to 40%); Hartland (9% to 20%); Braunton (21% to 36%); and Hayridge (17% to 31%). Additionally, the proportion of locative surnames derived from places outside the hundred also increased. In every hundred, these increases were more than 20%, and so quite significant, although the proportion of locative surnames from outside the county rose only insubstantially. The level of locative surnames from outside the county varied by region, from a low of 1% of locative surnames in Exminster Hundred to 19% in Coleridge Hundred, with a median of 7% and mean of 7.6%. The total number of taxpayers with surnames from outside the county was 510, appreciably below 2% of the total of taxpayers in 1524–5. The highest concentrations of extrinsec surnames were in the South Hams and east Devon, in Roborough (12%), Plympton (11%), Ermington (11%), Coleridge (19%), Colyton (15%), and Ottery St Mary (16%), but there were high levels also in the northern coastal hundreds of Hartland (18%) and Braunton (13%). Most were hundreds open to external influence through maritime activity. In nine other hundreds, the proportion of external locative surnames fell below 4% of all locative surnames.

There seems to be a correlation between the intensity of decline and regionalism. The decline of locative surnames as a whole affected all hundreds, but was most severe in precisely those hundreds where locative surnames had been most concentrated in 1332, and where dispersed settlement was most emphatic. The most distinctive correlation is in Black Torrington, Hartland, Lifton, South Molton, Witheridge, Crediton and Tiverton Hundreds.

Table 5.5

Severest Decline of Locative Surnames: 1332 and 1524–5

Hundred	Total locative as % of total taxpayers		CP as % of locative	
	1332	1524–5	1332	1524–5
South Molton	42	28	62	12
Witheridge	54	33	75	23
Tiverton	43	25	60	28
Lifton	46	28	66	16
Black Torrington	57	25	57	18
Hartland	61	15	75	32

Where CP refers to locative surnames relating to places within the same parish in which the surname occurred.

In these hundreds, the structure of locative surnames was different, in that there were equal proportions of surnames derived from within and outside the hundred, whereas in many other hundreds a higher proportion derived from parishes in other hundreds, as in Colyton (80% from other hundreds), Axminster (82%), Tavistock (79%), Stanborough (60%), East Budleigh (67%), Halberton (69%), although the small size of some of these hundreds may have been a critical factor in the levels of locative surnames from outside.

Table 5.6

Hundreds where less than 45% of Locative Surnames were derived from Outside the Hundred (that is, from another Hundred in Devon)

Hundred	From outside	CP	Another parish within the same hundred
Black Torrington	35%	18%	40%
Hartland	30%	32%	20%
Witheridge	33%	23%	42%
Haytor*	44%	14%	33%
Braunton	42%	9%	36%

* Haytor presents one of the principal difficulties in using hundreds for analysis, because of the relative differences between communities toward the coast and upland communities (see below).

From this analysis, it seems possible that the decline in locative surnames was mostly associated with those hundreds which had a heavy concentration of such bynames in 1332 related to the pattern of dispersed settlement. The effect of demographic contraction within some of these small settlements and communities may have been the loss of some locative bynames. For example, in the early fourteenth century, a tenant of a dispersed tenement or farmstead may have been known by that minor placename. The demise of that tenant, and the substitution of another tenant from elsewhere on the manor with a different byname, may have resulted in the loss of the locative byname. The actual desertion of some small communities may also have resulted in a diminution of the number of locative bynames, although this argument cannot be pressed too far, as some deserted settlements had already provided locative surnames which persisted within the corpus of Devon surnames (such as Winsor).[36] The contraction of locative surnames was undoubtedly also related to a change in naming patterns. The process can be better illustrated by some longitudinal studies of particular communities over the later middle ages (see below).

The absolute effect of the change can perhaps be illustrated by analysis of the position in two hundreds which were severely affected, Black Torrington and Hartland.

Table 5.7

Locative Surnames: Comparison of the Late Medieval Transition in Hartland and Black Torrington Hundreds

Hartland Hundred

1332

Taxpayers	Locative	% Taxpayers	CP	Hundred	Devon	Outside Devon
168	102	61	76	9	8	9
			75%	8.5%	8%	8.5%
1524–5						
380	56	15	18	11	17	10
			32%	20%	30%	18%

Black Torrington Hundred

1332

505	284	56	161	71	36	16
			57%	25%	13%	5%
1524–5						
1527	379	25	69	151	134	25
			18%	40%	35%	7%

N.B.: % = % of total locative

CP relates to surnames derived from places within the same parish where the surname occurred.

In Hartland parish, considerable depopulation occurred during the later middle ages, resulting in the desertion of a large number of dispersed settlements. This sort of contraction of settlement may have been one cause of the decline in locative surnames. It must be emphasized, however, that the diminution of locative surnames resulted from multi-causal variables, as discussed above.

The pattern of locative surnames in 1524–5 represented the short-distance, localized migration of surnames during the later middle ages. The distance of migration was often only into adjacent parishes. The major *caveat*, however, was the structure of surnames in some upland communities in Haytor Hundred, on the periphery of Dartmoor, around Ashburton, such as Widecombe in the Moor and Buckland in the Moor. In these communities, a high percentage of the locative surnames still related to dispersed settlement within the parish, rather anachronistically redolent of the pattern of 1332 (see further below).[37]

From the analysis above, it seems evident that the vast proportion of locative surnames in Devon were originally associated with dispersed settlement. Consequently, a high proportion of these locative surnames derived from the smaller settlements within Devon, although locative surnames did also originate from larger communities such as Kelly, Bovy, the Huishes, Membury, Hatherleigh and other parishes. The *corpus* of locative surnames in Devon was thus characterised by these minor placenames. In the early sixteenth century, these were the predominant locative surnames according to the criterion of the number of taxpayers bearing them. Even in 1524–5, these locative surnames from minor placenames tended to cluster around their original location. This localization is illustrated in the distribution maps of some twenty such surnames in 1524–5.

The influence of external locative surnames in Devon was minimal; the stock was mainly generated internally. Excluding the surnames of French seignorial taxpayers, the total of taxpayers with locative bynames from outside Devon in 1332 was about 126, or 1.2% of the total of taxpayers. With the Anglo-Norman seignorial surnames, the total of taxpayers amounted to 214, or 2% of the total of taxpayers.

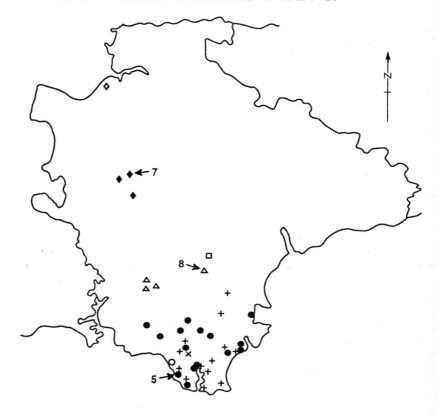

Figure 11(i)
Common Locative Surnames in 1524-5.

Distribution of the locative surname from Northam
- ✦ Incidence of the surname
- ◊ Location of Northam

Distribution of the locative surname from Hingston in Bigbury
- ● Incidence of the surname
- ○ Location of Hingston in Bigbury

Distribution of the locative surname from Wakeham in Aveton Gifford
- × Incidence of the surname
- + Location of Wakeham (including 3 occurrences of the surname)

Distribution of the locative surname from Hannaford in Widdecombe in the Moor
- ▫ Location of Widecombe (including 3 occurrences of the surname)
- △ Incidence of the surname Hanworthy.

Figure 11(ii)
Common Locative Surnames in 1524–5.

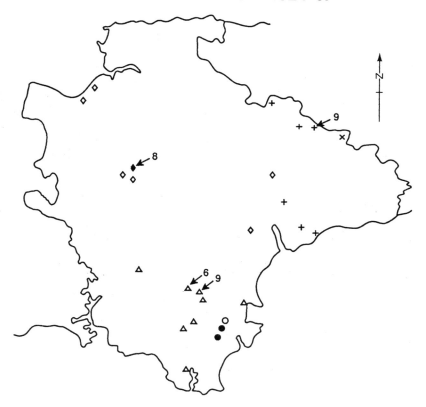

Distribution of the locative surname from Sharpham (House) in Ashprington
- ○ Location of Ashprington (including 5 occurrences of Sherpham)
- ● Incidence of the surname

Distribution of the locative surname from Trykehay in Churchstanton
- × Location of Churchstanton
- + Incidence of the surname.

Distribution of the ? locative surname Wyndgate, Wynyeatt and variants △

Distribution of the locative surname from Medland in Hatherleigh
- ♦ Location of Hatherleigh (including 8 occurrences of the surname)
- ◇ Incidence of the surname

Figure 11(iii)
Common Locative Surnames in 1524–5.

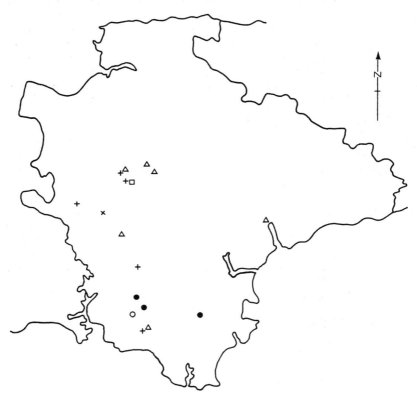

Distribution of the locative surname Sholbeare, Shulbeare and variants from Shillibear (deserted hamlet) in Meavy
        ○ Location of Meavy (including 1 occurrence of the surname)
        ● Incidence of the surname

Distribution of the locative surname from Axworthy in Thrushelton
        × Location of Thrushelton
        + Incidence of the surname Arkysworthy

Distribution of the locative surname from Wadland in Ashbury
        □ Location of Ashbury
        △ Incidence of the surname

Figure 11(iv)
Common Locative Surnames in 1524–5.

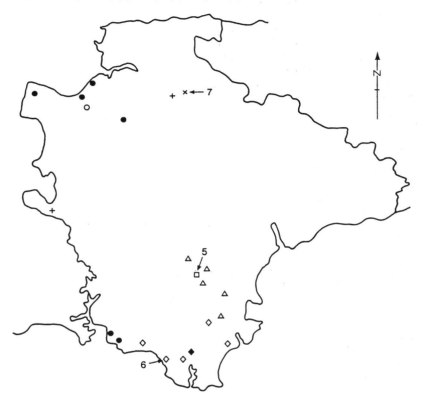

Distribution of the locative surname from Galsworthy in Buckland Brewer
- o   Location of Buckland Brewer (including 3 incidences of the surname)
- ●   Incidence of the surname

Distribution of the locative surname from Clatworthy in South Molton
- x   Loaction of South Molton (including 7 occurrences of the surname)
- +   Incidence of the surname

Distribution of the locative surname from Natsworthy in Widdecombe in the Moor
- □   Location of Widdecombe (including 5 occurrences of the surname)
- △   Incidence of the surname

Distribution of the locative surname from Lidstone in Buckland - Tout - Saints
- ◆   Location of Buckland - Tout - Saints
- ◇   Incidence of the surnames

Figure 11(v)
Common Locative Surnames in 1524–5.

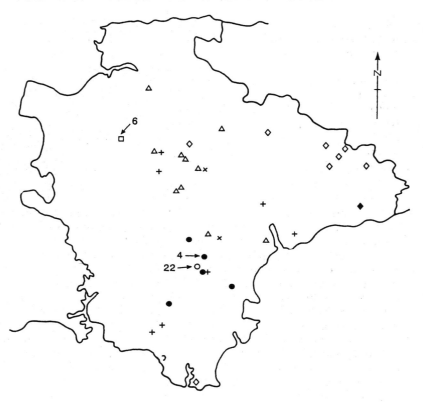

Distribution of the locative surname from Colyford in Colyton
     ◆ Location of Colyton
     ◇ Incidence of the surname

Distribution of the locative surname from Longworthy in Widdecombe in the Moor
     o Location of Widdecombe (including 22 occurrences of the surname)
     ● Incidence of the surname

Distribution of the locative surname Coplestone (either Colebrooke or Bridford)
     × Location of Colebrooke and Bridford (Colebrooke includes one occurrence
         of the surname)
     + Incidence of the surname

Distribution of the locative surname from Bramblecombe
     □ Location of Bramblecombe (including 6 occurrences of the surname)
     △ Incidence of the surname

Table 5.8

Non-Devon Locative Bynames in 1332

Category	No. of taxpayers	% of external locative bynames
Anglo-Norman seignorial	88	41
Continental generic	21	10
Continental regional	15	7
England placenames	31	15
Cornish	24	11
Welsh	15	7
Irish	9	4
Scot*	6	3
le Jeu	4	2
Engleys	1	0.5

* However, this could also be a personal name (OE).

The lay subsidy may, however, be an under-representation of the Cornish, Welsh or Irish, if some of these bynames were borne by poorer social groups. The Anglo-Norman seignorial locative surnames have been discussed above. The continental generic bynames included Frensh and Fraunceys (although the implication of these bynames is problematical), Flemyng, Gascoigne (2), Britayne, Lombard, Bourgoynoun, Peyteuyn (3), and more specifically Aungers (3), Toulous (2), and Boloigne. Fleming was concentrated in north Devon, which suggests that it was closely associated with seignorial bearers; the rest reflect commercial contacts.

Bynames from specific placenames elsewhere in England were insignificant in 1332, but the incidences conformed to several clusters. Bynames from places along the south coast of England were confined to the coastal settlements in the South Hams and east Devon, reflecting commercial contacts. Winchelsea, for example, occurred twice in East Budleigh Hundred and once in Haytor; Bosham (also Sussex) in Ermington Hundred. Bynames from places in Somerset were concentrated close to the county boundary, predominantly in North Tawton Hundred, where Wellington occurred three times and Mollington once. De Troubrigg', however, would seem to derive from Trobridge in Crediton rather than from Wiltshire.[38] Huntingdon, on the other hand, does not seem to have related to Huntingdon (Warren) in Devon, since the earliest known reference to this placename is of the fifteenth century.[39] Windsor in Devon, nevertheless, although only recorded as a placename from the 1520s according to the research of the English Place-Name Society, must derive from that hamlet in Devon rather than from

Berkshire.[40] Accordingly, bynames derived from places elsewhere in England accounted for only 0.3% of the total taxpayers in 1332, and this figure illustrates the localized nature of Devon society and the lack of penetration of external naming patterns until much later.

Bynames from the west, from Cornwall, were almost exclusively generic, although some may have been specific (Trenghier, Tremenet, Tregony, and possibly Trewynt). Penris is more likely to have its etymology in Penrose in Black Torrington Hundred than from Cornwall (or Wales).[41] The predominant forms of Cornish bynames were thus de Cornubia, Cornyssche, Cornwaille, Corneys and Corneis, or Cornu and variants. Like the other generic ethnic bynames (Waleys, Walsh, Irlande, Irreys), the distribution of Cornish bynames was throughout Devon, but with some concentration in the north and west. The numbers, however, were very small.

The impact of external locative surnames had not increased significantly by 1524–5. Then, some 1.5% of taxpayers bore this kind of surname, compared with 1.2% in 1332 (excluding in both cases Anglo-Norman seignorial surnames). The pattern, because of the higher absolute numbers, is, however, more discernible.

Table 5.9
'Origins' of External Locative Surnames in 1524–5

Location	No. of taxpayers	% of total external locative
Dorset	24	5.6
Wiltshire	6	1.4
Somerset	22	5.1
Guernsey	12	2.8
Cornwall	112	26.0
'Northern'	14	3.2
Other English specific	75	17.4
'England' (generic)	9	2.1
Continental	68	15.8
Welsh	51	11.8
Ireland	23	5.3
Scot	15	3.5

Where 'Northern' includes Northeren and Norreys; Other English specific comprises origins further east and north than Somerset or Wiltshire; 'England' generic consists of Ynglande and variants.

The figures for other specific English placenames relate almost exclusively to the south coast of England: from ports on the south

coast 23 (30.7%); from other inland places in the south of England 7
(9.3%); from the midlands and north 28 (37.3%); Buckingham 17
(22.7%). Combined, the surnames derived from the midlands and
the north comprised only 9.8% of all external locative surnames,
although the surname Buckingham had a high incidence for a
single surname.

The extrinsic surnames were clustered in Devon, with surnames
from the south coast and Guernsey concentrated in the South Hams
and east Devon, still reflecting the commercial linkages. Those from
the midlands and north tended to be confined to the northern
perimeter of Devon. The clusters of these surnames in 1524-5 is
represented on the map. Buckingham was restricted to north Devon
with the exception of two occurrences in Lifton Hundred.
Northampton was confined to east Devon. Waymouth occurred 17
times, located exclusively in the South Hams, especially at Cockington, Coffinswell and Brixham, adjacent coastal parishes in Haytor
Hundred. The surnames from Somerset — Wellington, Quantock,
Bridgwater, Portbury — were concentrated in north Devon. Even in
the early sixteenth century, therefore, these surnames were localized
and clustered at their point of entry into Devon. Their penetration
had not advanced very far. To some extent, this distribution was
influenced by the fortunes of individual families, but the pattern also
suggests the very localized social organisation within Devon. The
influence of external (that is, non-Devon) locative surnames was
rather insignificant.

The development of occupational bynames during the later
middle ages has significance for a number of reasons. Firstly, there is
the question of dialect terms, discussed by Fransson and Thuresson,
and possibly encompassing such occupational bynames as Tucker,
Helier, Dyer, Webbe or Webber, Crokker, and Clouter.[42] In the early
fourteenth century, before bynames had developed generally into
hereditary surnames, they may have derived from and reflect the
regional economy at that time, by comparison with the rank order of
such bynames in other regions. Perhaps more important, however,
are later developments in the regional economy or economies of
Devon, particularly the expansion of some specialised 'industries',
such as the production of woollen cloth, the extractive industries (tin
and quarrying), and leather. These industries had varying influences
on bynames and surnames within the regional community. Some
produced large quantities of occupational surnames which
'ramified' throughout the county, whilst others had little impact on
the nomenclature of the county. In a few cases, the occupational
surname remained extremely localized.[43]

Figure 12
The Distribution of Common Locative Surnames from Outside Devon in 1524.

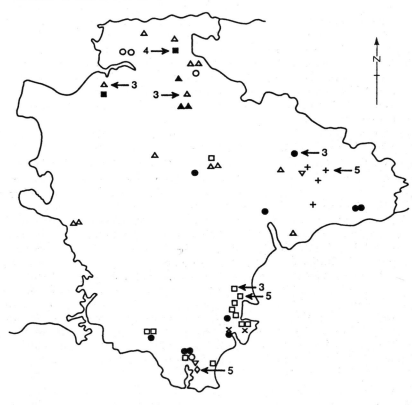

+	Northampton (Northants)	▲	Wellington (Somerset)
△	Buckingham (Bucks)	■	Quantock (Somerset)
□	Weymouth (Dorset)		
●	Guernsey		
×	Winchester (Hants)		
○	Chichester (Sussex)		
▽	Bridport (Dorset)		
◇	Winchelsea (Sussex)		

Tucker was the dialect term for fullers in the south west of England, compared with fuller in eastern England and walker in the northern region of the country.[44] The Latin form, however, occurred briefly in Exeter in the thirteenth century, in the guise of Thomas *fullo*, and at Hockworthy in the person of Michael *fullo*, and isolated examples of fulle and fullonere occurred in the lay subsidy of 1332. On a manor of Newenham Priory, a rental recorded Richard *fullonarius* who held a fulling mill in 1293.[45] Moreover, during the fifteenth century, the surname Walker intruded into east Devon, but only in isolated instances. In the coinage of tinners in 1523, however, two Walkers were assessed, but may have been immigrants into Devon.[46] Tucker was the exclusive byname and surname derived from this activity and had a profound effect on the naming pattern of Devon. The allied activity of weaving was represented in the byname Webbe(r), although Wever was also introduced in the fifteenth century.[47] The form with the suffix -ster did not appear in Devon, as -ster bynames here were infrequent and related to a specific context and gender.[48] Similarly, dyer (degher) remained the predominant byname, although in 1332 lister occurred in five instances.[49] According to Fransson, lister belonged to eastern England, and its incidence in Devon was transient.[50] Helier was associated with the quarrying and slate industry in the south west, and became a characteristic byname. The Latin term *sutor* constantly appeared in the vernacular as clouter or clouterman, although from the fifteenth century the byname cordwainer was introduced into Devon, probably in association with alien residents, in particular the Dutch.[51] Nevertheless, the Latin form, Sutor, persisted as a byname and surname in Devon into the early modern period. Similarly, the Latin form Pistor (more usually Pestor or Pester) continued beside the vernacular Baker. These two Latin forms were not confined to the middle ages but entered the modern stock of surnames in the county.

The significance of crocker or crokker dialectally is more ambivalent. In 1332, potter occurred amongst the taxpayers 19 times, crokker 16, but some metonymic forms also occurred (crok, crokke and crouk, but not pott, which might in any case have derived from the personal name Pot). The divergent usage may have reflected different occupational functions; potters may have been predominantly urban and crockers rural. The former may also have been distinguished since they produced metal pots as well as earthen, and their product may have been of a higher quality. Some dialectal difference may also have been involved.[52] The placename element potter occurs throughout England, except the south west; the element crocker, however, occurred in placenames predominantly in the south and west, in Oxfordshire, Sussex, Herefordshire, Wiltshire and Devon. The pattern of the distribution of potters and crockers in 1332 is not consistent with the possible differences of function. The two terms were used indiscriminately, it seems, in east Devon; on a manor of Newenham Priory there were listed Richard Potter', William le Croker, John le Pottere, *Relicta Thome le pottere*, another John Pottere and William Crocker.[53] Potters did occur in the urban context in Teignmouth, Ilfracombe, Exeter, Totnes, Ashburton, Teigncombe, Ottery St Mary, and on the ancient demesnes of East Budleigh and Axminster. Crocker, however, appeared in other towns, Kingsbridge, Plympton (3), Tavistock (3), Bideford (2), and Honiton, as well as in the rural manors which formed part of the boroughs of South Molton, Colyton and Ashburton. Potter equally occurred in many rural manors.

Difference in the quality of the product may still have been important, but it is difficult to assess the socio-economic position of the bearers of the byname. Much of the industry was dispersed in rural vills, and was probably a by-employment. Some crockers may have been either landless or smallholders; production may have been seasonal and gender-related within the household. For these reasons, the lay subsidy of 1332, because it was wealth-specific, undoubtedly excluded many of the poorer crockers and potters. The bynames are therefore under-represented. The nature of the craft, seasonal and a dual occupation, probably meant that it had less impact on the development of surnames. Some insight into the nature of the craft, however, can be elicited from the court rolls of Uplyme. Here, Joan la Crockestere was mentioned in 1340 as the previous tenant of a messuage and two and a half acres of land. Her position may therefore concur with the concept of the poor female, crocker-cottager, although, if she was a widow, she may have assumed the byname of her late husband. Walter Crockere occurred later on the manor, holding a cottage in the 1360s, but had probably died by 1387, when he is mentioned as the previous tenant. By that time, however, the byname may have become hereditary, not reflecting actual occupation. At Uplyme, however, the byname seems to suggest that crockers, perhaps by comparison with potters, were small tenants with a dual occupation.[54]

By 1332, many occupational bynames were becoming asyndetic. Only about 17% of such bynames were then prefixed by the definite article 'le'. It is possible that, as in Exeter, this transition from syndetic to asyndetic reflected the increasing heritability of such bynames, but it may simply have been part of a more general change in the form of bynames. In the case of occupational bynames, however, the transition seems to have been more precocious than in the case of locative or topographical. Equally, however, nicknames had predominantly become asyndetic, without the prefix 'le'.

In 1332, only 10% of taxpayers bore occupational bynames, including those from office or status, but these latter accounted for only 1%. Excluding bynames derived from the woollen cloth industry, the rank-order does not exhibit a regionally specialised economy. The list is dominated by the common occupations of any region, but the crafts associated with leather and woodland are represented.

Table 5.10

Rank Order of Occupational Bynames in 1332 excluding Woollen Cloth

More than ten occurrences for each byname

Total taxpayers: 10614

Smith	34	Chepman	18
Faber	32	Skynner	18
Taillour	34	For(e)ster	11
Cissor	32	Wodeward	5
Mouner	3	Shepesman	1
Mileward	24	Shephurd	9
Molendinarius	12	Lambard	4
Muleward	7	Bercarius	2
Baker	29	Woleward	1
Pistor	2	Hurdwyk	2
Pestour	5	Hurde(r)	2
Cook, Cocus	35	Cowherde	2
Potter	19	Maysterhyne*	1
Crokker	16	le Hyne	6
Soper	29	Parson	13
Clerk, Clericus	28	Marshal	12
		Haiward	10
Hoper	25	Tanner	10
Carpenter	15	Tournour	10
Coruyset	2		
Sutter	10		
Sutor	5		
Clouter	5		

* This unusual byname occurred at Stoke Fleming; it recurred there in an extent of a third of the same manor in 1374 and Hamon(d) Maisterhyne appeared in the court rolls in the 1380s and early 1390s.[55]

The most formative occupational influence on the pattern of surnames in later medieval Devon was the expansion of the woollen cloth industry. This industry had existed in Devon from at least the twelfth century. Production was concentrated in the north of the county, producing coarser cloths, and, later, in east Devon, specializing in finer cloths. Although the productive side of the industry was rural in the later middle ages, commercial control was exercised from the major towns. In the aulnage accounts of 1394-5, 75 merchants were assessed in Devon. The three leading merchants then, all based in Barnstaple, controlled one third of the trade. The main customs port for the south west was Exeter, although separate accounts were enrolled for Plymouth from 1404. The volume of exports increased from a nominal level in c.1350 to over 20,000 cloths c.1500, controlled almost exclusively by denizens, and directed mainly to markets in western France and the Iberian peninsular.[56]

The extent to which different processes in the manufacture affected the pattern of naming in Devon varied. The most profound influence was exerted by tucker. The absolute number of taxpayers called Tucker increased from 38 (0.35% of all taxpayers) in 1332 to 182 (0.65%) in 1524-5. This level in 1332 was higher than for the equivalent bynames in other counties producing woollen cloth, such as Lancashire and Yorkshire.

Table 5.11
Incidence of Equivalent Occupational Bynames for Fulling in 1327-32[57]

Surname	County	Incidence per 1000 taxpayers
Walker	Lancashire	3.0
Walker	Yorks WR	2.5
Walker	Warwickshire	1.0
Walker	Staffordshire	0.5
Tucker	Devon	3.5
Fuller	Norfolk	3.1*
Fuller	Suffolk	2.7*

* The total number of taxpayers is not known, but was probably about 10,000 in each county; in both, Fuller was the most numerous occupational byname.

Figure 13
The Distribution of the Surname Toker (Tucker) in 1524.

The widespread distribution of the surname by 1524-5 testifies to the impact of the occupation. The surname was heavily represented in most regions of Devon, except the central massif, and the density of its distribution reflected the general density of population in Devon. Its representation was slightly more concentrated in the cloth-manufacturing districts and less intense in those areas not directly involved in manufacture. By and large, the incidence was scattered, that is there was usually not more than one taxpayer called Tucker in each parish. Some concentrations did exist, and are illustrated by the matrix table.

Table 5.12

Frequency of the Surname Tucker in 1524-5

Number of incidences per parish	Number of parishes
1	61
2	26
3	5
4	4
5	1
6	1
7	0
8	1
9	1
10	1

The surname never became a core surname within a parish. This relative lack of concentration perhaps reflected still the scattered distribution of the occupation, since there would often have been only one fulling mill within each community. The highest incidence of the surname occurred at Membury (6 incidences, 8.5% of the taxpayers), Tiverton, (9, 3.1%), Morchard Bishop (8, 8.1%), and Crediton (10, 2.3%). *In toto*, the surname occurred 182 times in 1524 as Toker, 11 as Tokerman, three as Tockett and once as Tucke. In 1332, the 38 instances had been distributed throughout 28 parishes; by 1524-5, the incidence was through 101 parishes. In 1332, the bearer of the byname was probably more likely to have pursued the occupation, as Toker may not have become comprehensively an hereditary surname. By 1524-5, its incidence owed something to the fortunes of individual families and kinship networks as well as to the original distribution of the industry.

No other process had the same impact on naming within the county, although Dyer also became a widely distributed surname from 12 occurrences in 1332.[59] Although Toser and Webbe existed,

they did not influence naming so greatly.[60] The commercial surnames — Mercer, Draper — remained fairly concentrated and
minor, since they represented only a limited and controlled part of
the industry.[61] The reasons for this differential impact was, initially,
the organisation of the industry, and, also to some degree, the
fortunes of individual families during the later middle ages. Fulling
was probably a full-time occupation, whilst weaving, teasing, card-
ing and other processes were by-employments. Although the capital
investment may not have been high, a fulling mill was required for
tucking. It is possible that mills may have been used for different
processes, according to economic conditions. Tin mills may thus
have been converted to tucking mills and vice-versa. Between 1350
and 1500, 120 fulling mills have been detected in Devon, of which
only a quarter are known to have been in existence before 1400.[62] An
interesting aspect of the surname Tucker is that, even during the later
middle ages, it continued in some cases to be associated with the
process. Tavistock Abbey, for example, leased a fulling mill to three
generations of a Tucker family between 1416 and 1517.[63] At
Werrington, in 1462, John Toker was involved in an action of
covenant with John Tregarell

> de eo quod non fregit ei conuencionem promittendi ei j
> molendinum fullonicum et j Racke per plegium J Cotell.[64]

And at Priorton

> Thomas Toker tenet ij molendina unum bladarium et aliud
> fullonicum.[65]

This correlation of surname and activity in the later middle ages may
have reflected either the continuous association of some families
with fulling mills, or may be testimony to a persistent flexibility of
some surnames, whereby the surname was adopted on taking up the
occupation.

Table 5.13
Comparison of the Incidence of the Surname Tucker in 1332 and 1524-5[58]

| Date | Incidence | | % | Total |
	Total number	Per 1000 taxpayers	taxpayers	taxpayers
1332	38	3.6	0.35	10614
1524-5	182	6.5	0.65	28000+

The factor increase in the population of taxpayers between 1332 and
1524-5 was 2.8, but the surname Tucker increased by a factor of 4.8.
Although the taxable base was different in 1332 and 1524-5, yet the
factor increase does reflect the diffusion of the surname.

By contrast with the high numbers of Tuckers in 1524–5, Webbe occurred only 93 times in 63 different parishes, almost exclusively rural, although there were concentrations at Tiverton (5), Pyworthy (5) and Broadhempston (8). Almost a third of the occurrences were located in east Devon (30 of 93), partly reflecting the concentration of the woollen cloth industry in the later middle ages, but also owing something to the fortunes of individual families during the later middle ages. Dyer (in this form, no longer Degher) occurred at least 50 times, in 34 parishes. Again, a third (18 of about 50 incidences) was concentrated in east Devon. The distribution generally correlated to that of Webbe. Both surnames occurred in predominantly rural areas, with often only one incidence per parish in the lists of taxpayers in 1524–5. At this date, therefore, the distribution of the surnames may still have reflected the location of the processes. The impact of the processes on surnames, however, was relatively low, perhaps reflecting the nature of the processes as by-employment. The other functions in the industry had a more marginal influence on bynames and surnames. Draper occurred only 14 times (in 10 parishes), the incidences not correlating at all with where the actual occupation would be expected: they were often in rural vills rather than urban centres, and half occurred in Hartland and Black Torrington Hundreds. Similarly, Toser (teaser) had little influence on surnames: only 15 incidences amongst the taxable population of more than 28000.[66]

Several of the processes involved in the production of woollen cloth thus had only minimal impact on the formation and distribution of specific surnames in Devon, with the exception of Tucker. Their marginal influence may be attributed to the nature of the occupation — a by-employment. The failure of the tin industry to produce significant numbers of distinctive occupational surnames in Devon may have resulted from the same situation.[67] Tin, despite becoming a principal industry of Devon, remained a predominantly seasonal occupation and by-employment.[68] To some extent, the industrial base in Devon was superseded by activity in Cornwall during the later middle ages, but extraction and smelting continued as a distinctive occupation in Devon through into the seventeenth century. The tinners were exempt from taxation, but were subjected to lay subsidies in the mid fourteenth century. The lists of coinages and great courts allow the recovery of some of their bynames and surnames.[69]

The lay subsidy of 1339 included the bynames of some 444 men assessed as tinners.[70] Of these, 274 were taxed in rural parishes, 75 in taxation boroughs, and 95 on ancient demesne. The total number of those assessed as tinners in 1339 was equivalent to about 4% of all the other taxpayers in the lay subsidy of 1332. Since tinners had been previously exempt from taxation, however, some non-tinners may have claimed the status of tinners to avoid taxation. It is not absolutely certain, therefore, whether all those listed were actually tinners. The coinage rolls of the sixteenth century usually comprised over a thousand names, although the exact number of individuals is difficult to assess since a number of tinners recurred throughout the rolls. The reason is that each different piece of tin submitted at each Stannary town for coinage, was listed separately.[71] Moreover, the coinage of 1523 consisted of only about 479 individual tinners, so its comprehensiveness may be suspect.[72] The list of jurates at the great court on Crockerntor on 11 September 1494 provides additional selected surnames, as does the list of subscribers to the Guild of St Katherine of Tinners.[73]

In 1339, those who were probably actual tinners can be ascertained from the low sums at which they were assessed, many at only 3d., others up to 1s. About half were assessed at 1s or below, concentrated in Holne, Peter Tavy, Whitchurch, Sampford, Meavy, Tavyton and South Tawton. The level of assessment in the boroughs was higher, reflecting, perhaps, a more commercial rather than productive interest. Some individuals assessed at Barnstaple and in Shebbear and Shirwell Hundreds, were either not tinners or had a commercial role in tin, reflected also in the level of their assessment.[74] None of the bynames of the tinners derived from their stated occupation, except perhaps Richard Broker, of Tavistock, assessed at 18s., reflecting the commercial role of one of the Stannary Towns. The bynames correlated to a large extent with those of the other taxpayers of Devon assessed in the lay subsidy of 1332, with a very similar taxonomy (see table). Nine percent of the tinners of 1339 bore occupational surnames, the same proportion as the other taxpayers of 1332.

Table 5.14
Taxonomy of the Bynames of those Assessed as Tinners in 1339[75]

Classification	No. of taxpayers	% of total taxpayers
Locative	160	36
Topographical	79	18
Personal	87	20
Occupational	41	9
Nicknames	46	10
Relationship	3	>1
Uncertain	9	2
Illegible	19	4
Total	444	100

Only 9% of those assessed as tinners in 1339 bore occupational bynames, but all were derived from other activities: yetman, tucker, pipere, pottere, harpere, forster and forestere, heliere, sopere, crokere, drapere, for example. The implications are therefore that either these bynames had already developed into hereditary surnames or the tinners had other by-employments, or, more likely, both influences bore upon tinners' names.

By 1523, the entire corpus of tinners' surnames had changed. Very few of the bynames of 1339 recurred in the coinage of 1523. In particular, the locative surnames of tinners in 1523 differed almost completely from those in 1339. In this turnover of names, the pattern concurred with the general change in Devon as a whole.

Table 5.15
Taxonomy of Surnames of Tinners in 1523[76]

Stannary	Total tinners	Locative	%	Occupational	%	Topographical	%
Chagford	77	30	39	14	18	3	4
Ashburton	154	52	34	16	10	9	6
Plympton	100	19	19	12	12	7	7
Tavistock	148	55	37	15	10	9	6
Total	479	156	33	57	12	30	6

The distinctive feature of the taxonomy of tinners' surnames in 1523, however, was the very high level of locative surnames, principally derived from very localized hamlets. At Chagford, such surnames were held by 39% of the tinners in the coinage, at Ashburton 34%, and 37% in Tavistock. This level of locative surnames, derived from local dispersed settlement, related back to the pattern in the fourteenth century, and was different from the lower level of locative surnames (26%) held by the other taxpayers of Devon in 1524–5. Moreover, many of the surnames of tinners were isonymous within the local communities. At the coinage at Ashburton, for example, tin was presented by eight Langworthies, seven Mans, five Wegers, and four Wynyates, exactly those surnames which dominated the communities around Widecombe at this time. These same surnames recurred at the other Stannaries also, but those coinages also had their own concentrations of surnames, such as Seynthill, Lugger, Elforth, *et al.*[77] The same surnames dominated the great court of 1494 and the guild of tinners. At Crockerntor in 1494, for example, the jurates for Asburton included Brabam (Abraham), Bearde, Hamlyn (2), Carpenter, Miller, Voxford,

Thamlyn (Tomlyn), Hanworthy, Langworthy (2), Wyndeyeate, all isonymous surnames around Widecombe; moreover at Chagford, another Langworth and Hamlyn.[78] At Ashburton in the mid sixteenth century, the largest coinages were presented by Robert Hamlyn and Richard Langworthy, both isonymous surnames in the area around Widecombe.[79] The Stannary at Tavistock was dominated by the Petersfield kinship group from 1512 through to 1642.[80] In this respect, the pattern of surnames of tinners in Devon by the early sixteenth century was particularly distinctive.

The development of the surname Salter during the later middle ages is representative of the localization of very specific and unusual surnames in Devon at that time. The reasons for its localization may reside both in the fortunes of individual families during the late middle ages, but also, to some extent, in its very circumscribed origins. Its localization persisted through the early modern period. The surname was restricted, it seems, to a prescribed geographical area in east Devon, possibly at the routes from Somerset (and the West Midlands) into Devon.

In 1332, the byname occurred at Rawridge, Dawlish and (in the syndetic form le Salter) Morebath, apparently concentrated in east Devon, although the figures are minute. By 1524–5, the surname was borne by 36 taxpayers, concentrated in 15 parishes in a corridor in east Devon. The most intensive concentration was at Buckerell (six of 36 taxpayers), Feniton (two), Plymtree (six of 47), Payhembury (six of 67, but the list is defective), and Cullompton (five of 245). In these five parishes were thus concentrated 70% of the incidences of the surname. In the lay subsidy of 1543–6, taxpayers bore the surname in 18 parishes, of which two thirds were located in the same corridor in east Devon. In Payhembury, 11 of the 61 taxpayers were called Salter. In the subsidy of 1581, the surname occurred in 14 parishes, 13 being in the same corridor. By 1674, the surname had become slightly more diffused, now occurring in 28 places. In many of those parishes into which it seems to have been introduced recently, the surname was borne by poor inhabitants exempt from the hearth tax of 1674, as at Halberton, Uffculme, Crediton, Great Torrington, Lifton, Kenton, Ashburton and Highweek. The diffusion may therefore have resulted from the migration of the poor, in some cases possibly betterment migration from rural to urban parishes. In these parishes, the surname was represented by a single person in the listing for the hearth tax.

Figure 14
The Distribution of the Surname Salter: 1524–1674.
(Taxation Assessments)

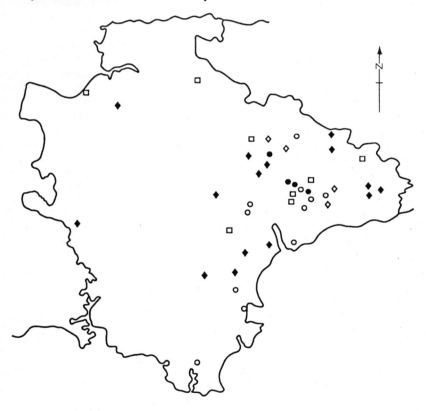

○ 1524 lay subsidy
○ 1524 lay subsidy (several taxpayers)
□ 1543-6 lay subsidy additional to distribution in 1524
◇ 1581 lay subsidy additional to distribution in 1524-46
◆ 1674 hearth tax additional to distribution in 1524-81

Table 5.16

Incidence of the Surname Salter in Taxation Listings 1332–1674

Taxation	No. of taxpayers with the surname	Of which in east Devon	No. of places of incidence	Of which in east Devon
1332	3	2	3	2
1524–5	36	29	15	9
1543–6	46	40	18	13
1581	27	26	14	13
1674	48	27	28	15

The taxation lists were produced for different purposes, so that there is some inconsistency; the taxation of 1581 was also an under-enumeration.

The very gradual diffusion of the surname reflects in part the exclusiveness of its origins. The occupation of saltmaking in Devon suffered a decline during the later middle ages. In 1086, numerous saltpans were located along the coast of Devon, principally in east Devon and the South Hams, but to a lesser degree in the Taw-Torridge estuary in north Devon. These pans were recorded in Domesday Book in 22 places and implied in six others. A total of 61 saltworkers were mentioned, including 33 at Otterton and 11 at Seaton. Some inland manors had contributory saltpans on the coast. The antiquity of this industry is reflected in a number of placenames in east and south Devon.[81] The industry here, however, was smaller than in the counties along the east coast of England.[82] Production in Devon was devastated by the importation of salt from the Bay of Borgneuf during the later middle ages. By the fifteenth century, substantial quantities of Bay salt were being imported to Exeter by Breton merchants. Until the late fourteenth century, Exeter was second only to London as an entrepot for imported salt, but during the fifteenth century, was superseded by Bristol and Southampton.[83] North west Devon was dependent by the fourteenth century on salt transshipped from east Devon.[84] Bay salt was coarse, not a suitable table salt, which still had to be sought from the wiches, presumably imported along the land routes into east Devon. It was precisely here that the surname Salter became concentrated.

The concentration also owed something to the fortunes of individual families during the later middle ages; in particular, the Salter family of Payhembury was very influential in the localization of the surname, a process already underway by the late fourteenth century. At that time, Henry Salter was a substantial tenant of lands there. William Salter of Clist William held a tenement of 30 acres called 'yea lond' in the same parish. Ellis Salter held a tenement called 'Hemock ys place'. Additionally, William Malerbe, lord of Feniton, granted to Ellis Salter, his wife Denise and son John, a tenement called Nitheryea in Payhembury, which Henry Salter had held, for a term of three lives. In a rental of *c.*1498, John Salter held 11 acres there. In another rental, in the fifteenth century, Elizabeth Salter and William Salter both held lands called 'le yea', at an annual rent of 30s., whilst Henry Salter held the tenement called 'Hemyokysplace', at an annual rent of 40s.[85] In a division of the lands formerly of Martin Ferrers, the tenants included several Salters. In Charlton, Ellis Salter held a messuage, garden, close called 'Bowode', half the close called 'Horghelond', two closes called 'Grenecliffis', a close called 'Lipilston', another called 'Vyne' and a *virga* (*sic*) of land. At Hill, John Salter held two messuages, a garden, six and a half closes, a meadow, three other closes called 'Bromhill', another called 'Bowton', the meadow called 'Grenemede', a close 'At Crosse', three crofts, a moor, and common of pasture for 100 sheep.[86] An inquisition was taken into 'Hemyokysplace' at Payhembury, *ex parte* William Malerbe

> ther being present Harry Salter being the aige of lxxx yer William Salter off Clist Willm being the aig lxxxx yer

and two other named tenants as well as 'diuers Wother'.[87] The longevity of these Salters must have contributed to their becoming core families in Payhembury in the later middle ages, combined with their substantial holdings of land there.

The importance of the Salters in the vill is confirmed by a memorandum by the lord of the vill, with the simple *incipit* 'Willelmus Salter at Hille.' The memorandum recorded that William held lands at Feniton and elsewhere, but had been evading the obligations which he should have paid, including Peter's Pence. Moreover

> Wher as the sayd William Salter was suyd in the Sher For hurting off a prist within his hous causid the sheriff to strike him out off his bokis Mor ouer when he was byffor the Kynges commissioner Maister Wood etc & euery man made ther Fyne For ther offences For my Faderys sake hit cost hym but .xx.s. Wher he shuld haue payd .xl.s. For he sayd that he was my Fader ys tenaunt.[88]

The Salters were thus very influential in the local community. In 1524, six out of 67 taxpayers in Payhembury were Salters; in 1543-5 11 of 61; in 1581 at least nine; but in 1674 only three were assessed to the hearth tax, of whom two were poor. The concentration of Salters here persisted through the sixteenth century, but by the late seventeenth, the surname had become more diffused.[89]

The development of occupational bynames in Devon during the later middle ages was thus influenced by a number of variables. The specific origins of the occupation — whether it employed large or restricted numbers of people — was one important influence. The nature of the employment was of some importance, since by-employments might have a lesser effect on naming. The fortunes of individual families would also affect the survival and persistence of surnames. These influences have been demonstrated through the different developments of the bynames relating to woollen cloth, tinmining and salters.

Surnames derived from personal names may elucidate the question of downward or upwards cultural conflation, elision or pluralism in late medieval society, as well as cultural diffusion spatially. The adoption of personal names by different social groups, and the timing of their reception by those different sectors of society, may reflect implicitly upon questions of cultural integration or pluralism. Personal names — or at least some specific forms of personal names — may be a more sensitive indicator of those processes than any other form of name. The problem is complicated, however, by the mechanics by which bynames and surnames were derived from forenames or font-names. The transformation may have arisen from the elision of patronymics: so that Robert *filius Willelmi* became Robert William(s) (with or without the genitival inflection) rather than Robert Williamson. In the north of England, such patronyms may have tended to be represented in the vernacular as -son, but in the south and south-west the translation may have been towards bynames from personal names. Thus, in Devon, and adjacent counties, such as Dorset and Somerset, patronymics in -son are extremely rare, whilst bynames derived from personal names quite profuse.

Consideration of the development and changes in bynames derived from personal names during the later middle ages might include the following possibilities. Firstly, what was the relationship between bynames and surnames from personal names and the total stock of bynames and surnames in Devon? Secondly, what was the proportion of bynames and surnames from personal names over the later middle ages? Thirdly, how far was there was a regional variation of these bynames and surnames, which was distinctive to Devon? Fourthly, what was the precise relationship between bynames and surnames derived from personal names, and the stock of personal names in Devon?

The final question is very significant, since changes did occur in the pattern of forenames in Devon (and elsewhere) during the later middle ages. It seems clear that there was no direct correlation between this pattern of forenames and the pattern of bynames and surnames derived from personal names. Even in 1332, some of the most frequent bynames are not evidently derived from frequent forenames. The question therefore arises whether these bynames reflected an earlier pattern of forenames. This implication might be important as the range of forenames in use narrowed during the later middle ages. Nevertheless, there still seems to be no direct correlation between earlier patterns of forenames and the most frequent bynames from personal names. Consequently, one implication might be that some forenames were selectively transformed into bynames, but such a suggestion would run counter to the concept of bynames from personal names being elisions of patronymic bynames.

The question could then be related to regionally significant forenames and consequential bynames. Discounting the very common forenames (John, William, *et al.*), there may have been a second tier of forenames, which became bynames, which may have been distinctive, to some degree, to Devon, which produced such bynames, possibly, as Cole, Saunder(s), Se(a)rle (Serell) and others. These distinctive bynames related back to cultural influences in Devon which affected the formation of forenames, possibly 'ethnic' influences, which became sociological influences, through some degree of downwards cultural conflation. This conflation was not a precise mechanism. In the case of Cole, the important question is the nature of the persistence or extinction of OE and OSc personal names. Additionally, did some of these earlier names have regional importance, which might be expected *ex hypothesi*: such as Alfred (and its variant Alured) or Arthur? Some of these insular names, such as Edmund and Edward, may have initially declined, to experience a recrudescence later from wider cults. The sparsity of OSc personal names in the south-west may be interesting, in that pockets of bynames from that source did continue. The cultural origins of some other forenames were not insular. It is commonly known that a new stock of Continental-Germanic and Christian personal names was introduced into England from the eleventh century and largely displaced the indigenous stock. Below the very common names introduced, some less common ones may have assumed some regional significance. Some may have been introduced from sources other than Normandy, reflecting the cultural diversity of the new nobility in Devon: Breton in particular, such as Joel (Jule, Jole, Jewell). Some OCeltic personal names may have derived from Britanny or from the Celtic fringes around Devon, introducing personal names which became important as bynames such as David (mainly as the hypocoristic Davy), Alan and, to a small degree, Brian. Amongst the insular OCeltic personal names, Colman (hypocoristic of Columban, OIr), had a lesser significance in Devon. Some Welsh names became bynames in Devon, such as Morgan and Maddock. These introductions from outside reflect one aspect of cultural diffusionism. This sort of cross-cultural transmission, is, however, very difficult to document. More easily explicable is the very low impact which women's forenames had in the development of the stock of bynames from personal names, a matter of the sociological position of women.

The influence of lordship and ecclesiastical dedications, even localized cults, had little overt impact. Saints' names (that is, Christian names *stricto sensu*) became established amongst the second tier of forenames and bynames from personal names in the county, but there is little evidence of direct local influence. Martin became an important byname here, but the localized dedications (such as German and Petroc) had a lesser impact. Biblical names were also involved at a lower level, especially Adam, and, to a lesser degree, and possibly through Breton influence, Sampson. Some of these influences were not confined to Devon, but had a wider application.

The persistence of these surnames from personal names through the later middle ages owed something to the fortunes of individual families, as well as to their original formation. The pattern emerging in the early sixteenth century thus developed in the adversity of demographic change and how some kinship groups survived those challenges. Nevertheless, some other developments during the later middle ages suggest some continuing cultural influences. In particular, the high level of hypocoristics in use as surnames, even and especially the more recently introduced Continental-Germanic personal names, suggests perhaps some degree of popular culture, popular perception of naming, and, by this time, some degree of upwards cultural conflation, or at least, cultural pluralism. The infusion of a high proportion of diminutives in bynames may also reflect this popular influence, both with the ME -cok, -kin and the French -el, (double diminutive) -erel, and -en (-on). Indeed, these diminutives were so frequently attached to hypocoristics that, it seems, popular naming was further involved.

The relative proportion of bynames and surnames from personal names altered over the later middle ages. In 1332, about 1150 taxpayers held such bynames, comprising an average of 11% throughout the county (or a median of 9–10% through the Hundreds). These forms were borne more highly in the South Hams and east Devon, ranging from 10% to 21% of the taxpayers.[90] Conversely, they were lower in the west, north and mid-Devon. Consequently, their incidence was in inverse relationship to the density of locative bynames. By 1524–5, surnames from personal names were borne by 16% of taxpayers, but ranging from 7% to 26% in different parts of the county. In direct contrast with the pattern in 1332, these surnames now had the highest incidence in the north, west and mid-Devon, such that they were borne by 18% of taxpayers in Hartland Hundred, 19% in Braunton Hundred, and 26% in Tavistock Hundred, although some parts of east Devon and the South Hams still had high levels.[91]

The patterns were probably multi-causal. One explanation was the relative decline in locative bynames in parts of Devon, leading to a higher proportion of other forms, especially those from personal names. The fortunes of individual kinship groups is another. The levels in east Devon and the South Hams may have resulted from these areas being more open to external cultural influences.

Table 5.17
Distribution of Surnames derived from Personal Names in 1524–5

Hundred	TT	PS	% TT	H(%)	D(%)	IS(%)
East Budleigh	1155	208	18	19	11	8
Colyton	507	71	14	33	8	15
Ottery	250	38	15	29	18	11
Axminster	740	133	18	32	8	14
Hemyock	402	61	15	20	2	30
Hayridge	920	133	15	17	2	5
Tiverton	370	26	7	39	12	8
Halberton	278	33	12	16	6	6
Bampton	451	56	12	23	5	11
West Budleigh	330	33	10	10	6	0
Crediton	713	74	10	11	8	5
Wonford	1850	252	14	19	8	5
Cliston	317	55	17	27	15	4
Witheridge	461	41	9	39	0	10
South Molton	847	102	12	27	7	4
Braunton	1146	214	19	30	8	4
Shirwell	274	38	14	7	3	>1
Shebbear	1050	144	14	31	9	0
Fremington	650	91	14	26	8	6
North Tawton	707*	74	12	21	1.5	5
Hartland	380	69	18	57	14	0
Black Torrington	1527	200	13	24	7	4.5
Lifton	799	129	16	17	13	>1
Tawstock	304	78	26	27	19	5
Roborough	1155	208	18	23	8	2.5
Plympton	663	111	17	16	6	>1

Hundred	TT	PS	% TT	H(%)	D(%)	IS(%)
Ermington	1177	195	17	14	8	1.5
Stanborough	1262	298	24	21	5	2
Coleridge	1650	394	24	13	8	4
Haytor	2050	401	20	22	13	3
Exminster	896	181	20	14	9	5
Teignbridge	991	107	11	20	10	3

Where: TT = total taxpayers; PS = number of taxpayers bearing surnames from personal names; % T = % of taxpayers holding surnames from personal names; H = % of total of surnames from personal names which were hypocoristics; D = % of total of surnames from personal names which were diminutives; IS = % of total surnames from personal names which had the suffix -s (inorganic or genitival).

* Some 100 taxpayers illegible and therefore omitted from these figures. A similar table for 1332 is not worthwhile because of the much smaller numbers.

The formation of bynames and surnames from personal names was a complicated process. In general, the introduction of C-G personal names from the eleventh century brought a radical change in the composition of personal names.[92] The insular names (OE) were gradually displaced over the course of the twelfth century.[93] During the later middle ages, moreover, the actual range of personal names in common use narrowed considerably, with particular domination by John, William and a small number of other names.[94] Influences on this changing pattern may have been diverse: lordship and patronage, cults and saints, patrilineal naming, spiritual kinship, and other variables.[95] The transformation of these personal names into bynames did not seem to follow any direct lineal progression.

5.18

Forenames of the Holders of Knights' Fees in 1242–3
Source: *Book of Fees*, ii, 755-97.

A — Fees arranged by Hundred.

Total holders of fees or parts of fees		223		
Number of different forenames		47		

Rank order:	William	16%		
	John	10%	Roger	7%
	Robert	9%	Henry	5%
	Richard	9%	Sub-total	56%

B — Fees arranged by barony

Total holders of fees or parts of fees	621
Number of different forenames	64

Rank order:

William	14%			
Robert	10%	Ralph	6%
Richard	10%	Henry	5%
John	6%	Roger	5%

The table illustrates the selection of forenames for the issue of families of the lesser nobility in the late twelfth and early thirteenth century. There was a concentration of forenames, which was, however, slightly less marked than amongst the general body of taxpayers in 1332. Some forenames which became significant bynames in Devon, were each borne by less than 1% of the tenants of fees or parts of fees in 1242-3: Alan; Joel; Jordan; Warin; Martin; David (hypocoristic Davy); Alexander (hypocoristic Saunder); Adam; Stephen; Ellis; Benedict (hypocoristic Benet).

Table 5.19

5.19.1 — The Forenames of Male Taxpayers in Selected Hundreds 1332
Rank order

Forename	No. of taxpayers bearing that name	% of taxpayers
John	766	21
William	566	16
Richard	389	11
Robert	310	9
Walter	249	7
Thomas	224	6
Henry	163	5
Roger	160	5

5.19.2 — Statistical Analysis of the same Forenames

N	$\bar{x}$	median	s	Q1	Q3	Min	Max
94	39	4	114	1	14	1	766

Where: N = the number of different fornames; $\bar{x}$ = mean of the number of taxpayers per forename; median = the median number of taxpayers per forename; s = the standard deviation; Q1 = the first quartile; Q3 = the third quartile; min and max = the minimum and maximum incidence of taxpayers for a forename.

The sample of taxpayers in both 5.19.1 and 5.19.2 is 3,625.

The Hundreds selected as a sample are: N Tawton; Witheridge; Crediton; Stanborough; Black Torrington; Hartland; East Budleigh; Colyton; Ermington; and Braunton. The sample is expected to have similar numbers of taxpayers from different parts and *pays* of Devon.

The pattern of forenames amongst Devon taxpayers in 1332 was much more concentrated than amongst the lesser nobility a century earlier, since eight forenames were borne by 77% of the taxable male population. In particular, John and William were held by a much higher proportion of the taxpayers. Whereas Walter had not been prominently held by holders of fees, many taxpayers still bore that forename. The selection of forenames by taxpayers did not therefore directly imitate that of the lesser nobility, although there was a similarity in the narrowing of use. Amongst taxpayers, some 70 forenames occurred fewer than 36 times, that is were each held by less than 1% of taxpayers. Many occurred fewer than five times. Those held by less than 1% of taxpayers included Martin, Ellis, David, Augustine, Benedict, Warin, Laurence, Alexander and Serlo, which all became significant bynames; they also included Edward, Joel, Jordan, Simon, Alan and Andrew.

The same pattern of concentration can be perceived amongst the unfree tenantry on some manors in Devon. At Uplyme, the narrowing of forenames was quite marked between the mid thirteenth and fourteenth century. In the mid thirteenth century, the most frequent forenames had included Richard and Roger (each held by seven tenants), Walter and John (six), Thomas, Philip and William (four). Thus seven forenames were held by about 50% of the tenants. Some unusual forenames still existed: Jordan, Alfred, Beymund, Gervase, Ellis, Seward, Salmay, Reginald, Maci and Gilbert. By the early fourteenth century, the position had altered; John was now held by 14 tenants, accounting thus for 21% of the tenantry. Thomas, William and Robert comprised the second tier, each held by seven tenants. Four forenames now accounted for 50% of the tenantry.

Table 5.20

Stock of Forenames in use at Uplyme

	Mid 13th cent.	Early 14th cent.
Total tenants	77	67
Total different forenames	35	21
Coefficient	2.2	3.2

Source: British Library Add MSS 17450 and 37053.

Table 5.21a

Frequency of Forenames at Berry and Stockleigh Pomeroy in 1293

	Frequency distribution of forenames					TT	TF	Co
Incidence	1	2	3	4	5+			
BP Burgesses	10	4	1	1	2	43	18	2.4
BP Villeins	3	2	1	1	2	29	9	3.2
BP *operarii*	1	2	3			14	6	2.3
BP free	5					5	5	1.0
SP customary	8	1	1	1		18	11	1.6

The frequency distribution shows how many forenames were held
by several tenants. Thus, ten different forenames were each held by
one burgess, but four different forenames were each held by two
burgesses, one forename was held by three burgesses, one forename
by four burgesses, and two forenames were each held by more than
five burgesses. TT = total tenants; TF = total of different forenames;
Co = coefficient (burgesses divided by forenames).

Table 5.21b

The Use of Male Forenames on the Manor of 'Plenynt'

1 — 1302

No. of tenants — 33

No. of different forenames — 18

Coefficient — 1.8

Rank order: Richard (6 tenants), John and Roger (4 each), the rest
only 1-2 tenants (including William — 2 tenants).

2 — Early fourteenth century

No. of tenants — 31

No. of different forenames — 14

Coefficient — 2.2

Rank order: John (9 tenants), Richard and Thomas (4 each), the rest
1-2 tenants (including William — 2 tenants).

Source: BL Arundel MS 17, fos 18v-20r.

By contrast, few of even the most common forenames had produced significant numbers of bynames by 1332. Bynames from
Richard, Henry, Robert, Roger, John , Thomas and William were
respectively held by only 11, 19, 16, 15, 13 and 8 taxpayers. The
second rank of forenames produced much higher numbers of
bynames, as tabulated on following pages.

Table 5.22

Incidence of Bynames from Personal Names in 1332

All taxpayers in Devon (10614)

Byname	Incidence as forename		Incidence as byname
Adam	251		15
Alexander	47	(Alesaundre)	7
		(Saundre)	8
Andrew	39		9
Ellis	54	(Ellis)	15
		(Eliot)	10
David	41	(David)	9
		(Davy)	12
Gilbert	87		8
Martin	39		23
Michael	40		14
Nicholas	220	(Nichol)	12
Philip	57		20
Stephen	133		15
Jordan	36		14

Even some relatively unimportant personal names produced higher numbers of bynames, such as Gerveys (20 incidences as a byname), Giffard (11), Isaac(13), Laurence (11), Matthew (10), Pain and Pagan (13).

There was therefore no exact correlation between popular forenames and common bynames from personal names.

The pattern of surnames from personal names in 1524–5 exhibited a confirmation of these characteristics. The most common surname did not relate in any way to the rank order of forenames in the thirteenth and fourteenth centuries during the formation of bynames.

Table 5.23

Rank Order of Surnames from Personal Names in 1524–5

Surname	Occurrences	% TPS
Martin	170	4
Harry(s)	133	3
Peirs	107	2.5
Waren	100	2.5
Stephen	94	2

Surname	Occurrences	% TPS
Philip	93	2
Adam(s)	90	2
Davy	88	2
Sander	88	2
Benet	86	2
Eliot	81	2
Ellis	70	1.5
William	68	1.5
Nichol	65	1.5
Pain	63	1.5
Richard	60	1.5
Simon	59	1.5
Geoffrey	57	1.5
Thomas	53	1.5
Hodge	53	1.5
Serle	50	1.5

The table excludes hypocoristics and diminutives of William, John and Thomas.

% TPS = % of total taxpayers who bore surnames from personal names. The table lists only those surnames borne by more than 50 taxpayers. Variants (e.g. Serell, Sarle) are included.

In 1524–5, 21 surnames were borne by 40% of the 4,248 taxpayers who held surnames from personal names. Some of these surnames from personal names tended to be localized. Serle occurred throughout 14 Hundreds, but was concentrated in east Devon. It was isonymic in some communities, such as Awliscombe, where it was borne by 12 of the 56 taxpayers, and at Dunsford, where 6 of 85 bore this surname.[96] Consequently, its highest incidence occurred here in Hemyock Hundred. Martin, although dispersed through 25 Hundreds, was more highly concentrated in east Devon and the South Hams; Waren through 25 Hundreds, but highest in Haytor (15 per 1,000 taxpayers); Piers in 22 Hundreds, but highest in the South Hams. Sander existed more widely through 24 Hundreds, with its highest incidence in Hartland Hundred (24 per 1,000 taxpayers) and Hayridge Hundred (10 per 1,000). Davy existed in 25 Hundreds. The distribution of these surnames from personal names was thus higher in east Devon and the South Hams. German was more localized, occurring in eleven Hundreds, whilst Jule (Juyll, Jewell) appeared in 19 Hundreds, but weakly through all.

Some contrast existed in the incidence of these second tier surnames from personal names in the south-western counties, in the
early fourteenth century, although the numbers are so small as to
be possibly insignificant. In 1327 and 1332, for example, Saundres
(as the equivalent of Saunder) occurred only once and twice respectively, the taxable constituency in Dorset being nine-tenths the size of
that in Devon.[97] The incidence was similarly low in Somerset in
1327.[98] By contrast, Terry, derived from Continental-Germanic
Terric, a hypocoristic of Theodoric, was more frequent in Dorset
than in Devon, occurring in Dorset in 22 and 20 instances in 1327
and 1332.[99] Both Davy and German had low incidences in both
Devon and Dorset, however.[100] In Somerset, German was equally
infrequent, but it occurred more frequently as a forename in some
tithings in the manor of Taunton *c.*1245–52.[101] Sampson (Breton)
and Potel (OFr diminutive of Philip) were more evident in Dorset
than Devon.[102]

The formation of bynames from personal names before the early
fourteenth century was influenced by several cultural transitions.
Amongst these was the changing attitude towards native or
indigenous or insular personal names, mainly Old English (OE), but
also some Old Scandinavian (OSc). These types of byname and
personal name persisted at a very low level.[103] In the lay subsidy of
1332, only about 2% of Devon taxpayers bore bynames derived from
these insular personal names, about 166 taxpayers in all, although
the etymology of some bynames is uncertain. If some forms, such as
Dodde, Dobb, Babb, Copp, originated in that way, then some 3% of
taxpayers in 1332 may have borne bynames derived from OE and
OSc personal names.[104] The total stock comprised some 33 personal
names. In rank order, the most frequent was Cole (68), followed by
Ailward (13), Ailmere (6) and Edward (5). The remainder survived in
isolated incidences. In the lay subsidy of Somerset in 1327, some 228
taxpayers bore such bynames; here the total stock consisted of about
62 bynames, but Cole (42 taxpayers) was the most frequent,
followed by Ailward (11), Arthur (12) and Alfred with its equivalent
Alured (12), Siward (11), Osbern (10), and Edward (10). In Dorset, in
1327, 104 taxpayers held similar bynames, about 1% of the total of
taxpayers. Cole comprised some 20% of the taxpayers with bynames
from insular personal names, Osbern 12% and Osmund 7%. In all
three counties, Arthur, Edward and Edmund had a low incidence.[105]
The most significant feature in all three counties, and possibly
Cornwall also, is the higher incidence of the byname Cole, which is
discussed further below. Edward and Edmund had failed to make
an impact on Devon naming by the early fourteenth century, despite
their adoption by the Crown. Neither the cult of Arthur nor Alfred

affected personal naming at that time, although the south-west may have provided the economic basis for the resurgence of Alfred's kingdom.[106] Other aspects of OE personal naming were more evident in Dorset than Devon. The element -wyne occurred much more frequently in Dorset than Devon.[107] There too, and in some other counties within the region of Southern ME dialect, such as Surrey, the element -grom occurred more frequently.[108]

An unusual aspect of Devon bynames was the survival of those derived from OSc personal names, although they existed at a very low level. In Somerset, however, 25 taxpayers held such bynames in 1327, the stock comprising 13 different names (such as Ordlof, Thurkyld, Colbern, Thurstan, Colebrand, Asketil). In Fulford tithing, in the same county, Richard Ketell was a customary tenant c. 1245-52.[109] About 18 taxpayers in Devon in 1332 held similar bynames, whilst contemporary taxpayers in Dorset bore the bynames Thurstan, Anketil, Colswain *et al.* In parts of Cornwall, Colbren was the byname of several tenants in 1334.[110] Their existence in the south-west was unusual, although at a low level.

The overall decline of bynames from insular personal names had occurred well before the early fourteenth century. The survival may have been higher in the twelfth and early thirteenth century, although the evidence is impressionistic rather than quantifiable. When, in 1168, the estates of Roland de Dinant were confiscated, the principal tenants of the manor of Hartland were assessed to the aid for the marriage of the daughter of Henry II, Matilda. Of the 15 tenants listed, 11 bore OE personal names, two Continental-Germanic, and two Biblical ones. In 1166, the *Carte Baronum*, however, included only one knight, Edward de Wotalta, who had an OE personal name.[111] Plaintiffs and deforciants to final concords relating to lands in Devon did include a large number who were known by OE and OSc personal names and derivative bynames: Everard Cole in 1195-6; Matilda daughter of Wolverich, Richard son of Edric, Alured le Mederwiricte in 1198; Edward Beivin in 1199; Ailward son of Edith in 1201. Even in the second and third decades of the thirteenth century, several of these personal names were held by conusors and conusees: Alured the chaplain, Robert son of Osmund, Arthur de Winton, Alward, Richard son of Edmund, all in 1219-20; Edmund de Thudeham in 1224-5; John Turbern in 1228; Gervase Turbern in 1238. In some final concords, the description of the land included the names of the (villein) tenants. At Galmpton in 1198, the four tenants, each holding a ferling, were Walter de la Bara, Robert Haluwe, William Raunde, and Osbert son of Edmund. Two tenants of ferlings at Coffinshayne in 1224–5 were Alured de Fonte and Osbert de Fonte. Those parties to fines who bore insular names seem without exception to have been small, free tenants, at the lower end of the economic spectrum of freedom.[112]

The imputation of the fines is a heavy diminution in the persistence of insular personal names in Devon by the end of the twelfth century. In many cases, the personal name occurred as the patronym of a bearer who had been given a Continental-Germanic personal name: such as Richard son of Edric or Richard son of Edmund. The OE personal names were possibly being eclipsed as unfashionable. Their decline by 1238 amongst those of free status is attested by the names of jurors and suitors to the eyre of that year. Of 640 electors and suitors, only 15 bore indigenous personal names. An even smaller number bore bynames from such personal names.[113] A slightly different aspect, however, is presented by the names of offenders who were presented at the eyre. About 120 had either a forename or a byname of OE or OSc provenance; amongst these, 11 had the forename Alfred, 15 Osbert, and 14 Edward.[114] Osbert may be ambiguous, since it had been current in both England and Normandy before the Conquest.[115] More exotic was Swetric Segar who was presented for theft.[116] The jurors for Plympton Hundred presented Ailward Sampson, Richard Ailwarde, Robert Swein, Osbert the cobbler, Osbert Crespin, Seward Slug, and Edward le Peitevin.[117] Although only a small proportion of those presentments, these instances suggest the continuation of insular personal names amongst the less privileged social groups into the early thirteenth century.

By the late thirteenth century, the level of persistence had diminished further. Of 950 burgesses admitted to the freedom of Exeter before 1348, only ten had such names, limited to the narrow corpus of Edward, Osbert, Edmund and Alfred *als* Alured.[118] Distinctive amongst these, perhaps, were Alured *custos* and Alured Aylward, a clerk, the latter admitted in 1307.[119] In the mid thirteenth century (perhaps *c.* 1265), a small number of tenants in a fragmentary rental of land of the Dean and Chapter in Exeter, had also borne insular names.[120] On the rural manor of Uplyme, in the thirteenth century, only a few tenants had insular forenames or bynames from insular personal names: Alfred de Tudewell, Edward Trus and Walter Edmar.[121] By contrast, Alured and Ailmer were quite common forenames on the manor of Taunton in Somerset *c.* 1245–52, perhaps reflecting a more localized association with the cult of King Alfred.[122] The exclusion of insular names happened fairly swiftly and comprehensively, therefore. These names may have persisted longer amongst lower social groups. Overall, however, such names had only a very limited impact on the formation of bynames and personal names in Devon, with the important exception of the OE personal name Cole. By 1524, Cole and its derivatives accounted for 60% of this residual corpus of surnames derived from insular personal names, whilst Edward, the second most frequent, comprised only 11%.

Table 5.24

Rank Order of Surnames derived from Insular Personal Names in 1524

Surname	No. of taxpayers bearing that surname
Ailward	5
Arthur	9
Cole	160
Coles	5
Collin	83
Collins	4
Edmund	12
Edward	41
Edwards	5
Godwin	2
Herward	23
Ketel	2
Seman	10*
Seward	28*
Swain	6
Thurstan	1
Turpin	15
Total	411+

* Both Seman and Seward are ambiguous, the latter possibly derived from Siward. For Seman, see B Seltén, *The Anglo-Saxon Heritage in Middle English Personal Names, passim*.

+ The total taxable population exceeded 26,000 in 1524.

The displacement of insular personal names was most commonly achieved by newly introduced Continental-Germanic personal names. Even the less usual of these new personal names affected the development of surnames in Devon more importantly than insular personal names.[123]

Table 5.25

Numbers of Taxpayers in 1524 bearing Surnames derived from the less usual C–G Personal Names

(more than 10 taxpayers per name)

Crispin	(12)		Norman	(12)
Geoffrey	(57)		Pain	(63)
Gervase	(22)		Piers	(107)
Hamelin	(36)		Perkin	(12)
Hamond	(28)	(possibly OSc)	Perot	(32)
Harding	(21)		Randel	(59)
Harvy	(36)		Raynold	(45)
Gibb(s)	(40)	(see also Gilbert)	Roland	(10)
Gifford	(13)		Serle	(50)
Gilbert	(24)		Waren	(100)
Gill	(23)	(see also Gilbert)		
Maurice	(42)			
Lewis	(12)			

N.B. 1 — The list includes some OFr hypocoristic forms of C–G personal names, such as Piers and Perot.

2 — Figures in parenthesis refer to the number of taxpayers bearing this surname.

In 1524, some 1,010 taxpayers bore surnames derived from the less usual Continental-Germanic personal names, from a taxable population of more than 26,000. This figure includes the very infrequent forms of surnames such as Corbin, Ilberd, Maynard, Bertram, Clifford, Gamlin, Herbert, Giles, Ingram, Jocelin, Miles, Terry, Vivian and Walrand.

Other 'ethnic' or 'national' influences also affected the pattern of naming in Devon, to smaller or greater degrees. The heterogeneity of the feudal lordships of Devon in the late eleventh century produced some interesting and unusual features in the formation of surnames in Devon, introducing Breton (and from Brittany, possibly also PCeltic) and Flemish forms. It is also possible that some PCeltic forms survived independently within Devon or were introduced from the Celtic fringes surrounding Devon. Cade, for example, has been interpreted as a possible OE hypocoristic of Celtic compounded personal names Cad- (for example, Cadwallader).[124] Cade occurred eight times amongst Devon taxpayers in 1332 and persisted as a byname and surname throughout the later middle ages. By 1524, 33 taxpayers bore this surname, as well as two called Cadding, possibly an associative of Cade. The etymology of Bate is ambivalent, but it too may have derived from PCeltic.[125] The difficulty of interpretation is increased by the form of some of the earlier occurrences. Osborn le Bat is mentioned in the Pipe Roll of 1234; in the Crown Pleas of 1238, presentments were made of Nicholas le Bate, Gilbert le Batur, and Roger le Batur.[126] These forms, however, may be consistent with derivation from an OE uncompounded personal name ultimately received from PCeltic *bat* or *bata*, a cudgel. The other potential etymology, as a hypocoristic of Bartholomew, is more likely even though that personal name was apparently rarely used in Devon. Unlikely is derivation from ON *bati* (fat) in this part of England. In 1332, the byname Bate was borne by seven taxpayers, Bade by one, Batecok, the diminutive form, by seven, Batyn (an associative) by 24. Batyn and Batecok were also each the forenames of a single taxpayer. By 1524, the surname Bate had 23 incidences, Badcock 12 and Batyn 29. Bate occurred in the court rolls of Werrington as a core surname during the later middle ages.[127] In the lay subsidy of 1524, 10 out of 92 taxpayers in North Petherwin had the surname Batte. Other taxpayers named Batte were located then in Okehampton and Lamerton.[128] Even in 1524, therefore, the surname seems to have been concentrated near the county boundary with Cornwall, although the form Batin was more widely distributed. Bate and Cade may thus represent residual PCeltic influence on personal naming in Devon. Other potential PCeltic survivals, Wase, Wade and Charles, occurred only two or three times each in the lay subsidy of 1332. Charles might have originated as a locative byname derived from the PCeltic placename Charles, in Shirwell Hundred. Wase may have persisted at Uplyme through the later middle ages in the form Gache, a core surname within that community.[129]

The most important PCeltic bynames, however, were probably re-imported during the later middle ages, from Breton, Welsh and Irish sources. Bryan occurred very infrequently, only eight times in the lay subsidy of 1524. Davy, by contrast, was much more prolific, accounting for 88 taxpayers in 1524, and David for an additional five. The incidence of Alan (Aleyn) may be complicated by alien, but this surname was also extensive in 1524.[130] Davy and David were introduced into Devon at an early stage. Until the mid thirteenth century, the placename Culm (Davy) remained simply Cumbe, but from at least 1285 had acquired the modifier Davi or David, since it had been held by 1242 by David de Wydeworth'.[131] In the Crown Pleas of 1238, the following had been presented: David the Welshman, David the tailor, another David the Welshman, William David, and Osbert David. By that time, the personal name had developed into a byname, but its origin may still have been reflected by the association with the byname 'the Welshman'.[132] In 1208, David Aaron had been involved in a final concord relating to land in Devon.[133] Two of the suitors to the Crown Pleas of 1238 bore the forename David.[134] By 1332, nine taxpayers had the byname David and 12 Davy, whilst the forename David was held by 41 taxpayers. Amongst the latter, significantly, were enumerated David Walshe, David Irlond and David de Cornwaille.[135] By the end of the later middle ages the hypocoristic form, Davy, had almost completely excluded the extended form, David, both as forename and surname.[136] By 1674, the form David hardly existed at all.[137] Alan had been held by 14 taxpayers as a forename in 1332, and by 18 as a byname. Several offenders and three suitors at the Crown Pleas of 1238 bore the forename. Its introduction into Devon followed the same pattern as David.[138]

Other personal names from the Celtic fringes surrounding Devon had a lesser impact. In this county, Colman seems implicitly a hypocoristic of OIrish Columban, but it was relatively sparsely held. In 1524, only 20 taxpayers bore this surname, although it had been a core surname at Werrington at the end of the later middle ages (1462–1524).[139] Another OIr personal name, Patrick, occurred only once in 1524 as a surname.[140] These personal names featured so insignificantly since most of the innumerable Irish immigrants into Devon were known by a generic locative byname — Irish, Irlond or similar. Similarly, most Welsh immigrants were accorded a generic locative byname, although a small number introduced Welsh personal names which became established in a small way in the lexicon of names in Devon. Whilst the static population in Wales persisted with patronymic naming patterns, the emigrants to Devon largely accepted a different naming pattern, but a few migrants bore bynames from personal names which may have originated as patronyms.[141] Amongst the taxpayers of 1332, sporadic Welsh personal names occurred, such as Morgan and Maddock (each held by one taxpayer, although Maddoc was also the forename of another taxpayer), Kinnock and its variants, and, more problematically, Iuon and variant forms (Hywyn, Iuoun). A Robert Morgan had held land in Romansleigh in the early thirteenth century. The byname and surname Morgan persisted through much of the fourteenth century at Uplyme in east Devon.[142] In 1238, Iwein de Remstorre, Iwein Bedel and Iwein le Bleu were presented for a breach of the peace in Bampton Hundred, as elsewhere was Iwan son of Ascelo.[143] By 1524, Maddock was held by 29 taxpayers as a surname, Evan(s), Ewan *alias* Ewin by 33, but Morgan only by three.[144] The numbers are too small to be categorical, but it seems that Welshmen migrating to the South Hams may have assumed a byname from a personal name, whilst those immigrating into west Devon and the interior of the county may have been attributed a generic locative byname.

Joel was an import from Brittany, which had a minor, but regional, impact on personal naming patterns. It became a placename element at Jewelscombe, now a deserted medieval hamlet in Modbury. In 1166, the enumeration of knights' fees included those held by Joel de Sancto Winnoco and Joel de Moles.[145] In 1332, 19 taxpayers had the forename Joel. By 1524, in all its variant forms (Jule, Juyll, and Gele), the surname was held by 53 taxpayers (and by one in the inflected form Joly).[146] Originally restricted to the Breton nobility in Devon, the personal name was rapidly adopted by other social groups. It continued to be associated with knightly families in the thirteenth century: thus Warin son of Joel, a justice itinerant, Joel, prior of Plympton, Joel de Vautort, and Joel de Veteri Ponte. By 1249, however, Joel le Mascun, a free peasant holding a half ferling in Nutcot, was party to a fine.[147] Suitors to the Crown Pleas in 1238 included Thomas son of Joel, Joel Giffard, Joel de Langfurlang, Joel le Mazun, and Joel Kyde, whilst those presented for offences encompassed Joel de Curforde, Joel de Paseforde, Joel de Stanhuse, Joel de Buketone, Joel the miller and Joel de Toritone.[148] In 1312, Joel de Tetteburne was admitted a freeman of Exeter.[149] By the early fourteenth century, the personal name had permeated downwards to the unfree peasantry. Joel Bysouthcolm was a customary tenant of the Dean and Chapter of Exeter on their manor of Stoke Canon, who came into dispute with his lords in 1306. One of the manorial jurors elected to decide this issue was Joel le Yurl. In the early fourteenth century, Joel Poddyng was one of the tenants of Cowick Priory.[150] During the later middle ages, the personal name became more extensively used as both a forename and byname: Walter Jul, an unfree tenant at Melbury in 1364; Richard Jule who compounded for his tithes to the Dean and Chapter in 1441; burgesses with the bynames Jul and Juyll admitted to the freedom of Exeter in 1369, 1380 and 1425. Nicholas Jule entered the tithing of Dawlish in 1461 and was a brewer there in 1514–15; John Jule held a messuage and ferling in Sidbury in c.1350.[151] Although having numerically only a small impact, the development of the surname in Devon was distinctive. Having been introduced by an aristocratic elite, it became diffused through social groups both as a forename and surname.

In a similar way, the personal name Jordan percolated through social groups, having been introduced at a relatively late time, after the Crusades.[152] By the early thirteenth century, it had been assumed by the free peasantry of Devon, such as Jordan de Wonford (1219), Jordan de Wodeburn (1228), as well as by the *buzones* such as Jordan Oliver, a justice itinerant.[153] Seven of the suitors to the Crown Pleas in 1238 had this forename.[154] By 1332, 14 taxpayers had a byname from this personal name, whilst 36 held the forename.[155] At Werrington in 1384, one of the transient unfree suitors to the manorial court was Jordan Ilond; earlier, in 1306, Jordan atte mille had been a manorial juror at Stoke Canon; in 1309, Jordan de Tadiaport held land in 'Tadiaport' in Buckland, to a moiety of which was admitted his son, whose pledges included Jordan *carpentarius de Tadiaport*.[156] By 1524, the surname, Jordan, was held by 14 tax-payers.[157] Although the personal name had only a limited impact on the development of surnames within Devon, it illustrates the adoption of personal names by all social groups, whether through cultural conflation, elision of pluralism.

Finally, a further extrinsic accretion to the stock of Devon surnames derived from personal names was Jakeman, introduced from Flanders during the later middle ages, possibly through trading connections. By 1524, however, only 15 taxpayers held this personal name as a surname.[158]

Extrinsic personal names thus had, by and large, only a marginal effect on the naming patterns of Devon. None of the external personal names formed a very large corpus. On the other hand, some contributed to the distinctive nature of naming in Devon. In this, they reflect the pace of horizontal diffusion of names — spatially and geographically and regionally, the variables which influenced this diffusion (such as immigrant nobility and trading connections and geographical location). More interestingly, they allow some idea of the acceptance of new personal names through all social groups, although the exact agency (conflation, elision or pluralism) is not always evident. In some cases, such as Joel, for example, it seems quite clear that the process of diffusion must have been downwards conflation, since the personal names were confined initially to an immigrant nobility.

This process of cultural integration cannot really be discerned even in the case of the new Continental-Germanic personal names. It seems, however, that variables external to the kinship group, such as lordship and ecclesiastical dedications, had little influence.[159] There is no correlation between the personal names of lords and taxpayers in the lay subsidy of 1332. For example, no taxpayers in St Marychurch or Fremington had the same personal name as Philip de Columbers, nor any in Plympton, Tiverton, Colyton, Exminster or Okehampton that of Hugh de Courtenay. Nor was any seignorial influence evident in Bratton Fleming or Croyde (Baldwin Fleming) or Dodbrooke (Roger Prideaux or Roger Rohant). Even William Pipard had no imitators at South Milton, despite the common nature of his forename.[160] The difficulty here is that any potential influence may have been received from earlier generations of lordship, whereas the listings in 1332 are of contemporary lords and tenants.

Dedications of local parish churches seem to have exerted little influence on local naming patterns. The most prevalent dedications in Devon comprised:

Table 5.26
Dedications of Parish Churches

Saint	Number of churches with this dedication*[161]
Mary	86
Peter	45
Michael	33
Andrew	28
John	24
All Saints	23
James	17
Paul	13
George	12
Thomas	11
Petrock	11
Martin	10

* Only listing those with more than ten dedications.

Many of these dedications were hardly replicated through personal names; there was very little correlation between local dedications and localized naming patterns. For example, in 28 parishes with a dedication to St Andrew, only three taxpayers bore this forename in 1332. At Sampford Courtenay, five taxpayers at that time had the forename Stephen, although the local dedication was to St Andrew.[162] Although there was only one dedication to St Stephen, this forename was more popular in Devon than many other Christian (that is, Saints') names. None of the taxpayers named David in 1332 inhabited one of the three parishes with that dedication (Exeter, Alphrington, Thelbridge).[163] The inverse correlation, in fact, is illustrated by the very high number of taxpayers in 1332 with the forename Martin by contrast with the relatively low number of dedications to that saint. Martin consequently also developed into a common surname derived from personal name.

Table 5.27

Rank Order of Surnames derived from Christian (Saints') Names in 1524

Andrew	46	Laurence	45
Austin	22	Lucas	15 ⎱
Bartholomew/		Luke(s)	3 ⎰
Bate	24	Mark	5
Benet	86	Martin	170
Christopher	5	Matthew	31
Clement	17	Michael	40
Gabriel	1	Nichol	65
German	28	Paul	1
Gregory	23	Paulin	9
John	33 ⎰	Peter	32
Jones	4	Philip	93
Jane	15	Sim, Simcok, Simkin, Simon,	
Littlejohn	8	Sims, Simson	78
		Stephen	94
Petyjohn	1 ⎰	Thom, Thomas, Tomme,	
James	26	Tomkin	85

The formation of bynames from Biblical names provides little further elucidation of cultural patterns, except to confirm that in Devon, as in many other parts of England, Adam(s) became a common byname and surname.

Table 5.28

Rank Order of Surnames from Biblical Names in 1524

Surname	Number of taxpayers with that surname
Abraham	11
Adam(s)	90
Daniel	13
Isaac	15
Sampson	21

(Some, of course, are ambivalent, affected by etymology in the Old Testament and ethnicity (Jewish), and Sampson may have been Breton).

During the later middle ages, one of the characteristics of the surnames from personal names in Devon was the relatively high proportion of hypocoristic forms. About 22% of taxpayers holding such surnames in 1524 had the hypocoristic form. In some localized areas, the proportion was much higher; in Hartland, the level was 57%. Diminutive forms varied from 0 to 19% by area within the county. All the forms, both hypocoristic and diminutive, had existed in 1332. During the later middle ages, however, the hypocoristic forms were intensified.

Table 5.29

Rank order of Hypocoristic forms (Surnames) in 1524

Extended form	No. of taxpayers	Hypocoristic form	No. of taxpayers
Alexander	3	Sander	88
Bartholomew	1	Bate	23
David	5	Davy	88
Peter	32	Piers	107
		Perin	7
		Perot	32
Gilbert	24	Gibb(s)	40
		Gill	23
		Gibbon(s)	7
		Gillett	2
Benedict	0	Benet	86
Nicholas	0	Nichol	65
Augustine	0	Austin	22
Henry	7	Harry(s)	133
Robert	24	Hobbs and variants	53
Roger(s)	32	Hogg(s)	56
Walter	40	Watts	26
William(s)	79	Wil-	47

In some cases, only the hypocoristic form was employed. Similarly, only the diminutive form of Ellis survived through the later middle ages (Elliot, held by 81 taxpayers in 1524). Moreover, diminutive forms were usually compounded with hypocoristics. Forms of personal names in use as surnames had thus been heavily affected by popular culture and perceptions, reflecting the form of address used in social discourse.[164]

One of the most prevalent hypocoristic forms was Sander, of which the etymology is not entirely uncomplicated. This form may also be influenced by the agrarian practice of depositing sand to improve arable land, perhaps initiating the occupational byname 'sander'.[165] It seems more likely, however, that Sander derived from· the personal name Alexander, which was represented almost without exception in Devon as Alesaundre.[166] More conclusively,

Saunder occurred as a forename in the lay subsidies of both 1332 and 1524, as did the diminutive Saundercok.[167] The military survey of Exeter in 1522 listed Saunder Gryston.[168] Moreover, Alexander Juyll, who occurred frequently in records relating to Dartmouth *c*.1390, appeared once as Sander Juyll.[169] The surname Saundercok (*alias* Sondercok) appeared in the court rolls of Werrington during the later middle ages, the diminutive form suggesting its origin as a personal name.[170] Since sanding the arable was probably not a full-time occupation, more a by-employment, the occupational surname may may have been quite rare.

Many of the hypocoristic forms of surnames from personal names have a distinctly Breton or OFrench character, such as Gibb or Piers. It may be that the evolution of these forms was influenced by the trading connections of east Devon and the South Hams with those foreign parts. In particular, it is interesting that many of the Breton traders involved in maritime disputes in the region had the forename Piers.[171]

The formation of surnames from personal names in the later middle ages thus provides some illumination of some of the questions of cultural change in the county, even superficial glimpses of popular culture. To some degree, external influences, from outside the county, contributed to the distinctiveness of Devon surnames. For the most part, however, the exact agency of change is concealed, but some assumptions can be hazarded in some specific cases.

In general, therefore, OE personal names did not affect the stock of bynames and surnames in Devon to any significant extent. The solitary exception was the byname and surname Cole, derived from the OE personal name indicating black or swarthy, which also developed at an early date into a byname. By 1332, Cole was one of the most predominant single bynames in Devon, held by 68 tax-payers.[172] In addition, Couling and Coling occurred very frequently, possibly as associatives or diminutives of Cole. In eastern England, Cole may have derived from ONorse Koli or Kolr, but in the south-west must presumably have had an OE etymology. It seems unlikely that Cole was a hypocoristic of Nicholas here, as the more usual form was Nicol.[173] Moreover, the early development suggests OE etymology, although Redin doubted its existence as a pre-Conquest uncompounded personal name.[174] Cole occurred in Domesday Book as a personal name in several counties, including Devon and Cornwall.[175] The thegn Cola held lands in Henscott, Collaton (eponymously) and Lupridge in Devon, as well as in five places in Cornwall, all TRE.[176] By 1086, however, he held only Hele in Cornwall.In some counties in the south-west, the associative form occurred in 1086 as a byname, as Alfward Colling.[177] The later occurrence of OSc personal names as bynames in Devon and Cornwall, in small numbers, cannot exclude the possibility of this Cole being OSc, but OE seems more likely.[178]

Table 5.30

Cole recorded as a Thegn in Domesday Book

County	No. of places	Date
Sussex	7	TRE
Surrey	3	TRE
Derbyshire	6	1086
Gloucestershire	1	TRE
Somerset	2	TRE
Berkshire	3	1086
Kent	1	1086
Yorkshire	1	1086
Essex	4	TRE
Lincolnshire	1	TRE
Wiltshire	5	TRE
Dorset (Colling)	1	TRE
Salop (Colling)	1	

Source: Phillimore Domesday volumes. Cole is not recorded in any other county.

By the late twelfth century, Cole had developed into the byname and hereditary surname of a knightly family in west Devon, where Cola the thegn had held his lands: Osbert son of Cola in 1162, but later (1162–83) as Osbert Cola; William Cola (1159–81); Reginald Cole (1170–86); Roger Cole (1185); William Cola (1199–1246); Richard Cole, who presented to oratories and chapels in 1228–1238, and who attested charters *c.*1228–67; William Cole *alias* Cola who attested other charters *c.*1244–91. In 1242–3, Roger Cole held a third of a fee in Chulmleigh, a tenth of one at Hamptonsford, Coleton in socage, and other fragments of fees. The family pertained to that group of knights which became *buzones*: William Cola, knight, served on several inquisitions in the late thirteenth century; Roger was a justice itinerant in 1219. Everard Cole levied a fine relating to a ferling in la Hille in Fremington in 1195–6.[179]

By 1238, the byname had become more widely dispersed: Richard Cole of Cadeleigh; Richard Cole, a pledge in Black Torrington Hundred; Roger Cole who had been robbed in North Tawton; Thomas Cole who had fallen from his horse at Colaton

Raleigh in the east; Walter Cole arraigned for a breach of the peace in Shebbear Hundred; William Cole who maimed Drogo de Dikeport in Lifton Hundred; Adam Colle who died by misadventure at Teignmouth.[180] This evidence from the Crown Pleas of 1238, by its nature, only hints at the widespread distribution of the byname by the early thirteenth century.

Table 5.31
Occurrence of Cole in Lay Subsidies

County	Date	Cole	Total taxpayers
Lincolnshire (part)	1225	0	
Wiltshire (part)	1232	4	
Derbyshire	1327	0	2657
Devon	1332	68	10614
Suffolk	1327	16	11000
Bedfordshire (part)	1297	0	
Yorkshire	1297	4	
Buckinghamshire	1332	8	
Surrey	1332	3	
Warwickshire	1327–32	6	3385
Sussex	1296	2	
Sussex	1327	4	
Sussex	1332	4	
Worcestershire	1280	14	
Worcestershire	1327	17	
Dorset	1327	24	7399
Dorset	1332	20	7681
Somerset	1327	42	

Sources: F A Cazel, *Lay Subsidy Rolls, 1225,1232* (Pipe Roll Soc, ns 45, 1983); J C Cox, 'Derbyshire in 1327-8: being a lay subsidy roll', *Journal of the Derbyshire Archaeological and Natural History Society*, 30 (1908), 23-96; E Powell, *Suffolk in 1327* (Suffolk Green Books, 9, 1906); A T Gaydon, *The Taxation of 1297* (Beds Historical Record Society, 39, 1959); W Brown, *The Yorkshire Lay Subsidy 25 Edw I* (Yorks Arch Soc Rec Soc, 16, 1894); A C Chibnall, *Early Taxation Returns* (Bucks Rec Soc, 1966); *Surrey Taxation Returns* (Surrey Rec Soc, 18, 1922, and 33, 1932); I Hjertstedt, *Middle English Nicknames in the Lay Subsidy for Warwickshire* (Uppsala, 1987); W Hudson, *The Three Earliest Subsidies for the County of Sussex . . .* (Sussex Rec Soc, 10, 1910); J W Willis-Blund and J Amphlett, *Lay Subsidy for the County of Worcester c.1280*; F J Field, *Lay Subsidy Roll for the County of Worcester 1 Edw III* (Worcester Hist Soc, 8-9, 1893-5); *Dorset Lay Subsidy 1327*; *Dorset Lay Subsidy 1332*; 'Somerset Lay Subsidy 1327'.

By the late thirteenth century, and through the later middle ages, almost every community contained a Cole, not as core families, but as single instances in each vill. Isabella Cole appeared in the court

The Surnames of Devon

Figure 15
The Distribution of the Byname Cole/Cola/Coule/Coula in 1332.

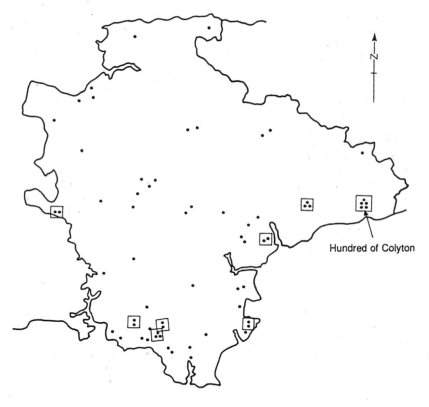

Each dot represents one occurrence of the surname.
Source: Lay Subsidy 1332

rolls of Uplyme, attached for stray beasts in 1307–8. In 1292, Nicholas Cole and John Cole held a ferling and two ferlings at Berry Pomeroy. The byname persisted at Werrington from 1365–98, through Adam, Richard and John, Walter having been taxed there in 1332. Thomas Cole occurred at Stoke Canon in 1455. John and Stephen Cole were senior inhabitants of Pilton, who gave testimony in a dispute about the parish boundary.[181] John Cole held a tenement at Schaugh Prior in the very early fifteenth century. Cole existed at Dartmouth throughout the fourteenth century: Ilary (1314–18); Simon (1322); William (1391); John (1377–91). Subsequently, the town was host to Thomas in 1409, several Williams, Johns, Thomases, Peter and Reynell in the later fifteenth century, Thomas having become mayor in 1460. In the early sixteenth century, Hugh (1501–9), Thomas (*c.*1514), Margaret and Helen (1508) all occurred there, the women presented for being common gossips.[182] The rental of Sidbury *c.*1394 enumerated Richard Cole, holding a messuage and half ferling, Bartholomew Cole a messuage and ferling, and Thomasia daughter of Bartholomew, holding another messuage and ferling.[183] At Staverton in 1441, Robert Cole farmed the tithes of 'Were' from the Dean and Chapter of Exeter, whilst William, Thomas, John and Benedict Cole all compounded for their tithes.[184] Robert Cole, Isolda Cole, John Cole and Thomas Cole all inhabited Yarcombe in the fourteenth century.[185] Richard Cole was a *nativus* at Bovy Tracey *c.*1400 and Thomas Cole acted as pledge at Colebrooke *c.*1500.[186] The Coles at Ottery St Mary formed a core surname: Henry held seven ferlings and other lands as five separate tenures in two hamlets; William Cole held two ferlings in another hamlet; Richard Cole a ferling in that same hamlet; and Thomas Cole a messuage and five acres in Ottery itself.[187] In 1339, Thomas, Geoffrey and Henry Cole were assessed as tinners at Okehampton, and in 1282, the accidental death of Ralph Cole was presented at Bradninch.[188] The byname thus became scattered throughout the county during the later middle ages as one of the commonest surnames. It was also significant in adjacent counties, although not as preponderant as in Devon, occurring on several manors of the earldom of Cornwall in the mid fourteenth century, and in high numbers in both Dorset and Somerset at the same time.[189]

The byname was still associated also with the lesser nobility in the later middle ages. Sir Adam Cole had been the steward of the household of the earl of Devon. He married Margaret Pomeroy, of another gentry family, and their son, John Cole, was a liveried familiar of the earl. This connection with the earl's household continued throughout the 1380s, until the disintegration of the earl's affinity.[190] In 1428, Coles were represented amongst the holders of fees in Devon: Roger a co-parcener in Tavyton Foliot; Nicholas a co-parcener in Sprey; Margery a co-parcener in Hurnford; John similarly in Wilbury and East Stodleigh.[191] In the 1420s, John and Roger Cole were ordained subdeacons and William a priest.[192]

By the end of the middle ages, the surname had become dispersed throughout Devon and through all social groups. In 1524–5, the subsidy included 141 taxpayers called Cole, 87 Collin, 25 Cowell or Coyll, and five Collis, or variants.[193] The incidence was scattered, not concentrated as a core surname, although there were eight at Brixton (of 83 taxpayers) and 13 at Ipplepen (of 145 taxpayers). Where status or occupation was mentioned in the subsidy, Coles held a variety of positions, a mason at Denbury, thatcher at Ipplepen, aliens at Branscombe, Northleigh, Dartmouth and Ashburton. It remained in the early sixteenth century one of the most prolific surnames in Devon. This byname had developed from an OE personal name in the south-west generally, but more particularly in Devon, and, although not numerically significant in terms of the total number of taxpayers, yet illustrated the regional differences in naming patterns in Devon, Cornwall, Somerset and Dorset combined, possibly as originally part of the south-western extension of the Old English kingdom.

Change during the later middle ages is well reflected in the developments in patronymic forms of byname and surname, although such forms only comprised a very small content of the total stock in Devon. The evolution of patronymic forms involved both local usage and the introduction of new forms from outside. Patronymics (including metronymics) in the lay subsidy of 1332 were held by less than 0.2% of the taxable population, in whatever form (Latin *filius*, Anglo-Norman *fitz*, or vernacular -son). In only four instances was the byname represented in the vernacular -sone, including William Euesone and Anastasia Hobsone.[194] It seems, however, that patronymics may have been more extensive earlier, but had declined by the early fourteenth century. Of the knights listed in the *Carte Baronum* of 1166, 21% held patronymic forms (and 4% no byname at all). In feet of fines for Devon, about 9% of the parties, both plaintiffs and deforciants, had patronymic bynames, that is between 1195 and 1250, comprising some 95 of 1044 conusors and conusees. Even after 1250, patronymic forms recurred in feet of fines: one in 1252, two in 1254, seven in 1256, one in 1259, two in 1262, one in 1263, five in 1270.[195] As well as including modest free tenants, the bearers of patronyms comprised also a number of the lesser nobility, such as Warin son of Joel, who compromised two actions by fine in 1219 and was also a justice itinerant in 1226. Andrew son of Richard recovered a knight's fee in Morchard in 1226. Gilbert son of Stephen took the homage of Nicholas de Wydimore and was lord of Dartmouth, one of the fines in 1244 settling a dispute with William de Cantilupe concerning Gilbert's market in that borough. William son of Warin levied a fine with Walter son of Warin, the former being lord of Little Marland. John son of Matthew was lord of Stokenham, his fine allowing his villeins to perform suit to the mill at Blackawton from 1259. Guy son of Guy held the manor of Portlemouth in a fine of 1262. Richard son of Stephen, a party to a fine of 1270, was lord of Dawney, Tunstal and Dartmouth, successor to Gilbert son of Stephen. John son of John held a serjeanty tenure in Morton. Others were more modest free tenants such as Laurence son of Richard, whose fine related to four acres in 1270.[196] In the Modbury cartulary, Peter *filius Lucie* is mentioned in 1285.[197] The continued use of hereditary patronymic forms shows that these had been more widespread at an earlier time.

An unknown factor is how far the lay subsidy, because of the basis of the assessment, may have excluded precisely that part of the population which may have held higher levels of patronymic bynames. Some evidence of the existence of this form amongst the medieval peasantry of Devon is contained in the court rolls of Uplyme. There John *filius Isolde* occurred between 1307 and 1315, once in the vernacular form John Isoldesone. Thomas *filius Clementis* appeared there in 1313–15, and John *filius Joyote alias filius Juliane* in 1307 (Joyote being a hypocoristic form of Juliana). Thomas *filius Sibille* occurred briefly in 1307. All these suitors to the manorial court were poor and unfree, all *garciones*. In three of the four cases, the bynames continued there as surnames from personal names. Thus John Clement appeared in court between 1332 and the 1350s; Isabella Joyote, Walter Joyote, Thomas Joyote and John Joyote between 1300 and 1315; John Sibilie in the lay subsidy of 1332, and in the court rolls, listed as a *garcio* in 1350–2, William Sybeli.[198] In an extent of the early fourteenth century for the manor, Walter Joyote held a messuage and five acres and Isabella Clement a messuage and half a ferdel. In the same document, William Richesone held a messuage and two acres.[199] Evolution at Uplyme confirms that patronymics and metronymics may have been residually associated with the unfree, as bynames which later developed into surnames from personal names, and that the vernacular form -son was largely not used.

Additional confirmation comes from the lay subsidies of adjacent counties. In Somerset in 1327, only about 28 taxpayers held patronyms or metronyms, 10 in Latin and 18 in the vernacular form, the latter form including Claricesone, le Revesone (five), Levesone (possibly from OE Leofgifu, ME Leveva), Luesone, Gibbeson (two), Tibbesone (OFr hypocoristic of Theobald), Hobbesone (hypocoristic of Robert), and Joneson.[200] The level was equally low in contemporary Dorset, but including Symesone, Emesone, Johanesone, Euesone, and Deyesone.[201] By contrast with Uplyme, some patronymic forms in Wiltshire became hereditary in that form. The *perquisita* paragraphs in the accounts of Monkton Deverill referred successively to entry fines paid by the Maggesones (William, Walter and John) between 1352 and 1369, for customary messuages and virgates.[202] Anastasia Hobbesone, however, also seems to have had an hereditary surname at Cornworthy (Devon) in 1332.[203]

The element -son, however, was mainly inconspicuous in Devon in the fourteenth century, by contrast with, for example, Warboys in Huntingdonshire, where new bynames were being produced within the community with this element in the late fourteenth century in some profusion.[204] Such surnames infiltrated into Devon from external sources during the fifteenth century. The churchwardens' accounts of Ashburton recorded 16d. paid to Matthew Gibbison for work in 1487–8, and he served the masons there in 1490–1.[205] At Stoke Fleming, Joan Robynson allowed her houses to fall into disrepair in *c.*1521–2.[206] In the lay subsidy of 1524–5, some 12 tax-payers had surnames with the element -son, still a small number amongst 28000 taxpayers, but including Edmanson, Greyson, Jacson, Pateson, Ricson, Symson, Tomson, and Wylson.[207] A few more occurred additionally in 1544.[208] The distribution, although somewhat concentrated in east Devon, was scattered throughout Devon in 1524–5.

The introduction of these surnames with -son, however, must be closely related to the trading communities of east and south Devon. By 1402, a John Joneson paid aulnage for trading in wool through Exeter. In the mid fifteenth century, three Dutchmen, William Dirykkesone, Peter Jonessone and William Jonessone, were all taxed as aliens resident in Devon.[209] From the late fifteenth century, several new freemen with these forms of name were admitted in Exeter, including Peter Johnson in 1492, Peter Johnson junior in 1495, William Richardson in 1495, John Wilkinson in 1484, William Wylkenson in 1497, John Filson .in 1493–4, Henry Johnson in 1510–11, Anthony Peterson in 1519–20, and Robert Johnson in 1520–1.[210] Similarly, at Dartmouth, the surnames with the suffix came into evidence in the late fifteenth century: Gilleson (1464); Jonson (1491); Richardsone (1415, the earliest). A later Richardsone (fl 1484–1502) was bailiff of the town in 1502 and constable in 1484. William Robynson (fl 1502–17) was an attorney for livery of seisin in several charters, bailiff in 1503, mayor in 1517, an arbiter in 1510, a witness to several charters (1504–11) and described as 'of the Castle' in 1502.[211]

The same pattern of introduction seems to occur in other coastal towns in the south of England, such as Winchester, where surnames with the element -son appeared for the first time from *c.*1462.[212] The port books of Southampton reveal that these new forms were being introduced by Dutch merchants, as early as 1439–40.[213] The trading communities in Devon had contact through Southampton, an entrepôt, with the Dutch, and by the late fifteenth century some Dutch aliens were resident in Exeter. In 1438, Thomas Jacobysson of Middleburg became involved in a dispute concerning his trade to Dartmouth.[214] By 1522, the military survey of Exeter included several bearers of -son surnames, many of whom were Dutch: Barberd Johnson, Harry Johnson, Hugh Johnson, Anthony Peterson.[215] In the lay subsidy of 1524–5 for the City, 14 taxpayers had surnames with -son, of whom three were specifically aliens; in the subsidy of 1587–8 there, six such surnames occurred, two explicitly held by aliens.[216] By *c.*1568, Thomas Richardson had become warden (*custos*) of the Leper Hospital in the City.[217]

The element -son had therefore been introduced as a patronymic form into Devon during the later middle ages, probably through commerical contacts. Patronyms in their Latin form had existed sparsely in Devon at earlier times, and may have been more significant in the twelfth and thirteenth centuries. In this respect, Devon was similar to many other counties in southern England, since the element was more extensively developed in northern England.[218]

The relative use of Anglo-Norman during the later middle ages is an indicator of cultural patterns, both over time and through society. The use of the language amongst the higher and lesser nobility has been well attested, both as an oral and written expression.[219] More importantly, anthroponymy allows a discrete window into how far through society the use, to some extent, penetrated, and over what period of time.[220] Attempting to define the influence in these terms may be too deterministic about downwards cultural conflation, however, and medieval society may have been pluralistic or, at least, may have experienced cultural elision in the use of language. The effect of Anglo-Norman was basically exerted on four aspects of naming: those bynames and surnames derived from personal names, especially hypocoristics (as opposed to general Continental-Germanic personal names); occupational forms; some topographical forms; but principally nicknames (omitting for this purpose the

Anglo-Norman locative surnames and locative surnames derived from placenames in England formed from Anglo-Norman or Old French). The most formative and illuminating influence may have been on nicknames, since these related very closely to how society and individuals saw other individuals within their community, and were possibly originally what anthropologists have designated reciprocal names.[221]

In global terms, all these forms in Anglo-Norman in 1332 were held by about 1% of the taxpayers of Devon. Some 11% of the taxpayers who bore occupational bynames did so then in Anglo-Norman form; 4% of those with nicknames had them in Anglo-Norman as did a similar proportion of those taxpayers holding topographical bynames.

In 1332, taxpayers held some two dozen different occupational bynames in Anglo-Norman. About half of these persisted into the sixteenth century. Some common ones proliferated, such as bocher, barber, taillour. Caperon existed in Willand, Mary Tavy, Exeter and Plymouth in 1332, and had become localized around Tiverton, Burlescombe and Bampton in 1524–5. This byname (for a cloak-maker) had appeared in Devon from at least 1174, and a Denis Caperon had been murdered at Plympton in 1302. It had also, however, been associated with the nobility (see below). Although Ganter occurred almost as frequently as Glover in 1332, it had been excluded by 1524–5. Other bynames which did persist over the later middle ages included Jouter, Pretre, Sommaster, Gamoner, Spicer.[222] The byname Pleydur occurred at Molland in 1332.[223] Its disappearance is not surprising because of its very specialized nature.[224] It also seems to have been transient elsewhere.[225]

More significant, perhaps, were nicknames construed in Anglo-Norman. In London and Canterbury, such names developed within a 'milieu' that was largely Middle English, with French forms occurring alongside insular forms.[226] It has been suggested that this combination and the general nature of the use of Anglo-Norman nicknames may imply at least a minimal acquaintance with Anglo-Norman amongst lower social groups.[227] Moreover, the suggestion has been advanced that Anglo-Norman nicknames were more limited, narrow and conventional than the livelier and less inhibited Middle English ones.[228] Although occupational bynames were restricted, possibly, to the craft sector, the burghal elite, nicknames may, by their nature, have been applied to individuals from a wider social spectrum. In Devon, in 1332, the stock of nicknames in Anglo-Norman comprised some 60 names. Although originally applied quite specifically to individuals, some became hereditary bynames and persisted throught the later middle ages: Amadeu (Amadas);

Beaupel (Beaple); Belamy; Blanchard; Blaunche (Blanke); Blaunc-payn (Blampyn); Bonefaunt; Maudu(i)t (Maudet); Chanterel; Compaignon (Company); Copyner (Copner); Fynamour (Finmore, but possibly also locative); Parleben (Parlybyn); Proucz (Prowse); Quent (Quant, Quint); Plaicz (Plays, Plees); Queynterel (Quintrell); Rous (Rowse); Pouleblanc (Pullyblank); Sage; Bonclerk (Bondclerk); Courteys; Grosse; Tropinel.[229] Russell may have derived from a nickname, but possibly also later as a personal name. Most were held by single taxpayers in 1332, but by two to seven in 1524–5, although still localized, often in the same place as earlier. Others which did not recur in 1524–5 included Beaufitz, Oysel, Partout, Jaumbe, Malerbe, Merveil, Peau, Portioye, Purprise, Beaus, Tort, Beausire and Garsoun. Some of these, however, are known to have survived from other sources.[230]

Some of these nicknames were certainly held by or associated with the nobility in Devon, such as, for example, Beaupel and Coffin.[231] Both thus became hereditary surnames from an early time, but, during the later middle ages became more diffuse, possibly because of the social transformation of the lesser nobility (see below). Nevertheless, many of the Anglo-Norman nicknames in 1332 were borne by lesser taxpayers, and this evidence is confirmed by other sources. Tenants at Yarcombe in 1334 and Uplyme in the late thirteenth and early fourteenth centuries were Walter Carlemayn and Gregory Charlemayn. Gregory Charlemayn was probably a free tenant at Uplyme, since he was involved in charters in the late thirteenth century.[232] Porteioye was also a common byname of unfree tenants. Amongst other unfree tenants at Uplyme in the early fourteenth centuries were enumerated Thomas Dieuleseit, Roger Porteioye, Nicholas Roys, Hugh and Edith Propechaunte, Thomas Quenterel, William Trenchemer, and John Pertenaunt.[233] Between 1307 and 1315, the court rolls of Uplyme referred to three *garciones*, Richard, John and Gervase Dieuleset, indicating that this byname may have become hereditary amongst the unfree tenantry.[234] Thomas Dieuleseit had held only a messuage and five acres in villeinage. The byname seems to have disappeared from the manor, possibly as a result of the emigration of the *garciones*. This byname occurred in Canterbury, Marlborough in Wiltshire, and London, and one of its equivalents, Godwot, in More Crichel in Dorset in 1327. Its vernacular equivalent in Uplyme may have been represented in Robert Godfelagh, who occurred once as a pledge in 1313.[235] The surname Papeiay became established at Dawlish during the later middle ages. In 1385, Joan and Richard Papeiay were placed in mercy for trespasses with their avers and trespass in the lord's *defensum*. Richard was involved in three cases of debt, and also neglected to take oath in the office of reeve, having been elected by the homage. In 1461, Thomas Papeiay appeared in the court rolls. In 1514-15, Richard Papeiay was a party to a *licencia concordandi* in a case of trespass; was placed in mercy for brewing; and was at law in another case of debt. John Papeiay junior was involved in cases of debt and trespass, Thomas in trespass, and John Papeiay was a brewer.[236] All were customary tenants in the rentals of the fifteenth century.[237] This surname probably derived from the parrot or peacock on a wooden stick used as target practice or for running at the quintain.[238] An unusual Anglo-Norman nickname thus became hereditary amongst a kinship group of unfree peasants which became a core family in the community.

The lay subsidy of 1332 comprised many taxpayers with Anglo-Norman names assessed at very small amounts, although the subsidy excluded the very poor. Assessed at between 8d. and 12d. were taxpayers with the bynames: Partout; Herigaud; Queynte; Peuerel; Proucz; Amadeu; Fynamour; Queynterel; Tropinel; Porteioye; Graunt; Coffyn; Tailleboys; Beaufitz; Belamy; Barbarel; Peau; Petipas; Mortimer; Copyner; Parleben; Bonefoys; Maudut; Blaunchard; Bonefaunt; Compaignon; Blancpayn; Beausire; Curlepays *et al.* Peuerel, Prouca, Fynamour and Copyner were held by several taxpayers, Proucz by as many as 16, Peuerel by eight.[239] Although Coffin pertained to a knightly family, the nickname had extended, independently, through Devon by 1332, some five Coffins assessed at only 8d.-12d. Similarly, Pomeray, a surname of the higher nobility, was held by seven taxpayers assessed at only 8d.-12d.

At Stoke Fleming, the minor inhabitants called Pourpilion seem to have existed there partly through brewing.[240] John and Ralph Copyner were transient there in 1368-9. A kinship group called Copener comprised smallholders at Axminster in the early fourteenth century (Roger, Walter, Adam).[241] The byname Amadas had humble origins in 1332 at Tavistock, later recurred in Dartmouth in the later middle ages, and at Plympton in the sixteenth century, having become hereditary in a very circumscribed locality.[242] John and Robert Snoublench were assessed at Bradninch in 1332, and a petition from the men of Bradninch, a petty borough, in 1358, included John Snoublench. This composite surname may reflect a conflation of ME and Anglo-Norman.[243] In 1351, a presentment was made of Philip de Doune, bailiff of John Chambernoun, who had hired Thomas Coffyn for 60s. to kill his lord, Chambernoun, the task completed at Stone — hardly a Coffyn of chivalric status. John Coffyn, his wife Joan, and first-born (*primogenitus*) son, John, held two tenements from Plympton Priory in Schaugh.[244] Tenants at

Feniton in *c.*1498 included Thomas Pomerey (two ferlings and other lands) and John Tropinel (a cottage and one acre). The surname Tropynell *alias* Tropenell was held by two former tenants in Plympton Grange in the early fifteenth century.[245] The hereditary surname Bonefant existed in Exeter from the early fourteenth century through to the early modern period.[246] In the early thirteenth century, a number of burgesses there had borne Anglo-Norman nicknames, such as Belebuche.[247] In 1293, a customary tenant at Berry Pomeroy bore the nickname Hautemere.[248] These Anglo-Norman nicknames thus extended down the social scale, through burgesses, even to the unfree peasantry.

Anglo-Norman nicknames had begun to appear from at least the early twelfth century in Devon. In final concords in the early thirteenth century, parties included Richard Marchepais (1208), Philip Chaucebof (1219), John Malherbe (1219), Richard Beaufiz (1233), Peter le Bon and Walter le Bon (1255).[249] The earlier forms seem to have been livelier and less conventional. The clergy in the thirteenth and fourteenth century in particular held compounded forms which were lively constructions: Cachefreins, Chaceporc, Chauceboff, Coupegorge, Marchepais, Metlefrein, Parleben, Pernegarde, Sachebien, Sanzfaille, Deulegarde.[250] Amongst the earlier types are found a number of compositions of verb and noun (the 'Shakespeare' form), which Seltén assumed to be of OFr origin, but Clark has suggested may also be equally ME, and, indeed, the clergy included Master Simon Shakespeare, rector of Arlington, from 1308.[251] The clergy, however, may have been to some extent drawn from a higher social group at this time. By 1238, however, more conventional forms appeared such as Pulein and Curtis.[252] Perhaps indicative is that almost all the metonymic bynames of the later middle ages were constructed in ME: Beangrout; Whetebred; Hotebathe; Whithod; Hotybaker; Siluerlok'; Honycod' (but also a few compounds in both languages such as Whetepayn and one fully Anglo-Norman example, Blancpayn).[253]

Some nicknames existed in both languages, in use simultaneously, such as red and russel or rous, graunt and long (and also speare, a common surname at Werrington during the later middle ages); tropinel and snell (to a lesser degree quyk). Compounded ME forms occurred in 1332, such as Rennewell, Fairefot, Herdhead, Whitebrother, Maidegod, Fairmaid, Friethoght, Kinrich, Truwelove, Shortboard (*sic*). More distinctive of ME constructions, however, was compounding with the element -man, or, in a few cases, -grom (Whitegrom, Redegrom), and, once, Redwyne.[254] In 1332, taxpayers thus included several Fairman, several Lytelman, Langeman, Stilleman, many Selimans, Truman, several Whitemay and Godman.[255]

At Berry Pomeroy, in 1293, some complex ME forms were borne by customary tenants: Laysebagge, Dulle Sparke, Wytfot and Wyteking.[256] At Axminster, Roger Biggffysch made an agreement with Newenham Priory in the late thirteenth century. At Dartmouth, in 1289, the Shakespeare construction occurred in ME in the persons of Hervey and Ralph Makeglad.[257]

Topographical bynames in Anglo-Norman were extremely limited, comprising only Mareis, Boys, Pomeray and Roch. All except Mareis seem to have persisted into the sixteenth century. Pomeray was as common as Orchard, increasing from 11 taxpayers in 1332 to 22 in 1524–5.[258] Its development, however, was complicated by its association with the higher nobility (see below).

An indicator of the extent of assimilation of Anglo-Norman bynames and surnames can be derived from the admissions to the freedom of Exeter. Of some 950 freemen admitted before 1348, only 69 had bynames in Anglo-Norman, whether occupational, nickname or topographical.[259] Although all social groups may have had some knowledge of Anglo-Norman, its influence on the stock of bynames and surnames in the county was quantitatively limited. The commercial connections with western France do not seem to have exerted a significant influence in this respect, nor the levels of alien immigrants during the later middle ages. Nevertheless, Anglo-Norman bynames extended right down the social scale, to the unfree peasantry and poor tinners, especially the byname Porteioye. A small proportion of these bynames persisted into the sixteenth century.

As indicated above, however, the diffusion was complicated by the association of some surnames with the nobility. This connection sometimes resulted in the very slow diffusion of the byname and its relative localization. In some other cases, the surname became dispersed independently of the noble family. The particular bynames concerned here were Pomeray, Coffin, Malerbe and Beaupel. The diffusion of these surnames was in part connected with the change in the social composition of the lesser nobility during the later middle ages.

In 1166, Henry de Pomeray was both a tenant in chief and mesne tenant, a similar tenurial position to that existing in 1086. The *Carte Baronum* described his honour of Berry as comprising some 32 knights' fees in Devon, held by 20 mesne tenants. Most of the mesne tenants originated from the Cotentin, so that his own feudal *caput* may have been at La Pommeraye in Calvados in Normandy, thus a locative surname.[260] By the fifteenth century, the surname no longer reflected the same status, various Pomerays holding only fragments of fees as co-parceners.[261] Simultaneously, the surname had 'ramified' amongst other social groups independently, possibly as a topographical byname.[262]

In 1166, Richard Coffin held two knights' fees and Ellis Coffin half a fee, both of Robert, the king's son.[263] The Coffins made endowments to Tavistock Abbey and were constantly involved in final concords.[264] By 1332, the byname was held by five taxpayers in five vills. By 1428, the social status of the noble family had declined, since John Coffin held a fee with five co-parceners in Alvington and a third of a fee with two others in Rouston, now parish or petty gentry.[265] The surname elsewhere became more widely distributed.

The Malerbe family remained localized throughout the later middle ages, and the surname accordingly. In 1166, Ralph Malherbe held an eighth of a fee from William de Traci.[266] By 1428, William Malerbe was one of five co-parceners in a fee in South Pool and three quarters of a fee in Feniton. John Malerbe, with two co-tenants, held three quarters of a fee in Payhembury.[267] The tenurial basis of the family was localized in Feniton, Sherford and Payhembury, and the surname remained more or less localized here.

The surname Beaupel was also associated with the lesser nobility. In the late twelfth and thirteenth century, the family was tenant of lands throughout North Devon, in at least fourteen vills.[268] By 1298, the surname had entered Exeter amongst the freemen.[269] In 1332, taxpayers with the surname were still concentrated in North Devon, at Brendon, South Molton, Shirwell and Whiddon.[270] By 1428, a large number of the fees previously associated with the surname were no longer so, as the family was reduced to the status of parish gentry. In 1524-5, Beaples contributed to the subsidy at Alwington, Monkleigh, Northam, and, significantly, six in the small borough of Fremington.[271] Even in the subsidy of 1581, the surname was geographically circumscribed, three taxpayers in Barnstaple, two in Fremington, one each in Peters Marsland, Abbotsham, Shebbear and Thornbury, still predominantly in North Devon.[272]

The surname Copenere had been associated with the nobility in Robert le Copenere, who held a fee in 1242-3. William le Caperun had the wardship of Henry de Pomeray at the same time.[273] Simultaneously, Hugh Peverel held a fee in Devon.[274] All these bynames, however, developed amongst other social groups independently within Devon.

Despite the strong connection with the nobility, Anglo-Norman bynames were held by all social groups within Devon, alongside ME forms. The development, distribution and decline of these forms reflect some of the social and cultural changes in Devon during the later middle ages, although the actual proportion of bynames in this language was always fairly marginal.

Significant changes in the pattern of naming thus occurred throughout the county during the later middle ages. The proportions of the different forms of surname ostensibly altered, with a decline in locative surnames and a compensatory increase in other types. Some particular surnames, of all types, proliferated, such as Tucker, whilst others became less evident. Others remained extremely localized, through the influence of social and geographical constrictions, such as Beaupel (Beaple). Some forms of bynames and surnames — especially patronymic forms in the vernacular (-son) — were never prominent in Devon, but were introduced during the later middle ages through commercial linkages. Although insular personal names were almost completely displaced by the newly introduced Continental-Germanic personal names, yet one particular OE personal name, Cole, persisted to become a very significant localized byname and surname in Devon, and the south-western counties more generally. By the end of the later middle ages, some regionally distinctive aspects of naming had developed. Throughout the county, the massive demographic and economic changes of the later middle ages had wrought a profound effect on the pattern of surnames. Within particular communities, the disjunction was even more evident.

References

1   For the most recent discussion of late medieval demography, R M Smith, 'Human resources' in G Astill and A Grant, eds., *The Countryside of Medieval England* (1988), 208-11; see also J Hatcher, *Plague, Population and the English Economy 1348-1530* (1977).
2   McKinley, *Oxfordshire*, 199-200.
3   *Lay Subsidy 1332, passim; Dorset Lay Subsidy 1332, passim.*
4   H S A Fox, 'The chronology of enclosure and economic development in medieval Devon', *Economic History Review*, 2nd ser, 28 (1975), 181-202.
5   M Aston, 'Deserted farmsteads on Exmoor and the lay subsidy of 1327 in west Somerset', *Proceedings of the Somerset Archaeological and Natural History Society*, 127 (1983), 71-104.
6   O Padel, 'Cornish surnames in 1327', *Nomina*, 9 (1985), 82-6.
7   McKinley, *Lancashire*, 78.
8   J F Willard, *Parliamentary Taxes on Personal Property 1290 to 1334*, (1934).

9 McKinley, *Oxfordshire*, 200; J A Raftis, 'Geographical mobility in lay subsidy rolls', *Mediaeval Studies*, 38 (1976), 385-403.

10 *Lay Subsidy 1332*, 43-5.

11 *Ibid*, 74.

12 *Ibid*, 20-1, 68-9, 74.

13 *Feudal Aids*, I, 473-5 (Wonford Hundred only).

14 *Lay Subsidy 1332*, 3.

15 *Ibid, passim.*

16 *Ibid*, 4-5, 7-8, 9-10, 23.

17 L C Loyd, *The Origins of Some Anglo-Norman Families*, (Harleian Society, 103, 1951), 42.

18 *Ibid*, 78-9.

19 R Bearman, 'Charters of the earls of Devon', unpub. PhD thesis, London, 1981, 147; *Book of Fees*, ii, 761-2, 787-8, 790; *Register of Edward the Black Prince, IV, 1351-65* (HMSO, 1933), 75; *Caption of Seisin*, 12; *Feudal Aids*, I, 477, 480, 488, 490.

20 DRO M1438; *Crown Pleas Devon 1238*, 60 (no 342); Dartmouth Records computer database.

21 *Canonsleigh Cartulary*, xxiv-xxv; *Book of Fees*, ii, 767, 769, 777, 786, 795; *Feudal Aids*, I, 452, 464, 467, 491.

22 *Book of Fees*, ii, 767-8, 772, 796.

23 *Black Prince's Register*, IV, 2, 59; BL Add MS 28838, fos 77v and 79v.

24 *Feet of Fines Devon*, I, 292; *Feudal Aids*, I, 467-70; *Lay Subsidy 1332*, 28; *Lay Subsidy 1524-5*, index, sn Clotworthy; DRO 217/3/19, fo 53r; *Chancery Decree Rolls: Elizabeth I* (List and Index Society, 198, 1983), 133; PRO C78/16.

25 *Feudal Aids*, I, 452, 454, 466, 488.

26 BL Add MS 28838, fo 43r: 'Henricus de Thurleston dedit Ricardo at yea et Philippe uxori eius omnia terras et tenementa apud le yea in parochia de Payhembur'.'

27 BL Add MS 28838, fo 49r: 'nuper tenementa Willelmi Collesworthi'.

28 BL Add MS 28838, fos 77v, 79v, 82v, 83v, 84r.

29 PRO Chancery Miscellanea Bundle 55, File 9, No 350.

30 DRO Bedford MSS Werrington court rolls: 'Decenarius et tota decenna de Markesworth in misericordia quia concellauerunt (per xx^ti annos elapsos) quod Rogerus Knyght residens in eadem decenna tanquam liber ubi ipse est natiuus et omnes successores sui prout idem Rogerus hac instanti die propria sua recognicione fatebatur . . .'; 'Rogerus Knyght venit in plena Curia et dat domino de fine ut patet in capite (12d.) de inquirendo quale Ius habuit in terris et tenementa in Knyghtyscote.' *Calendar of Inquisitions Post Mortem 7-15 Richard II*, (1974), 438-9.

31 D&C Exeter Archives 2961.

32 BL Harley MS 4766, fos 3r, 13v, 14v, 19r-v, 23r. See also the *conventionarius* at Newton St Cyres, Walter Rowhorn, who held one ferling *apud Rowhorn nuper Roberti Rowhorn*: BL Harley MS 4766, fo 4r.

33 See also below, ch 6; Z Razi, 'The erosion of the family-land bond in the late fourteenth and fifteenth centuries: a methodological note' and C Dyer, 'Changes in the link between families and land in the west midlands in the fourteenth and fifteenth centuries', both in R M Smith, ed., *Land, Kinship and Life-Cycle* (1984), 295-312.

34 R Faith, 'Berkshire: fourteenth and fifteenth centuries' in P D A Harvey, ed., *The Peasant Land Market in Medieval England* (1984), 147. For the association at an earlier time, in the late thirteenth century, Walter de Bacalre gave all his lands in 'Bacalr' to Newenham Abbey in exchange for a corrody; Richard de Wrangheie was associated with the hamlet of 'Wrangheie'; the suitors to Axminster Hundred included Ellis de Comb' for a tenement in 'Comb', Robert de Grenewey for one in 'Grenewey', and William de Tril for 'Tril' (all probably *hundredarii*): Bodl Lib MS Top Devon d 5, fos 42r-47r, 112v-113r. For the same concurrence in the early thirteenth century, the charter of Reginald de la Putte, leper, *pro terra de Putte* (1205): H P R Finberg, 'Some early Tavistock charters', *English Historical Review*, 62 (1947), 375.

35 C W Brackley, 'The manor of Plympton Grange', *TDA*, 70 (1938), 247.

36 *Lay Subsidy 1332*, 3, 13, 56.

37 See below.

38 *PND*, II, 406; *Lay Subsidy 1332*, 2, 32, 49, 52, 56, 109.

39 *PND*, I, 195; *Lay Subsidy 1332*, 17.

40 *PND*, I, 262 and see note 35.

41 *PND* I, 159 ; *Lay Subsidy 1332*, 25, 79, 80.

42 G Fransson, *Middle English Surnames of Occupation 1100-1350*, (Lund Studies in English 3, 1935); B Thuresson, *Middle English Occupational Terms*, (Lund Studies in English 19, 1950).

43 See the example of Salter below.

44 Fransson, *Middle English Surnames of Occupation*, 42, 81-110.

45 *Lay Subsidy 1332*, 70, 73; BL Arundel MS 17, fo19r; BL Harl MS 3660, fo 79v.

46 H P R Finberg, 'The Stannary of Tavistock', *TDA*, 81 (1949), 173-82, e.g. 179.

47 As Richard Whyte weuere at Werrington *c.*1490: DRO Bedford MSS Werrington court rolls.

[48] See above.

[49] *Lay Subsidy 1332*, 34, 79, 82, 89, 105.

[50] Fransson, *Middle English Surnames of Occupation*, 87-8, 100-5.

[51] PRO E179/95/100.

[52] J Le Patourel, 'Documentary evidence and the medieval pottery industry', *Medieval Archaeology*, 12 (1968), 101-26; E Gooder in P Mayes and K Scott, *Pottery Kilns at Chilvers Coton, Nuneaton*, (Society for Medieval Archaeology Monograph Series 10, 1984), 3-5; C C Dyer, 'The social and economic changes of the later middle ages and the pottery of the period', *Medieval Ceramics*, 6 (1982), 33-42. In 1327, in Dorset, ten taxpayers bore the byname Crocker and one Pottere: *Dorset Lay Subsidy 1327, passim*.

[53] *Lay Subsidy 1332*, 10, 27, 37, 43, 57, 60, 73, 76, 81, 83, 88-9, 97-8, 108, 110-13, 115, 116, 120, 124-6; see also *Crown Pleas Devon 1238*, 6, 7, 105, 111-12. By 1524-5, there were 34 Crockers as taxpayers and 44 Potters: *Lay Subsidy 1524-5, passim*. BL Arundel MS 17, fos 36r, 47r-48v.

[54] Longleat MSS Uplyme court rolls computer database. See also the William Crocker who paid only 12d. rent for the tenement formerly held by Ralph Calue: BL Arundel MS 17, fo 48v (1334).

[55] DRO M902M/E/5, M4.

[56] E M Carus-Wilson and O Coleman, *England's Export Trade 1275-1547* (1963), 188-91 and graphs; W G Hoskins, *Devon*, 124-6; H P R Finberg, *Tavistock Abbey*, 147, 152.

[57] McKinley, *Norfolk and Suffolk*, 32, ,41; *idem, Sussex*, 225.

[58] *Lay Subsidy 1332, passim*; *Lay Subsidy 1524-5, passim*.

[59] *Lay Subsidy 1332, passim*; see also, for example, John Degher at Modbury, as illustrative of the numerous Dyers during the later middle ages: Eton College Records 1/139 (1398).

[60] For Toser: *Lay Subsidy 1524-5*, 67, 70, 126, 137, 170, 173-4, 180, 183-4, 188, 201, 230 (15 incidences in 12 parishes); *Lay Subsidy 1332*, 2, 61, 97, 100, 113, 119 (7 incidences).

[61] For Draper: *Lay Subsidy 1524-5*, 9, 49-50, 104, 127, 130, 134, 138, 200, 202 (14 incidences in 10 parishes).

[62] *Ex inf* H S A Fox.

[63] H P R Finberg, *Tavistock Abbey*, 154-5.

[64] DRO Bedford MSS Werrington court rolls computer database.

[65] BL Harley MS 4766, fo 13v; but see also *ibid*, fo 15r, where John Hakeworthy held a cornmill and a fulling mill at Thrushelton. These two entries rather suggest that fulling may not always have been a full-time occupation, but that some tuckers may also have been millers of other products.

[66] *Lay Subsidy 1524-5, passim*, and notes 19-20 above.

67 I Blanchard, 'Labour productivity and work psychology in the English mining industry, 1400–1600', *Economic History Review*, 2nd ser, 31 (1978), 1ff. See also note 74 below.

68 For what follows, G R Lewis, *The Stannaries: A Study of the Medieval Tin Miners of Cornwall and Devon*, (1908); T A R Greaves, 'The Devon Tin Industry 1450–1750', unpub. PhD, Exeter, 1981; J Hatcher, *English Tin Production and Trade before 1550*, (1973). There is some difference of opinion about seasonality, but see Greaves, 'Devon Tin Industry', 289.

69 PRO E179/95/15; H P R Finberg, 'Stannary of Tavistock', 173-82; Greaves, 'Devon Tin Industry', 380-1 (great court of 1494).

70 PRO E179/95/15.

71 Greaves, 'Devon Tin Industry', 282-4.

72 Finberg, 'Stannary of Tavistock', 173-82.

73 Greaves, 'Devon Tin Industry', 380-1; DRO 14294/PW2.

74 For different views on the economic position of miners and organisation of the industry, I Blanchard, 'The miner and the agricultural community in late medieval Engand', *Agricultural History Review*, 20 (1972), 93-106; *idem*, 'Rejoinder: Stannator Fabulosus', *AgricHR*, 22 (1974), 62-74; J Hatcher, 'Myths, miners and agricultural communities', *AgricHR*, 22 (1974), 54-61. For Richard Broker, MP for Tavistock, Finberg, 'Stannary of Tavistock', 184.

75 PRO E179/95/15.

76 Finberg, 'Stannary of Tavistock', 173-82.

77 For the dominance of Elforth *alias* Elford, Finberg, 'Stannary of Tavistock', 172.

78 Greaves, 'Devon Tin Industry', 380-1.

79 Greaves, 'Devon Tin Industry', 291.

80 Greaves, 'Devon Tin Industry', 292.

81 *PND*, I, 311, II, 583, 595; H C Darby and R W Finn, *The Domesday Geography of South-West England*, (1967), 269-73.

82 A R Bridbury, *England and the Salt Trade in the Later Middle Ages*, (1955), 19.

83 *Ibid*, 109, 115-16, 120 and Appendices E—F.

84 B Putnam, *Proceedings before the Justices of the Peace*, (1938), 64, 67 · (large quantities of salt imported through Appledore in Northam for sale in Barnstaple, Bideford and Great Torrington and the countryside there — *patria*).

85 BL Add MS 28838, fos 42v, 43v, 49r.

86 BL Add MS 28838, fo 141r.

87 BL Add MS 28838, fo 177r (*Participacio*); BL Add MS 28838, fo 126r.

88 BL Add MS 28838, fo 172r.

[89] The surname had, however, been introduced into Exeter by the mid fifteenth century. In 1455, John Hilman *alias* Salter was apprenticed to John Salter, saddler: *Exeter Freemen*, 40-1, 44, 52; and it recurred there in the military survey of 1522: *Tudor Exeter*, 24.

[90] *Devon Lay Subsidy 1332, passim.*

[91] *Devon Lay Subsidy 1524-5, passim.*

[92] See, for example, B Seltén, *The Anglo-Saxon Heritage in Middle English Personal Names: East Anglia 1100-1399*, Part 1 (Lund Studies in English 43, Lund, 1972).

[93] C Clark, 'Willemus Rex? vel alius Willelmus?' *Nomina*, 11(1987), 7-33, and the references in her notes to her previous research.

[94] P Franklin, 'Normans, saints and politics: forename choice among fourteenth century Gloucestershire peasants', *Local Population Studies*, 36(1986), 19-26.

[95] Clark, 'Willemus Rex?'; Franklin, 'Normans, saints and politics'; Seltén, *Anglo-Saxon Heritage*.

[96] T Forssner, *Continental-Germanic Personal Names in England in Old and Middle English Times*, (Uppsala, 1916), sn Serlo; Reaney, *DBS*, sn Serle. For Serlo, Dean of Exeter, in 1228, and Walter Serle, attorney in 1255, *Feet of Fines Devon*, I, 110 and 284 (nos 226 and 559); Serlo de Holne, a knight in 1166, *Red Book of the Exchequer*, (Rolls Series, 3 vols, 1896), 258. For Richard *filius Serlonis c.*1107-13 H P R Finberg, 'Some early Tavistock charters', *English Historical Review*, 62(1947), 355-6. The personal name had become a byname by the mid thirteenth century (Walter Serle above). For its descent down the social scale, John Serell, who held three closes in Wolston in east Devon in the early sixteenth century: BL Add MS 28838, fo 177r ('Participacio terrarum et tenementorum Martini Ferrers . . .').; and John Serle, former tenant on the manor of Plympton Grange, in the early fifteenth century: BL Harley MS 4766, fo 22r. And so Serlys Lane in Exeter: DRO Magdalen Hospital Deeds 100.

[97] *Dorset Lay Subsidy 1327, passim; Dorset Lay Subsidy 1332, passim.*

[98] 'Somerset Lay Subsidy 1327', *passim.*

[99] *Dorset Lay Subsidy 1327, passim;* M Pope, *From Latin to Modern French*, (1934), 140; E(ton) C(ollege) R(ecords) 1/32, fos 4v-5v and 7v-8r: 'Helewysia que fuit uxor Terrici de arboribus', 'Willelmus de arboribus filius et heres predicti Terryci', William *de arboribus* as tenant of the land 'que vocatur De arboribus in parochia de Modbyr' ', 'Helewysia que fuit uxor Terryci de Arboribus'; at fo 18v. William quitclaimed the land *de la Wyke* under the style William Terry atte Trawen. See later John Tyrry in the rental of Modbury *c.*1398 (ECR 1/139). See also John Tyrry att' Trewyn,

who held lands by knight service from Plympton Priory in the very early fifteenth century: BL Harley MS 4766, fo 19r. *Feet of Fines Devon*, I, 149 and 303 (nos. 297 and 596) (Andrew Terry and Robert Terry, 1238 and 1256); *Crown Pleas Devon 1238*, 1, 5, 66; Forssner, *Continental-Germanic Personal Names*, 228, 232.

100 *Dorset Lay Subsidy 1327, passim*; *Dorset Lay Subsidy 1332, passim*.

101 T J Hunt, (ed.), *The Medieval Customs of the Manors of Taunton and Bradford-on-Tone*, (Somerset Record Society, 66, 1962), 3, 7-8, 10, 13, 15.

102 *Dorset Lay Subsidy 1327, passim*; *Dorset Lay Subsidy 1332, passim*.

103 Seltén, *Anglo-Saxon Heritage, passim*.

104 M Redin, *Studies on Uncompounded Personal Names in Old English*, (Uppsala, 1919), *passim*. Browning, which occurred frequently as a byname and occasionally as a forename, may also have been OE.

105 'Somerset Lay Subsidy 1327', passim; *Dorset Lay Subsidy 1327, passim*; *Dorset Lay Subsidy 1332, passim*; *Lay Subsidy 1332, passim*.

106 J R Maddicott, 'Trade, industry and the wealth of King Alfred', *Past & Present*, 123 (1989), 3-51.

107 *Dorset Lay Subsidy 1327*, 49, 52, 57, 97, 100, 105, 111-14, 121, 141.

108 *Ibid*, 10, 52, 63, 67, 144; *Surrey Taxation Returns* (Surrey Record Society, 33, 1932), 21, 65, 85 (1332).

109 'Somerset Lay Subsidy 1327', *passim*; Hunt, *Medieval Customs*, 15.

110 *Dorset Lay Subsidy 1327, passim*; *Caption of Seisin*, 110, 112, 115 (Stoke Climsland); the Colbern family was still at Stoke Climsland in 1354 — *Register of Edward the Black Prince Part IV (1351-1365)* (HMSO, 1933), 67.

111 J Insley, 'Some Scandinavian personal names from South-west England', *Namn och Boyd*, 70 (1982), 78-93.

112 *Feet of Fines Devon*, I, *passim*, but, for example, 4, 12, 21, 23, 26, 31, 39, 43, 49, 54, 59, 66-8, 72-4, 82, 90, 97, 104, 127, 134. See also Edwin Coaching (*c*.1155-62) and Osbern Goyo (*c*.1174—86): H P R Finberg, 'Some early Tavistock charters', *English Historical Review*, 62 (1947), 357-8, 367-8. R P Chope, 'The early history of the manor of Hartland', *TDA*, 34 (1902), 421. *Red Book*, I, 249.

113 *Crown Pleas Devon 1238*, 3-8.

114 *Ibid, passim*.

115 Forssner, *Continental-Germanic Personal Names*, sn Osbert.

116 *Crown Pleas Devon 1238*, 12.

117 *Ibid*, 89.

118 *Exeter Freemen*, 1-28.

119 *Ibid*, 9.

[120] D&C Exeter Archives 3710. See also the proportion of C-G personal names in Winchester, Battle and Canterbury cited by C Clark in a review in *Archives*, 57(1977), 87.

[121] BL Add MS 17450, fos 218-221.

[122] Hunt, *Medieval Customs*, 24-6; O Padel, 'Geoffrey of Monmouth and Cornwall', *Cambridge Medieval Celtic Studies*, 8 (1984), 1-3; see, however, the several Alfreds who attested charters to Canonsleigh Priory in north Devon and Somerset: BL Harl MS 3660, fos 38v, 76r, 81v (Arthur de Aysforde *alias* de Esseford, who was both a donor and a witness, Alured de Nyweton, Alured *custos*, Alured de sancto Georgio).

[123] Forssner, *Continental-Germanic Personal Names*, *passim*, esp. 101, 110-11, 113, 142-3, 152, 208, 211, 219, 224, 246-7. Drew (from Dreu, Drogo) became established as a surname around Widecombe in the Moor; for this personal name, Forssner, 60. War(r)en often occurred with a spurious final 'g' during the later middle ages; see also *Ashburton CW Accounts*, xxi.

[124] The evidence has been reviewed most recently by O von Feilitzen, 'Some Old English uncompounded personal names and bynames', *Studia Neophilologia*, 40 (1968), 1.

[125] Reaney, *DBS*, sn Bate.

[126] *Crown Pleas Devon* 1238, 57, 114, 127, 137; *Dorset Lay Subsidy 1327*, 12 (le Bat); For le Batur as an OFr occupational term, C Clark, 'Some early Canterbury surnames', *English Studies*, 57 (1976), 296; C Spiegelhalter, 'Surnames of Devon', *TDA*, 68 (1936), 397-410.

[127] *Lay Subsidy 1332, passim*; *Lay Subsidy 1524-5, passim*; DRO Bedford MSS Werrington court rolls computer database — Bate 1365-86 and 1462-96.

[128] *Lay Subsidy 1524-5*, index, sn Batte.

[129] Longleat MSS Uplyme court rolls computer database; Forssner, *Continental-Germanic Personal Names*, 237 and 249, suggests derivation from C-G personal name Wazo; Reaney, *DBS*, 366 (sn Wace) admits either OCeltic (Cornish) or O Fr (i.e. C-G).

[130] *Lay Subsidy 1524-5, passim*.

[131] *PND*, II, 616.

[132] *Crown Pleas Devon 1238*, 1, 68, 91, 102, 104, 110, 112.

[133] *Feet of Fines Devon*, I, 36 (no 59).

[134] *Crown Pleas Devon 1238*, 1.

[135] *Lay Subsidy 1332, passim*.

[136] *Lay Subsidy 1524-5, passim*. And so the charity called Davie's Almshouses founded by John Davye, citizen, alderman and merchant of Exeter: DRO Exeter Deeds (Davie's Almshouses) 342-352.

137 *Hearth Tax 1674, passim.*
138 *Lay Subsidy 1332, passim.*
139 Reaney, *DBS*, sn Colman; DRO Bedford MSS Werrington court rolls computer database, Colman 1462–1524.
140 *Lay Subsidy 1524–5*, index, sn Patrick; Patrich also occurred at Tarrant Gunvile cum Pentridge in 1332, but possibly as a locative byname: *Dorset Lay Subsidy 1332*, 92-3.
141 P Morgan, 'The rise of Welsh hereditary surnames', *Nomina*, 10 (1986), 121-35, esp. 121-3.
142 Longleat MSS Uplyme court rolls computer database, Morgan 1312–1408.
143 *Crown Pleas Devon 1238*, 32, 110.
144 *Lay Subsidy 1524-5, passim.*
145 *PND*, I, 280.
146 *Lay Subsidy 1332, passim*; *Lay Subsidy 1524-5, passim.*
147 *Feet of Fines Devon*, I, 22, 45, 49-50, 74, 88, 246.
148 *Crown Pleas Devon 1238*, 4, 7, 35, 43, 45, 87, 95, 101, 109, 116, 117.
149 *Exeter Freemen*, 12.
150 D&C Exeter Archives 1712-1714; Oliver, *Monasticon*, 157.
151 D&C Exeter Archives 5249; *Exeter Freemen*, 33, 35, 44; DRO M889; D&C Exeter Archives 4785-4786; D&C Exeter Archives 2944. And so, later, Roger Juell of Exeter, cordwainer (decd by 1637): DRO Inventories of the Court of Orphans, Exeter, inventory no. 186.
152 Reaney, *DBS*, sn Jordan; *Red Book*, I, 249.
153 *Feet of Fines Devon*, I, 54, 82, 90.
154 *Crown Pleas Devon 1238, passim.*
155 *Lay Subsidy 1332, passim.*
156 DRO Bedford MSS Werrington court rolls computer database: Jordan Ilond, transiently, 1384-6; D&C Exeter Archives 1712-1714; DRO M1277.
157 *Lay Subsidy 1524-5, passim.*
158 *Ibid, passim*; Reaney, *DBS*, sn Jakeman.
159 Clark, 'Willemus Rex?'; Franklin, 'Normans, saints and politics'.
160 *Lay Subsidy 1332*, 5, 11-14, 22-4, 36-7, 43-5, 55-8, 62, 80, 83, 94.
161 Oliver, *Monasticon*, 444-5.
162 *Lay Subsidy 1332*, 73; Oliver, *Monasticon*, 452.
163 *Lay Subsidy 1332*, 30, 51, 109-10; Oliver, *Monasticon*, 444, 448, 454.
164 For the frequency of A-N diminutives in the fourteenth century, Forssner, *Continental-Germanic Personal Names*, 280 (-et, -ot, -(e)let, -e(lot), -inet).

[165] But see William le Sonder who held a ferling in 1302: BL Arundel MS 17, fo 19r.

[166] *Ibid, passim*; Reaney, *DBS*, sn Saunder.

[167] *Lay Subsidy 1332, passim*; *Lay Subsidy 1524–5, passim*.

[168] *Tudor Exeter*, 23.

[169] Dartmouth Records computer database.

[170] DRO Bedford MSS Werrington court rolls computer database (Saundercok 1462–1470).

[171] *West Country Shipping, passim*, but, for example, 52-3, 60-4 (Piers).

[172] See Figure 15; *Lay Subsidy 1332, passim*.

[173] G Fellows-Jensen, *Scandinavaian Personal Names in Lincolnshire and Yorkshire* (1968), 176-7, 345; O von Feilitzen, *The Pre-Conquest Personal Names of Domesday Book* (Uppsala, 1937), 217-18; C Clark, 'Women's personal names in post-Conquest England: observations and speculations', *Speculum*, 53 (1978), 249-50.

[174] M Redin, *Studies on Old English Uncompounded Personal Names* (Uppsala, 1919), iii, vi, 46, 166; W G Searle, *Onomasticon Anglo-Saxonicum* (1897), 141; for placename elements incorporating the element cole: M Gelling, *Signposts to the Past* (1978), 171-2; A H Smith, *English Place-Name Elements, part I, A—IW* (English Place-Name Society, 25, 1970), 105-6; E Ekwall, *The Oxford Dictionary of English Place-Names* (4th edn., 1966), 115-18; for Cornwall, where coll may indicate hazel-trees, O Padel, *Cornish Place-Name Elements* (EPNS, 66-7, 1985), 62. For Devon placenames, *PND*, I, 3, 50-1.

[175] See Table 5.30.

[176] *DB*, Devon, 3/12, 17/35, 20, 24; Cornwall, 5/3/5, 5/3/8, 5/3/18, 5/3/23, 5/24/3 (Phillimore editions).

[177] *DB*,Cornwall, 5/3/5, 5/3/8, 5/3/18, 5/3/23, 5/24/3 (Phillimore editions); Wiltshire 67,14.

[178] See also J Insley, 'Regional variation in Scandinavian personal nomenclature in England', *Nomina*, 3 (1979), 52-60.

[179] *Launceston Cartulary*, 12, 14, 20, 27-30, 32-4, 86, 108, 111, 115, 121, 129, 131, 153, 165, 171; *Feet of Fines Devon*, I, 4, 39, 49, 97; *Book of Fees*, ii, 758-9, 761, 783.

[180] *Crown Pleas Devon 1238*, 11 and *passim*.

[181] Longleat MS 11253; DRO Bedford MSS Werrington court rolls; D&C Exeter 5007-5008; see also Walter Cole, a free tenant of Hartland in 1301: R Chope, 'The early history of the parish of Hartland', *TDA*, 34 (1902), 443; Oliver, *Monasticon*, 245.

[182] Dartmouth Records computer database. BL Harley MS 4766, fo 12r.

[183] D&C Exeter Archives 2945.

184 D&C Exeter Archives 5249.
185 DRO CR1430, 1432, 1433, 1435; 346M/M1.
186 PRO SC11/161; Nottingham University Library Dept of MSS MiM 6/173/272.
187 BL Add MS 28838, fos 77v, 81v, 82r; DRO M1288.
188 PRO E179/95/15.
189 *Caption of Seisin*, 13, 31, 37, 87, 89, 110-15 (1337); and see Table 5.31.
190 M Cherry, 'The Courtenay Earls of Devon: the formation and disintegration of a late medieval aristocratic affinity', *Southern History*, I (1979), 71-97, esp. 77.
191 *Feudal Aids*, I, 448, 451, 459, 463, 496-7.
192 G R Dunstan, ed., *The Register of Edmund Lacy, Bishop of Exeter, 1420–1455*, IV (Canterbury and York Society, 63, 1971), 82-3, 93, 107, 115.
193 *Lay Subsidy 1524–5, passim.*
194 *Lay Subsidy 1332, passim.*
195 *Red Book of the Exchequer*, (Rolls Series, 3 vols, 1896), I, 248-61; *Feet of Fines Devon*, I, 1-372.
196 *Ibid*, I, 45, 49-50, 74-5, 193, 213, 297, 313, 320, 346, 363, 372 (nos 77, 87, 143, 315, 386, 426, 582, 615, 626, 675, 703, 721).
197 Eton College Records 1/32 fo 1v; O J Reichel, *TDA*, 28 (1896), 373-4.
198 Longleat MSS Uplyme court rolls computer database.
199 BL Add MS 37053, fo 279.
200 'Somerset Lay Subsidy 1327', 90, 103, 109-10, 139, 142, 144, 163, 175, 201, 213, 226, 240-2, 249-51, 261, 266, 276.
201 *Dorset Lay Subsidy 1327, passim*; *Dorset Lay Subsidy 1332, passim*; e.g. 1327, 40, 43, 138, 142.
202 Longleat MSS 9747, 10715, 10716. See also Edward son of Edward Agneysesone at Longbridge Deverill: Longleat MS 10604 (1342-3).
203 *Lay Subsidy 1332, passim.*
204 J A Raftis, *Warboys. Two Hundred Years in the Life of an English Village*, (1974), 67.
205 *Ashburton CW Accounts*, 11-12, 16.
206 DRO M902/M33.
207 *Lay Subsidy 1524–5, passim*; McKinley, *Sussex*, 332-3.
208 *Lay Subsidies 1544–5, passim.*
209 'Kowaleski database' (citing PRO E101/338/11).
210 *Exeter Freemen, passim*, e.g. 59-62, 65, 68-9, 72-3; PRO E179/95/100.

211 Dartmouth Records computer database.

212 D Keene, *Survey of Medieval Winchester* (Winchester Studies, 2, ii, 1985), 1274-5, 1306, 1333, 1379, 1394-5.

213 H S Cobb, ed., *The Local Port Book of Southampton, 1439-40* (Southampton Record Society, 5, 1981), *passim*.

214 *West Country Shipping*, 43.

215 *Tudor Exeter*, 7, 9, 23, 30, 32.

216 *Ibid*, 36, 40, 46, 47, 52, 53 and *passim*.

217 DRO Exeter Deeds, Magdalen Hospital, 121(b); DRO Exeter Deeds, Borough Charity, 327.

218 C Clark, review of McKinley, *Oxfordshire*, in *Nomina*, 3 (1979), 114; McKinley, *Sussex*, 332-3. For Wiltshire in the sixteenth century, G D Ramsay, ed., *Two Sixteenth Century Taxation Lists, 1545 and 1576*, (Wiltshire Archaeological and Natural History Society, Record Series, 10, 1954), *passim* (24 taxpayers with surnames with -son).

219 M T Clanchy, *From Memory to Written Record 1066-1307* (1979), 151-74.

220 C Clark, 'People and languages in post-Conquest Canterbury', *Journal of Medieval History* 2 (1976), 1-34, esp. 13-21.

221 Reciprocal naming is an anthropological term.

222 *Lay Subsidy 1332, passim*; *Lay Subsidy 1524-5, passim*. For Caperun in 1174, C Spiegelhalter, 'Surnames of Devon', *TDA*, 68 (1936), 401; at a later date, Chancery Miscellanea Bundle 55, File 5, No. 136, and DRO M1277 (1370).

223 *Lay Subsidy 1332*, 74.

224 For the complicated nature of pleading even in lower courts by the thirteenth century, see R Palmer, *The County Courts of Medieval England* (1982), 89 ff; J S Beckerman, 'Customary law in manorial courts in the thirteenth and fourteenth centuries', unpub. PhD London, 1972, *passim*; Dr Paul Brand suggests to me that this byname may have been a nickname based on loquacity and ability to represent others rather than from formal office. I have encountered the byname in isolated instances in Berkshire in the 1240s and Leicestershire and Dorset in the early fourteenth century.

225 As in Berkshire, Leicestershire and Dorset: *Dorset Lay Subsidy 1327*, 71, 122; M T Clanchy, *The Roll and Writ File of the Berkshire Eyre 1248* (Selden Society, 90, 1973), 347 (no. 876); Merton College, Oxford, MM 6556 ff.

226 Clark, 'People and languages', 13-21; E Ekwall, *Early London Personal Names* (Acta RSHLI, 43, Lund, 1947), 173.

227 Clark, 'People and languages', 13-21.

228 Clark, 'People and languages', 13-21.
229 For Copiner (paramour), see also *Crown Pleas Devon 1238*, 5, 67, 70. Compare the wider variety of bynames with the OE/ME element leofu/love, as in 1332: Luuing, Triweloue, Luueriche, Louekyn, Luuenet; at Uplyme in 1307-15: Roger, Felicia and Adam Louehous and Henry Louescheft; the tinner at Whitechurch in 1339, John Welbeloued: *Lay Subsidy 1332*, 11, 30, 51, 57, 113; Longleat MSS Uplyme court rolls computer database; PRO E179/95/15.
230 *Lay Subsidy 1524-5, passim*; for William Beaufitz at Ottery St Mary in the late fourteenth century, DRO M1288; a Richard Blompayn received 20s. under the will of John Hyl, vicar of Colyton in 1428: G R Dunstan, *The Register of Edmund Lacy, Bishop of Exeter, 1420-1455*, IV (Canterbury and York Society, 63, 1971), 31. For Quaintrelle, which existed in King's Lynn and was common in northern France, C Clark and D Owen, 'Lexicographical notes from King's Lynn', *Norfolk Archaeology*, 37 (1978), 61.
231 Coffin (a basket or box) also occurred in medieval Canterbury and Arras: Clark, 'People and languages', 16; see also the tinner in Whitechurch, John Coffyn: PRO E179/95/15.
232 DRO M1429; Longleat MSS Uplyme court rolls computer database; A Watkin, ed., *The Great Chartulary of Glastonbury*, (Somerset Record Society, 3 vols, 59 and 63-4, 1947-56), 3, 582; but T Forssner suggested Carleman as a C-G personal name: *Continental-Germanic Personal Names*, 54.
233 BL Add MS 17450, fo 220v; see also the poor tinner in Tavistock Hundred in 1339, Simon Porteioye: PRO E179/95/15; and John Porteioye, customary tenant at Sidbury *c.*1350: D&C Exeter Archives 2944.
234 BL Add MS 17450, fo 220v; Longleat MSS Uplyme court rolls computer database.
235 M W Farr, letter in *Local Population Studies*, 42 (1989), 74; *Dorset Lay Subsidy 1327*, 126; Clark, 'People and Languages', 20 ('God-given' or 'God save him', i.e. in the latter case, Dieu-le-saut).
236 D&C Exeter Archives 4784-4786.
237 D&C Exeter Archives 3684, 5053.
238 Reaney, *DBS*, 261-2.
239 For Peverel developing independently of nobility, especially in France, with some sexual implications, C Clark, 'Social stratification, personal identity, and the study of ME personal naming', paper to conference on Naming, Society and Regional Identity, July 1990. For Richard and Gilbert Quynta *alias* Quynte, BL Harley MS 4766, fos 12r-v (early fifteenth century); for two

tenants of a ferling and half ferling at Newton St Cyres in the early fifteenth century, who were called Prudham, both *conventionarii*, BL Harley MS 4766, fo 4r.

240 DRO M902.

241 DRO Bedford MSS Werrington court rolls; for the Copeners at Axminster, BL Arundel MS 17, fos 35v-36r, 47v-49r.

242 *Lay Subsidy 1332*, 115; Dartmouth records computer database; C W Brackley, 'The manor of Plympton Grange', *TDA*, 70 (1938).

243 *Lay Subsidy 1332*, 120; *The Register of Edward the Black Prince IV (1351-1365)* (HMSO, 1933), 144.

244 B H Putnam, *Proceedings before the Justices of the Peace*, (1938), 62; BL Harley MS 4766, fo 12v.

245 BL Add MS 28838, fos 49r et seqq.; BL Harley MS 4766, fo 22r.

246 *Exeter Freemen*, 26, 100; *Tudor Exeter*, 1-2, 68.

247 D&C Exeter Archives 3721.

248 *Book of Fees*, ii, 1310-11.

249 *Feet of Fines Devon*, I, 36, 43-4, 126, 284-5 (nos. 59, 74, 76, 257, 559, 561).

250 C Spiegelhalter, 'The surnames of Devon', 407-8.

251 B Seltén, *Early East Anglian Nicknames: 'Shakespeare' Names*, (1969); C Clark, 'People and languages', 21; Spiegelhalter, 'Surnames of Devon', 408.

252 *Crown Pleas Devon 1238*, 2, 7, 65, 102. For the derogatory use of Polein by this time in France, M R Morgan, 'The meanings of Old French Polain, Latin Pullanus', *Medium Aevum*, 48 (1979), 40-54.

253 *Lay Subsidy 1332, passim*; see also the bynames of some criminals in the thirteenth century, constructed in ME: William le Wikkede; Ralph Ronneaway; Robert Godbithamungus; William Routaboute; William Swengebagge; John Luggespurs (see above, p.76, n.20); see also William Hurlebat, a tinner assessed at only 6d. in 1339 in Tavyton: PRO E179/95/15; which all witness to the vitality of ME nicknames from an early time, including Shakespeare forms.

254 For Speare, for example, DRO Bedford MSS Werrington court rolls computer database.

255 One Anglo-Norman equivalent, Prodhomme, was to be found amongst the lesser nobility, the burgesses of Exeter and also as customary tenants in Yarcombe in the 1330s: H P R Finberg, 'Some early Tavistock charters', *English Historical Review*, 62 (1947), 377; *Lay Subsidy 1332, passim*; for Exeter, see below, pp.256-8; DRO M1432.

256 *Book of Fees*, ii, 1310-11, 1314.
257 Bodl Lib MS Top Devon d 5, fo 37r; Dartmouth Records computer database; also William Fishpond (fl 1410-65), MP for Tavistock and John Brounbrom, of Tavistock, fl 1492: J J Alexander, 'Tavistock in the fifteenth century', *TDA*, 69 (1937), 280, 282.
258 See also the tinner at Fernhill, John Mareis: PRO E179/95/15.
259 *Exeter Freemen*, 1-28; no attempt has been made here to correlate Anglo-Norman nicknames with those existing in France on the lines of C Clark, 'Thoughts on the French connections of Middle English nicknames', *Nomina*, 2 (1978), 40, or C Clark and D Owen, 'Lexicographical notes from King's Lynn', 56-79, esp. 57.
260 *Red Book of the Exchequer*, I, 249, 252, 261; *Book of Fees*, ii, 763-6, 769, 776, 791-2, 795, 1307-15; L C Loyd, *The Origins of Some Anglo-Norman Families*, (Harleian Society, 103, 1951), 78-9.
261 *Feudal Aids*, I, 449, 451, 453, 458, 480, 486, 491, 493.
262 *Lay Subsidy 1332, passim*; *Lay Subsidy 1524-5, passim*.
263 *Red Book*, I, 252; *Book of Fees*, ii, 784, 791, 795.
264 H P R Finberg, 'Some early Tavistock charters', 363-4; *Feet of Fines Devon*, I, *passim*.
265 *Feudal Aids*, I, 459. 461, 470.
266 *Red Book*, I, 254; *Book of Fees*, ii, 782.
267 *Feudal Aids*, I, 481, 487; BL Add MS 28838, *passim*, but esp. fos 43r-v, 47v, 51v, 65r-v, 88r, 126r-127v.
268 *Feet of Fines Devon*, I, 61, 102-3, 108, 123, 134; II, 20, 55, 86; *Book of Fees*, ii, 773-5, 784.
269 *Exeter Freemen*, 5.
270 *Lay Subsidy 1332, passim*.
271 *Lay Subsidy 1524-5, passim*; *Feudal Aids*, I, 460, 464, 466-9, 491.
272 *Lay Subsidy 1581, passim*.
273 *Book of Fees*, ii, 757-9, 781, 791.
274 *Ibid*, 786.

CHAPTER 6

CHANGE WITHIN COMMUNITIES
DURING THE LATER MIDDLE AGES

Significant changes thus occurred in the pattern of naming in Devon during the later middle ages. These changes affected almost every community, so that there is very little correlation between bynames in a community in the early fourteenth century and surnames there in the early sixteenth. Such a comparison, however, presents a number of methodological problems, since the compositions of the two lists of taxpayers in 1332 and 1524–5 are not totally consistent. One principal difference was the change in the basis of assessment in relation to total population at the two dates. In 1332, some 10614 taxpayers were contained, comprising those with taxable disposable wealth over 6s. in boroughs and 10s. in rural areas. In 1524–5, some 28,000 were assessed, the lowest limit for inclusion being 20s. on wages, goods or land. Both subsidies may thus have excluded a large element of the population. More serious, however, is the apparent difference between the number of taxpayers as a proportion of the total population at the two dates. It can be assumed that the population of the county may have been considerably higher in 1332 than in 1524–5, if national demographic trends were reflected in Devon.[1] Whilst the population was thus much lower in 1524–5, the number of taxpayers had increased by a factor of 2.6. The two taxations thus capture a different proportion of the population. Secondly, the culture of naming changed during the later middle ages, as has been illustrated above, so that a proportion of the bynames of 1332 disappeared. Finally, the economic, social and cultural changes of the later middle ages were so dramatic as to cause considerable social inversion. Individuals and kinship groups responded differently to the challenges of that time. Some bynames which occurred in 1332 may been held by taxpayers who subsequently declined in economic and social status, whilst others, omitted in 1332, rose, either for the life-cycle of individuals or inter-generationally. These changes were quite radical.

Taking Devon as a whole, there was little correlation between bynames and surnames in the two assessments. The vast proportion of the communities contained no bynames or surnames which

Figure 16
The Relative Location of Werrington.

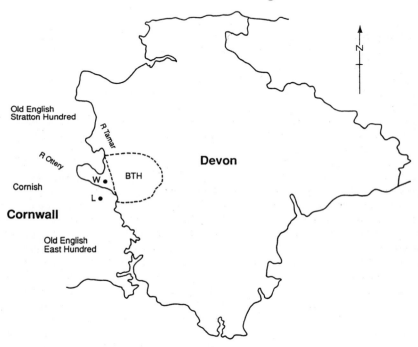

Old English
Stratton Hundred

R Tamar

R Ottery

Devon

W ● | BTH

Cornish

L ●

Cornwall

Old English
East Hundred

Old English }	Placename Element	- Svensson		BTH = Black Torrington Hundred
Cornish		- Cotes		L = Launceston
		- Worthy		W = Werrington

Figure 17
Werrington in its Region.

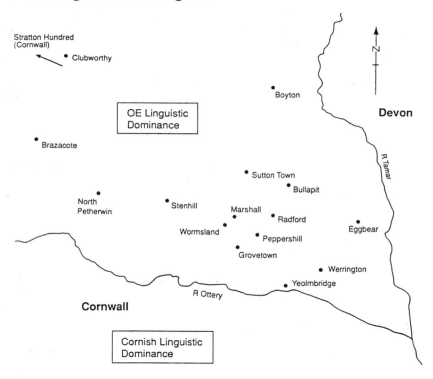

Stratton Hundred
(Cornwall)

• Clubworthy

• Boyton

OE Linguistic
Dominance

Devon

• Brazacote

R Tamar

• Sutton Town
• Bullapit

North
Petherwin
• Stenhill
Marshall
• Radford
Eggbear
Wormsland
• Peppershill

Grovetown

• Werrington

• Yeolmbridge

R Ottery

Cornwall

Cornish Linguistic
Dominance

Approximate scale is 1 : 50,000
Areas of linguistic dominance follow place - name etymology after Svensson

occurred at both dates, according to a comparison of the subsidies. Some continuity is visible in the persistence of a few surnames in a few communities, excluding, for this purpose, the surnames of the lesser nobility which tended to have a higher rate of survival (for example, Beaupel, Malherbe *et al*). A very small number of surnames persisted in the parish of Hartland (see below); the surname Lillycrop ('whitehead') continued at Sourton and expanded in this localized area.[2] In the vast majority of cases, however, there was dissonance between the two taxation lists.

It is important, therefore, to assess these changes at the level of the microcosm by studying sample communities in detail as a corrective and amplification to the static listings in the subsidies. A more dynamic assessment depends on the survival of a reasonable series of manorial records, but Devon is not fortunate in that respect. To some extent, the communities have thus tended to be self-selecting — Uplyme, Werrington, and Stoke Fleming — but, fortuitously, all are located in different *pays* of the county, east Devon, the South Hams and the west, respectively. *Ceteris paribus*, these would have represented good examples of the contrasting developments in different regions, which were more or less accessible or remote, but the sample is corrupted by some other variables. Lordship and seignorial control were possibly greater in Werrington, even though this was the most remote of the communities. Stoke Fleming was adjacent to the rapidly developing borough of Dartmouth; indeed, the periphery of the borough was within the manor of Stoke Fleming. Despite these complicating variables, a comparison of developments in the composition of surnames in these communities is instructive. In all, a very small proportion of surnames persisted and provided an element of continuity and stability, but it was only a thread in each.[3]

Werrington was located in the extreme west of Devon adjacent to the boundary with Cornwall (Figure 16). Indeed, until the late twelfth century, the parish was contained within Cornwall in Stratton Hundred, but was transferred into Devon (but returned to Cornwall in 1966).[4] The parish was situated across the Tamar, which thus physically divided Werrington from the rest of the county. The chapelry of St Martin at Werrington was dependent on its mother church, St Stephen's, Launceston, in Cornwall. The parishioners of Werrington were buried in the cemetery at Launceston and contributed to its maintenance. The parish, particularly in the fourteenth century, became embroiled in disputes with Launceston Priory, which held the rectory, concerning the repair of the church. In a case in the Consistory Court in 1366, parishioners complained about the state of repair of the chapel as they could not reach the mother church because of inundations.[5] Some tenants of Werrington illicitly pursued their suits, especially debt and detinue, in the borough court of Launceston.[6] Contained within the court rolls, for a manor held by Tavistock Abbey, are many pleas of detinue of tithes prosecuted by Launceston Priory against tenants of the Abbey.[7] The networks of Werrington were thus as closely related to Launceston and its hinterland as to Devon. In this sense, Werrington was physically more remote than the other manors under consideration.

Strong lordship was exercised by Tavistock. Settlement was highly dispersed; the manorial structure comprised three tithings, each with its own chief pledge, reeves and beadles. A high proportion of locative bynames and surnames reflected the nature of dispersed settlement. The court rolls are extant from 1365, but rentals only from the late fifteenth century. Manorial or seignorial control may have been important in influencing demographic replacement and immigration, and attempting to retain the bond between land and family. The evidence of the court rolls suggests that the exercise of lordship was maintained through the fourteenth century, but began to decline in the fifteenth. Fines for brewing may be an indicator of the change in the nature of seignorial control. During the fourteenth century, the level of fines for brewing, the assize having deteriorated into a licensing system, was high, but in the fifteenth the level declined dramatically. By 1472, tenants were taking advance licences to brew. The decline may also have been caused by the increasing specialization and monopoly of brewing and the demographic contraction of the later middle ages. The very small number of amercements such as merchet and leyrwite after the late fourteenth century, however, supports the suggestion of a decline in enforcement. These fines had been fixed at a very high level in the late fourteenth century. Leyrwite was fixed at 5s. 1d. and closely associated with pregnancy, not simply fornication outside wedlock. Merchet for permission to marry inside the lordship ('oundede') was lower, often 15d., but licence to marry whomsoever the woman wished ('cuicunque voluerit') (presumably outside the lordship) incurred a fine of 4s. or 5s. Some collective challenge to this lordship insinuated from the late fourteenth century, with collusive withdrawal of works, particularly harvesting and reaping; seven tenants failed to perform these works in 1365, 23 in 1368, 26 in 1392 and 34 in 1395.[8]

The stock of surnames in the court rolls might depend on a number of variables discussed by others. The levels of appearances by women may not be critical, even if they were of independent status, since the surname might still be represented.[9] Decline in amercements for brewing might be more critical, depending on the nature of production. In the fourteenth century, the lists for both Werrington and Stoke Fleming contain numerous people, ostensibly landless or smallholders or undertenants, who do not appear elsewhere in the rolls, and for whom brewing was important for their subsistence. In the fifteenth century, the concentration of the industry may, however, mean that surnames of brewers would also be represented elsewhere in the court rolls.[10] The most serious deficiency may have been the obvious decline in personal pledging on all these manors, induced either by a decline of solidarity, dissolution of kinship ties, or, more plausibly, the increased use of presentment in manorial courts during the later middle ages. At Werrington, 344 personal pledges provided surety, of which almost half occurred between 1365 and 1385 (202 pledges). At that time, two pledges were required for most offences, but from the 1380s the beadle increasingly appeared as one of the pledges, with a personal pledge as the other, and from 1392 one pledge only was all that was often required. Pledges by the beadle are excluded from the figures, since this was evidently a pledge *ex officio*. In 1365, 1368, 1369, 1384 and 1385, pledges numbered 69, 28, 27, 32 and 46 respectively. Thereafter the highest number in one year was 16 (1392); in the late fifteenth century the number of pledges only attained double figures in one year. By this time, most tenants preferred to initiate their suit through presentment; juries of presentment comprised fewer tenants than had been contained in the homage. On the other hand, other causes of decline were also in action. The volume of business of the court had declined.[11] Some free tenants were seeking their justice in more efficient courts.[12] It seems, however, that these changes did not seriously affect the number of surnames represented in the business of the court. Personal pledging had been performed predominantly by the more substantial tenants on the manor. Pledging did continue on the manor into the late fifteenth century, involving some pleas of pledge for failed pledges.[13] The rise in default of suit did not withdraw surnames from the rolls, since defaults were consistently reported. The rolls enumerate 515 reports of default of suit, almost two thirds occurring between 1365 and 1395 (297 reports, including 92 in 1365, 55 in 1369, and 62 in 1395). The numbers of reports were lower in the late fifteenth century, although 36 reports were made in 1479. These figures reflect both the demographic collapse of the late middle ages and the resistence to seignorial control from the late fourteenth. Similarly, there is no difficulty caused by respite or relaxation of suit since fines were collected and enrolled. A combination of demographic decline and diminution of seignorial control resulted in an overall contraction of the volume of business in the manorial court, but did not ostensibly affect the level of surnames appearing in the rolls.

External relations of the peasantry were limited, but not totally proscribed. The evidence of pleas of debt reveals that most of these transactions were intra-village rather than outside. Fugitives mainly migrated within a very short radius of the manor. Litigation in courts other than the manorial court is only revealed when tenants were placed in mercy for pursuing litigation outside the manorial court. These instances, although few, seem to have increased in the later fifteenth century; thus peasants were fined for impleading in the borough court of Launceston, the Peculiar Court and the County Court. These pleas related to debt, the litigants seeking a more expeditious justice than that provided by the manorial court. Pleas of debt above 40s., however, were probably removed from these manorial courts since none was an ancient demesne manor with jurisdiction for pleas of that level.[14]

The population of Werrington may have been decimated in the late 1360s, by heavy mortality in 1368-9. The mortality of tenants may not be an absolute reflection of overall mortality, but is an indicator. The inheritance of land was temporarily disturbed, whilst a high proportion of tenements remained in the lord's hands; tenants were elected to vacant tenures by their peers *(per pares suos)*. Moreover, a high proportion of tenements remained with the widow, sometimes as custodian with wardship of a minor, sometimes as sole tenant.[14] Tenures were, therefore, for a short time, susceptible to movement with the re-marriage of widows, and hence to be disassociated from the surname. By the late fifteenth century, however, inheritance of holdings had been re-established as the normal route of movement. The mortality of 1368-9 affected the persistence of some surnames. In that year the deaths occurred of John, Eleanor and Richard Baron; William Eyrigge de Brasyngcote and William son of William Eyrigge; William Godefray, William Godefray de Durkyston, and William Godefray de Pattecote; John and Richard Hamlyn; John and Nicholas Yunge; Richard Wyngcote and Juliana widow of Walter Wyngcote; thus resulting in the eclipse of some of these surnames within the community, as well as the temporary dislocation between land and family. The difficulty of obtaining heirs to take up land is illustrated by two examples in 1369; on the death of William Barbel, the court rolls required:

> Et nichilominus distringet unum proprinquiorem heredem ad faciendum domino fidelitatem per plegium Christine Barbel

and so also on the death of John Sutton in the same year. The re-establishment of inheritance in the fifteenth century was complicated by the introduction of terms of lives, the purchase of reversions and the insinuation of remainders.

Table 6.1

Changes of Tenures at Werrington 1365–1498

Date	Lord's hands	Taken	Inherited	Elected	Lease /sale	Remainder /reversion	Main- tenance
1365–6	1	0	3	1	0	0	0
1368–9	15	0	11	3	0	0	0
1384–6	0	2	9	11	1	0	0
1392–6	1	0	8	0	0	0	0
1469–80	1	1	12	0	0	0	0
1486–98	1	2	5	0	1	6	1

Table 6.2

The Mortality of Tenants at Werrington 1365–1498

Year	no. of tenants decd.
1365–6	6
1368–9	31
1384–6	5
1392–3	4
1395–6	8
1462–80	16
1486–98	11

Table 6.3

Inheritance by Women in Werrington 1365–1498[15]

To widows	8 tenures
To widows with wardship	2 tenures
To other female *consanguinee* (including men *de iure uxoris* and daughters)	14 tenures

Tenures at Werrington were diverse. Tenure by knight service was held by at least the Edward family in the fourteenth century. There was an element of other forms of freedom. Tenures were slightly complicated by the intrusion of conventionary tenures from Cornwall.[16] Nevertheless, conventionary tenure seems to have been rather residual. William Mysteauwe was described as *conuencionarius domini* in 1365; Hamelin atterbrigge was also a conventionary tenant, when he died in 1368, when his widow, Margery, was admitted *per scriptum domini*. The court rolls provide no further references to conventionary tenants. The vast majority of the tenants were *nativi*, but there were occasional references to tenure in socage, which, in one instance, was qualified as tenure *libere in socagio*, confirming that here socage was free tenure rather than the socage of eastern England.[17] The standard holding in Werrington was of two types, the ferling and half Cornish acre. Multiple tenures or tenements were held from the late fourteenth century, although most tenants until the late fifteenth continued to hold a single tenure. Six tenants who died in the 1360s held more than one tenure, although only one had as many as three. Through the fourteenth and fifteenth centuries, five tenants were recorded as holding two or three tenures at their death. John Louya held four when he died in 1393. Extreme engrossing did not occur until the 1490s, when, for example, William Whitchurche held eleven tenures; John Canon held six in reversion and John Uppecote four. In the rental of 1522, John Cloteworthy held eleven tenures. All, however, seem to have related to the life-cycle of individuals rather than dynastic or family holdings. Unlike in some other parts of England, fragmentation of holdings did not happen in Werrington; there was no visible land market in small parcels of land, perhaps, as on some other estates, an indicator of seignorial influence.[18] This consolidation of holdings was facilitated during the later middle ages by the excess of land over demand. Inheritance customs may have affected the transmission of forenames more than bynames and surnames. At Werrington, as also at Uplyme and Stoke Canon, the custom was ultimogeniture. The stimulus of ultimogeniture in some circumstances may have been to induce the migration of elder siblings, especially during the later middle ages.[19] In the fourteenth century, strong seignorial pressure may have been exercised to prevent the confusion of personal status and the status of the land. When free and unfree married, the lord required a warranty that neither the status of the land nor that of the unfree partner would be affected. In some cases, free tenants were prohibited from inheriting unfree land, to prevent land being subtracted from seignorial control.[20]

Throughout the period, the existence of some core surnames within the community was associated closely with office-holding.[21] Offices were notionally elective, in that tenants were elected to offices by the homage, but no doubt as a seignorial strategy to hold the homage accountable for the misdemeanours of manorial officers. The offices were obviously onerous, and heavy fines paid for relief or remission from office; thus in 1365, William Besant paid 40s. and William Roberd 26s. 8d.; in 1384, Thomas Burgeys 40s. and Thomas Gode 60s.; in 1392, John Piper 50s. and Richard Baron 46s. 8d.; thus these fines contributed one of the largest elements from the perquisites of courts in the later middle ages. The offices tended to be held by the principal tenants within the community;

the homage may have preferred such men to save itself harmless. Pledges, included in the table below, were not really officers, but their selection reflects position within the community.

Table 6.4

Office-holding at Werrington 1366–1497
Concentration in the hands of substantial tenants.

Office	Total	Louya	Canon	Colman	Tommas
Jurors	177	30	41	16	16
Swarmen	73	0	2	2	0
xij pro rege	316	0	6	0	0
beadles	41	6	10	2	0
reeves	25	2	4	0	1
chief pledges	64	8	9	6	6
rent collectors	20	6	7	1	2
pledges*	344	73	15	15	8

* Pledges includes only personal pledges (i.e. omits the beadle as a pledge).

Personal pledging was mainly between unrelated tenants rather than through ties of kinship. For example, between 1365 and 1393, there were cumulatively 150 pledgings, of which the beadle accounted for some; of the remainder, only 18 entailed a pledge with the same surname as the pledged, such as John Cotel senior being a pledge for John Cotel in 1393, John Kyea for Alice Kyea in 1369. Even John Louya, a principal pledge of substantial status in these years, pledged for kin on only four occasions, a very minute part of his total activity as a pledge.

These were consequently some of the variables which affected the persistence of surnames within the community at Werrington. The following analysis shows the pattern of these surnames within Werrington through the later middle ages. The enumeration of surnames of taxpayers in 1332 reveals a highly localized content. Some 20 to 24 of this stock in 1332, that is about 50%, consisted of local locative bynames, mostly deriving from hamlets and tenements dispersed within the parish and manor. The remainder originated in small settlements in the adjacent parishes, especially North Petherwin. At this time, heritability was still nascent, but many of the bynames of 1332 were still in existence when the court rolls become extant in 1365–6, many persisting to the end of the fourteenth century. By the time of the earliest surviving court rolls, in 1365–6, surnames had become entirely heritable in Werrington. The persistence of the bynames of 1332 reflects several important points.

Firstly, bynames were becoming heritable in west Devon between 1332 and 1365; secondly, the locative bynames in use in the lay subsidy in 1332 were replicated in the court rolls of the late fourteenth century, so illustrating that in this area locative bynames were the forms by which tenants were actually known; thirdly, these locative forms represent the extreme localization of the community in the fourteenth century.

Table 6.5

Persistence of the Bynames in the Lay Subsidy of 1332

Total bynames	45
Immediate loss*	10
Further loss by 1396	18
Further loss by 1498	13
Further loss by 1525	4

* That is, by the time of the first extant court rolls in 1365–6.

The table represents the persistence and loss of the bynames of 1332 over the middle ages. Four persisted into the lay subsidy of 1524–5: Vele *alias* Vela *alias* Veele; Colacott *alias* Coulecote; Sutton *alias* Sotton; and Cotel(l); seven persisted into the 1480s and 1490s: Morches; Gode; Panston; Bolepytt; Hamme; Louya; and Tommas *alias* Thomas.

The survival of locative bynames from 1332 illustrates the continued localized nature of surnames. Mostly derived from within the parish, a few related to Petherwin, and reflected the intensely localized nature of society within the isthmus intruding into Cornwall: de Stauenhall (Stenhill); de Hulscote (Hellescote); de Clobury (Clubworthy); de Wynnesdon (Winsdon); de Gotecote (Godcott). The extent of survival and loss is tabulated below:

Table 6.6

Persistence and Loss of Locative Bynames of 1332

Total of locative bynames in 1332	20–24*
Immediate loss	6
Further loss by *c.*1385–95	8
Further loss by 1469–94	8
Further loss by 1524–5	2

* Some may represent either locative or topographical forms (e.g. atte Lete might relate to Leat in Werrington, Graue *alias* de la Groue, de Topehille, de la Hamme).

This analysis reveals principally the very slow process of loss of bynames and surnames from the community. Although only four persisted from 1332 through to 1524–5, yet many others persisted over very long periods of time. In particular, a number survived into the 1490s. Looking retrospectively from the lay subsidy of 1524–5, the subsidy contained a total of 31 surnames, of which ten originated by 1365, four from between 1366–1400, seven in 1462–96, whilst eight appeared only after 1500.

The demise of some surnames can be directly attributed to the mortality. The surname Red disappeared after the death of John Red in 1365, since he left only a sister Joan (although Rede recurred from 1462). The surname Carpenter was extinguished on the death of William in 1365, it seemingly being impossible to distrain his son to assume the holding (although this surname too recurred from 1462). The surname Briton disappeared on the death of William in 1365 and Robert in 1369. The heir of William had been Joan, daughter of Robert, Robert receiving custody of her. Robert died in 1369, his heir being Joan, wife of Walter Salle. The Yunge family and surname was a similar casualty of the mortality. Both Nicholas and John died in 1369, effectively the end of the surname in Werrington. The death of William Berbal marked the finality of that surname, since, although he left a female relative Christine, no heir could be distrained to take the holding. Some, such as Agnes Priope and Agnes Plouete, who were also consumed by the mortality, seem to have been landless, and their surnames transient on the manor, leaving no record on the court rolls other than their death. By contrast, Alana Laundrey, daughter of Nicholas, held two ferlings at her death in 1369. The family comprised Alwyta, John, Walter, and Juliana, but John and Walter were *fugitivi* from the manor. Alwyta was presented for default of suit in 1369 and Juliana for leyrwite, but thereafter, with presumably no males with that surname remaining in the community, the surname lapsed. John Yunge had held two ferlings and Nicholas Yunge half a Cornish acre. Carpenter, Briton and Berbal had all held ferlings. Hamelin ate Brigge, a conventionary tenant, had held half a Cornish acre, but died in the mortality and with him the surname. The surname Godefray, however, persisted, despite the loss of Agnes in 1365 and William in 1369. The mortality thus removed some surnames indiscriminately from the community.[22]

The court rolls throughout the later middle ages recorded the deaths of 81 tenants. About 25 deaths were associated with the demise of a surname, including those of the 1360s: such as, Walter Mistauwe (1385); William Yungcote (1393); Nicholas Parkeman (1395); William Bodyer (1395); Joan Spear (1395); Richard Wylcok (1469); Joan widow of John Tredythen (1472); Walter Page (1479);

and John Carter (1479). Some surnames, such as Parkeman, Tredythen and Carter, related to transient or life-cycle tenants. The 1390s was another period of heavier mortality of tenants, some surnames disappearing in close association, others lingering for a short time longer. Storm had appeared in the court rolls from 1365. Its principal bearer, John, died in 1392; John son of John Storm had been a *fugitivus* from the manor in 1384, but may have returned since a John Storm was involved in actions of trespass in 1395–6. Isabella Storm paid a fine to compromise an action in 1393. Thereafter, the surname did not recur. Isabella was the widow of John, who had held half a Cornish acre in Penrice by her right (*ut de iure Isabelle uxoris sue*), and she probably received the tenement after his death. The mechanics of loss of surnames in the later middle ages thus involved mortality, ultimogeniture and female heirs.

Throughout the later middle ages, a number of surnames persisted and represented core or focal families in Werrington. Amongst unfree tenants, the most significant surname was Louya, although it disappeared in the 1490s. One criterion of the status of the family is office-holding, although there are different perceptions of its reliability. Of 344 pledges on the manor, 73 involved the Louyas. Thirty jurors held the surname; a Louya was beadle six times, reeve twice, chief pledge eight times and rent collector on six occasions. The family was inter-related with the Notte, Baron, Taylour, Wolf, Wyledon, and, importantly, Canon families, the latter being another dominant family in the community. These social networks complicated the movement of land. When Joan, widow of John Notte, died, William Louya inherited the ferling as *proximus heres* in 1384. When Christine Baron died, Roger Louya inherited; when John Taylour died, his ferling was inherited by William Louya through the right of his wife, Emma (*de iure dicte Emme*), in 1385. Margery, daughter of Richard Louya, was married to John Baron in 1393.[23] When Stephen Canon died, Stephen Louya was the next heir (*heres proprinquior*) to his land in Heele in 1489. Conversely, John Wolf and his wife, Alice, inherited on the death of Roger Louya, and Jocelin Wyledon and his wife on the death of William Louya, Wyledon through the right of his wife (*de iure Isabelle uxoris sue*). These kinship ties and social networks reflect the importance of the Louya family within the community. The patterns of inheritance tend to confirm Razi's suggestion, for this community at least, that changes in surnames at inheritances do not necessarily reflect the dissolution of the bond between land and family.[24]

Umfrey Louya was enumerated amongst the taxpayers of 1332. The first extant court rolls in the 1360s record John Louya as the head of the kinship group. When John died in 1393, he held four ferlings. Although a few tenants had accumulated two or three holdings previously (Alana Laundrey, John Yunge, William Ayrig, William Godefray, Richard Hamelyn, and William Carpenter), Louya was the first to engross four tenures. His holding was divided between several heirs: two ferlings went to Thomas Louya, one to Thomas son of Robert Louya, and one to John's own son, John. This inheritance strategy was important for a family which was bifurcating in the late fourteenth century. John Louya was a pledge on some 60 occasions between 1365 and 1392. He was beadle in six years during that time, affeeror in three years (1365, 1368 and 1384), although not recorded as chief pledge in the court rolls (but these are defective for many years). The foundations of the socio-economic importance of the family seems to have been laid by John. The family was already proliferating before his death. Roger and Juliana Louya had died in 1365, Walter a year before John. Isabella had been manumitted in 1384.[25] Despite this influence, younger sons were required to follow the normal adolescent life-cycle, reflected in John Louya junior being assaulted by his employer, John Robin, in 1369.[26] The Louya surname thus provided a strong element of continuity from at least 1332 through to the 1490s.

Further stability was provided by the surname Canon, inter-related by the 1490s with Louya. Canons provided 41 jurors in the annual lists, ten beadles, nine chief pledges and seven rent collectors. In their continuations in the later middle ages, they persisted through to at least the lay subsidy of 1524–5. Members of this kinship group held half a Cornish acre. A similar influence was exerted by the Colman and Cotel families, through tenure of land and office-holding. Colmans existed from 1365 to the 1490s, Canons from 1365 to 1525, Cotels from 1332 to 1522. The Suttons, although genealogically longevious from 1332 to 1524–5, exercised less influence through office.

During the fifteenth century, these families bifurcated and 'ramified'. Combined with the demographic contraction, their continuance and expansion increased their importance within the community. Amongst the various branches of the kinship group, a predilection for a limited number of common forenames, perhaps through patrilinear naming, led to the need to use affixes, at least for the purposes of some records.[27] Isonymy of both forename and surname otherwise made it difficult to identify inhabitants in the record. Affixes for these families were frequently locative ones. Thus for the Colman family, the court rolls differentiated between John Colman, John Colman de Raddon, John son of John Colman, John Colman de Druxston, all in the 1460s. William Colman had to be distinguished from William Colman de Hilliscote in the early 1470s.

The affixes applied to the Canons included: Richard Canon de Kylwere; Richard Canon de Panston; John Canon de Hamme; John Canon de Brasecote; John Canon myller; John Canon de Nytherbrygge; as well as John Canon and John Canon junior. Other appearances in court involved Reginald Canon, Stephen Canon, Robert Canon, and Thomas Canon. The Cotells included John Cotell de Launceston, John Cotell de Fursdon, John Cotell Bocher, John Cotell de Yomebrigg (de Brygg), and John Cotell. In fact, the Cotells required affixes from the late fourteenth century, in the form of John Cotel de Radeforde, John Cotell de Wytston, John Cotell atte Brigge, and John Cotell *clericus*. The Suttons had fewer complications, but affixes were still necessary; thus by the 1490s, John Sutton de Groue, John Sutton de Sutton, John Sutton and John Sutton junior. This surname had obviously originated as a locative form from the hamlet of Sutton in Werrington, with Robert and Ralph de Sutton in 1332. By 1365, the surname had become asyndetic, although the syndetic form, de Sutton, still occurred four times in the court rolls in 1369. By the 1490s, the locative surname was insufficient and curiously a new affix, employing the same placename, had to be applied. To some extent, this requirement for affixes was a reflection of the very intense localization of society in this part of Devon. Nevertheless, similar affixes became prevalent in some other communities, such as Stoke Fleming, and in these other cases, affixes developed because of the existence of core families and the predilection within those families for the transmission of common forenames.

By the late fifteenth century, a concentration of surnames still existed within the community. The rental of 1494 enumerated seven Canons, who thus comprised 11.5% of the tenantry (Richard, Stephen, two Johns, Thomas, Robert, and Reginald); whilst the surname Cotell occurred three times (Robert, John and Richard), but had been listed six times in the incomplete rental of 1486.

Table 6.7

Isonymy in Werrington: Rental of 1494

Total tenants	61
Total surnames	41
Coefficient of surnames against tenants	1.49

Despite this concentration of surnames, there were some fifty other surnames which occurred only transiently within the community; in all cases, they are evident only because their bearers were presented a few times for not being in one of the three tithings, and occasionally also for debt or brewing. Poos has suggested that these transients may have been servants in the early stages of their life-cycle.[28] Jordan Ilond is a typical example, occurring in the court rolls between 1384 and 1386, in cases of trespass, assault and debt, and presented for brewing three times. Richard Vicary was presented in 1384 for not being in tithing, subsequently appeared in pleas of debt and trespass, and was presented for brewing twice, before dis-appearing from 1392. During the fourteenth century, the lists of brewers had drawn from all socio-economic status, but in the fif-teenth century life-cycle brewers from the lower echelons of society, often seemingly landless, featured more dominantly in the lists, a phenomenon more significant still in Stoke Fleming.[29] These tran-sient surnames may thus have represented servants in husbandry, who received part of their subsistence through brewing. Explicit references to servants are by their nature sporadic, since they would only be entered in the court rolls through misdemeanours, most usually assault. Only 19 references related to servants; in 11, the servant was simply identified by a forename and the qualifier *serviens*. In the other seven cases, the servant seems to have belonged to one of the existing families, thus Thomas Sondercok in 1365, John Piper also in that year, Joan Louya in 1395, and Margaret Sutton in 1480. John Beaux, who occurred in litigation in 1395, was possibly an immigrant, and some of the anonymous servants may also have been new to the community.

Towards the end of the fifteenth century, the intrusion of some new transient surnames seems to have been more closely related to life-cycle landholding. When Walter Page died in 1479, his tenure in Ford was inherited by John Rooche through the right of his wife, Katherine, sister of Walter (*cuius proprinquior heres est Katerina uxor Johannis Rooche soror eius*). Rooche was a new introduction to Werrington. Between 1479 and 1496, this surname occurred in the court rolls for default and respite of suit twelve times, once for brewing and twice in actions of trespass; he was also listed in the rental of 1494. Equally recent were the surnames of Pedeler, Taltarne and Wyllyam. Richard Pedeler was presented for poaching in the lord's warren in 1474 and 1478; in the latter year, John Pedeler was appointed one of the *xij pro rege*, continuously appearing on that panel from 1489 to 1496. John was listed in the rentals of 1486, 1494 and 1522. John Taltarne appeared initially in the court of 1489, recurred consistently as one of the *xij pro rege*, and in the rentals of 1494 and 1522. William Wyllyam served also as one of the twelve in 1492, when he was also admitted to land, was presented for respite of suit in 1493-6, and seems to disappear from 1496. The best example of these new life-cycle introductions, however, was John Cloteworthy. Occurring first for an infraction of the tithing in 1496, he subsequently became a principal tenant on the manor. Although he only appeared once in the court rolls, in 1497 in a case of trespass, he was a substantial engrosser of tenures by the rental of 1522, in which he held eleven tenements owing rents of 19s. 9d., 10s. 8d., 16s., 7s. 9d., 10s. 7d., 33s. 4d., 10s., 40s., 6s. 8d., 10s. and 18s. He was still there in the lay subsidy of 1524–5.[30] The introduction of some new surnames in the late fifteenth century was thus closely associated with the life-cycle landholding of some individuals.

Stoke Fleming was situated in an entirely different region, in the coastal South Hams, adjacent, moreover, to the developing borough of Dartmouth, part of that town, indeed, being within the manor of Stoke Fleming. By 1377, Dartmouth had a population of about 1,000, and increased its prominence as a port and trading community during the later middle ages.[31] The pattern of naming at Stoke Fleming thus had many differences from that at Werrington, yet some similarities too. The major similarity was the usage of affixes to differentiate members of some dominant kinship groups during the later middle ages, as preferred forenames led to some confusion. On the other hand, the turnover of surnames in Stoke was much more frequent and at a higher level. There was less persistence and continuity here, but, despite this general pattern, one surname, Elyot, persisted from at least 1332 through to the end of the fifteenth century. Another feature here was the high proportion of surnames ostensibly of landless and undersettles who existed in the community partly, it seems, from income from brewing, and which would not have been revealed had they not been presented for brewing.

By contrast with Werrington, and in close approximation to many other manors in east Devon, there was a dissolution of the relationship between tenures and surnames in Stoke during the later middle ages; inheritance never became revivified as at Werrington.

Table 6.8

Changes of Tenancy in the Court Rolls of Stoke Fleming

Tenancy to another surname	21
Inherited by same surname	4
In lord's hands	17
Elected by homage	1
Purchase of reversion	3
To widow	3

Table 6.9

Changes of Tenancy in the Review of Tenures of c.1466

Regrants	24
Previous tenant not stated	11
Previous tenant different surname	8

Admissions to tenancies at Stoke, after the commencement of the extant court rolls in 1384, almost comprehensively involved a new surname. In c.1466, the tenures were reviewed, and regranted for terms of lives (mainly three), but even in this document some of the tenures were delivered away from the surname.[32]

Despite the greater volatility in Stoke Fleming, some of the same features which existed at Werrington were also exhibited here. In 1332, for example, a considerable proportion of the taxpayers bore locative bynames derived from dispersed settlement within the manor and parish, such as the two named (de) Imerigge (Embridge), de Esse (Ash), Bogheton (Bowden), three called Wodebury (now Woodbury Farm), atte Cotene (now Cotton), and Swaneton; additionally, two other taxpayers bore locative bynames derived from hamlets in adjacent Stokenham, such as de Yernecombb' (Yarnscombe) and Kynebogh (Kernborough).[33] In toto, a third of the 34 taxpayers in the subsidy bore localized locative bynames. Many of these persisted into the late fourteenth century, as, for example, John Swaneton, who died in 1394. At that time, the surnames Wodeby and Kenboghe, from amongst those listed in 1332, still persisted on the manor.[34] Amongst the 19 nativi listed in the extent of 1374, however, only two bore locative surnames, Ralph Buggeford (Bugford in Stoke Fleming) and Isabella atte Fenne (Venn in Stoke Fleming).[35] It seems, however, that the extent, relating only to that third of the manor provided as dower, omitted a great number of locative bynames of customary tenants, since many more occurred in the court rolls.

During the later middle ages, there was a complete change in the pattern of surnames on the manor, but the process was protracted. Several surnames persisted over several generations before disappearing. Only one, however, persisted from 1332 through to the early sixteenth century. Elyot was connected with a core, substantial kinship group throughout this period. In 1332, Richard Elyot was assessed at 18d., the fourth highest contribution in Stoke, but two payments (5s. and 2s.) were exacted from taxpayers called (de) Carru, lords of the manor. If these are excluded, then Elyot was second highest after another assessment of 2s. The range of assessment on the 32 taxpayers (excluding de Carrus) was 8d. to 2s., the mean and median both 12d. In the extent of 1374, a Richard Elyot, a *nativus*, held one and a half ferlings, and this Richard was constantly embroiled in pleas of debt, some of which he prosecuted illicitly outside the manorial court. In some of these cases, he was acting as the executor of the will of Agnes Elyot and as co-executor of the will of Gervase Elyot, who had died in 1395. By the early fifteenth century, a Richard Elyot held three tenures *ad voluntatem*, and, in the process of engrossing these holdings, had allowed some of the houses to fall into disrepair. In the mid fifteenth century, Stephen Elyot took a ferling at South Ash from the lord. Both William and Richard Elyot featured on the list of the *xij pro rege* at that time. When tenures were reviewed and regranted as leases for lives in *c.*1466, Richard Elyot held two ferlings, John Elyot senior one, and John Elyot junior one. On the renewal of fealty of tenants in *c.*1470, Walter Elyot held freely, but John senior, John junior and Richard all held *secundum consuetudinem manerii*. The family had proliferated so much that affixes were required in the court rolls from the 1470s. In *c.*1470, the rolls had to differentiate between John Elyot de Stoke, John Elyot, Stephen Elyot, John Elyot Bocher, and Walter Elyot. Between 1476 and 1491, the court rolls distinguished John Elyot senior, John Elyot junior, John Elyot Bocher, John Elyot de Stoke senior, John Elyot de Wyche, John Elyot de Worthyn, John Elyot de Imerygge, John Elyot Brewer, and John Elyot de Court. Accordingly, some cases of trespass and debt in *c.*1477–8 involved John Elyot de Wyke *v* John Elyot junior de Court, John Elyot de Worthyn pitted against John Elyot junior de Court, and John Elyot de Worthyn with John Elyot de Wyche. The family continued to recur frequently in the court rolls.[36]

Other surnames ostensibly appear initially at the end of the fourteenth century and persisted into the early sixteenth as core elements. Thus the close of Richard Comb was broken into in 1384, and the surname continued into the sixteenth century.[37] The surname Coleton only occurred, it seems, towards the middle of the fifteenth century, but rapidly expanded within the community to become an important element. William Coleton, who died in 1438, held two ferlings *secundum consuetudinem manerii* and one tenement at 'Whytalond'. Some seven years before William's death, Richard Coleton had taken two ferlings from the lord. At that time, both Gervase and William Coleton served as *xij pro rege*. When John Coleton junior died in 1447, he held a ferling in 'Swaneton' *ad voluntatem*. In that year, another John Coleton (de Combe) was placed in mercy to satisfy the lord for 20s. 2¾d. *de arreragiis suis de tempore quo fuit prepositus*. In the regranting of tenures in *c.*1466, William Coleton held a ferling, John three ferlings, Richard three ferlings, and Thomas two ferlings, thus dominating the tenure of customary land in the community in the mid fifteenth century, and continuing as a core kinship group and surname into the sixteenth century.[38]

Not all core families were continuously substantial, however. The Hunte family illustrates those which experienced changing fortunes, but were genealogically longevious within the community, thus providing a stable surname. The position of the H(o)untes seems generally to have deteriorated over the later middle ages. In 1374, David Hounte had held a standard holding of one ferling. In the 1390s, John Hounte had acted as a *collector domini Regis*, and had employed at least one servant, Laurence. John subsequently offered the lord an increase of rent of 12d. to be exonerated from serving as reeve (but most tenants in the later regranting of tenures in the mid fifteenth century achieved the same exemption). By the regranting of tenures in 1466, however, the Huntes had declined to a lower economic status as cottagers; John senior held only an *aula* (basically a house) and garden; John junior a cottage; and Andrew a cottage and close. By 1476, however, Andrew had abandoned his cottage for some three years (*Et illum reliquid per tres annos elapsos . . .*), and it remained in the lord's hands. Despite their lower position, the Huntes had still expanded within the community, so that affixes were necessary for formal identification: thus in the 1480s, John Hontte de Aysshe, John Hontte weuere, John Honte junior, Thomas Hontte, John Hontte de Stoke, Richard Hontte de Stoke, John Hontte and Richard Hontte.[39]

The social dominance of these three kinship networks and surnames is thus reflected in the regranting of tenures in 1466.[40] Of the 43 tenures involved, including cottages, three were held by Elyots, four by Coltons and three by Honttes. Elyots had existed on the manor from at least the early fourteenth century, the other two from at least the late fourteenth. All continued as core surnames through into the early sixteenth century. Other surnames persisted over several generations (such as Trenda, Shuter *alias* Sweter, Spyre), whilst, however, the *corpus* of surnames in the community was gradually transformed. By the late fifteenth century, innumerable new surnames had been introduced into the community, whilst a small lingering core provided some continuity.

An equally significant feature at Stoke, however, was the substratum of surnames which was revealed only intermittently and at specific times — for licensing for brewing, which the assize of ale had become. Thus, whilst the extent of a third of the manor comprised 23 tenures and the regranting of tenures on the whole manor in 1466 43 tenures, innumerable individuals were amerced for brewing:

130 different people between *c.*1384–1407; 142 from the 1430s to *c.*1477; 88 from *c.*1477–98. With the exception of some constant substantial brewers, including the Coletons and the Elyots, a very large number of these individuals were occasional brewers, constant but fined for only one brewing at each court; none seems to have held land within the manor; many can be supposed to have been landless, servants or undersettles. Income from brewing allowed their existence within the community by supplementing their income from non-landed sources. Some of these surnames survived over two generations, most only related to an individual, perhaps a life-cycle servant.[41]

The process of change in Stoke Fleming thus involved a radical turnover of the stock of surnames over the later middle ages, but with some continuity provided by some more longevious core surnames. Only one surname, however, survived throughout the entire period. Simultaneously, there was a high volume of very transient surnames. The pattern at Uplyme resembled that at Stoke, but the pace of turnover was more rapid. Uplyme was located in the very eastern extremity of Devon, on the coast and adjacent to the county boudary with Dorset.[42] Here too, although located in the more nucleated parts of Devon, there was still some dispersed settlement, reflected in some locative surnames which persisted over the fourteenth century, so that one third of the 31 taxpayers in 1332 had localized locative bynames.[43]

The overall turnover of surnames over the secular trend was almost comprehensive. Only two of the bynames listed in the lay subsidy of 1332 persisted into the early sixteenth century, as described below. Of the surnames existing in the rental of 1516, only the same two had seemingly existed on the manor at an earlier time, although the data are inadequate since there is a long gap between the previous extant court roll (1408) and the rental. All these surnames in 1516, with the exception of two, were, nevertheless, introduced to the manor in the fifteenth century at the earliest — that is, 32 of the 34 surnames listed in 1516. Further introductions continued in the early sixteenth century, since an additional 20 surnames appeared in the court rolls of 1530–6 which were not included in the rental of 1516, although it is possible that the omission of some may be explained by their being borne by landless or under-tenants. Some 22 of the surnames in the rental recurred in the court rolls of the 1530s, whilst nine seem to have been lost. By the sixteenth century, the stock of surnames had thus almost completely changed, and the fluidity still continued in the early sixteenth century.

More detail of this fluidity and volatility can be accumulated for the fourteenth and fifteenth centuries. In particular, the rapid change of the stock in the early fourteenth century is evident.

Table 6.10

Survival of Bynames listed by the Lay Subsidy of 1332

Listed only in the lay subsidy of 1332	5
Disappeared before the 1340s	9
Disappeared in the 1350s	4
Disappeared in the 1370s–1380s	5
Disappeared between 1380–1408	1
Persisted into the sixteenth century	2

* It should be noted, however, that some of these bynames of 1332 had existed in the community from at least 1300–15, and, indeed, in the case of de Carswill from at least 1275.[44]

Nevertheless, many more bynames existed in the community than were enumerated in the lay subsidy, as illustrated by a comparison of the extents of the mid thirteenth and early fourteenth century and the lay subsidy, as considered above.[45] A more detailed perspective can be obtained by consideration of the bynames which occurred in the court rolls during the fourteenth century, from 1307 to 1408. Between 1307 and 1350 some 240 bynames are entered on the rolls. During the fourteenth century, however, some 162 bynames and surnames were extremely transient, and of these, 61 occurred in the early fourteenth century. For example, Thomas Alseluer appeared only between 1307 and 1315; John Anthony, a *garcio*, and therefore possibly only on the manor transiently in service, had an equally short existence at Uplyme. Many bynames at this time existed on the manor for only one generation: thus Geoffrey Artur 1313–44; Richard Broun from the 1340s to 1370s, despite being reeve and a constant pledge; Gregory Charlemayn from 1279–1340; John Colprest from the 1340s to 1370s; Walter Crokkere, a cottager, who received his smallholding in the 1360s, and died by 1387. These subtractions of bynames and surnames probably had several causes. First, bynames were still fluid and unstable in the first decades of the fourteenth century, so that some may have related only to individuals. Secondly, some of the bynames and surnames were borne by transient inhabitants of the manor, especially by *garciones*. Finally, some surnames were lost by mortality in the 1340s, when widows inherited.

The change in the stock of surnames was thus reflected in changes of tenancy of holdings on the manor, although the number of transactions in land in the court rolls is small.

Table 6.11

Changes of Tenancy at Uplyme 1344–75

Changes where the new tenant had the same surname as the previous	15
Changes where the new tenant had a different surname	28

* These figures omit land remaining in the lord's hands.

In fact, the changes which involved no disruption of surname comprised almost exclusively inheritances within the Gache and Lilling families, and remainders to widows in 1344–7 (five widows). It was these two kinship groups which provided the continuity in the community between the early fourteenth and early sixteenth centuries, both still existing there in 1536. With the exception of 1408–1516, when the court rolls are defective, almost continuous genealogies can be constructed of these two persistent families and surnames. Throughout, both were substantial holders of land, although siblings had constantly to go through the life-cycle process as *garciones*.

The difference between the three manors, located in different regions of Devon, was thus the pace of change and turnover during the later middle ages. In Werrington, in the west, the change was slower, whereas it was swifter in Stoke Fleming and Uplyme. Moreover, the volume of transient bynames and surnames in the latter two was higher than in Werrington, which still, however, had numbers of transient surnames. In all, however, the almost total replacement of the stock of surnames was counterbalanced by the persistence of a few surnames throughout the entire period into the sixteenth century. Such processes may have occurred on other manors in similar *pays*, but it is not feasible to assess the nature of change by a simple comparison of the lay subsidies of 1332 and 1524–5.

References

1 R M Smith, 'Human resources', in G Astill & A Grant, eds., *The Countryside of Medieval England*, (1988), 190-1; the national population may have declined from 5-6 millions in 1348 to 2.8-3.1 millions in the 1540s.

2 *Lay Subsidy 1332*, 62; *Lay Subsidy 1524-5*, index, sn Lillycrop.

3 For some aspects of Werrington, H P R Finberg, *Tavistock Abbey*, (1951), *passim*. The sources used here comprise: DRO Bedford MSS Werrington court rolls; DRO W1258M/D69 (rentals); *Lay*

Subsidy 1332, 68; *Lay Subsidy 1524-5*, 4; Finberg, 'The early history of Werrington', *English Historical Review*, 59 (1944), 248; H P R Finberg and W G Hoskins, *Devonshire Studies*, 19-29; H P R Finberg, 'The Devon-Cornwall boundary', *D&C Notes and Queries*, 23 (1947), 104-7; *Launceston Cartulary*, xxiii-xxiv, xxix.

5 *Launceston Cartulary*, xxiii, xxxv-xxxvi, 112-16 (nos. 291-6).

6 *Ibid*.

7 *Ibid*. Launceston prosecuted at least eleven cases of debt against tenants of Tavistock Abbey in the Abbey's manorial court at Werrington; in four cases, the debt was specifically *pro decima (decimis) vendita (venditis)*; the amounts ranged from 2s. 8d. to 30s., with a median of 15s. 8d.

8 For brewing, J M Bennett, 'Village ale-wives', in B Hanawalt, ed., *Women and Work in Pre-Industrial Europe*, (1986), 20-36; R M Smith, 'Some issues concerning families and their properties in England 1250-1800', in *idem*, ed., *Land, Kinship and Life-cycle*, (1984), 27-30; R H Hilton, *The English Peasantry in the Later Middle Ages*, (1975), 45-6; C Dyer, *Lords and Peasants in a Changing Society*, (1980), 346-9; N Denholm-Young, *Seignorial Administration in England*, (1937), 89-91; J B Post, 'Manorial amercements and peasant poverty', *Economic History Review*, 2nd ser, 28 (1975), 308-9. For a recent discussion of merchet and leyrwite, R M Smith, 'Marriage processes in the English past: some continuities', in L Bonfield, R Smith and K Wrightson, eds., *The World We Have Gained*, (1986), 52-8; for the development of leyrwite, T North, 'Legerwite in the thirteenth and fourteenth centuries', *Past & Present*, 111 (1986), 3-16.

9 L R Poos and R M Smith, ' "Legal windows onto historical populations"? Recent research in medieval England', *Law & History Review*, 2 (1984), 144-8.

10 D Postles, 'Brewing in the peasant economy on some manors in late medieval Devon'. (unpub. paper).

11 R M Smith, 'Kin and neighbours in a thirteenth century Suffolk community', *Journal of Family History*, 4 (1979), 219-56; M Pimsler, 'Solidarity in the medieval village? The evidence of personal pledging at Elton, Huntingdonshire', *Journal of British Studies*, 17 (1) (1977), 1-11; E B DeWindt, *Land and People at Holywell-cum-Needingworth*, (1972), 249; J Beckerman, 'Customary law in English manorial courts in the thirteenth and fourteenth centuries', unpub. PhD thesis, London, 1972, 63-116.

12 For example: Robert Groue v John Bordeuyle 'quod ipsum non vexerit nec implacitauit alibi quam in Curia domini sui ad dampnum xl.d . . .' (1368); John Robin att' Ford' v Nicholas Spear 'extra manerium domini' (1369); Matilda Mylle 'tenens domini implacitauit et vexauit Ricardum Tallan alterum Tenentem

domini extra Curiam domini in Curia de Launceston' de rebus determinandis infra manerium domini' (1490); Nicholas Courtes de Tamerton 'per excitacionem Johannis Courtes de Heele tenentis domini perturbauit et vexauit Ricardum Hobbe Tenentem domini (et) alios Tenentes domini extra Curiam domini apud Launceston' et aliis diuersis locis contra consuetudinem manerii' (1475); 'Item presentant quod Johannes Whyte de Eggebear tenens domini implacitauit et vexauit Reginaldum Canon natiuum domini extra Curiam domini in Curia peculiari de materiis determinandis in Curia domini contra consuetudinem manerii' (1490); 'xij manerii venerunt Et presentant quod Willelmus Esseworthy tenens domini implacitauit et vexauit Robertum Canon alterum Tenentem domini extra Curiam domini in Comitatu Deuon' &c' (1494); the same William prosecuted a case against three other tenants 'extra Curiam domini in Comitatu Deuon' de materiis determinandis infra Curiam domini contra consuetudinem manerii' (1494).

¹³ Pimsler, 'Solidarity in the medieval village?'.

¹⁴ J S Beckerman, 'The forty-shilling jurisdictional limit in medieval personal actions', in D Jenkins, ed., *Legal History Studies 1972*, (1975), 110-17; E Clark, 'Debt litigation in a late medieval English vill', in J A Raftis, ed., *Pathways to Medieval Peasants*, (1981), 247-79; M K McIntosh, 'Money-lending on the periphery of London', *Albion*, 20 (1988), 557-67.

¹⁵ P Franklin, 'Peasant widows' "liberation" and remarriage before the Black Death', *Economic History Review*, 2nd ser, 39 (1986), 186-204.

¹⁶ See also, J Hatcher, 'Social structure: F South-west England', in H E Hallam, ed., *The Agrarian History of England and Wales II 1042-1350*, (1988), 677.

¹⁷ D C Douglas, 'The social structure of medieval East Anglia', in P Vinogradoff, ed., *Oxford Studies in Social and Legal History*, 9 (1927); but see also, J Williamson, 'Norfolk: thirteenth century', in P D A Harvey, ed., *The Peasant Land Market in Medieval England*, (1984), 71-2.

¹⁸ P D A Harvey, in *idem*, ed., *The Peasant Land Market in Medieval England*, (1984), 346-8.

¹⁹ Thus also at Stoke Canon: '. . . dicunt quod cum aliquis Natiuus decedit junior filius eius vel filia succedit' (D&C Exeter 1712-1714); Werrington 'Et venit Radulphus Besant natiuus de stipite junior filius (et) heres predicti Willelmi secundum consuetudinem manerii et admittitur tenere tenuram predictam secundum consuetudinem manerii predicti' and 'cuius proprinquior heres est Johannes Louya filius eius Juvenissimus' on the

death of John Louya de Troswell in 1496; Uplyme 'Adam filius
Ricardi Richeman de Hertcomb' petit uersus Willelmum fratrem
suum unum mesuagium et dimidiam virgatam terre unde predictus Walterus pater suus obiit seisitus ut de villenagio cuius
proprinquior ipse est secundum consuetudinem manerii istius
eo quod postnatus'. (*c.*1315, Longleat MS 10771). See also R Faith,
'Peasant families and inheritance customs in medieval England',
Agricultural History Review, 14 (1966), 83-4, who takes a different
view about the effect on the siblings of ultimogeniture.

20 'xij sware(men) presentant quod Robertus Opi liber maritauit
    Ammotam Salle natiuam domini. Et secundum consuetudinem
    manerii debet inuenire pleggios domino alioquin dimittet terram
    suam'; 'Johannes Dauy dat domino de fine xl.d. de inquirendo si
    ipse proprinquior ius habet ad tenuram quam Willelmus Page
    natiuus domini tenet in Colecote. Jurati dicunt quod idem
    Johannes liber est ex parte patris et matris per quod nullum habet
    Jus ad tenuram predictam secundum consuetudinem manerii
    nisi pater vel mater natiui fuissent' (both cases in 1365).

21 There are different opinions whether office-holding reflected
    social status, a thesis originally propounded by J A Raftis, 'The
    concentration of responsibility in five villages', *Mediaeval Studies*, 28
    (1966), 92-118, and pursued by others in the 'Toronto School', as,
    inter alia, A DeWindt, 'Peasant power structures in fourteenth-
    century King's Ripton', *Mediaeval Studies*, 38 (1976), 236-67; but
    this concept has been criticized by Z Razi, 'The Toronto School's
    reconstitution of medieval peasant society: a critical view', *Past &
    Present*, 85 (1979), 141-57, and K Wrightson, 'Medieval villagers in
    perspective', *Journal of Peasant Studies*, 7 (1978), 203-17. At
    Werrington, it seems there was some correlation between socio-
    economic status and officeholding.

22 'Et est eius heres de Stipite secundum consuetudinem manerii
    Johanna uxor Walteri Salle'; 'Et nichilominus distr' unum pro-
    prinquiorem heredem ad faciendum domino fidelitatem per
    plegium Christine Berbal'.

23 See note 21.

24 Z Razi, 'The erosion of the family-land bond in the late four-
    teenth and fifteenth centuries: a methodological note', in R M
    Smith, ed., *Land, Kinship and Life-cycle*, (1984), 295-304; *idem*, 'The
    Toronto school's reconstitution of medieval peasant society: a
    critical view', *Past & Present*, 85 (1980), 142-9.

25 'Isabella Louia venit in plena Curia et dat domino de fine essendi
    liber simul cum bonis et catallis preter si predicta Isabella
    pregnans est soluet domino v.s. ob. prout consuetudo manerii est
    per plegium Johannis Louia Et sic proclamatum est in Curia.'

26 R M Smith, 'Some issues . . .', in *idem*, ed., *Land, Kinship and Life-cycle*, 32-9.

27 I argue elsewhere for patrilinear naming amongst a small core of peasant society.

28 L R Poos, 'Population turnover in medieval Essex', in L Bonfield, R Smith and K Wrightson, eds., *The World We Have Gained*, (1986), 17.

29 D Postles, 'Brewing in the peasant economy on some manors in late medieval Devon'.

30 P D A Harvey, in *idem*, ed., *The Peasant Land Market in Medieval England*, 338-44.

31 M Kowaleski, 'The 1377 Dartmouth poll tax', *D&C Notes and Queries*, 35 (1985), 288-9; the sources for Stoke Fleming used here comprise: DRO 902M/M3-33; 902M/E/5; *Lay Subsidy 1332*, 93; *Lay Subsidy 1524-5*.

32 DRO 902M/M21.

33 *Lay Subsidy 1332*, 93.

34 DRO 902M/M5.

35 DRO 902M/E/5.

36 As n 31.

37 DRO 902M/M3.

38 DRO 902M/M15, 19, 21.

39 DRO 902M/E/5, M6-8, M21, M24 et seqq.

40 DRO 902M/M21.

41 Postles, 'Brewing'.

42 H S A Fox, 'The boundary of Uplyme', *TDA*, 102 (1970), 35-48.

43 *Lay Subsidy 1332*, 47. The sources used here comprise: Longleat MSS Uplyme court rolls; BL Add MS 17450, fos 218-221, 37053, fos 273-9.

44 A Watkin, ed., *The Great Chartulary of Glastonbury*, (Somerset Record Society, 3 vols, 59 and 63-4, 1947—56), 3, 584-6.

45 BL Add MSS 37053, fos 273-9; *Lay Subsidy 1332*, 47.

CHAPTER 7

BYNAMES, SURNAMES,
SOCIAL GROUP AND REGION

Amongst the variables affecting naming patterns, considerable importance must be attached to the influences of social group and region.[1] Both were agencies which had a significant impact on cultures of naming. In some areas of England, the impact of social group was more pronounced. For example, in Oxfordshire a higher proportion of free tenants bore locative or occupational bynames, whilst the unfree tended to have bynames from personal names.[2] In some areas, the nobility, both higher and lower, continued to bear predominantly locative surnames, and so too did the secular clergy, although this special social group may have had wider social origins. On the other hand, the effect of regional cultures had a more profound influence in some other areas. In counties such as Lancashire and Durham, patronymic forms of byname were prolific.[3] The secular clergy in Lancashire and Cheshire may have exhibited a different pattern of naming from those sampled in a recent study of the clergy in Worcestershire in the fourteenth century (although the pattern is corrupted by numbers of unbeneficed clergy in the northern sample which are not contained in the Worcester sample).[4] In Devon, the variables interacted in a complex manner and their respective influence changed over time during the later middle ages. For example, whilst the nobility tended in the early middle ages to have predominantly locative or A-N nickname bynames and surnames, the lesser nobility during the later middle ages exhibited a pattern no different from other social groups in Devon, a change reflecting the transformation in the social composition of the lesser nobility and its transition from a military elite through chivalric social group to gentry. The secular clergy in Devon at the earlier time bore predominantly locative and A-N nickname bynames, but in the later middle ages had the same pattern as other social groups. The naming patterns of different social groups are therefore considered over time: the free and unfree peasantry; the nobility; and the clergy.

Some comment has been made concerning the nature of the sources, but more is necessary. The sources for the nobility comprise the various inquests from the *Carte Baronum* of 1166

231

through to the Feudal Aid of 1428. The latter, however, reflects not necessarily wealth and social status as much as tenure of fees or parts of fees, many of which had become fragmented by the fifteenth century. Analysis of the bynames of the clergy is compounded by similar problems, since the evidence available for the earlier middle ages comprises mainly the beneficed clergy, whilst that for the later period includes numbers of unbeneficed clergy. Similar problems are presented for the study of the bynames of the peasantry. Unlike the case of Oxfordshire, there is no general survey which covered the entire county and differentiated by legal status, such as the *Rotuli Hundredorum* of 1279–80.[5] On the other hand, the *Rotuli* are a static source, which do not account for changes over the later middle ages. For Devon, a large number of survey-type documents (surveys, rentals, extents and custumals) have been analysed, covering several regions of Devon and different times during the later middle ages.

The discussion commences with the naming patterns of free and unfree peasantry.

Table 7.1

Classification of Bynames and Surnames borne by Customary Tenants on some Manors in Devon during the Later Middle Ages[6]

Manor	Date	Loc	Top	Occ	Pat	Pers	Nick	Rel	Unc	Total
Bratton										
Clovelly	1229	8	5	2	0	1	3	0	0	19
Berry Pomeroy	1292	7	10	12	1	11	12	0	4	58*
Stockleigh										
Pomeroy	1292	3	9	3	0	1	4	0	0	20
Modbury	c.1304–8	10	7	1	0	4	6	0	0	28
Modbury	c.1398	7	4	7	0	7	5	0	3	33
Uplyme	mid 13th c.	15	24	7	1	5	16	4	6	78
Uplyme	early 14th c.	13	9	5	1	10	19	0	10	67
Sidbury	c.1350	10	19	14	0	15	11	0	2	71
Sidbury	c.1394	10	23	14	0	11	15	0	3	76
Sidbury	15th c?	22	27	13	0	17	16	0	4	99
Ottery										
St Mary	c.1381	32	47	29	0	29	39	0	6	182
Tawstock	1392	7	8	9	0	8	7	0	0	39
Bovey Tracey	c.1400	5	8	0	0	1	0	0	0	14
Lidford	1447	6	7	9	0	2	9	0	2	35
Stoke Fleming	c.1464	8	5	6	0	17	7	0	0	43
Monkleigh	15th c.	8	6	3	0	6	5	0	3	31

Manor	Date	Loc	Top	Occ	Pat	Pers	Nick	Rel	Unc	Total
Berry Pomeroy	1496	2	9	4	0	2	5	0	0	22 †
Feniton	*c.*1498	4	8	4	0	6	4	0	3	29

* *Villani* and *operarii*; one widow whose byname is not supplied.
† One third of the manor (dower).

Notes to the table: loc = locative; top = topographical; occ = occupational (including status and office); pat = patronyms and metronyms; per = bynames and surnames from personal names; nick = the same from nicknames; rel = the same from relationship; unc = uncertain etymology.

Modbury *c.*1304–8 comprises several manorial inquisitions, so does not include all tenants and does not define status.

Tawstock 1392 relates to part of the manor, at least two-thirds.

Sidbury 15th cent: status is not identified, the rental being arranged topographically rather than, as previously, by legal and economic status. The status of tenants during the later middle ages is frequently complicated by the variety of tenures: at will, *in bondagio*, as *villani*, for lives (assumed to be copyhold for lives), and *conventionarii*.

Berry Pomeroy 1496: again status is not described, and there is some difficulty in distinguishing between locative and topographical; the distinction has been established by reference to *PND*.

In the above table, the status of tenants was, by and large, differentiated. On some other manors, status was not clarified, in particular the manor of Newenham Priory in Axminster.

Table 7.2
Bynames of Tenants at Axminster (Undifferentiated Status)

Taxonomy	1260	late 13th c.	1315	(1332)	1334	Total
Locative	6	6	17	6	18	53
Topographical	13	16	25	7	12	73
Occupational	13	4	25	6	26	74
Patronymic	0	0	0	0	0	0
Personal	5	3	10	2	6	26
Nickname	16	8	23	3	13	63
Relationship	0	0	0	0	0	0
Uncertain	7	6	10	6	16*	45
No byname	2	0	0	0	0	2
Total	62	43	110	30	91	336

Source: BL Arundel MS 17, fos 33v-49r.

(1332) relates to the lay subsidy of 1332.

* This figure is enlarged by the expansion of the bynames Pyw and

Wrang(he), borne by several tenants, both bynames being of uncertain etymology. Pyw could derive from a nickname for magpie, or be metonymic for piemaker, or even be an elision of ApHugh. At Uplyme, however, the byname occurred in the early fourteenth century as le Pyw, which would eliminate the suggestion of ApHugh.

In the case of some estates, the figures for individual manors are so small as to be insignificant except when agglomerated.

Table 7.3

Tenants on the Estate of Canonsleigh Priory 1323 and Plympton Priory 1408 (All Status)

	Canonsleigh	Plympton
Locative	37	54
Topographical	59	46
Occupational	22	27
Nickname	24	34
Personal	16	50
Relationship	1	0
Uncertain	4	12

Source: BL Harley MS 3660, fos 141r-174v; BL Harley MS 4766.

This tabulation of the taxonomy of bynames and surnames of customary tenants illustrates two aspects: first, unfree status did not preclude locative bynames and surnames in Devon; secondly, however, the level of locative surnames did decline amongst the unfree during the later middle ages. Numerous tenants in some vills in the thirteenth and fourteenth centuries bore locative bynames in Devon. This pattern must be related to the dispersed nature of settlement throughout Devon. Even in east Devon, where there was more nucleation, although still some degree of dispersal, many unfree tenants at that time had locative bynames associated with their holding dispersed tenements or inhabiting hamlets within the manor. An excellent example of this phenomenon is the manor of Uplyme, situated in the easternmost part of Devon, adjacent to the county boundary with Dorset.[7] This manor, co-terminous with the parish, now contains a number of scattered farmsteads such as Cannington Farm, Yawl, Carswell Farm, Harcombe Bottom, Holcombe, all of which had existed as hamlets in the thirteenth and early fourteenth centuries.[8] Accordingly, the extent of Uplyme of the mid thirteenth century enumerated customary tenants, identified by their *opera* and weekworks, called Walter de Holcumbe, John de Holcom', Adam de

Holecom', Roger de Holecumb', Peter de Hale, Beymund de Hale; whilst the extent of the early fourteenth century included *dimidii virgatarii tenentes in villenagio* named Matilda de Canyngton and Hugh de Canyngton, *tenentes ferdella terre* called William Pikeston, Sampson de Eston, Robert de Holecombe, William de Holecombe and Isabella de Holecombe, *quinque acrarii* including Thomas de Canyngton, and *cottarii* known as Christine Carswell and Richard de Obecombe.[9] In nearby Yarcombe, customary tenants or *nativi* included John de Churlebrok, John son of Walter de Wyllyngbear, William Bremillore, Matthew de Crawecumb', William de Hockelegh, Alice de Bradeleghe, and several others with locative bynames, in the early fourteenth century, although many others bore syndetic topographical bynames, such as atte Wode, atte More and many others. These locative bynames persisted in Uplyme and Yarcombe through the fourteenth century.[10]

Similarly on the manor of Hockford Waters, a manor of Canonsleigh Priory in the north-east of Devon, *nativi* in the extent of 1323 included John de Slancombe (now Slantycombe), John de Loscombe as well as Robert and Nicholas de Wonham (from Wonham in adjacent Bampton).[11] In the west, a high percentage of surnames in the manor of Werrington originated from dispersed tenements within the manor. William de Lumene gave to Canonsleigh Priory a half ferling with its tenant, Walter *filius Jacobi de Wytenehe, nativus*, and his *sequela*.[12] This pattern was replicated throughout Devon, both in highly dispersed areas and more nucleated areas; all, to some degree, contained some element of dispersed settlement, which affected the pattern of naming of even the unfree social groups.

The regional nature of naming had an impact also on the higher echelons of society, causing a considerable change in the composition of the surnames of the nobility, particularly the lesser nobility, over the course of the later middle ages. Such a transformation, however, was also influenced by the change in the social composition and status of the lesser nobility, as it changed from a military class through chivalric knighthood to gentry.

The fragmentation of fees had progressed some way in Devon by 1242–3, exhibiting a considerable increase by comparison with the degree of disintegration in the *Carte Baronum* of 1166.[13] By 1242–3, some 620 mesne tenants held fees or fragments of fees within the county. A transition in the pattern of naming of these tenants was already developing. Most of them still bore locative surnames with also a small proportion having Anglo-Norman surnames derived from nicknames. A perceptible change, however, was the introduction into the listings of locative bynames and surnames derived from the placenames of minor settlements in Devon. In these cases, the surname was eponymous with the settlement, as these new mesne tenants held a fee or part of a fee predominantly in one settlement only. Fees were arranged in two ways in the listing of 1242–3: by hundred and by barony (although there was considerable overlap between the two arrangements). The arrangement by hundred comprised some 276 fees, of which 60 fees or parts of fees (22%) were held in minor settlements eponymous with the surname of the holder of the fee.[14] For example, the heirs of Geoffrey de la Hoke held a sixth of a fee in la Hoke; William de Ospital held le Ospital; Henry de Goreland held part of a fee in that eponymous place; Henry de Yerd held half a fee in Yard; Ralph de Esse held in Ash; Umfrey de la Shete held four-fifths of a fee in la Shete; Henry de la Hille was co-parcener of half a fee in la Hille and Exton.[15] Arranged by barony were 761 fees or parts of fees, of which 147 (20%) were held by mesne tenants with surnames eponymous with the settlement in which the fee was located.[16] Jordan de Hode, for example, held in la Hode; Roger de Hele held a fee in Hele; Richard de Worth a fee in Worth; John de Dune three-quarters of a fee in Down.[17] The change in nomenclature also involved the initial intrusion of forms of byname more widely associated with lower social groups: Lucy de la Bere; Robert le Marchant; Oresia Crok; Nicholas de la Ya.[18] These latter introductions were only limited, however, in comparison with the more radical change in the stock during the later middle ages. The social composition and surnames of the lower nobility were incipiently being transformed.[19]

During the later middle ages, there occurred a radical change in the surnames of the lesser nobility in Devon, in the form of the gentry and pseudo-gentry. Some tenants in chief and mesne tenants (knightly families) of the twelfth century gradually declined in importance, with some notable exceptions.[20] With their decline, and occasionally demise, went their surnames, particularly some Anglo-Norman surnames. Some families, such as the Pomeroys, Coffins and Malerbes, persisted amongst the gentry, but with diminished status. In the early middle ages, feudal society in Devon had been dominated by the Redvers, earls of Devon; in the late fourteenth, the Courtenay earls exercised a similar influence, although through different social mechanisms; by the early fifteenth century, however, their influence had waned because of a minority.[21] By the early fifteenth century, the gentry of Devon were fragmented, with a level of moderate gentry, but also a very numerous parish or petty gentry, without political leadership or affinity, and considerable political rivalry.[22] The petty or parish gentry existed in other counties, but they were especially widespread in Devon.

Consequently, in many cases, there was a discontinuity between surnames and lordship within communities. This disjuncture happened particularly as fees in some places became even more fragmented, whereas there had previously been a single tenant. Concomitantly, a smaller group of Anglo-Norman surnames survived at this level; where they did survive, it was in reduced circumstances. The vast proportion of the gentry of Devon, because of the innumerable petty or parochial gentry, bore common Devonian surnames which were borne by most other social groups, comprising not only locative surnames predominantly from (often minor) places in Devon, but also topographical and occupational surnames, the latter often derived from simple craft occupations. This process of change is most evident in the feudal aid of 1428.[23]

This aid enumerated the holders of fees and parts of fees by hundred, although a smaller number was listed by vills without reference to hundred. The list therefore approximates to an index of lordship, a rough counting of manors, and a profile of the pseudo-gentry. The list provides the surnames of the current holders of the fees and also the surnames of the former (*quondam*) holders. In the first section, the fees were predominantly fragmented; in the second, the fees had mainly remained undivided. Virtually all the divided fees had been held previously (*quondam*) by a single tenant. In many cases, the co-parceners of these divided fees in 1428 numbered as many as five to seven. Thus, for the total of 419 divided fees or parts of fees in a vill, some 1,324 co-parceners were enumerated, a mean of 3.2 tenants per fee or part of a fee within a vill; most co-parceners held their portions separately rather than jointly.[24] The earlier continuity between surnames, lordship and community was thus severely disrupted; but this continuity was higher, not surprisingly, in those vills where fees had remained intact and undivided.

Table 7.4

Continuity and Discontinuity of Surnames, Lordship and Community in Late Medieval Devon (1428)

1 Divided fees:

Change of surname associated with the fee/community	333	(81%)
Continuity of surname, lordship and community	78	(19%)
Total	411	(100%)

2 Intact fees:

Change of surname associated with the fee/community	168	(70%)
Continuity of surname, lordship and community	71	(30%)
Total	239	(100%)

3 Combined totals:

Change of surname associated with the fee/community	501	(77%)
Continuity of surname, fee and community	149	(23%)
Total	650	(100%)

Continuity was greatest amongst the lesser gentry who held fees in only one vill, lowest where the previous tenant had held fees in many vills — but which were now (in 1428) held by several different tenants, reflecting the decline of importance and status of some former principal mesne tenants and even tenants in chief. The new tenants in these latter cases, where there was the lowest continuity, bore mainly locative surnames from places within Devon, whilst the previous tenants had been distinguished by a high proportion of Anglo-Norman surnames, including several de Ferrers, de Bryan, de Sancto Amando, Pypard, Beaumond, de Monte Acuto, Pomeray, Vautort, Trenchard, de Albemarle, Tyrrell, Daumarle, Champernon, Coffyn, Beaupel, Despencer, Polayn, Chalouns, Malerbe, Dynham. The displaced surnames did not completely disappear, but were replaced within some communities. The surnames of the new gentry were derived from within the community and were often particular to Devon. Nevertheless, despite the enormous changes in the composition of the gentry, a core of stability persisted in about a fifth to a quarter of communities. The surnames of the gentry, however, now consisted of a high Devonian content.

Table 7.5

Taxonomy of Surnames of the Gentry of Devon in 1428

Locative	43%	Topographical	17%
Occupational	8%	Personal	15%
Nicknames	17%	Patronymic	>1%

This taxonomy now reflected the wider pattern within Devon. Perhaps indicative of this pattern were those topographical names which incorporated either syndetic forms (at Yeo, atte Wode) as late as 1428, or the element -man (Bryggeman, Crosseman, Putteman,

Hayman, Rygman, Waterman, Buryman, Mureman, Moreman, Douneman, Rodman, Hilman).[25] Equally, surnames derived from occupations reflected humble origins (several Toukers, Suter, several Crockers, Hoper, Teser, Baker, several Coterells, several Haywards, Cotell, Wright, Helyer, Deyman).[26] Holders of knights fees in Devon in the fifteenth century thus held surnames no different from those borne by other social groups in the county.

By the fifteenth century, the gentry of Devon had a very mixed composition. Hypothetically at least, the secular clergy of Devon may have been composed from diverse social groups, as a career open to all, despite seignorial restrictions on the ordination of the unfree. The caveat in any analysis of the surnames of the clergy is the difficulty of capturing those of the unbeneficed clergy as well as the beneficed, a difficulty which changes over time; the analysis here is compounded by that difficulty. Three different sources have been employed: samples of ordinations in the registers of the Bishops of Exeter; lists of incumbents of sample benefices; admissions to Exeter College.

The latter can be used first to illustrate the taxonomy of a sample of those clergy from Devon who received an education at University between the early fourteenth century and 1530, a database comprising some 203 fellows and members of the college.

Table 7.6
Taxonomy of Clergy who were Graduands of Exeter College, Oxford, to 1530

Type of surname	Number	% of total
Locative	64	32
Topographical	46	23
Personal	41	20
Nicknames	25	12
Occupational	16	8
Patronymic	1	
Uncertain	9	5
Total	203	100

Very broadly, the taxonomy of the clergy reflects the wider pattern of naming in Devon. More detailed diachronic analysis reveals that the level of locative bynames or surnames was higher before *c.*1360, but declined thereafter, again consistent with the general changes within naming in Devon. These locative surnames began to become asyndetic from the 1340s, but syndetic forms still lingered until the 1360s. Occupational surnames had humble associations, such as Pester, Gardiner, Sawyer, Taylor, Prentys, Toker, Wodeward,

Chepman, Helier, Glover. Bearing in mind that such surnames had become hereditary, the pattern in Devon correlates quite closely during the later middle ages with that exhibited by the clergy of Lancashire, as well as the wider pattern of naming within Devon.[27]

This pattern in the later middle ages is confirmed by ordinations in the bishops' registers. The taxonomy of the surnames of ordinands, including *tonsurati*, acolytes, subdeacons, deacons and priests, between 1420 and 1455, replicates the pattern of surnames generally throughout Devon in the later middle ages. The locative surnames almost all derived from within Devon, although some ordinations in Devon also involved Cornish locative surnames. A few locative surnames originated at a greater distance, such as Lancastr', Crukern, Shirborn, Lamport, Derby, but other external locative surnames, such as Chichestr', Bokyngham, Wynchelsee and Dorsete, had already become established in Devon.[28] The few Anglo-Norman surnames from nicknames which were borne by ordinands at this time were residual from the wider corpus at an earlier time, such as John Parlesbyn, who was ordained on the title of St Frideswides Priory in Oxford, or Bonefont and Graunte.[29] The topographical bynames were characteristically Devonian: Bere; Combe; forms with the suffix -man, such as Beryman and Holman; syndetic forms still such as John atte Wille, John atte Hille, and Nicholas Nytheway; forms with the final -ing such as Ralph Hillyng and Richard Willyng.[30] Occupational surnames had humble associations, such as Crocker, Toker, Deyman, Dyer.[31] The proportion of locative surnames had declined by the fifteenth century, as had Anglo-Norman surnames from nicknames.

This later pattern contrasted strongly with the taxonomy of the bynames of the secular clergy in the thirteenth and fourteenth centuries. At that time, the vast preponderance of the clergy bore locative bynames, although from places within the county.[32] The incumbents of parishes almost universally bore locative bynames until the late fourteenth century, comprehensively from placenames in Devon, although Sir Robert de Wylyngtone, rector of High Bickington, represented an extrinsec locative byname which had been introduced to Devon at an earlier time.[33] The preponderance of locative bynames amongst the secular clergy at that time was impinged upon only by a number of Anglo-Norman nickname bynames borne by some clergy, such as Cachefrens, Chaceporc, Chauceboff, Coupegorge, Marchepais, Metlefrein, Parleben, Pernegarde, Sachebien, Sanzfaille, Taillebois, Taillefer, and Trenchemer. Most of these were transient, bynames applying strictly to an individual; in some cases, they transparently reflected the pre-occupations of their clerical bearers.[34] By the 1360s, however, other forms of byname and surname were intruding into the corpus of locative and Anglo-Norman nickname surnames, represented by Robert atte Crosse who was presented to Widworthy in 1361–2.[35]

Urban craftsmen were not a social group *per se*, but they may have formed a definite cohort, which, in the early fourteenth century, had a different pattern of bynames. In particular, the craftsmen collected together for work on the fabric of the Cathedral in Exeter had a quite distinctive pattern of naming.[36]

Table 7.7
Taxonomy of the Bynames of Craftsmen working on the Cathedral fabric 1279–1320

Taxonomy	No. of different bynames
Locative	116
Topographical	22
Occupational	23
Personal	15
Nicknames	20
No byname	7
Uncertain	10
Total	213

Thus, 55% of the different bynames held by these craftsmen at this time were locative. Of these locative bynames, 80 derived from places within Devon and 36 (31%) from places outside the county. Of these latter, nine related to places of origin in Somerset, eight in Dorset, five in Wiltshire, one in Cornwall and thirteen from other counties. A number derived from other ecclesiastical or religious centres, reflecting the organization of their work: de London; de Christechurche; de Hereford; de Taunton; de Wells; de Gloucestr'; de Sarum; de Malmesbiri. The probable explanation for the pattern of their bynames resides in the continued instability of their bynames and the nature of their social status and occupation. At this very time, the bynames of most of the burgesses of Exeter were developing into hereditary surnames. These craftsmen, some attracted to Exeter from elsewhere as well as some denizens, were lower down the social scale; their bynames were correspondingly still unstable and fluid. Their craft required some movement between ecclesiastical centres. Accordingly, these craftsmen tended to have a preponderance of locative bynames, which were still unstable and not hereditary. The nature of their bynames is confirmed by the small percentage of occupational bynames; these were all often still directly related to their actual trades, such as le Daubere, carpenter, le Tournour, sawyer, mason, painter, tiler, sculptor. Only a very few were obviously hereditary, such as le Bailif, Pestour, and the metonymic Crok. This distinctiveness was associated with a specific time, before the development of hereditary surnames amongst this cohort.

It may seem anomalous also to treat of women within the framework of social groups. Differences of gender are covered here for convenience only. The difficulty of exploring the names of women is their elusiveness and exclusion from the records, except for specific stages of their life cycle; they are therefore grossly under-represented. Generally women only appear in the records if they remained independent as spinsters but held land, if they paid their own merchet and leyrwite, or in their widowhood as tenants of land.[37] In Devon, only a small proportion of women appeared as brewers; those who paid the fines for licences to brew were usually presumably responsible for the production of their household.[38] Women were only included in the lay subsidies if they were independent (either as spinsters or widows) and had accumulated sufficient personal estate, so that their numbers are particularly low.

Table 7.8

Female Taxpayers in the Lay Subsidies of Devon and Dorset in 1332

	Total taxpayers N	Women N	% of total taxpayers
Devon*	10614	499	4.7
Dorset†	7621	536	7.0

* *Lay Subsidy 1332, passim.*   † *Dorset Lay Subsidy 1332*, vii.

The taxonomy of the bynames of these female taxpayers differed slightly from the mean of all taxpayers.

Table 7.9

Taxonomy of Bynames of Female Taxpayers in Devon in 1332

	Loc N	Loc %	Top N	Top %	Occ N	Occ %	Nick N	Nick %	Pers N	Pers %	Others* N	Others* %	Total N	Total %
Rural	170	40	102	24	34	8	75	17	34	8	15	3	430	100
Urban	16	23	19	27	8	12	19	28	7	10	0	0	69	100
Total	186	37	121	24	42	8	94	19	41	8	15	3	499	100

* Thirteen known simply as widows; two as wives.

Superficially, the proportion of female taxpayers with locative bynames, especially in rural communities, seems slightly higher: 37% as compared with a mean for all taxpayers of 34%. This difference might suggest that migration tended to be female-led. A small proportion of the female taxpayers belonged to the higher and lower nobility, and may be discounted from the analysis. Of the rest, over 60% bore a byname derived from a local, dispersed settlement situated within the parish in which they were assessed, such as Joan de Gatecomb' in Little Hempston, Alice de Coperenesland in Dartington, and Isabella de Wyggeworthi in Loddiswell.[39] The origins of their locative bynames were thus the same as those of male taxpayers. In part, this feature is not surprising since bynames may have been incipiently heritable about this time, so that no real differences might be expected in taxonomy related to gender.

Nevertheless, very few women, enumerated in rentals, extents or surveys, bore locative bynames, even contemporaneously with the lay subsidy.

Table 7.10
Female Tenants on some Manors of Canonsleigh Priory in 1323[40]

Manor	No. of female tenants	Of which with locative bynames
Dunsford	10	1
Hockford	3	0
Canonsleigh	5	1
Nitherton	3	0
Rokebear	4	0

Table 7.11
Female Tenants of Newenham Priory in Axminster

Date	No. of female tenants	Of which with locative bynames
1260	14	2
late 13th cent.	9	0
1316	8	2
1334	17	2

Table 7.12
Female Tenants at Uplyme

Date	No. of female tenants	Of which with locative bynames
mid 13th cent.	8	2
early 14th cent.	9	4

Similarly, few women who were tenants at Sidbury in *c*.1350 bore locative bynames. It seems, however, that most of these women were known, by the early fourteenth century, by incipiently hereditary bynames. At a slightly earlier time, there had been more imprecision in the rentals, female tenants being acknowledged by their former dependent status, as the widow of a male tenant, but in an often imprecise form. Thus, at Axminster, the rentals enumerated *Relicta Pope*, Luuelote *vidua, Relicta Beste, Relicta Ailward', Relicta Thome le Potter, Relicta Ade le Garenter, Relicta Ricardi Shalden, Relicta Willelmi fabri, Relicta Walteri Pyw, Relicta Thome Stede*; and at Uplyme, Edith *vidua* and Warennia *vidua*.[41] This form of address emphasized their previous dependent status, with a demonstrable lack of concern for their own identity. By the later middle ages, however, a slight change may have occurred, illustrated, for example, by entries in the court rolls of Werrington.[42] At and for a short time after the onset of their widowhood, women were known by their previous dependent status as the widow of a male tenant; a short time thereafter, however, they became acknowledged simply by their own identity: thus Agnes widow of Robert Cobbethorn' became Alice Cobbethorn'; Alice widow of John Wolf as Alice Wolf; Isabella widow of Robert Harry as Isabella Harry; Emota widow of John Churcheton as Emota Churcheton. Such a change does not necessarily imply any change in their social position as women, but may have been purely an administrative change.

In Oxfordshire, some widows who remarried retained the surname of their first husband, which was also adopted by their new husband, as a surname associated with a tenement.[43] No instances of this custom have been found in Devon. Thus, when John Swytere died in Stoke Fleming, his widow and executrix, Nichola, married Richard Slota, and became henceforth known as Nichola *uxor Ricardi Slota*.[44] The sources, however, are not particularly helpful. More independent women seem to have appeared in court in the late fourteenth century, but very few during the fifteenth century, a trend illustrated by appearances in Werrington.

Table 7.13

Females Appearing in the Manorial Court of Werrington

Dates	No. of different women appearing
1365–1392	80
1462–1498	17

In the late fourteenth century, many women had appeared because they were widows inheriting land through the mortality of the 1360s and 1390s, who did not remarry.[45] Others were mentioned as *fugitive*, for paying leyrwite (associated at Werrington with becoming pregnant), or for paying their own merchet.[46] In 1384, for example, eight women paid a fine for relaxation of their suit of court: Emma Canon; Matilda Barbel; Isabella Weryng; Argentilla Gille; Rosa Wyteleys; Sibilla Page; and Isabella Cot. In the fifteenth century, few women inherited as widows, as opportunities became restricted again; a decline in seignorial control resulted in no recorded payments of merchet or leyrwite. In the rentals of Werrington between *c.*1487 and 1522, less than a handful of women were tenants.[47]

Throughout the middle ages, bynames and surnames of different social groups were still in flux, in that the taxonomy of bynames and surnames was transformed, from being specific to social groups to convergence between social groups. The naming pattern of the secular clergy was thus transformed during the later middle ages, from one dominated by locative bynames to one consisting of locative, topographical, and occupational surnames and surnames from personal names in similar proportions to the composition of the surnames of other social groups in the county. The same radical transition had occurred with the surnames of the nobility, especially the lower nobility, in association with the evolution of that social group from a military, then later chivalric, class, to a gentry comprising a large number of parochial gentry. The naming pattern of the unfree peasantry of Devon exhibited a higher level of locative bynames than in some other counties in the thirteenth and fourteenth centuries, concomitant with the greater degree of dispersal of settlement in this county. A proportion of locative surnames persisted amongst customary tenants through the later middle ages. In Devon, consequently, the effect of social group on the pattern of bynames and surnames was moderated by an equivalent influence of regionalism. Both influences bore on the pattern of naming. Moreover, the patterns were not static, but altered over time. It might be suggested that the influence of social group operated initially, but that the effect of region became more important during the later middle ages, although the process was more sophisticated than this simple periodization.

References

[1] For social group, R McKinley, *Oxfordshire*, 199-200.

[2] *Ibid.*

[3] McKinley, *Lancashire*, 322-34; T Lomas, 'South-east Durham: late fourteenth and fifteenth centuries', in P D A Harvey, ed., *The Peasant Land Market in Medieval England*, (1984), 291-3.

[4] M Bennett, 'The Lancashire and Cheshire clergy in 1379', *Lancashire and Cheshire Historical Society*, 124 (1973), 1-30; R Keep has analyzed the bynames of the secular clergy of the diocese of Worcester who were presented to livings in 1348-9, in her unpub. project, Leicester University, Dept of English Local History.

[5] McKinley, *Oxfordshire*, 199-206, analyzed bynames of unfree peasants in Bampton Hundred in the *Rotuli Hundredorum*.

[6] The sources are: *Feet of Fines Devon*, I, 121-2 (no. 249); *Book of Fees*, ii, 1307 ff; Eton College Records 1/32, fos 5v-7r; Eton College Records 1/139; BL Add MS 17450, fos 218-221v; BL Add MS 37053, fos 273-9; Exeter D&C Archives 2944-2945, 2961; BL Add MS 28838, fos 77v-84r; *Inquisitions Post Mortem, 7-15 Richard II*, 438-40; DRO 902M; PRO SC11/161, 165; *Inquisitions Post Mortem Henry VII*, I, 438-9; BL Add MS 28838, fos 49r-51r.

[7] H S A Fox, 'The boundary of Uplyme', *TDA*, 102 (1790), 35-48.

[8] *PND*, II, 649.

[9] BL Add MSS 17450, fos 218-221, and 37053, fos 273-9; DRO CR 1435, 346M/M1.

[10] Longleat MSS Uplyme court rolls computer database.

[11] BL Harley MS 3660, fos 148r-149v.

[12] See above, pp.212-13; For the gift to Canonsleigh, BL Harl MS 3660, fo 42r.

[13] *Book of Fees*, ii, 755-97.

[14] *Ibid*, 755-71 (by hundred).

[15] *Ibid*, 756, 758-9, 762-3.

[16] *Ibid*, 771-97.

[17] *Ibid*, 781, 786, 790-1.

[18] *Ibid*, 758, 775, 778.

[19] For a resumé of recent research, C Given-Wilson, *The English Nobility in the Late Middle Ages*, (1987), 69-83; unfortunately, the particular account of the income tax of 1436 does not survive for Devon, so I am obliged to rely on the tenure of fees and fragments of fees in 1428: H L Gray, 'Incomes from land in England in 1436', *English Historical Review*, 49 (1934), 607-39.

[20] See above, pp.186-7.

[21] M Cherry, 'The Courtenay Earls of Devon: the formation and disintegration of a later medieval aristocratic affinity', *Southern History*, 1 (1979), 71-97.

22 Given-Wilson, *op. cit.*, 69-83.

23 *Feudal Aids*, I, 442-98.

24 The mean number of tenants per fee was 3.0, mainly *quam tenent separatim inter eos*. The tenancies of fees were as follows: 46 fees held by one tenant, 87 by two, 153 by three, 51 by four, 60 by five, 13 by six, six by seven, one by eight, two by nine.

25 *Ibid*, 443, 448, 453, 457, 459, 461, 465-6, 471, 484-5.

26 *Ibid*, 445-6, 449, 452-3, 456, 461-2, 464, 466-8, 472, 477-8, 480, 483-5.

27 C W Boase, *Registrum Collegii Exoniensis*, (Oxford Historical Society, 27, 1894), 1-59; M Bennett, 'Lancashire and Cheshire clergy in 1379'.

28 G R Dunstan, ed., *The Register of Edmund Lacy, Bishop of Exeter, 1420–1455*, IV (Canterbury and York Society, 63, 1971), 69, 72-5, 78-9, 85, 87-8, 94, 97.

29 For example, *ibid*, 68-72, 79-80.

30 For example, *ibid*, 68, 72, 88-9.

31 For example, *ibid*, 69, 72, 78.

32 Compare Table 7.6.

33 J Ingle Dredge, 'The rectors of High Bickington', *Devon and Cornwall Notes and Gleanings*, 5 (1892), 101.

34 C Spiegelhalter, 'The Surnames of Devon', *TDA*, 68 (1926), 407-8.

35 W Jones, 'List of the rectors of Widworthy', *D&CNG*, 4 (1891), 35. See also, W Jones, 'Account of the rectory and vicarage of Ilsington', *ibid*, 3, (1890), 85-90; *idem*, 'The vicarage of Harberton', *ibid*, 130-6; Dredge, 'The rectors of Wear Giffard', *ibid*, 152-3; Dredge, 'The rectors of Huntshaw', *ibid*, 5 (1892), 113.

36 A M Erskine, *The Accounts of the Fabric of Exeter Cathedral, 1279-1353*, (2 vols, D&C RS, NS 24 and 26, 1981 and 1983), Part I, 1279–1326, 175-211.

37 J M Bennett, 'Medieval peasant marriages: an examination of marriage license fines in the *Liber Gersumarum*', in J A Raftis, ed., *Pathways to Medieval Peasants*, (1981), 193-246.

38 For peasant brewers in Devon, D A Postles, 'Brewing in the peasant economy on some manors in late medieval Devon', unpub. paper; J M Bennett, 'Village ale-wives', in B A Hanawalt, ed., *Women and Work in Pre-Industrial Europe*, (1986), 20-36.

39 *Lay Subsidy 1332*, 5, 8, 9 and *passim*.

40 This and succeeding tables from BL Harley MS 3660, fos 142v, 144r-v, 145r-147r, 149v, 167r-174v (Canonsleigh); BL Arundel MS 17, fos 33r-49r (Axminster); BL Add MSS 17450, fos 218-221, and 37053, fos 273-9 (Uplyme).

41 BL Arundel MS 17, fos 33r-49r.

[42] DRO Werrington court rolls.

[43] McKinley, *Oxfordshire*, 186-90; P D A Harvey, *A Medieval Oxfordshire Village. Cuxham, 1250–1400*, (1965), 126-8; T Lomas, 'South-east Durham', 292.

[44] DRO 902M/M8.

[45] DRO Werrington court rolls.

[46] Bennett, 'Medieval peasant marriages'; R M Smith, 'Marriage processes in the English past', in L Bonfield, R M Smith and K Wrightson, eds., *The World We Have Gained*, (1986), 52-5.

[47] DRO W1258M/D69.

CHAPTER 8

NAMING AND THE URBAN HIERARCHY

The urban hierarchy in Devon was as differentiated as in most other counties, but complicated by the very high number of boroughs and towns.[1] More than seventy settlements achieved burghal status, defined by the lowest limits of burghality.[2] This development was partly in response to the commercial and economic changes of the late twelfth and thirteenth centuries, partly a confirmation of existing small communities in their function of low-level exchange, and partly a result of seignorial opportunism.[3] At the apex of the urban structure was Exeter, set apart from the other urban communities. A second tier comprised such trading communities as Dartmouth, Barnstaple and Totnes, the latter ceding something of its commercial position to the rise of Dartmouth.[4] The residue comprised a motley amalgamation of lesser boroughs and market towns. The function and structure of these towns was reflected in the pattern of bynames and surnames within them. Some were thus differentiated from their surrounding rural hinterland, others distinguished less completely from rural communities.[5] Immigration into the larger boroughs was likely to be higher and for different reasons. The density of population and demographic structure of the larger boroughs differentiated them. In some cases, the increasing population of boroughs was sustained more by immigration than natural increase.[6] The more complex urban topography of the larger boroughs contrasted with the simpler forms of the smaller towns and rural communities.[7]

Bynames and surnames in the urban context elucidate and reflect these urban characteristics. The change from bynames to hereditary surnames may have been more precocious in urban communities than rural, as stabilised *cognomina* became necessary for the unimpeded commercial organization of boroughs.[8] Moreover, the high levels of immigration into boroughs may have elicited a higher level of locative bynames and surnames. Before the general heritability of surnames, such bynames may have reflected the general patterns of migration into boroughs and may thus assist in defining the sociological and commercial hinterlands of boroughs in the urban hierarchy.[9]

By contrast, however, there may be a less distinctive correlation between the complex urban form of some boroughs and

Figure 18
Locative Bynames as a Percentage of the Total Taxpayers in Taxation Boroughs and Ancient Demesnes in 1332.

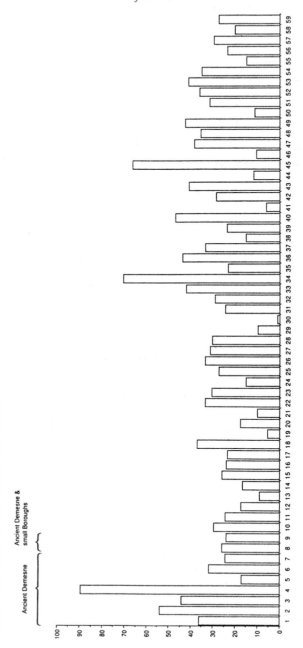

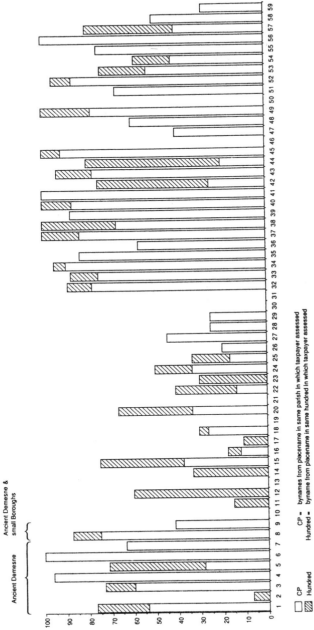

Figure 19
The Composition of Locative Bynames in Taxation Boroughs and Ancient Demesnes in 1332.

CP = bynames from placename in same parish in which taxpayer assessed
Hundred = byname from placename in same hundred in which taxpayer assessed

Figure 20
Locative Bynames in some Taxation Boroughs
and their Rural Appendages in 1332.

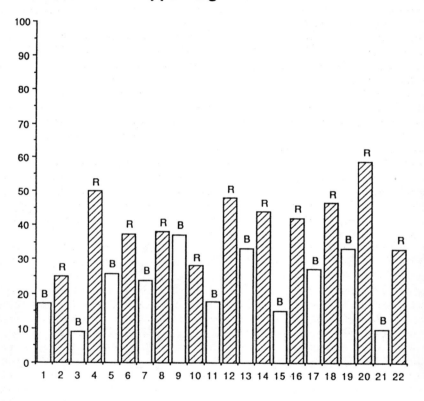

B   Boroughs
R   Rural appendages

topographical bynames.[10] *Ex hypothesi*, therefore, there are reasons to expect the pattern of bynames in the larger urban communities to be different from that in rural ones. During the later middle ages, however, there may have been more convergence between urban and rural patterns, as the characteristics of naming in boroughs became closer to that in other communities. Although the population and personnel of the larger boroughs was volatile, with rapid social change, yet there may have been a subcurrent of continuity even over quite long periods, reflected in the persistence of some core surnames.

Exeter was at the apex of the urban hierarchy of Devon. A comparison of the taxonomy of bynames and surnames of the City over the middle ages reveals some significant changes. Between the mid thirteenth century and the late fourteenth, some classes of byname and surname increased, whilst others contracted, it seems.

Table 8.1
Analysis of Bynames and Surnames in Exeter c.1265–1377

Taxonomy	c.1265		1303		1332		1377	
	No.	%	No.	%	No.	%	No.	%
Locative	42	23	12	28	44	37	115	27
Topographical	10	5	1	2	11	9	49	12
Personal	17	9	1	2	11	9	44	11
Nicknames	64	34	10	23	19	16	80	19
Occupational	30	16	19	44	31	26	108	26
Patronymic	8	4	0	0	0	0	0	0
Relationship	2		0	0	0	0	0	0
Metonymic	1		0	0	3	3	3	
No byname	6	3	0	0	0	0	0	0
Uncertain	6	3	0	0	0	0	21	5
Totals	186	100	43	100	119	100	420	100

Sources:
D&C Exeter Archives 3721 (rental of the burgage property of the Dean and Chapter, *c.*1265).
DRO ECA Misc Roll 2/28 (rental of City property in 1303— 'Rentale Ciuitatis Exon' . . .').
Lay Subsidy 1332, 109-10.
DRO ECA Misc Roll 72 (murage roll 1377).

The evidence, however, presents a number of problems, not least because it is extracted from different types of document compiled for different purposes. The fragment of the rental of the burgage property of the Dean and Chapter comprises obviously only a part of the urban population in c.1265. Nevertheless, with the names of previous tenants and those names derived from abutments and adjacent properties, it allows a wider indication of the urban populace.[11] The lay subsidy was wealth-specific, compounded by the problems of levying the tax in urban situations.[12] The murage roll is possibly more complete, being levied on a large proportion of heads of burgess households.[13] The rental of the City's property in 1303 is self-evidently unreliable because of its inherently narrow basis. Analysis is further complicated by the different time at which bynames developed into hereditary surnames within the different burghal groups within the City. In c.1265, some burgess kinships had already developed hereditary surnames, but many others had not; by 1377, hereditary surnames were almost universal within the City.

The principal long-term changes concerned the level of nicknames and occupational bynames. In the mid thirteenth century, there seems to have been a greater tendency to identify an individual burgess by an individual nickname. As more urban characteristics developed, however, these bynames from nicknames declined as occupational bynames increased from about 16% to about 26% over the late thirteenth century. This urban level of occupational bynames contrasted strongly with the much lower level (10%) in rural communities in 1332. Over the long term, the proportion of locative bynames may also have altered. In the City in 1332, according to the lay subsidy, 37% of taxpayers bore locative bynames, compared with 34% in contemporary rural Devon. In the early thirteenth century, however, only 23% of the burgesses may have held locative bynames. It is possible that the apparent increase in locative bynames in the City over the thirteenth century reflected an increase in immigration. By 1377, the level of locative surnames had diminished to 27%, reflecting, perhaps, the more general cultural change away from locative surnames in Devon. The level of topographical bynames and surnames remained consistently low, paradoxically in view of the complex urban form of Exeter.

Some other changes which occurred are less perceptible from these sources. In the mid thirteenth entury, a very small proportion of burgesses were still identified by a forename only, without a byname. The identification of some of the officials and burgesses of the City in the late twelfth century clarifies this change from an earlier pattern. Between c.1090 and 1120, the portreeves and other officials comprised Aignulf, Aelfger, Aelfwaerd *alias* Alfword, Alwin, Dirling, Swegen, Wulfeg, Saerla, Pain and Gildeberd. From c.1130, some of these officials assumed bynames. This transition is illuminated by William son of Dirling, who was portreeve in *c.*1141. Witnesses to and donors in charters relating to burgage property in the late twelfth century included many with insular forenames combined with newly introduced bynames: Alured Tanner; Segar de Insula; Deorling Tanur; Alured Pictor (all *c.*1160). A gift by Probus homo son of Segar was attested by Ailwar Leureke and Alfred Quinel, also *c.*1160. Later witnesses included Alfred Furbur, Ancatil son of Ivelin, Ailward Ruf, and, before 1206, Edmer de Mouton and Walter Thurbern. Alured Slug was a burgage tenant in the late twelfth century.[14] In the rental of *c.*1265, a few inhabitants were still known only by a forename. Thus Walerand held three selds in the *magnus vicus* near the goldsmithy *(iuxta aurifabros)*. Rent was due from the heirs of German. This change to the use of bynames was also associated with the decline of insular personal names. A residual persistence of insular names can be detected in *c.*1265, in such as Edward faber; Wulfred *iuxta hellam*; Askatil de Bomme; John Thurbarn; Alured de Brente; and a grant of rent which had been made *pro anima eadmeri et uxoris sue*; Alured *custos; quam eadwardus tenet*.[15] Edmer Chie's tenement was mentioned in a charter of *c.*1200; Alured Bubbe had bought land at the west gate in the early thirteenth century from Aedwi Golde; Alured de Pasford was a party to several charters *c.*1200; Ralph Wlfric was mentioned in a charter of the same time, but in *c.*1227–33 as Ralph son of Wlfric.[16] By the mid thirteenth century, the displacement of insular names was almost complete, with only a few reflections of the former pattern; thus Dirling became a byname of a civic family in the City; Alured de Porta became a steward of the City in 1275, and mayor in several years between 1276 and his execution in 1285 for complicity in the murder of the precentor.[17]

In the early thirteenth century, patronymic bynames were much more frequent than later. Parties to charters then included Roger son of Henry, Eustace son of Herbert, Jordan son of Ralph, Gervase son of Henry, Roger son of Henry, Eustace son of Gillian, Richard son of Arnulf, Abraham son of Denis, Philip son of Ralph, and John son of Simon (*c.*1200–53). In the rental of *c.*1265, 4% of the burgesses bore patronymic bynames. Thereafter, such bynames almost disappeared within the urban community, as also in rural areas; only a small proportion of patronyms still persisted. It seems that such forms were more prevalent before the mid thirteenth century and declined thereafter.[18]

The development of bynames into hereditary surnames in the urban context was a complicated and uneven process. It seems that the bynames of some of the civic elite were inherited over two or more generations from the early thirteenth century. This heritability at that time may have affected only a small proportion of the population of the borough, however. Some of these families may originally have been lesser nobility with houses in the borough, part of the tenurial heterogeneity of the borough. Some of the inheritance is well documented, some inferred from the proliferation of unusual bynames held by several individuals, especially nicknames. The OE personal name Deorling became established as an inherited byname by the early thirteenth century. Dirling had been an official of the borough *c.*1090–1100. William son of Dirling acted as portreeve in *c.*1141. William Derling was subsequently reeve in 1189 and mayor between 1207 and 1218. Another William Dirling owed 9d in rent to the Dean and Chapter in *c.*1265. Martin Dirling had become reeve in 1217–18 and 1221–2. Another Martin Durling was appointed reeve between 1263 and 1270 and mayor between 1272 and 1278.[19] Belebuche was an unusual Anglo-Norman nickname. Its bearers included Philip, reeve between 1207 and 1212, Nicholas, reeve in 1215–16 and who owed rent to the Dean and Chapter from a house in *c.*1265, and Roger, who in the same rental held two houses and acted as reeve in 1225–6.[20] The byname Boschet was held by William, who was reeve in 1232–3 and 1236–7 and held houses from the Dean and Chapter in *c.*1265, Alice who held another house in *c.*1265, and Gilbert who attested a charter before 1206 and was reeve in 1211–12. This byname recurred later in the form of Roger Boschet in 1291 and, in 1318, when Vincent Boschet, son of Nicholas Boschet, was admitted to the freedom of the City by succession.[21] The Quinel kinship became important in Exeter, providing Peter, Bishop of Exeter, (1284–92). Alfred Quinel attested a charter of *c.*1190; William held a house near the cemetery in *c.*1265; at the same time, John held a *hostium*; Peter held in the same rental a house outside the east gate, was reeve in 1234–5, and father of Peter, the Ordinary.[22] Prudhomme may have been a polyphyletic nickname and was also associated with the lesser nobility. Probus homo son of Segar attested a charter of *c.*1160, and this *cognomen* may have become corrupted to Prudhomme. William Prudhomme attested a charter of *c.*1200, Martin similarly *c.*1200–1206. In the thirteenth century, officials of the City represented this byname.[23] Roger Baubus attested a charter of *c.*1200 and another Roger was tenant of a house of the Dean and Chapter in *c.*1265. John Baubus became town clerk slightly later.[24] Several other bynames may have been polyphyletic within the borough. Blund was represented by Jordan who had died by *c.*1265, but Gilbert then held a house from the Dean and Chapter and and may have been that Gilbert who had been reeve in 1225–6; a Hilary Blund also held a house then, and another was reeve in 1215–16 and 1219–20, and mayor in 1224–30.[25] The proliferation of the byname Rof presents problems, as it too may have been a common nickname. Ailward Rof attested a charter in the late twelfth century, whilst William Rouf was reeve in *c.*1200. Martin Rof held selds and houses in the *magnus vicus* and Exeweystrete in *c.*1265, and John held a house in Strikene-strete then. A John Rof had been reeve in 1228–9 and 1234–5 and steward in 1226–8 and 1246–7. Thomas Rof acted as reeve in 1232–3 and 1244–5 and as mayor in many years between 1238 and 1253. Earlier mention was made to Richard son of Ralph Ruffus.[26] Another nickname, Strang, was held by several burgesses. The will of Geoffrey was mentioned in the rental of *c.*1265; he had been reeve in 1229–30 and 1238–9. John had acted as reeve in 1218–19. Richard held a house in *c.*1265 and had been appointed reeve in 1223–4.[27] The byname Lydena was held by two generations. Roger Lidena held a house and garden (*ortus*) in the rental of *c.*1265, in which Jordan was also mentioned. Jordan had been appointed reeve in 1218–19 and 1220–1. William Lidena, vicar of St Peter's, was later the executor of his brother, Roger.[28] Even some locative bynames may have been evolving into hereditary names. The rental of *c.*1265 referred retrospectively to a former tenant, Simneth de Rifford. Adam de Rifford had been steward in 1233–4 and 1243–4 and mayor in 1246–9 and 1253–4. Ellis de Rifford had been reeve in 1233–4. In *c.*1250, a charter revealed that William de Rifford was son and heir of Ellis de Rifford. It is possible that the byname developed independently as several immigrants came from the same place to Exeter, but the association with office-holding suggests a dynastic interest.[29] The rental of *c.*1265 mentioned both Nicholas and Walter Gervase; a Nicholas had been reeve and steward in 1214–15 and 1226–8; in *c.*1265–9, Thomas Gervase, son of Nicholas Gervase, was a donor of burgage property.[30] Richard Podding had held a house and cellar in *c.*1265, whilst John Podding had been reeve in 1210–11 and 1227–8. This byname, from a not unusual OE personal name, occurred infrequently in the City.[31] Some of these bynames may have been held independently by unrelated burgesses, but, in view of the probable size of the population of the City at that time, it seems more likely that these bynames represented dynastic families, particularly because of the close association with civic office. In many other charters of the early thirteenth century, bynames were explicitly transmitted over at least two generations: Roger Giffard son of Baldwin Giffard (*c.*1250); Baldwin Trenchard son of John Trenchard (*c.*1200); Robert le Bucar son of Roger le Bucar (1234); Alexander *cementarius* son of John *cementarius* (*c.*1260). Pauline, widow of John Turbert made a conveyance to her son, Mr John Turbert, in 1253–4; charters in *c.*1250 referred to Richard Bubbe and

Pagan Bubbe, sons of Alured Bubbe, as well as to Robert Sukerspye (*c.*1220–7) and Robert II Sokespiche (1252), the latter byname becoming hereditary in the Clists, but associated with the lesser nobility.[32] Such evidence suggests that bynames amongst a small civic elite were becoming hereditary in the early thirteenth century, and that bynames of some other burgess families were also becoming hereditary about the middle of that century.

The transformation from unstable bynames to hereditary surnames accelerated from the middle of the thirteenth century. For example, the locative byname de Okeston became hereditary in the 1260s and 1270s, when John and Walter held civic office as reeve and mayor. John was mayor in 1254–5, whilst Walter held this office almost continuously between 1264 and 1272. Walter's father, Geoffrey de Okeston, had held a tenement in Exeter, from which a rent was assigned to the leper hospital. Both Walter and John had been burgesses from the 1230s. Michael, John, Geoffrey, Vincent, Clarice, Alice and Amice de Okeston were all parties to a charter in favour of Canonsleigh Abbey relating to property in the City.[33]

Locative bynames may reflect the active hinterland of Exeter and its sphere of influence. Such *noms d'origine* may reflect the general pattern of migration into the City.[34] Nevertheless, migration into the City, even in the late thirteenth century, may not be truly represented by locative bynames, since some of these, such as de Rifford, were already becoming hereditary, and many more did so by the early fourteenth. For example, in 1307, William de Gorhywysh was admitted to the freedom in succession to his father, Gilbert de Gorhywysh; in 1310, Henry de Gatepath similarly succeeded his father, W de Gatepath.[35] For locative bynames at this time, the principal source is the register of freemen. Not all freemen can be presumed to have resided in the City, however. Some were admitted through patronage, others belonged to the lesser nobility, that is, were honorary freemen. Thus the admission of a freeman called Doveria was at the instance of Walter de Stapledon, the future Bishop; John de Wallyngforde obtained the freedom by petition by Sir W Martyn and other 'great men' in 1316; Walter de Oxneford was promoted by the Bishop, reflecting the linkage between Exeter and Oxford.[36] Moreover, another difficulty is how far the freemen represented the total urban population. In York, Canterbury and other towns, different customs of admission resulted in different proportions of the urban populace achieving the freedom.[37] 'The freemen of Exeter', it seems, 'always constituted a substantial minority of the population of the city . . .'[38] The composition consisted of those who held the monopoly of retailing within the City, although others were allowed to trade on a more modest scale on

Figure 21
The Places of Origin of Locative Bynames in Exeter before 1332.

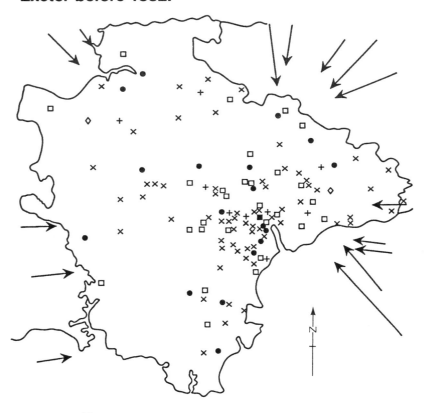

- ■ Exeter
- + Canonsleigh Cartulary c1215-80
- × Exeter Freeman 1266, 1284-1332
- □ Lay Subsidy 1332
- ◊ Easterling 'Officials" c1001 - 1300

For noms d'origine from outside Devon, see separate listing.

payment of a special fine. Although freemen were expected to be resident within the City and hold property there, yet it seems that from the late thirteenth century some were non-resident.[39] It has been estimated that those in the freedom in c.1300 comprised only several hundred burgesses.[40] These several hundred were the most influential and important burgesses, and the lists excluded women. A more accurate assessment has been made by Kowaleski, who has suggested that, in 1377, only 21% of the heads of household in the murage roll (that is, 4% of the total urban population) had the privilege of the freedom. These exclusive freemen may have held a different pattern of names from the rest of the urban population, so that using the locative bynames in the register may contain a margin of error. For example, freemen who migrated into the borough may have held a higher percentage of locative bynames from 'betterment migration'.[41]

The whole corpus of locative bynames before 1332 can be compiled from a number of sources: the rental of c.1265; the attestation of charters, especially those of Canonsleigh Priory; admissions to the freedom; the lay subsidy of 1332; the list of civic officials compiled by Easterling; and the early charters relating to burgage tenements in the borough. From these, a distribution map has been compiled, which records the occurrences of locative bynames (that is, it represents the *noms d'origine*, not the number of burgesses). These different sources were compiled for different purposes, and are therefore not totally comparable. Nevertheless, some patterns do emerge.

The locative bynames in the rental of c.1265 suggest that the regional role of Exeter had already become well established. Places of origin were scattered throughout Devon, as well as some non-Devon places. The charters of Canonsleigh confirm this pattern, but provide also evidence of wider immigration into the City from outside Devon. These external locative bynames, however, may reflect only the connections of Canonsleigh rather than those of the City. Extra-regional immigration is more apparent in the locative bynames in the lay subsidy of 1332. The greatest intensity of external origins, however, is reflected in the locative bynames in the admissions to the freedom. How far these origins existed at an earlier time, but were not revealed by the poorer sources, is an imponderable. Very few data have been included from the Mayors' Court Rolls, since it is difficult in this source to establish residence, particularly in the case of external locative bynames. *Magistri* have also been excluded from the data, because of the singularity of their type of migration, determined more by ecclesiastical careerism than the urban characteristics of the City.

Three patterns of migration and migrants can thus be discerned. Exeter had established its regional importance by the mid thirteenth century, reflected by a number of locative bynames from within and outside Devon. During the late thirteenth century, this regional role was increasingly reflected in locative bynames in the City. The origins of most immigrants lay within the county; the vast preponderance derived from east Devon, within a short distance of the City, but some from further afield. The concentration in east Devon was more intense, however. This concentration and the other bynames from within Devon may have reflected 'betterment migration'. The nature of this migration was substantially rural-urban.[42] A second pattern related to the migration from other places within the county to Exeter, reflecting the City's position at the apex of the urban hierarchy in the county, as the county town. Some of this migration was urban-urban, from the lesser boroughs to Exeter, although there must be some question as to whether the bearers of these locative bynames were actually resident or had simply been conferred with commercial privilege. A third pattern reflected extra-regional linkages, perhaps exhibiting chain migration along established commercial routes, although again the question of actual residence is important. Kowaleski, analyzing the data of locative bynames in Exeter in the register of freemen between 1266 and 1349, has arrived at a similar conclusion. She has found that, of those immigrants with locative bynames, 54% had their places of origin within 20 miles of the City. A further 40% derived from within 40 miles of Exeter. Her data thus reveal that, although Exeter was a regional capital, attracting immigrants from more than 25 miles from the City, yet its position was not as important as that of York, Winchester or Bristol.[43]

Further analysis of the locative bynames and surnames in the City through the register of freemen, until 1420, reveals additional patterns.[44]

Table 8.2
Locative Bynames and Surnames in the Register of Freemen c.1266–1420

Cohort years	Locative		Non-locative		Totals	
	N	%	N	%	N	%
To 1332	272	39	421	61	693	100
1333–1349	109	34	210	66	319	100
1350–1377	47	33	94	67	141	100
1378–1420	106	27	279	73	385	100

First, the freemen tended to have a higher proportion of locative bynames and surnames than the average for all inhabitants of the City. Second, the level of locative surnames, even amongst the freemen, declined during the fourteenth century, perceptibly by 1377, more significantly by 1420. Freemen still, in 1420, however, bore a higher proportion of locative surnames.

During the later middle ages, a number of extra-regional locative surnames were introduced into the City: Kendale (1332); Charteseye (1335); Wakefeld (1336); Ylminstre (1338); Oxneford (1338); Portes-mouth (1339); Leycestre (1348); Bemynstre (1350); Nyweport (1350); Londone (1353); Brideport (1359); Lyndeseye (1363); Faryngdon (1417); Skarburgh (1464); Warwike (1468); Bokynham and Horsham (1483-4); a Calys (1484-5); a Grauntham (1489-90); Bucnam (1513-14); Holand (1519-20).[45] Some of these probably existed in Exeter at an earlier time. These introductions reflect the migration of surnames rather than people. Some may have been borne by non-residents, but others were certainly resident: thus Richard Skarburgh son of William, was apprenticed; Christopher Faryngdon was apprenticed; William Bucnam son of William Bucnam of Rougham (Suffolk) was also apprenticed, to John Bucnam, merchant; Henry Holand son of Robert Holand, of Croydon (Surrey), was apprenticed. Others were admitted to pursue a craft, but their actual residence is unknown: Richard de Wakefeld, cutler; Robert de Portesmouth, potter. Some other surnames had already become established in the county around Exeter.[46] Bokynham existed already in north east Devon in the early fourteenth century.[47] Kendale was well established in Devon and Cornwall.[48] Horsham was introduced to the region around Ashburton and Widecombe at the same time as it entered Exeter.[49] Nonetheless, very few of these surnames persisted in the City over any period of time, but seem to have been largely transient.

One measure of the persistence of surnames in Exeter over the secular trend is the longevity of surnames introduced by appren-tices. These figures relate purely to the persistence of surnames rather than, necessarily, individuals or kinship groups. The surnames of apprentices from 1358 to 1500 have been selected as a sample. By this time, when apprentices began to appear in the register of freemen, surnames had become hereditary throughout Devon, so there are no problems of continued instability. These surnames were not held exclusively by apprentices, since some would have been held by burgesses and freemen.[50]

Table 8.3

The Persistence of the Surnames of Apprentices in Exeter

Surnames held by apprentices in 1358-1500

Surnames which did not recur		63	63
Surnames which endured	less than 100 years	25	24
	more than 100 years	8	6
	more than 200 years	20	17
	more than 300 years	8	8
	more than 400 years	6	2
	into the 20th century	72	36
Total		202	156

For this analysis, the surnames of apprentices have been traced through the register of freemen only, which is a limited source. In column one, the analysis comprises all forms of surnames, both common and localized. In column two, the analysis relates only to localized Devon surnames, such as Row, Toket, Toker, Hilman, Pole, Bery, Davy, Hayne, Hele et al.

Despite the problems of common surnames, it seems that, beneath the volatily of urban demography and social change, there was an undercurrent of stability of some surnames over a long period of time. The results may be somewhat distorted since apprentices may have tended to become those freemen who were the principal actors within the urban community. A similar exercise can be undertaken with the surnames of those listed as apprentices and servants in the military survey of the City in 1522, who bore what seem to have been surnames new to Exeter at that time.[51] Of 251 employees in this survey, 245 bore surnames different from their master's, five had the same surname, and one had no surname.

Table 8.4

Persistence of 'New' Surnames of Apprentices and Servants listed in 1522

Transient surnames*	64
Short-term surnames**	10
Surnames only over one generation †	5
Surnames up to three generations	4
Persistent surnames (permanent)	9
Total	92

* Not in the lay subsidy of 1524-5, but this was produced for different purposes.

** In the register of freemen to *c.*1545 or the lay subsidy of that year, but the latter was produced for different purposes and is defective.

† In the register of freemen to *c.*1600.

The trends here are merely indicative of the continuity of an undercurrent of new surnames. For example, Venycombe existed in the City until at least the end of the eighteenth century; Glubbe, the surname of an apprentice dyer in 1519–20 as well as 1522, persisted into the eighteenth century. Paramore persisted into the nineteenth century; Horsey to at least 1688. John son of William Meryfelde was apprenticed in 1473, the surname persisting in the City until at least 1776. A Mountstephen entered the freedom in 1514, and one was an apprentice in 1522; in 1802, John Mountstephen, of Langport, Somerset, son of John Mountstephen, hairdresser, was admitted to the freedom by succession. John Hylman, *alias* Salter, was apprenticed in 1455 to Salter; a John Hilman, baker, was admitted in 1525–6; and in the nineteenth century, John Hilman, of St Mary's Steps, mariner, son of James Hilman, fuller, was admitted by succession.[52] These examples are representative of the undercurrent of persistent surnames. This persistence did not necessarily relate to single kinship groups, nor was it a considerable proportion of the total number of surnames in the City. Nevertheless, it did represent a small undercurrent of localized continuity, even in the City of Exeter.

Below Exeter, at the second tier in the urban hierarchy, were Plymouth, Dartmouth and Barnstaple, reflected in their taxable constituencies in the poll tax of 1377.[53]

Table 8.5
Taxable Populations of the Four Principal Towns in 1377

Town	Taxable population
Exeter	1666
Plymouth	1549
Barnstaple	680
Dartmouth*	506

* excluding Southtown and Norton.

Dartmouth developed rapidly during the fourteenth century, replacing Totnes as the port of distribution for the eastern side of the South Hams. The extant poll tax for the borough in 1377 allows an analysis of the taxonomy of surnames in the borough, but at a time when they had become hereditary.[54] Before that source, there is no comprehensive listing of the names of inhabitants of the borough, and some reliance has to be placed on the impressionistic and problematical evidence of the attestation of charters relating to property in the borough. There is no certainty that witnesses actually resided in the borough. The parties to and witnesses of such charters may also have tended to have been the civic elite, except when neighbours attested.[55] This social and economic exclusivity may thus affect the analysis to some degree.

The charters, commencing in the early thirteenth century, allow an insight into the eclipse of insular naming patterns. Thus Robert son of Siward and Adam son of Sebrith were involved in charters of 1210. Their patronymic bynames contain the vestiges of earlier OE personal names, but their own forenames consist of newly introduced C-G personal names and Biblical names. Other patronyms occurred at this time, 1210, suggesting that such forms of byname may have been more prevalent at that time: Richard son of Stephen; Adam son of Gilbert. By 1210, all those mentioned in charters had acquired a byname.

The incipient heritability of bynames in Dartmouth is reflected in some less usual ones being held by several burgesses. Thus a William Aubyn occurred in 1233-45, another in 1285, and a John Aubyn in 1233 and 1281. William Finamur, who was bailiff of the borough, attested charters between 1220 and 1244, whilst Walter and Thomas Finamur appeared in charters in 1280 and 1290-3. Charters referred to Richard Hurtebise in 1233, another of the same name in 1280 and 1300, and a Roger Hurtebise in 1210. Edward Rurde attested in 1244, another Edward in 1290 and 1300, Henry Rurde in 1250 and 1290, John Rurde in 1276-96, and Philip Rurde witnessed innumerable charters between 1276 and 1300. Roger Tubbe, reeve of the borough, witnessed between 1210 and 1243, whilst Martin Tubbe did so between 1280 and 1300. The continuity of these less usual bynames suggests that, among a civic elite at least, bynames were becoming heritable by the mid and late thirteenth century.

A high proportion of the bynames of inhabitants of Dartmouth before 1350 were locative ones. Because of the incomplete and random nature of the sources — charters — no precise percentage can be assigned. Moreover, there is no certainty that witnesses bearing locative bynames actually resided in the borough; so the bynames may in some cases reflect only trading linkages. With these caveats, the *noms d'origine* suggest two patterns: a high concentration in the rural hinterland of Dartmouth; a lower intensity reflecting the trading linkages of the borough. The very intense local concentration related to rural-urban migration for betterment. This concentrated pattern is much more localized than that around Exeter; this pattern continued to dominate locative bynames in Dartmouth through to the later middle ages. Although Dartmouth was a trading community, the locative bynames there did not exhibit the same widespread distribution of places of origin as did those in Exeter, which was a regional capital.

Figure 22
The Places of Origin of Locative Bynames in Dartmouth before 1350.
(Locative Bynames from Places in Devon.)

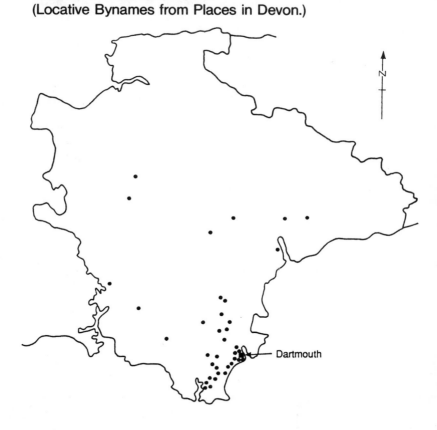

Very few extra-regional bynames occurred in Dartmouth, by comparison with Exeter — only Waleys, de Botisava, de Fowey, de Lanceston, de Bridaport, de Grouesende, de Jernemuth, de Boseham, de Medeway, de Touechestre (but borne by a cleric). Benedict de Botisava (Bossava, Cornwall), inhabited Dartmouth between 1320 and 1378. The byname derived from Fowy (also Cornwall) had a longer duration in the borough: Bartholomew occurred in 1233-44; Walter *c.*1245; Gilbert I 1280-1325; Robert 1320-29; William 1329; and Gilbert II 1354-95. Many of the other locative bynames which were external to Devon, however, were transient within the borough. During the later middle ages, Dartmouth attracted comparatively few extra-regional locative surnames, most still relating to places in the close, rural hinterland of the borough. New extra-regional locative surnames included Bristow, Esyngwold, Notynham, de Wight, Welyngton (1453-95), Wynchester (1509-33), Theukesburi, and Irland. Most of these surnames had, however, already been established in Devon at an earlier time. An additional, important, extra-regional locative surname was borne by Richard de London (fl 1401-1440), who attested many charters, was mayor in 1414, and an active participant in the urban land market. Single references, such as that to Lodwyg Portuygall in 1394, represent transient locative surnames connected to trading linkages, although many Iberian traders were interred in Dartmouth by the late fifteenth and early sixteenth centuries.

Some indication of the taxonomy of the bynames of the inhabitants of Dartmouth can be established from the lay subsidy of 1332 and the poll tax of 1377, although both were imposed after bynames were becoming hereditary surnames.[56]

Table 8.6
Taxonomy of the Bynames and Surnames of Inhabitants of Dartmouth

Date	Loc	Top	Occ	Nick	Met	Pers	Unc	Ill	Total
1332	5	4	3	7	1	9	0	0	29
1377	49(23)	22(10)	56(22)	57(26)	2	27(12)	2	3	218

Notes: Loc = locative; Top = topographical; Occ = occupational; Nick = nickname; Met = metonymic; Pers = personal; Unc = uncertain; Ill = illegible; figures in parenthesis are percentages of the total.

The taxonomy in the poll tax is very similar to that in the contemporary murage roll of Exeter, exhibiting a high level of locative and occupational surnames and surnames derived from nicknames.

By contrast with Exeter, the survival of surnames through the later middle ages in Dartmouth was much lower, but the sources are not conducive to proper analysis of this aspect. Some of the bynames which occurred in charters in the early thirteenth century still existed in the list of taxpayers in 1332. Amongst these were the less usual bynames (such as Finamur from 1220), as well as ones which may have been polyphyletic within the community (de la Pole from 1218, Crosse *alias* de Cruce from 1230, Wood *alias* de Bosco from 1243, and de Fouwy from 1233). The unusual diminutive byname from a nickname, Barbarel, did not occur in the lay subsidy, but existed in Dartmouth from 1235 to 1353. Of the bynames listed in the lay subsidy of 1332, only 40% persisted until 1377, although the different purposes for which the sources were compiled affects the analysis. The byname and surname Bacon, introduced in 1311 by William Bacon, King's sergeant, persisted over three generations; the byname and surname Rurde, which dominated the community in the thirteenth century, also persisted until the late fourteenth century. From the late fourteenth century, however, the entire corpus of surnames in Dartmouth was transformed, with the introduction of apparently new surnames associated with a new civic and mercantile elite: Brusshford; Hawley; Copleston; Savery; Stephyn; Robynson; London; Holand; and many more. Virtually none of the previous surnames persisted.

By contrast with the taxonomy of naming in the principal boroughs, the pattern of naming in small towns was much less differentiated, and hardly distinguishable from many rural communities. This difference is perhaps epitomised by the taxonomy of the burgesses at Berry Pomeroy in 1292-3.[57]

Table 8.7

Taxonomy of the Burgesses of Berry Pomeroy in 1292-3

Form of byname	No.
Locative	8
Topographical	11
Occupational	10
Nickname	14
Personal	7
Relationship	1
Uncertain	4
Total	55

Here, locative bynames were not significant and topographical bynames were quite important; occupational bynames were associated with crafts which might have been rural or urban. The higher level of topographical bynames of the burgesses of Berry Pomeroy may have been a significant difference between larger and smaller boroughs. Topographical bynames were comparatively unusual in the larger boroughs.

In the lay subsidy of 1332, some 16% of taxpayers in rural communities bore topographical bynames in Devon. In the larger boroughs, this proportion was very much smaller. In the rental of the urban property of the Dean and Chapter in Exeter in *c.*1265, only 5% of the burgesses held topographical bynames. In 1332, only 9% of the taxpayers of Exeter had this form of byname. In both sources, the topographical bynames were of a nature that might have been rural rather than urban (for example, de la broke, *iuxta hellam*). In the rental, only two bynames were ostensibly urban: *de tentis* and de paislestret'. In 1332, all the taxpayers with topographical bynames had ones which were essentially of a rural nature (for example, Torre, Birch, atte Hamme). Of the burgesses admitted to the freedom between 1266 and 1332, no more than a dozen bore topographical bynames, almost completely of a rural character (such as atte Ok, atte Brok). A few had ones which might have been urban: de Venella; atte Halle; de la Hurne; atte Porte. Some wills enrolled in the Mayors' Court, however, add slightly to this list of urban topographical forms. The testators included Alice Bythewall (1308), Wymarc Bythewall (1315), Alice atte Crosse (1332), Clarice atte Crosse (1349), and Ralph atte Lane (1331), although atte Crosse and atte Lane may have been equally of rural derivation.[58] The murage roll of 1377 comprised 420 contributors, of whom 49 held topographical bynames, but the only forms which were potentially urban were Crosse, atte Stayre, and Crosman. The same pattern obtained in Dartmouth, where the poll tax of 1377 enumerated 221 heads of households (the tax here listed only heads of households, not all persons over 14). Only eight taxpayers bore topographical bynames, mostly rural in character (such as Welle, Pole, Knolle, Forde, and Leyman). Most of the few witnesses of charters who bore topographical bynames in the thirteenth and fourteenth centuries also had predominantly ones from rural topography.

In all boroughs of Devon in the taxation of 1332, few inhabitants bore topographical bynames, and those that did had forms which could have been from rural features. A few incidental references suggest that some urban topographical forms did exist. In 1332, a taxpayer in Ottery St Mary was designated de Cobbestrete; David de Northstret lived in Totnes *c.*1260; John de Maydenestrete and John de Schamelis (Shambles) in Barnstaple in 1318 and 1329; Arnulph atte Shamele was appointed one of the searchers for counterfeit coin in Teignmouth in 1331–5.[59] The appellation of burgesses, however, was not profoundly influenced by the urban topography of the larger boroughs. The simple form of smaller boroughs, hardly differentiated from that of rural vills, was not a strong influence, but neither was the more complex urban form of the larger boroughs. Whether treated as proper nouns (locative) or topographical forms, street names did not feature significantly in naming in the borough. Some other urban features — particularly the walls — did induce topographical surnames which were distinctly urban, but these never accounted for more than 1–2% of the total urban population. The sources available, however, may have a bias against topographical bynames, since they emphasise mainly the wealthiest socio-economic groups in the borough. Even so, it seems unlikely that urban topographical bynames had any great impact. Burgesses were not normally known by their place of residence within the borough; they tended to be known far more frequently by locative and occupational bynames, reflecting the demography and functions of boroughs. The preponderance of the small number of topographical bynames in the borough were rural in nature; these may have reflected migration into the borough as did locative bynames. Topographical bynames from rural features may either have represented short-distance migration (assuming that migrants from further afield may have been known by a locative byname) or, perhaps, habitation of the suburban vills.[60]

The pattern of bynames and surnames in the larger boroughs thus differed from that in rural communities, although there was some convergence over time. One distinct difference was the level of topographical bynames in rural communities, which was very much higher than in the urban context. Before the middle of the fourteenth century, both locative and occupational bynames were more preponderant in the larger towns, but the proportion of locative ones declined during the later middle ages. The places of origin of locative bynames in the larger towns, however, were more widely distributed. Whereas those in rural communities tended to be from dispersed settlement within the parish or from the adjacent parish, those in towns were from further afield, although still concentrated within the rural hinterland of the borough. The pattern of distribution varied according to the role of the borough. The distinctive pattern obtained only in the upper echelon of the urban hierarchy; in the lesser boroughs, the pattern of naming was not differentiated from that in rural communities.

References

1   See, for example, R H Hilton, 'Medieval market towns', *Past &
    Present*, 109 (1985), 2-23; *idem*, 'Towns in English feudal society',
    in *idem, Class Conflict and the Crisis of Feudalism*, (1985), 175-86; R H
    Britnell, 'The proliferation of markets in England', *Economic
    History Review*, 2nd ser, 34 (1981), 209-21; S Reynolds, *English
    Medieval Towns*, (1977).
2   M W Beresford and H P R Finberg, *English Medieval Boroughs. A
    Handlist*, (1973), sub Devon. Dr H S A Fox has provided
    additional information about the small towns of Devon.
3   Britnell, 'Proliferation of markets'.
4   M Kowaleski, 'The 1377 Dartmouth poll tax', *D&C Notes and
    Queries*, 35 (1985), 288-9.
5   Hilton, 'Towns in English feudal society'.
6   E Miller, 'Medieval York', *VCH Yorkshire. The City of York*, (1961),
    41.
7   See, for example, M D Lobel, ed., *The Atlas of Historic Towns*, (2 vols,
    1969 and 1975), *passim*.
8   J A Raftis, *A Small Town in the Late Middle Ages. Godmanchester, 1279-
    1400*, (1982), 153.
9   P McClure, 'Patterns of migration in the late Middle Ages: the
    evidence of English place-name surnames', *EconHR*, 2nd ser., 32
    (1979), 167-82; S A Penn, 'The origins of Bristol migrants in the
    early fourteenth century: the surname evidence', *Transactions of the
    Bristol and Gloucestershire Archaeological Society*, 101 (1983), 123-
    30.
10 D A Postles, 'Topographical bynames in the medieval
    borough' (forthcoming).
11 D&C Exeter Archives MS 3721.
12 *Lay Subsidy 1332*, 109-10; J F Willard, *Parliamentary Taxes on Personal
    Property, 1290 to 1334*, (1934).
13 DRO ECA Misc Roll 72; R Easterling, 'The officials of the City of
    Exeter', *TDA*, 70 (1938), 455-94; *Exeter Freemen, passim*; R L Poole,
    Report on the MSS of the Dean and Chapter of Exeter, (HMC Reports,
    55, Reports on MSS in Various Collections, 8 vols, 1901-14, IV)
    (hereafter HMC D&C), esp. 49-59; database from Mayor's Court
    Rolls provided by Dr Kowaleski; DRO ECA Misc Roll 2/28 (a
    rental of 1303 comprising the bynames of some 50 burgesses, of
    whom 36 were current, 10 former tenants, and four added in a
    different hand: 'Rentale Ciuitatis Exon' confectum ad terminum
    sancti Michaelis Anno Regni Regis Edwardi xxxjᵒ . . .'). The
    Mayor's Court Rolls have not been used extensively, since many
    of the litigants did not reside in Exeter, their litigation relating to
    their trade to the City: M Kowaleski, 'Town and country in late

medieval England: the hide and leather trade', in D Keene and P Corfield, eds., *Work in Towns 800–1800* (1990); *eadem*, 'The commercial dominance of a medieval provincial oligarchy: Exeter in the late fourteenth century', *Mediaeval Studies*, 46 (1984), 369.

14 Easterling, 'Officials', 463-6; HMC D&C, esp. 49-59.

15 D&C Exeter Archives 3721.

16 'Exeter City Muniments', *D&C Notes and Gleanings*, 3 (1890), 189; 5 (1892), 20-1, 23 (hereafter ECM).

17 Easterling, 'Officials'.

18 ECM, 3, 99-100, 102-3, 120, 122; 5, 25, 40-1; D&C Exeter MS 3721.

19 D&C Exeter Archives 3721; Easterling, 'Officials', 463, 465, 467-70, 480-4.

20 D&C Exeter Archives 3721; Easterling, 'Officials', 467-8, 471.

21 D&C Exeter Archives 3721; Easterling, 'Officials', 468, 473-4; 5, 84 (Roger Boschet in 1291); *Exeter Freemen*, 15.

22 D&C Exeter Archives 3721; Easterling, 'Officials', 473; HMC D&C, 50.

23 HMC D&C, 50, 59-61.

24 D&C Exeter MS 3721; HMC D&C, 59; Easterling, 'Officials', 472.

25 D&C Exeter Archives 3721; Easterling, 'Officials', 471-2; and so in 1253, William 'called' le Blund *alias* Albus, son of Alice la Blunde: ECM, 5, 41.

26 D&C Exeter Archives 3721; Easterling, 'Officials', 471, 473-7; HMC D&C, 59.

27 D&C Exeter Archives 3721; Easterling, 'Officials', 469-70, 472, 474; and so, Geoffrey Stranga in 1292: ECM, 5, 84.

28 D&C Exeter Archives 3721; Easterling, 'Officials', 465-6, 468-71.

29 D&C Exeter Archives 3721; Easterling, 'Officials', 473, 475-7; ECM, 4, 9.

30 D&C Exeter Archives 3721; Easterling, 'Officials', 468, 471; ECM, 5, 45.

31 D&C Exeter Archives 3721; Easterling, 'Officials', 468, 471.

32 ECM, 3, 99-101, 120, 142, 190-1; 4, 10, 42; 5, 25.

33 D&C Exeter Archives 3721; Easterling, 'Officials', 474, 478, 480-3; *Canonsleigh Cartulary*, 72-3 (no. 198).

34 McClure, 'Patterns of migration'; Penn, 'The origins of Bristol migrants'.

35 *Exeter Freemen*, 9, 11.

36 *Ibid*, 9, 14, 24.

37 A F Butcher, 'Canterbury's earliest rolls of freemen admissions, 1297-1363 — a reconsideration', in F Hull, ed., *A Kentish*

Miscellany, (Kent Records, 21, 1979), 1-26; R B Dobson, 'Admissions to the freedom of the City of York in the later middle ages', *EconHR*, 2nd ser., 26 (1973), 1-22; H Swanson, *English Medieval Artisans*, (1990).

38 W G Hoskins, introduction to *Exeter Freemen*, viii, xiv.

39 *Ibid*, xiii-xviii, xx.

40 *Ibid*.

41 M Kowaleski, 'Women's work in a market town: Exeter in the late fourteenth century', in B A Hanawalt, ed., *Women and Work in Pre-Industrial Europe*, (1986), 146, 153; *eadem*, 'The commercial dominance of a medieval provincial oligarchy', 356-8. Admissions in Exeter were much more restrictive than in many other English boroughs in the later middle ages.

42 See Figure 21.

43 Personal communication from Dr M Kowaleski.

44 *Exeter Freemen*, 1-43.

45 *Ibid*, 21-2, 24, 28, 30-2, 42, 55, 56, 59-60, 67-8.

46 *Ibid*, 42, 55, 67-8.

47 For Bokyngham, see above.

48 For Kendale, see above.

49 For Horsham, see above.

50 *Exeter Freemen*, 31-63.

51 *Ibid*; *Tudor Exeter*, 7-33.

52 *Exeter Freemen*, sn Vinicombe, Glubb, Mountstephen, Hillman.

53 Kowleski, 'The 1377 Dartmouth poll tax', 288-9.

54 *Ibid*, 286-95.

55 Watkin, *Dartmouth Records*, *passim*.

56 *Lay Subsidy 1332*, 111; Kowaleski, 'The 1377 Dartmouth poll tax'.

57 *Book of Fees*, ii, 1307 ff.

58 *Lay Subsidy 1332*, 109-10; D&C Exeter Archives 3721; Kowaleski database from Mayor's Court Rolls; DRO ECA Misc Roll 72; Kowaleski, 'The 1377 Dartmouth poll tax'. E Masson Phillips, 'The stone crosses of Devon', *TDA*, 69 (1937), 289-34, 70 (1938), 299-340, 86 (1954), 173-94, 91 (1959), 83-91.

59 C Spiegelhalter, 'The surnames of Devon', *TDA*, 68 (1936), 403; *Lay Subsidy 1332*, 123-4 (Ottery St Mary had not received a charter, but was a quasi-borough with an urban core); A Beardwood, 'The royal mints and exchanges', in J F Willard, W A Morris & W H Dunham, eds., *The English Government at Work 1327–1336, III, Local Administration and Justice*, (1950), 65.

60 D A Postles, 'Topographical bynames in the medieval borough'.

CHAPTER 9

ISONYMY AND COMMUNITY

Isonymy in 1524-5; its probable causation; isonymy in
some communities into the late seventeenth century;
isonymy in two 'remote' communities into the nineteenth
century, Widecombe and Hartland.

The demographic decline during the later middle ages and the
consequent contraction of some communities produced isonymy —
the concentration of surnames — within a number of communities.[1]
The causal influences were a combination of the demographic
contraction and the varying fortunes of individual kinship groups,
and, sometimes, the life-cycles of individuals. The result was the
preeminence of some 'core' families within some communities,
reflected by the dominance of some surnames in the lists of taxpayers in 1524-5. The process of social change in some communities is described more fully below, as is the persistence and
localization of some surnames.[2] A comparison of the lay subsidies of
1332 and 1524-5 reveals little correlation between bynames and
surnames within communities at the two dates. In fact, there was a
great discontinuity in most settlements. The isonymy produced in
the early sixteenth century thus almost universally consisted of
surnames which had become dominant during the later middle
ages. Analysis here considers first the position in 1524-5.

In 1524-5, at least 50 communities exhibited some degree of
isonymy. In these communities, one or two surnames dominated
the lists of taxpayers in 1524-5; this isonymy is tabulated below. The
pattern of distribution of these communities is not confined to one
pays. There seems to be a tendency, however, for concentration
within some particular regions. One nexus occurred in mid Devon,
where some degree of depopulation and contraction may have been
expected. Here the communities were located at 400-700', the
physical relief dissected by small rivers and interrupted by moors.
Some settlements in the South Hams also exhibited isonymy, but
these were situated on the periphery of Dartmoor. In east Devon,
some communities on the higher contours also revealed a degree of

275

isonymy. These settlements tended to be those, such as Morebath, located at 600' on the edge of the Brendon Hills, or, like Awliscombe, at a height of 400–700', even 800', adjacent to Black Down. Finally, a very distinctive group of communities around Ashburton and Widecombe in the Moor, experienced a very high degree of isonymy and localized surnames. The network around Ashburton is discussed in more detail above.

The most intensive level of isonymy occurred within hamlets in Widecombe. This parish comprised a number of dispersed minor settlements, all quite isolated and remote. They were located on the 1200–1300' contours, and, at Natsworthy, even 1500'. The entire parish extended to some 11,000 acres, of which 4,000 were moor. Although there was a fair on the second Tuesday in September, for cattle, sheep and ponies, particularly from Dartmoor, the communities here were isolated physically not only by the height, but also by the deeply riven valleys, such as the Webbern and Bovey.[3] Isonymy here persisted into the late seventeenth century. What is particularly distinctive of this area is the high level of isonymic locative surnames. These surnames had declined elswhere in Devon during the later middle ages, except in this area. Here, in 1524–5 and later, a high proportion of the isonymic surnames were locative, derived from the hamlets within the parish: Langworthy, Catrew, Widecombe, Nosworthy (Natsworthy), and other adjacent settlements (Winyeat, Pethybridge). These isonymic surnames thus referred back to an earlier pattern of naming in Devon, and were rather anachronistic, although, curiously, some had existed in 1332.[4]

Communities adjacent to Widecombe had a similar pattern of isonymy, such as Manaton and Lustleigh, both at about 800', in upland country dissected by deep gorges. This nexus included Buckland in the Moor, Holne, North Bovey, Christow, Highweek, Manaton and Lustleigh.[5] The profile of the taxpayers in these communities was unusual. Throughout much of Devon, a high proportion of taxpayers were assessed in 1524–5 at 20s., the minimum level, on wages, indicating, perhaps, the high level of wage labour. In Widecombe and adjacent hamlets, the taxpayers with isonymic surnames all contributed quite high amounts on goods. In Widecombe, for example, none paid on land and wages, all on goods at varying values. The same pattern existed in Highweek, Manaton, Lustleigh and North Bovey, but Christow was a slight exception. In Christow, the isonymic Clampitts were assessed mainly on goods (six taxpayers, but two on wages), whilst the remainder of the taxpayers contributed for goods and wages (28 goods, 18 wages). The nature of the assessment suggests, with other sources discussed below, that the assessment of these isonymic taxpayers was predominantly on goods related to the tin industry. The isonymy also reflected the close extended kinship ties which elevated these families into core families within their communities.[6]

Table 9.1
Profiles of the Holders of some Isonymic Surnames in 1524–5[7]

Widecombe and hamlets

Surname	Land	Assessment on Goods	Wages
Langworthie		23	
Tomlyn		5	
Catrew		12	
Elyott		4	
Man		18	
Smardon		4	
Drew		4	
Wyndyate		7	
Hogge		8	
Milward		10	
Noseworthie		4	
Widecomb		3	

Highweek

Surname	Land	Goods	Wages
Carpynter	1	8	2

Manaton

Surname	Land	Goods	Wages
Foxford		5	
Langworthy		5	
Contor		6	

Pyworthy

Surname	Land	Goods	Wages
Gilbert		7	
Hartoppe		6	
Webber		5	
Jedde		4	

Figures represent numbers of taxpayers.

Isonymy persisted in a number of communities into the late seventeenth century. The extent of continuous isonymy in some communities is reflected in the lay subsidy of 1545.[8]

Table 9.2

Continuous Isonymy in Sample Communities 1545

Community	TT	Surnames	Coefficient
Widecombe	225	71	3.2
Buckland in the Moor	27	13	2.1
North Bovey	77	43	1.8
Manaton	67	32	2.1
Highweek	65	39	1.7
Lustleigh	38	24	1.6
Christow	82	40	2.1
Sourton	60	23	1.8
North Lew	70	34	2.1
Pyworthy	77	30	2.6
Payhembury	61	33	1.9
Welcombe	32	17	1.9
Hartland	219	100	2.2
Woolfardisworthy	68	40	1.7
Awliscombe	65	34	1.9

TT = total taxpayers; Surnames = total number of different surnames within the community; Coefficient = the mean of taxpayers per surname.

The mean of taxpayers per surname, however, is only a relative indicator of the level of isonymy; it disguises the absolute level of some isonmyic surnames in particular communities. In Widecombe, 17 surnames encompassed 62% of the taxpayers. These surnames were basically the same as those which dominated the community in 1524–5. Here, Man was borne by 11% of the taxpayers, Hodge by 6%, Langworthy by 5%, Catrew by 5%, and the continuity of surnames was completed by Widecombe, Wyndyeat, Tomlyn, Milward, Horssham, Drewe, Nordon, Abraham, Smardon, Knyght, Quynte, Nosworthy and Pethybridge. Thus also, in Buckland, Wyndyeat accounted for 22% of the taxpayers, whilst Catrew and Langworthy accounted for others. Pethebridge comprised 14% of taxpayers at North Bovey, Croyt another 12%, Teyngcombe and Nosworthy a further 9%, Hount and Elys each 8% and Tapper 7%. At Manaton, in 1545, 15% of taxpayers held the surname Langworthy, 9% Caunter, and Elytt, Wyndyeatt, Foxford, Caselegh and Soper were also isonymic here. Wetherdon, Carpenter and Babbe all accounted for at least 9% each in Highweek; Caselegh and Comyn together comprised 21% of taxpayers in Lustleigh. At Christow, Clampytt comprised 17% of all the taxpayers, and five surnames (Clampytt, Holeman, Osborn, Potter, Valans) contained 48%

of all taxpayers. In Sourton, Lyllyecroppe accounted for 20% of the taxpaying population, and had, unusually, existed in the lay subsidy of 1332, being a nickname reflecting a white head. In North Lew, the isonymic surnames were Northam (13% of taxpayers), Glawyn, Medlond, Newcombe and Tekell; in Pyworthy, Hortopp, Bonde, Crocker and Westlake (together 30% of taxpayers); in Payhembury, Salter (18%) and Mountstephen and Saunder (each 10%); in Welcombe, Trick and Peyrd each covered 16% of the taxpayers; in Hartland, a dozen localized surnames accounted for 30% of the taxpayers; in Woolfardisworthy, Nycoll (10%) with Cole and Peard (16% combined) were isonymic; in Awliscombe, Harrys (14%), Serle (12%), and Prynge (9%) were core elements amongst the taxpayers.

These figures related entirely to taxpayers, that is, generally male adults, often heads of households, who had sufficient wealth to be assessed. The figures do not relate to all inhabitants of the community. The context therefore enhances the level of isonymy reflected in the figures. Moreover, in some communities, the same level of isonymy of the same surnames was still exhibited in the late seventeenth century. In the hearth tax of 1674 for Manaton, 42 taxpayers held only 30 surnames; of these, nine were Nosworthys, a localized isonymic surname. John Nosworthy, who was born in Manaton in 1612, was educated at the grammar school, of which his relative, William Nosworthy, was master. After living in Oxford and Northamptonshire, John resigned his living at the Restoration and returned to Manaton. In 1665, he established a meeting house in Ashburton. Other surnames there included Pethbridge, Langdon and Mardon. At Highweek, four taxpayers were Nicholls, others Smardon, Pethbridge and Wetherdon. In Awliscombe, those assessed to the hearth tax in 1674 still included eight Prings and nine Searles.[9] Nevertheless, the degree of isonymy in some of these communities had begun to diminish, consequent on further demographic and social changes, and the change in the fortunes of individual families. In some communities, a stable demographic regime, evident from the beginning of the parish registers in 1538, combined with the relative remoteness of the parish, engendered continued localization and isonymy.[10] In other areas of Devon a different demographic regime operated, such as that in Colyton, where the upward demographic trend up to the crisis of 1646, combined with the relative accessibility of its location, discouraged stability.[11] The different, localized, demographic regimes, in combination with other variables, affected levels and persistence of isonymy, during the early modern period, just as the widespread demographic change of the later middle ages had initially assisted the development of isonymy.

Developments at Widecombe and Hartland have been described cursorily above, but both merit further attention as examples of the continuous localization of surnames in some of the more remote communities of Devon. Neither should, however, be perceived as typical of Devon in general. The characteristics of the pattern of surnames in these two parishes may only reflect on the general developments in some of the more isolated areas of Devon.

The lay subsidy of 1332 unfortunately contained very few taxpayers for either Widecombe or any of the hamlets within the parish. By contrast, the taxation of 1524–5 (and subsequent assessments) comprised very large numbers. By 1524–5, an evident pattern of isonymy had developed, but it seems likely that this isonymy was already emerging during the later middle ages. The Great Court on Crockentor in September 1494 was attended by tinners from the Stannary of Ashburton who bore surnames distinctively associated with Widecombe and its hamlets in the early sixteenth century: John Brabam (Abraham); William and Richard Hamelyn; William Thamlyn (Tomlyn); John Hanworthy; Alexander and Richard Langworthy; William Wyndyeate.[12] The coinage of 1523 at Ashburton was similarly dominated by surnames connected with Widecombe.[13] The two largest coinages at that stannary town in the sixteenth century belonged to Robert Hamlyn and Richard Langworthy, both of Widecombe, and who both acted as jurors at the great court of this stannary in 1532–3.[14] Subscriptions to the guild of St Katherine of Tinners of Melbury, Teingcombe and South Teign included, between c.1496 and 1525, John, Stephen and Richard Hamlyn, and Richard Horsham, all surnames later associated with the area around Widecombe.[15] In 1524–5, the structure of surnames at Widecombe exhibited two distinguishing features: first, the high level of isonymy; second, a distinctive corpus of localized locative surnames derived from the immediate vicinity, even still from hamlets within the parish (such as Langworthie, Smardon, Noseworthie, Catrew, Widecombe), and thus anachronistically redolent of the older pattern of naming of the early fourteenth century — which had become much more attenuated elsewhere in Devon. The local nexus of surnames thus seems to have been closely related to tinmining in the area, and so, not surprisingly, the vast majority of the taxpayers with these surnames in Widecombe, and adjacent parishes, were assessed in 1524–5 on goods. In the taxation of 1545, the 225 taxpayers in Widecombe bore only 71 surnames, the same ones dominating as in 1524–5. In 1588, when the parish was taxed towards the defence of the realm, the 76 taxpayers enumerated held 49 surnames, the list still predominantly the same ones.[16] Unfortunately, the hearth tax return for the parish is not extant.

Moreover, this trend continued over the long-term into the nineteenth century. In 1851, the census enumerator recorded some 174 households in Widecombe, although the details of the return are illegible for about 86.[17] Of the remainder, 51 heads of household held those surnames which had existed and dominated the community in the sixteenth century. The rank order had altered in some cases, with the changing fortunes of individual families, but the stock of surnames seems to have persisted over the secular term.

Table 9.3

Surnames of Heads of Households in Widecombe in 1851 which had Existed in the Sixteenth Century

Surname	Borne by heads of household (numbers)
Whiddon	1
Withycombe	1
French	3
Langdon	2
Hext	2
Easterbrook	1
Stancombe	1
Hamlyn	3
Pethybridge	1
Smerdon	6
Nosworthy	4
Caunter	4
Andrews	1
Laman *alias* Leaman	11
Hannaford	8
Potter	2

The enumerator's return for Widecombe in 1841 is equally defective and illegible in parts. Of the three books, only two are completely legible, substantial parts of the first being illegible. By and large, however, these three books provide more data than those of 1851.

Table 9.4

Analysis of Surnames in Widecombe in 1841

1. Global analysis

	houses	inhabitants	
First enumerator's book	67	387	
Second enumerator's book	38	286	719 (65%)
Third enumerator's book	76	433	
Totals	181	1106	

2. Isonymic surnames
(second and third enumerators' books)

N isonymic	N all surnames	Bearers	% total inhabitants
15	115	458	64

A large proportion — almost two thirds — of the population in the parish in 1841 was thus comprehended by some 15 surnames. The most frequently recurring surnames had existed there from the sixteenth or seventeenth centuries: Hannaford; L(e)aman; Nosworthy; Caunter; Andrews; Smerdon; Harris; Townsend; Widdecomb and Withycombe; Potter; Hamlyn; Cleave; Hext; French. Although no precise figures can be presented for the first of the enumerators' books, because of illegibility, many of these surnames were replicated there. For example, 24 inhabitants bore the surname Hannaford, 27 L(e)aman, 20 Nosworthy, 23 Townsend, 12 Potter.

This continuity of surnames in Widecombe resulted in large measure from the localized nature of society in this upland region. Hartland Hundred was remote and isolated in a different way; four of the five parishes (Hartland, Woolfardisworthy, Clovelly and Welcombe) were situated in the north-west of Devon, on the Atlantic seaboard. The exception (the parish of Yarnscombe) was located inland some twelve miles from the other four, a detached parish appurtenant to the hundred. Accordingly, the pattern of surnames in Yarnscombe developed differently from that in the other four parishes, reflecting the intensely localized nature of social organization here.

In the lay subsidy of 1332, a very high proportion of taxpayers within the hundred had locative bynames from local settlements. By the lay subsidy of 1524–5, this level of locative surnames had been decimated.[18] The pattern of naming had changed substantially, perhaps in some measure because of a change in the culture of naming, possibly also as a result of depopulation and desettlement.

The level of isonymy in the early sixteenth century thus again owed something to the demographic contraction of the later middle ages, as well as the fortunes of particular families.

Table 9.5

Changes in Demography and Social Structure in the Parish of Hartland during the Later Middle Ages

1. Changes in the structure of landholding

Date	no. of tenants	mean size of holdings (acres)
1301	128	13.7
c.1365	64	25.5
1566	19	46.3

2. Changes in the pattern of settlements

	before 1348	late 14th– 15th cents.	late 15th– 16th cents.
No. of occupied settlements	43	40	33
Contracted settlements	0	23	24
Settlements reduced to single farmsteads	8	14	20

Sources: H S A Fox, 'Devon and Cornwall: Peasant Farming', Table 7/1, and *idem*, 'Devon and Cornwall: occupation of the land', Table 2/3, in E Miller, ed., *The Agrarian History of England and Wales*, III (forthcoming).

Note: The survey of *c.*1365 is defective, relating to about one third of the parish and manor, so all figures cited here relate only to that part covered in that survey.

Despite this level of discontinuity, some continuity was ensured by the preservation of a small corpus of surnames of non-locative form in the parish of Hartland. In particular, a small group of surnames of free tenants, who had appeared in a rental of 1301, persisted into the early sixteenth century: (atte) Velye; Kynesman; Snow; Chepman; Cole; Baggelhole. Some of these thereafter continued to be localized surnames in the parish of Hartland; Snow and Baggelhole persisted into the mid nineteenth century, whilst Velly was a core and dominant family and surname there through the sixteenth century. By contrast, few surnames survived through the later middle ages at Clovelly. The *nativi* of the manor of Clovelly — some 15 in number — had borne only seven surnames in 1411; of these surnames, Wille and Andru accounted for at least eight of the customary tenants. These surnames did not remain as significant surnames in Clovelly.[19]

The process can be best illustrated firstly by reference to the parish of Hartland, for which there exists not only the lay subsidies of 1524, 1545, and 1581, and the hearth tax of 1674, but also a manorial survey compiled in the summer and autumn of 1566, which allows socio-economic status to be attached to surnames.[20] The lay subsidy of 1524 enumerated 90 different surnames in the parish, the survey of 1566 92, and the hearth tax 117, since the latter also included the surnames of the poor who were exempt. Some 31 (34%) of the surnames of 1524 still featured in 1674. In particular, some core surnames were held at all these respective dates by a number of tenants or taxpayers simultaneously: Baglehole, Atkin(s), Dayman, Herde, Holman, Husband, Mey, Nicholl(s), Prust, Row, Snowe, and Velly *alias* Veale. The survey reveals the correlation between several of these core surnames and substantial landholding within the manor and parish. The Pryst (Prust), Velly, Atkin, Bagilhole and Nicholl kinship groups especially held considerable land, comprising multiple tenures.

Table 9.6

The Persistence of Surnames in the Parish of Hartland: Specific Surnames borne by Multiple Taxpayers

	No. of taxpayers or tenants with this surname			
Surname	1524	1566	1581	1674
Baglehole	7	8	6	2
Atkin(s)	5	3	0	2
Dayman	1	3	2	6
Herde	5	0	0	7
Holman	4	0	0	2
Husband	5	0	1	2
Mey	4	0	0	1
Nicholl(s)	4	3	4	4
Prust	12	6	4	8
Row	1	3	0	8
Snow(e)	4	5	3	3
Velly/Veale	2	4	0	2

Table 9.7

The Linkage between Core Surnames and Landholding in Hartland in 1566

Tenant	Free tenure No. of free tenures	Customary tenure No. of half-ferlings	Demesne land – acres
Heirs of Hugh Pryst	9		
Katherine Pryst widow	2		
Hugh Pryst de Gorven	3		
John Pryst	1	2.5	
Hugh Pryst de Wullesworthy	2		
John Dayman de Hurston	1		
John Dayman	1	2	
Heirs of Velly	1		
Thomas Velly	1.5		
Philip Cole	6		
Heirs of Wm Cole	1		
Heirs of Rawe	1		
Thomas Rowe	1		
Agnes Dayman widow		1	
John Atkin		6	36
Alice Atkin		2	52
Joan Atkin widow		2	
John Nicholl		3	
John Nicholl de Eggeston		3	
Robert Nicholl		10.3	
Martin Snowe		2	
John Snowe		2.5	
Thomas Prust		3.5	
Alice Prust		2.5	
Henry Baggilhole		2.5	
William Baggilhole		5	
William Baggilhole de Loveland		3.5	
William Rawe		1	
Mark Dayman			5
Peter Atkin			28
Hugh Snowe			32
Patroc Snowe			35+
Thomas Snowe			30

Table 9.7 — continued

Tenant	Free tenure No. of free tenures	Customary tenure No. of half-ferlings	Demesne land – acres
George Baggilhole			12
Edmund and Richard Baggilhole			52
Peter Baggilhole			1
Edmund Baggilhole			a house
William and Elizabeth Baggilhole			60
Thomas Nicholl			28
Joan Vely widow			7
Robert Coole gent with Edward Baggilhole and Thomas Docton			40
John Prust de Emenscott			3

Throughout the whole hundred, there was a strong correlation of surnames, with the exception of Yarnscombe. The surnames Prust, Dennis, Heard, Velly, Cholwill, Cleavedon, Bagelhole, Holman, Tucker, and Nicholl occurred in several parishes. In Clovelly, Woolfardisworthy, and Welcombe, about half the taxpayers had surnames which occurred also in the parish of Hartland. Moreover, the same continuity existed in the other parishes; thus about 35% of the surnames which occurred in 1524 in Woolfardisworthy were still there in 1674, whilst at Welcombe the level was some 41%.

Table 9.8

The Correlation of Surnames between Parishes in Hartland Hundred in 1674

Parish	Total taxpayers	No. of taxpayers with surnames found in the parish of Hartland	Total surnames	No. of surnames which correlate with surnames in the parish of Hartland
Woolfardis- worthy	72	36	38	18
Clovelly	35	14	30	11
Welcombe	35	18	21	11
Yarnscombe	53	10	Different pattern	

Table 9.9

The Persistence of Surnames within some Parishes in Hartland Hundred 1524–1674

Parish	Total no. of surnames in 1674	Total no. of surnames in 1524	Surnames of 1524 persisting in 1674 No.	(%)
Hartland	117	90	31	34
Woolfardis-worthy	35	34	11	35
Clovelly	20	35	2	
Welcombe	17	17	7	41

During the later middle ages, therefore, a nexus of localized surnames was established in this remoter area of Devon. The extent of localization is reflected anecdotally by the principal tenure of Thomas Velly still being located at Higher Velly in Hartland in 1566.[21] During the sixteenth and seventeenth centuries, some distinctive surnames disappeared, it seems, from these parishes, such as Father from Hartland.[22] Conversely, a number of different surnames were introduced, perhaps as many as 80, many of which were transient, but some of which became established. These latter included, for example, Chollewyll, Toker, Davy, Kempthorne, Lapthorne, Jewell, Cullyford, Southcot, Vanstone, Mugford, Adams and Randall. All these more recent surnames, however, belonged to the local tradition. Moreover, some of the surnames which disappeared from a parish recurred in the adjacent parish; thus Cleverdon and Knapman which migrated from Woolfardis-worthy to Welcombe.[23] New introductions at Clovelly had a localized nature: Colwill, Branton, Cleverdon and Ashton. Despite these small discrepancies, therefore, there remained a large element of continuity within these four adjacent parishes.

The pattern of surnames in this area was influenced by inter-related variables of demographic movements, regional geography and social organization. The pattern of settlement in Hartland remained dispersed into the nineteenth century.[24] During the late middle ages, demographic change caused the complete desertion of some of the dispersed settlements and hamlets, but did not disrupt the general pattern[25] During the early modern period, the demographic trend in Hartland, it has been suggested, was remarkably stable. It was not until the 1750s that any upward move-ment happened. This late increase resulted in a population of 1546 in 1801, and a peak of 2200 in 1841.[26]

The stable demographic regime of the early modern period has been attributed to the remoteness and isolation of the area. Mean age at marriage remained high for both men and women through the sixteenth to eighteenth centuries.[27] Social organization was tight and confined, with little leakage or emigration before the nineteenth century, and little inward movement. Even in the nineteenth century, there was a strong presumption in favour of servant-giving and -taking within the community. Adjacent farms hired servants and labourers from neighbours; more isolated farms provided their labour resources from within the household or through extended kinship. The average size of households in 1851 was 4.9 persons, but some 22 households contained more than ten, usually the more isolated farmsteads providing labour from within their own resources. The occupational structure of the parish in 1851 was still dominated by agriculture and agricultural services. In that year, 280 adults were employed in agriculture, of whom 168 were labourers and 112 farmers. Some 184 adults were in trades, professions or non-farming activities, but many of these, in fact, had dual occupations, of which one was farming. More than half the farmers held fewer than 50 acres.[28]

During the nineteenth century, even more emphasis was placed on dairy farming and pastoral husbandry, but production remained at the primary, household level, and did not induce a sexual division of labour. Change was stimulated only from the 1880s when the London market became accessible for dairy produce from this remote location.[29] The persistence of these stable conditions over the secular trend contributed to the stability and localized pattern of surnames in Hartland.

In the large parish of Hartland in 1851, there were some 418 households.[30] The heads of households held between them only 51 surnames; of this total of 51, almost half (25) were held by five or more heads of household. Consequently, 196 heads (47% of the total heads of household) held these 25 recurrent surnames, of which the rank order is given below.

Table 9.10

Rank Order of Surnames of Heads of Households in the Parish of Hartland in 1851

Surname	No. of heads	Surname	No. of heads
Jeffery	14	Cook	11
Westlick/		Prouse	11
Westlake	12	William	10
Colwill	11	Howard	10

Surname	No. of heads	Surname	No. of heads
Heard	9	Prust	6
Shute	9	Moore	6
Short	8	Courtice	6
Littlejhons (*sic*)	8	Rendall	6
Row(e)	8	Dayman	5
Evans	7	Hop(p)er	5
Bayley	7	Pennington	5
Braund	6	Dennis	5
Harris	6	Ashton	5

More than half of these 25 recurrent surnames had existed in the parish in the sixteenth and seventeenth century, some having also been very concentrated at that time; Colwill, Heard, Row(e), Prust, Dayman and Dennis had all been isonymous in Hartland at some time before 1674. The Prust family was both a genealogically core family and significant tenants of Lord Dinham in 1566. The surname was still concentrated in the parish in 1674. In 1851, the surname still reflected a genealogically core family, since William Prust held Charles Farm, comprising 187 acres, Daniel Prust had a freehold farm of 50 acres at Cherrystow (with a wife and seven children), whilst Susan Prust was an annuitant living in the village. Joseph Prust, of Lutsford, however, was a farm labourer, aged 40, with a wife and three children. The surname of Dayman had been concentrated within the parish from the sixteenth century. In 1851, John Dayman held a tenant-farm of 50 acres, and was aged 72. In the adjacent household, John Dayman, aged 40, and his wife, were labourers, also at Philham, presumably labour supplied from within the kinship group. Richard Dayman farmed 200 acres, but Henry Dayman was another farm labourer, at Stoke, living in an extended household with his wife, four children, his brother-in-law, a widower, and his niece. Some surnames which had existed at a much earlier time in the parish, thus still predominated in the community.

As might be expected, however, some surnames failed to last the exacting course of the longue durée. Those of Atkin(s), Holman, Husband, May and Velly (Veale), isonymic at an earlier time, were insignificant by 1851. The position of some others had suffered a relative decline. Amongst those which did persist, some remained core surnames, such as Prust (six heads of household in 1851), Colwill (11), Row(e) (eight), Heard (nine), and Dayman (five). Some others had been less important at an earlier time, but had pro-liferated by 1851. Thus Littlejohn had existed in 1524–5 at a low level, but in 1851 Littlejhon (*sic*) accounted for eight heads. Cook and Westlick (*alias* Westlake) also expanded in this way. Some others, which had existed in Hartland and adjacent parishes in the earlier period, still existed in 1851 in the parish of Hartland; thus three heads bore the name Nicholas *alias* Nickle, two Cleverdon, two Galsworthy, five Dennis, three Baglole, three Snow, three Trick. Bagilhole had been isonymic in Hartland, and distinctive in this area, in the sixteenth and seventeenth centuries. In 1851, Samuel Baglole held Ford Farm (99 acres), although Charles Baglole was an agricultural labourer resident in the village. This byname had, indeed, existed in the parish in 1332. The most concentrated surnames in the parish in 1851 were Williams and Jeffery, more recent introductions into the parish in the early modern period. All the heads of households who bore these surnames had themselves been born in Hartland.

A large proportion of surnames within the parish had thus existed from an earlier time; some 50% of those listed in 1851 had featured in the seventeenth century. Some continued to be core surnames. On the other hand, some 83 surnames were held by a single head of household, but many of these had also existed in the parish at the earlier time.

Almost all the heads of household in Hartland in 1851 had been born in the parish. Those born outside the parish came exclusively from the adjacent parishes in the same Hundred, from Clovelly, Woolfardisworthy and Welcombe. From Clovelly came heads with the surnames Prouse, Jeffery, Burnard, Hamlyn, Ching, Pooley, Jewell, Beer, Oke, Lemon, Mugford, Dennis, and Headon. Many of these surnames had existed in Hartland already. Similarly, heads from Woolfardisworthy had the surnames Pennington, Fulford, Bayley, Goodenough, Gifford, Nichols, Prouse, Shute, Neal, Johns, Turner, Miller, Vanstone, and Glover, many pre-existing in Hartland. From Welcombe came heads called Downing and Gallsworthy. Most marriages in Hartland were endogamous, according to the places of births given in the census of 1851. Exogamous intermarriage, a much smaller proportion, was highest between these parishes — Welcombe, Clovelly and Woolfardisworthy; most spouses not born in Hartland came from one of these three other adjacent parishes, although a number of wives also derived from Cornwall. A small number of heads also originated in Cornwall, but some bearing surnames pre-existing in Hartland (Ashton, Hooper, Heard, Braund), others new surnames (Shaddick, Pasko). A very small number of heads had originated elsewhere in Devon, but always from places in north-west Devon: Parkham, Bradworthy, West Putford, for example. A tiny number came from more distant places: Northampton (the surname Burnard); Bury St

Edmunds (a Ryder who was an annuitant in the village); Plymouth (an Unstone); Hampshire (Baker). Overwhelmingly, however, the heads of households in Hartland were indigenous.

This localized social organization extended to the relationship between households and farm service.[31] Thus in 1851, John Cleverdon, farming 300 acres at Berry, employed as household and farm servants Elizabeth Williams, Elizabeth Snow, Richard Cook and Richard Jeffery. John Jeffery employed John Baglole, Sarah Colwill, Richard Jeffery and John Westlick. Altogether there were over 250 servants of all kinds (farm, household, general) in Hartland in 1851. Although the numbers of living-in farm servants had declined in general in England, Devon was one of the five counties where the employment of farm servants persisted strongly into the mid nineteenth century.[32] About 80% of the servants had been born in Hartland and bore surnames held by heads of household enumerated in 1851. Some 20% had been born outside the parish, but predominantly in the adjacent parishes of Woolfardisworthy and Clovelly, and to a lesser extent Welcombe. A few others had been conceived in other local parishes: Holdsworthy, East Woodhay, East and West Putford, and a very few in Cornwall. Most of those born in Woolfardisworthy or Clovelly bore surnames pre-existing in Hartland. A servant called Vanstone had been born in Luscombe, but the surname already existed in Hartland. Elizabeth Trick was a servant, a widow born in Portsmouth, living in 1851 in the household of the Moore family in Lower Velly, but Trick was an established surname in Hartland. Two new surnames introduced by immigrant servants were Gregory and Dayment: Ann Gregory from Derbyshire, a household servant to the same Moore family; John Dayment from Gloucestershire a farm servant of William Chope at Herscott Farm (but this surname may have been a phonetic spelling or corruption of the surname Dayman, common in Hartland).

Table 9.11
Origins of Servants in Hartland in 1851

Born in Hartland	202
Born elsewhere	54
Total	256*

* A few illegible.

In both Hartland and Widecombe in the Moor, a high level of localized surnames persisted into the nineteenth century. Both parishes were remote for different reasons, and developments there may represent those in other more isolated communities in Devon.

Even in the small town of Buckfastleigh, something of the same localization is evident. A proportion of the surnames in the late nineteeth century there seem to have been local ones, such as Arscott, Knowling and Furneaux. The economy of this town had depended on the manufacture of woollen cloth, which remained more buoyant here than in other places in Devon. Nevertheless, dislocation occurred in the mid nineteenth century, leading to much male out-migration, and a resultant unbalanced sex-ratio skewed towards women. Single women and widows thus comprised the majority of the population, and they were often engaged in the informal economy, with multiple occupations. Women had a more restricted social, geographical and occupational mobility than the men. Both widows and unmarried women raised offspring and tended to live in households of extended kinship. Consequently, unusually, women became the medium for the transmission of surnames in this small town.[33]

Widecombe belonged to the hinterland of another town, Ashburton. This hinterland was characterized by a high degree of concentration of localized surnames from the sixteenth century. In 1896, the Rev W M Birch remarked upon the continuity of surnames in Ashburton from 1603, when the registers are extant, through to his own time, including such surnames as Woodley, Tozer, Abraham, Knowling, Palk, Halse, Yolland, Smerdon, Cruse, Coaker, Ireland, Wotton, Tiddy, Soper, Furneaux, Egbeare, Sheelabeare, Eales, Luscombe, Bickford, Caunter, Edgecombe, Petherbridge, Perry, Gruit and Binmore.[34] This localization around Ashburton is discussed further above.[35]

Ipplepen, in close proximity to Ashburton, looked more towards Totnes than Ashburton, if marriage horizons are a reliable guide. The registers of Ipplepen in the seventeenth century do not illustrate an enormous degree of isonymy. The concentration of localized surnames was, however, sufficient for three isonymic marriages to be occasioned: in 1691 between Roger Cole and Mary Cole; in 1692 between Zachariah Wotton of Bovy Tracey and Martha Wotton; in 1694 between Francis Blackaller and Agnes Blackaller, both of Broadhempston. At Martinhoe, of 79 marriages between 1597 and 1700, two were isonymic: John Pyle and Clemas Pyle in 1598; Henry Rooke and Christine Rooke in 1613. At Uffculme too a few isonymic marriages occurred in the sixteenth century including that between John Rudge and Elizabeth Rudge in 1543.[36] Such isonymic marriages, although numerically few, are indicative of the level of concentration of surnames in some parts of Devon. In particular, the more remote, upland communities experienced some degree of isonymy in the early modern period, in some cases, extending even into the nineteenth century.

Table 9.12

Appendix: Examples of High Levels of Isonymy in some Communities in 1524–5

Parish	Tax-payers	Surnames	Isonymic surnames	% tax-payers	Coefficient
Widecombe	207	74	Langworthie	10.6	2.80
			Catrew	5.3	
			Milward	4.8	
			Hogg	3.9	
			Wyndyate	3.4	
			Tomlyn	2.9	
			Leman	2.4	
			Noseworthie	2.4	
Widecombe constituents:					
Widecombe	47	26	Langworthy	17.0	1.80
Lydford	56	26	Langworthy	12.5	2.20
			Man	14.0	
			Hogge	11.0	
			Drew	7.0	
			Wynyate	7.0	
Dewdon	41	18	Milward	19.5	2.30
			Langworthy	17.0	
			Leyman	9.5	
Spitchwick	63	30	Catrew	14.0	
			Man	9.5	
			Keys	8.0	
			Nordon	6.0	
			Beare	6.0	
Manaton	55	32	Foxford	9.1	1.70
			Langworthy	9.1	
			Contor	9.1	
			Caselegh*	5.5	
			Thomas	5.5	
			Elyott	5.5	
Highweek	77	39	Carpynter	13.0	1.98
Clist Honiton	32	22	Kelly	20.0	1.46
			Tryckhay	10.0	
Clist St George	37	16	Hount	24.0	2.30
			Gybbe	13.5	

(* See also Lustleigh, where Caselegh comprised 7.3% of taxpayers.)

Table 9.12 — continued

Parish	Tax-payers	Surnames	Isonymic surnames	% tax-payers	Coefficient
Culmstock	78	46	Trykehay	11.0	1.70
			Potter	7.5	
Beaworthy	32	17	Bycklake	19.0	1.90
Ashbury	10	5	Glanfel(l)(d)	50.0	2.00
Hatherleigh	119	68	Medlond	6.7	1.75
			Joute	5.8	
			Wadland	5.0	
Pyworthy	76	41	Gilbert	9.2	1.86
			Hortoppe	7.9	
			Webber	6.5	
Sourton	41	25	Lillicrop	12.2	1.64
Lapford	55	33	Mylford	12.7	1.67
Iddesleigh	46	23	Bremel-comb	13.0	2.00
			Herde	8.7	
			Tawton	8.7	
			Cupper	8.7	
Wear Giffard	32	21	Southcote	15.2	1.50
Parracombe	30	20	Thorne	16.7	1.50
Christow	46	27	Clampytt	19.6	1.70
Cheriton Bishop	65	40	Gorvyn	9.2	1.63
Awliscombe	55	22	Serell	21.4	2.50
			Pryng	14.3	
			Northamp-ton	8.9	
			Rode	7.1	
Morebath	55	32	Tymwyll	14.6	1.70
			Norman	10.9	
Stokeinteign-head	104	47	Zeve	8.5	2.20
			Cade	7.6	
			Kyrton (Crediton)	7.6	
			Fleccher	6.6	
			Martyn	5.7	

Parish	Tax-payers	Surnames	Isonymic surnames	% tax-payers	Coefficient
Southleigh	20	11	Wydeslade	20.0	1.80
			Batstone	20.0	
Zeal Mona-chorum	41	25	Hawkerugge	12.0	1.64
Chittle-hampton	120	73	Pellevyn	6.6	1.64
			Chapell	4.9	
Gidleigh	35	19	Parlebyn	20.0	1.80
Newton St Cyres	104	65	Prudham	6.7	1.64
			Payne	6.7	
			Brouns-combe	4.8	
Thurlestone	41	25	Lyston	17.0	1.60
			Tabb(e)	12.0	
N Bovey	42	24	Myller	9.5	1.75
			Tapper	12.0	
			Pethebrige	7.0	
			Tyncombe	7.0	
			Frenche	7.0	
Diptford	64	45	Lauerance	11.0	1.40
			Dustayn	8.0	
Axmouth	48	31	Abbot	12.5	1.60
			Seward	8.3	
Buckerell	38	25	Salter	16.0	1.50
Musbury	21	14	Frenche	19.0	1.50
Harberton	137	81	Turpyn	6.6	1.70
			Perys	3.6	
			Hervy	3.6	
			Dattyn	3.6	
			Voyse	2.9	
			Lauerance	2.9	
Winkleigh	89	57	Luxton	9.0	1.60
Hartland	190	99	Prust	6.3	1.90
			Bagylhole	3.7	
Abbotskers-well	41	24	Goteham	17.0	1.70
Little Hempston	42	26	Blackealler	16.7	1.60

Table 9.12 — continued

Parish	Tax-payers	Surnames	Isonymic surnames	% tax-payers	Coefficient
Holne	58	32	Hanworthie	11.8	2.10
			Berd	13.2	
			Flayccher	10.3	
			Harry	8.8	
			Pery	5.9	
Buckland in the Moor	30	13	Wyndyate	30.0	2.30
Dunterton	21	12	Sergeant	33.0	1.75
Stoke Gabriel	53	39	Churchward	11.0	1.40
Dunsford	85	54	Borugge	8.0	1.60
			Seryll	7.0	
			Smalruge	7.0	
			Mayne	6.0	
Seaton	74	54	Callegh	11.0	1.40
Cotleigh	30	23	Worthyall	17.0	1.30
Meavy	65	42	Eggecombe	9.0	1.10
S Milton	48	31	Henxston	10.0	1.60
S Huish	51	27	Yaberle	16.0	1.90
			Gervys	16.0	
Halwell	40	29	Ryder	13.0	1.40
Ashprington	62	41	Sherpham	8.0	1.50
			Tremyll	8.0	
Buckland Mona-chorum	144	78	Re(a)pe	7.0	1.90
			Dunruge	5.0	
			Crese	4.0	
			Topsham	4.0	
			Palmer	3.5	
			Stephyn	3.5	
			Petersfield	3.5	
			Laucrans	3.5	
Botterford	17	9	Toser	24.0	1.90
			Northcote	32.0	

Parish	Tax-payers	Surnames	Isonymic surnames	% tax-payers	Coefficient
Yealmpton	109	71	Deryng	7.0	1.50
			Thornyng	4.0	
			Treby	4.0	
Welcombe	32	17	Peerde	22.0	1.90
			Trycke	9.0	
			Pruste	9.0	

References

1 For the term isonymy, G Lasker, *Surnames and Genetic Structure*, (1985).

2 See also ch 6.

3 W G Hoskins, *Devon*, (1954), 514-16.

4 *Lay Subsidy 1332*, 5-6.

5 See Appendix, pp.293-7.

6 *Lay Subsidy 1524-5, passim.*

7 *Ibid, passim.*

8 *Ibid, passim.*

9 E Windeatt, 'Early Nonconformity in Ashburton', *TDA*, 28 (1896) 228-32; the author's name is significant. *Hearth Tax 1674, passim.*

10 I am grateful to Richard Wall of the Cambridge Group for the History of Population and Social Structure for providing the data relating to Hartland; E A Wrigley and R S Schofield, *The Population History of England 1541-1871*, (1989), 248, 249n, 261n.

11 E A Wrigley, 'Family limitation in pre-industrial England', in A R H Baker, J D Hampshere, and J Langton, eds., *Geographical Interpretations of Historical Sources*, (1970), 141-70, esp. 144.

12 T A R Greaves, 'The Devon tin industry 1450-1750', unpub. PhD Exeter 1981, 380-1.

13 H P R Finberg, 'The Stannery of Tavistock', *TDA*, 81 (1949), 173-5.

14 Greaves, *op. cit.*, 291.

15 *Ibid*, 289; DRO 14294/PW2.

16 J S Amery, 'Residents in Ashburton and the adjoining parishes in 1588', *TDA*, 28 (1896), 247-56. See also C D Lineham, 'A forgotten manor in Widecombe-in-the-Moor', *TDA*, 94 (1962), 475-8, for aspects of isonymy in the eighteenth century.

17 PRO RG 6/187/147 ff.

[18] *Lay Subsidy 1524-5*, sub Hartland; R M Chope, 'The early history of the manor of Hartland', *TDA*, 34 (1902), 443-5.

[19] PRO C260/1241/6.

[20] *Lay Subsidy 1524-5*; *Devon Lay Subsidy Rolls*; *Hearth Tax 1674*; (all sub Hartland); DRO 217/3/19, fos 51r-70v (Chope, 'The early history . . . Hartland', abstracts the section of this document for Hartland, but I have used the original).

[21] DRO 217/3/19, fo 51v.

[22] DRO 217/3/19, fos 51r-70v.

[23] *Hearth Tax 1674*, sub Hartland.

[24] M R Bouquet, 'The sexual division of labour: the farm household in a Devon parish', PhD Cambridge 1981, 113-14. (I have consulted the thesis in preference to the subsequent book, Bouquet, *Family, Servants and Visitors. The Farm Household in Nineteenth and Twentieth Century Devon*, (1985)).

[25] H S A Fox, 'Contraction: desertion and dwindling of dispersed settlement in a Devon parish', *Thirty-first Annual Report of the Medieval Village Research Group*, (1983), 40-2.

[26] Bouquet, thesis, 88-9.

[27] *Ibid*, 88-9, discussing the effect of the building and destruction of the quai at Hartland and the advent of the railway to Bideford.

[28] *Ibid*, 91 (Table 3.1), 110, 112 (Figure 4.2), 115, 118-23, 125A, 126-8, 131-2.

[29] *Ibid*, 57, 75-6.

[30] PRO RG 6/189/535 ff.

[31] Bouquet, thesis.

[32] A Kussmaul, *Servants in Husbandry in Early Modern England*, (1981), 6-7, 15 (Table 2.2), 20-1.

[33] D Gittins, 'Marital status, work and kinship, 1850–1930', in J Lewis, ed., *Labour and Love: Women's Experience of Home and Family, 1850–1940*, (1986), 249-67.

[34] W M Birch, 'The parish registers of Ashburton and Buckland in the Moor', *TDA*, 28 (1896), 241.

[35] See above, pp.146-7.

[36] W Phillimore, ed., *Devonshire Parish Registers I* (1909), *passim*; see also D Souden and G Lasker, 'Biological inter-relationships between parishes in east Kent: an analysis of Marriage Duty Act returns for 1705', *Local Population Studies*, 21 (1978), 30-9.

CONCLUSION

Given the geographical position of Devon, it would not be surprising that the county was opened to external influences only at a very late time. Mobility into and out of the county before the modern period was extremely limited. Patterns of migration and movement tended to be circumscribed and localized. The county comprised several pays and regional societies, which were affected by external influences to different degrees. East Devon and the South Hams, particularly the trading communities and their hinterlands, were more receptive to the external influences, whilst central and west Devon were more inhibited. North Devon may have been equally resistent, except in the immediate hinterland of some of the larger trading communities there. Consequently, some local societies within the county remained fairly isolated and remote until recent times, perhaps epitomised by those upland communities such as Widecombe in the Moor and those remoter places on the Atlantic seaboard such as Hartland.

Cultural influences in Devon thus continued to be particular, in, for example, such aspects as religion. Before the Reformation, religious practice in Devon was intense and devotional. The Reformation removed this intensity, but replaced it only by a sullen conformism and observance, resistant to Puritanism.[1] Old Dissent only slowly established any interest in the county, more especially in the larger trading communities.[2] In the religious census of 1851, patterns of observance in Devon were distinct.[3]

This provincial particularism produced similarly distinctive patterns of naming in Devon, with the persistence of some patterns forged in the middle ages. One distinctive aspect of naming in the county in the middle ages was the high proportion of locative surnames. Although the level declined over the later middle ages, yet a very large number of such surnames — derived from local places in the county — persisted into modern times. Amongst this *corpus* were surnames derived from place-names which were in turn derived from topographical features, such as Week, Comb, Torr *et al*. Distinctive forms of occupational byname, such as Tucker, also proliferated. This occupational term was in use throughout the entire region of Southern Middle English, but proliferated in those regions, such as parts of Devon, Somerset and Wiltshire, where the industry was concentrated. Some local usages became common forms in Devon through into the modern period. The suffix -ing on topographical bynames, in particular, was distinctive of surnames in the county. The absence of topographical forms with the suffix -er was a further feature.

At an earlier time, the taxonomy of bynames in Devon had been influenced by social group. During the later middle ages, its impact was moderated by the force of regionalism, with a consequent convergence of the types of surnames held by all social groups in Devon. All social groups tended thenceforth to hold distinctly Devonian surnames, of all types, many of ostensibly humble origins. By the sixteenth century, there was very little difference of types of surnames according to social stratification. At the same time, demographic change resulted in concentrations of surnames in some communities by the early sixteenth century. As local populations were decimated, and new opportunities of landholding were presented, some kinship groups expanded into the gaps, leading to isonymy of surnames. In some communities, because of their remoteness and endogamy, this concentration of localized surnames persisted into the nineteenth century. These characteristics have been detected in many other communities.[4] Perhaps, however, the degree and persistence of concentration was more exaggerated in some communities in Devon because of their greater isolation. Such communities, however, were not representative of the whole of Devon, since others, in the more accessible regions, had a higher influx and turnover of surnames. The sociological significance of this isonymy of surnames, it has been suggested, is that they seemingly reflect an endogamous society and the predominance of some core kinship groups within the community. This continuity of core families and surnames may have provided stability and the persistence of local customs, attitudes and norms. The persistence of core and localized surnames reflected local identity. Not all communities in Devon exhibited this pattern, but it was evident in many of the remoter ones.

Perhaps the most effective way of illustrating the regional nature of naming in Devon is to make a comparison with naming in another county on the periphery. In terms of cultural diffusion horizontally, England in the middle ages exhibited, in some respects only and certainly not exclusively, the characteristics of a core-periphery model. Both Devon and Northumberland were on the periphery. In the south-west, patronymic forms of byname were virtually non-existent amongst the taxpayers in 1332 — less than half a dozen taxpayers had such bynames out of more than 10,000. In the north-east, 23% of the taxpayers, that is 1,034 out of 4,455 taxpayers in Northumberland contributing to the lay subsidy of 1296, bore this form of byname. Considering that the poorest — probably those most likely to bear this form of byname — were omitted from the lay subsidy of 1296, the proportion of patronyms is undoubtedly under-represented. Additionally, 135 bore metronymic bynames, a further 3%. In Devon, in 1332, only a couple of taxpayers were known by a single personal name; in Northumberland in 1296, about 61 (1.4% of the taxpayers), usually bearing the less common names, such as Absolom, Bateman, Benedict, Vincent, Alexander, Thurbert, Siward, Edmund, Ingram and Anselm.[5] Such contrasts between patterns of naming in two counties on the periphery are illustrative of wider differences, despite conflation in other respects towards very common forenames.

References

[1] R Whiting, *The Blind Devotion of the People*, (1990).

[2] A Whiteman, *The Compton Ecclesiastical Census of 1676*, (British Academy Records of Social and Economic History, ns 10, 1986), 263-93; J M Triffit, 'Believing and belonging: church behaviour in Plymouth and Dartmouth 1710-1730', in S Wright, ed., *Parish, Church and People Local Studies in Lay Religion 1350-1750*, (1988), 179-202. In particular, the Hingstons, leading merchants and Quakers in Plymouth, who held a localized locative surname: Triffitt, 'Believing and belonging', 183.

[3] I owe this information to the density map of religious observance in 1851 produced by Dr Paul Ell using GIMMS software, in his research into religious observance in the whole country in 1851.

[4] M Anderson, *Family Structure in Nineteenth Century Lancashire*, (1971); G Lasker, *Surnames and Genetic Structure*, (1985); M Strathern, *Kinship at the Core*, (1981), esp. 18-24; McKinley, *Lancashire*, 385-421.

[5] *Lay Subsidy 1332, passim*; C M Fraser, ed., *The Northumberland Lay Subsidy Roll of 1296* (Publications of the Society of Antiquaries of Newcastle-upon-Tyne, Record Series 1, 1968), *passim*.

INDEX LOCORUM

In this index, all places are in Devon unless another county is given in parenthesis; units used are historic counties. Included here also are religious houses, cathedral chapters and similar institutions. Please also check under locative bynames and surnames for forms of names derived from places.

INDEX NOMINUM

This index comprises personal names (forenames), bynames and surnames. Syndetic elements (atte, de, etc) are omitted, except where they form an integral part of the name and to avoid confusion. Wherever possible, cross-references have been made between Latin and vernacular forms (both French and Middle English). In some cases, forms with the genitival -s have been consolidated with uninflected forms [e.g. Adam(s)] when it is not clear that there was an intended difference between these names; in the case of names of females with the inflected form, however, separate entries have been made.

Viroun, 105
Visacre, 20
Vischleigh, 20
Visere, 20
Visher, Viss(h)ere, Vyssher, 20
Visshe, 20
Vivian, 165
Vog(he)ler(e), 20
Voleslo, 20, *see* Foleslo
Voode, 40, *see* Wode
Vorn, 21, 76, *see* Thorn
Vorseman, 20, *see* Forsman
Vosse, 20
Voule, 20
Vowler, 20
Voxford(e), 20, 146, *see* Foxford
Voxhill, 20
Voyse, 295
Vrenshe, 20, *see* Frensh
Vromond, 20
Vrye, 64
Vyne, 54

Wada, Wade, 19, 54, 166
Wadland, 130, 294
Wakefeld, 262
Wakeham, 128
Walding, 24
Walerond, Walrand, 90, 165
Waleys, 8, 112, 134, 267
Walker, 137, 140
Wallyng, 23, 46
Wallyngforde, 258
Wals(c)h(e), 112, 134, 167
Walter, 172
Wangeforde, 88
Warde, 39, 49
War(r)en(g), 159, 161, 165, 195
Warwike, 262
Wascomb', 119
Wase, 166
Watere, 31, 56, 103, *see* Vatere
Waterman, 25, 239
Watta, 16
Watt(e)s, 42, 172
Waxmaker, 49
Way(e), Weye, 33, 118
Waymouth, 135
Webbe(r)(e), 36, 39, 135, 137, 142,
    144, 277, 294
Webbestere, 48
Week(e), Weke, Whyke, Wiche, Wika,
    Wike, 16, 22, 45, 59, 118, 299

Weger, 146
Weker, Whycher, Whyker, Wycher,
    Wyka, Wyke, 19, 22, 24, 25, 59, 118
Wekys, 22
Welbeloued, 200
Wel(l)in(g)ton, Welyngton, Wylyngton,
    119, 120, 133, 135, 136, 240, 267
Well(e), Wella, 18, 118, 269, *see* Will(e)
Weller, 25
Welshman, 166, 167
Wenman, 21, 26, *see* Fen(ne)man,
    Venman
Wer, 32
Weryng, 245
Westbroke, 34
Westlake, Westlick, 34, 279, 288, 290,
    291
Westlane, 34
Westway, 34
Wetherdon, 278, 279
Weuer, Wever, 36, 137
Whetebred, 185
Whetena, 16
Whetepayn, 185
Whiddon, 281
Whimple, 90
Whisleigh, 54
Whita, White, Whyta, Whyte, Wighta,
    Wita, Wyta, 16, 17, 18, 190, 227
Whit(e)churche, 211
Whitebrother, 185
Whitegrom, 28, 185
Whiteman, 26
Whitemay, 185
Whithod, 185
Whityng, 22
Wid(d)ecomb, Wydecombe, 72, 74,
    278, 280, 282
Wight, de, 267
Wiking, 23
Wilford, 39
Wilkinson, 180
Will(e), Willa, Wyll, Wylla, 17, 32, 33,
    34, 49, 54, 240, 283
Willesford, 62
William(s), 172, 288, 290, 291
Willing, Willyng, Wyllyng, 23, 24, 240
Winchelsea, Wynchelsee, 133, 136, 240
Winsor, 133
Winton', 36, 162
Winyeat, Wyndeyeate, Wyndyate,
    Wyndyeat(e), Wyndyeatt, Wynyate,
    Wynyeatt, 129, 146, 147, 276, 277,
    278, 280, 293, 296

INDEX RERUM